*The Supreme Court and
Public Funds for Religious Schools*

The Supreme Court and Public Funds for Religious Schools
The Burger Years, 1969–1986

by
JOSEPH E. BRYSON
and
SAMUEL H. HOUSTON, JR.

McFarland & Company, Inc., Publishers
Jefferson, North Carolina, and London

British Library Cataloguing-in-Publication data are available

Library of Congress Cataloguing-in-Publication Data

Bryson, Joseph E.
   The Supreme Court and public funds for religious schools : the
Burger years, 1969–1986 / by Joseph E. Bryson and Samuel H. Houston,
Jr.
      p. cm.
   Includes bibliographical references (p.).
   Includes index.
   ISBN 0-89950-257-1 (lib. bdg. : 50# alk. paper) ∞
   1. Church schools—Finance—Law and legislation—United States—
History.   2. Federal aid to education—United States—History.
3. Church and state—United States—History.   4. United States.
Supreme Court.   5. Burger, Warren E., 1907-   .   I. Houston, Samuel
H.   II. Title.
KF4124.B79   1990
379.1'21—dc20   89-43640
                                                                        CIP

Manufactured in the United States of America

McFarland & Company, Inc., Publishers
   Box 611, Jefferson, North Carolina 28640

Table of Contents

Preface

Church-state activities hang heavy in the wind of American political and religious history. From colonial America to modern Minnesota, New York, Ohio, Pennsylvania, Rhode Island, Missouri, and many other states, church-state relations encapsulating elements of established ecclesiastical organizations and political structures have existed. Dozens of sectarian legislative enactments have been caught in the vortex of religious and political activities.

The Burger years, 1969–1986, at least regarding Supreme Court church-state cases, represent an historical judicial watershed unprecedented in American history. Never in American history have there been as many Supreme Court decisions, with as far-reaching implications and decided effects on staunch sectarian legislative supporters. This part of the Supreme Court record is filled with many quality decisions.

The church-state issue is among the most important questions in Western civilization. Public funds for religious schools is one of the two antinomies in the church-state public-education struggle. The other encapsulates religious curricular and extracurricular imperatives.

This book details the American drama from 1620 to 1986. We have included (1) an analysis of public education's secularizing the public schools; (2) an analysis of federal and state constitutional and statutory provisions for separation of church and state; (3) an analysis of federal and state constitutional and statutory provisions permitting use of public funds for religious schools; and (4) the Supreme Court and the legality of using public funds for religious elementary and secondary schools, 1969–1986: the Burger years. Every Supreme Court case relevant to public funds for religious schools during the Burger years is recorded with analysis. Major questions indicated in Chapter I concerning future legislation, litigation, and Supreme Court response are answered in Chapter VI. Finally, church-state decisions during the Burger years are prefatory to the future, and that is the story we wish to chronicle.

Church-state history began many centuries ago. The historical light is dim and impossible to record accurately. From prehistoric human to Paleolithic hunter to Neolithic farmer to modern humans, it is not illogical to assume that all worshiped God and Caesar similarly. Indeed, as one travels the church-state-history road, one is impressed with remarkable similarities, regardless of church denomination, mysticism, superstitions, politics, cultural patterns, and human involvement. The church-state drama continues to unfold. It reminds us of Nickles in Archibald MacLeish's great play *J.B.:*

> I heard upon his dry dung heap that man cry out who cannot sleep: If God is God He is not good, if God is good He is not God; take the even, take the odd, I would not sleep here if I could except for the little green leaves in the wood and the wind on the water.

Joseph E. Bryson
Samuel H. Houston, Jr.

Chapter I

Introduction

Overview

The legality of using public funds for religious education has become a much litigated question in recent years. From 1969 to 1986, the U.S. Supreme Court handed down more church-state decisions than in the entire 179 years prior to 1969. Competition for financial aid by religious schools is not a new occurrence in American history and certainly not unique to the 1970s and 1980s, yet massive legislation and litigation concerning this topic did occur during this period.

On May 27, 1986, Chief Justice Warren Burger submitted his resignation to President Ronald Reagan, who subsequently nominated Associate Justice William H. Rehnquist to become the nation's sixteenth chief justice. On September 17, 1986, the United States Senate, after a vigorous debate, confirmed Justice Rehnquist's nomination by a vote of 65–33. Chief Justice Burger served seventeen years as chief justice, longer than any other chief justice in the twentieth century. As Chief Justice Burger relinquished the Court's stewardship, current political, religious, social, and financial conditions within American society seemed to indicate that there would be continued competition for tax money by nonpublic educational agencies.

For America this story began November 21, 1620, when the *Mayflower* anchored in Provincetown harbor. On December 21, 1620, the *Mayflower* pilgrims stepped ashore at Plymouth with the Mayflower Compact — a God-centered civil-government document — in hand. In 1647 the General Court of the Colony of Massachusetts Bay passed the Old Deluder Satan Act. Section 2 of that act provided that when a town increased to one hundred families or households, a grammar school would be established with a master capable of preparing young people for university-level study — the first public-funding act for education.[1] The colony of Massachusetts Bay was not unique in its concern for education. Other colonies provided unrestricted aid through land grants and money appropriations. Both

1

practices were later adopted by the Continental Congress and the Congress of the United States.[2]

By the time the federal Constitution was adopted in 1787, nine states had established churches with several denominations represented.[3] Moreover, in the very first public schools established in Massachusetts under the Old Deluder Satan Act, a chief purpose of the schools was to prepare students to read the Bible. Religious influences pervaded the curriculum of many public-funded schools during much of American history.[4] Early Americans were apparently happy to have any kind of school that would provide young people with an educational opportunity.[5] In certain instances, "public funds and other forms of public aid were turned over to private agencies and religious groups for support on non-public education."[6] In 1875, President Ulysses S. Grant, on the occasion of the first centennial celebration, proposed a constitutional amendment (constitutional amendments must be approved by Congress and the legislatures of three-fourths of the states) "forbidding the teaching in said schools of religious, atheistic, or pagan tenets."[7]

Even prior to President Grant's proposal, numerous educators voiced concerns about the necessity for separation of religion and education. In 1837, Samuel Lewis, first superintendent of the common schools of Ohio, supported the concept of nondenominational education in his *First Annual Report* to the Ohio Legislature. In New York, the Reverend Horace Bushnell published an article contending that "to insist that the state shall teach the rival opinions of sects and risk the loss of all instructions . . . would be folly and wickedness together."[8]

Because of political, social, and educational conflict during the second quarter of the nineteenth century, secularization of the public school began. Reading the Bible followed with prayer was often an accepted practice in public schools. However, religious conflicts emerged when Protestant approaches to biblical scripture and interpretation came in conflict with Catholic religious attitudes — both horns of the church-state dilemma began to emerge.

Americans were culturally unprepared to adopt and accept varied European lifestyles and group behaviors, which appeared when large numbers of Catholics immigrated to America. Immigrants often retained native customs, mores, language, family leadership, and educational desires. The view of education proposed by some American immigrants was not compatible with the "American dream." The new Catholic immigrants desired an education for survival and religious continuity. Moreover, as the Catholics clustered together in ghettos with subsequent growth in numbers, they were often seen as a threat to the new society.[9]

Native-born Americans had certain expectations of newcomers. Primarily, immigrants were expected to be hardworking, thrifty, and honest, and to assimilate democratic ideals. It was often perceived that immigrants could never be Americanized by keeping to themselves, retaining old customs, and continuing to use their native languages. Moreover, their religion was suspect. American Catholics were expected to send their children to public school where the young could be properly indoctrinated with an established process for living in a democratic society.[10]

In the 1830s and 1840s, Bishop John Hughes of New York led a fight for aid to Catholic religious schools on the basis that public schools were actually Protestant-oriented and anti–Catholic in nature. He was unsuccessful and initiated the Catholic church's system of schools separate from the public-school system.[11]

Protestant influence in public education was a continuing concern for Catholic leaders and theorists. Nineteenth-century Catholic political activities focused on (1) lobbying to remove Protestant leadership and doctrine from public schools; (2) gaining financial support for religious schools; and (3) concentrating on developing a religious school system. At first, American bishops merely urged each parish to establish a church school. However, in 1884, when the Third Plenary Council of the church hierarchy met in Baltimore, "the Church made it obligatory for each parish to set up its own school and for each Catholic to send his children to a parochial school."[12]

Elywn Smith, in his superior publication on religious liberty, insisted the difficulty between the participants in the controversy lay in the realm of civil liberties. Smith said:

> The touchstone of Freedom was conscience. If conscience should be taken captive by spirit of dogma, restrictive education, authoritative rule or coercion, freedom would die. Here was America's precise and most elemental quarrel with Roman Catholicism; in the American view — not solely the Protestant view, much less than that of a tiny band of propagandists — the Catholic conscience, both in principle and in fact was captive to the Pope.[13]

Moreover, continued Elywn Smith, "It was assumed that Protestantism had given birth to republicanism in government; Catholicism reflected the support of old monarchial tyrannies and had no understanding or appreciation of civil liberties."[14] And it seemed perfectly logical to men like Lyman Beecher that in order for Catholics to understand the meaning of America, they should "be assimilated, amalgamated and Americanized in the common schools."[15] The Jeffersonian basis for the American republic depended upon an "enlightened" citizenry. Therefore, all citizens should be required to learn the meaning of great documents such as the Constitution.[16] In addition, Catholics should be permitted and encouraged to engage in freedom of thought and expression, so the republic may continually renew itself.[17] Reluctance on the part of the Catholics to "mingle" with other Americans promoted the suspicion that they were indeed subject politically to a foreign power and therefore could not be trusted to become "good citizens."[18]

This brief historical sketch describes the beginnings of a battle for control of education by various interest groups. Well-defined theological differences that historically separated Catholics from other groups paved the way for what is presently a battle for public financial aid to religious elementary and secondary schools. Moreover, the recent emergence of New-Right fundamentalist schools provides an ally in the fight for religious schools at public expense. Herein lies the constitutional dichotomy the Burger court addressed from 1969 through 1986 and the basis of this study.

Purpose of the Study

The purpose of this study is to determine the legality of using public funds to support religious elementary and secondary schools in the fifty states through analysis of statutory provisions established by the states, juxtaposed against Supreme Court decisions involving state legislative action. This study is developed in a factual manner and will deal with the legal questions. No attempt is made to relate these questions to social or economic factors.

Questions to Be Answered

This is an historical study of the legal ramifications of using public funds to finance religious education in the United States as determined by Supreme Court decisions from 1969 through 1986. The research describes the extent to which these funding practices have been challenged and litigated, the reasons for the litigation, and the results of the Court decisions. The effects these judicial decisions will have on the use of public funds for religious education is also discussed.

The study is limited to litigation that has a relationship to the public funding of religious elementary and secondary schools. A major purpose of this study is the development of practical legal guidelines for educational decision makers to have at their disposal when faced with decisions concerning public funds for religious education. Listed below are several key questions the authors seek to answer in order to establish guidelines.

1. What are the major legal issues regarding public funding for religious elementary and secondary schools?

2. Which of these issues are likely to be included in court cases related to public funds for religious elementary and secondary schools?
3. Which of the legal principles established by the landmark decisions regarding public aid for religious elementary and secondary schools are applicable to the state constitutional and statutory provisions?
4. Based on the results of recent court cases, what specific issues related to public funds for religious elementary and secondary education are being litigated?
5. Can specific trends be determined from analysis of the court cases?
6. Based on established legal precedents, what are the legally acceptable criteria for using public funds for religious elementary and secondary schools?

Coverage and Organization of Issues

The remainder of the study is divided into five major parts. Chapter II contains a review of related literature dealing with the legal aspects of tax usage for education and includes a summary review of all Supreme Court decisions concerning the use of taxes for religious elementary and secondary schools prior to *Lemon I* of 1971.[19]

Chapter III encapsulates a thorough review and analysis of both state and federal constitutional and statutory provisions concerning church-state separation and public funds for religious schools. These data are presented in a continuum ranging from general prohibition against church-state involvement, to specific prohibition against public funds used to support sectarian education, to specific efforts allowing secondary education. Complete "codes" to all constitutional and statutory provisions are included in appendices A and B.

Chapter IV includes a narrative discussion of the major legal issues relating to public aid supporting sectarian schools. An attempt is made in this chapter to show the relationships between the legal issues and the state constitutional and statutory provisions and in some cases federal statutes that become questionable points in litigation.

Chapter V presents a literary narrative of the Supreme Court's decisions from 1969 to 1986 that relate to funding of sectarian schools. The narrative traces the judicial evolution of Supreme Court decisions that arise from simple school-funding practices—mandated by legislative enactments—to a more complex school-finance arrangement that has gradually expanded to include all Americans. Thus, in Chapter V, the narrative will detail the "rebirth" of a sectarian education system and will show to what extent public dollars assisted in the "rebirth." We now have two school systems in America—one public and one private, two ways of education foreign to each other, yet whose respective wholes should illustrate and explain each other. The narrative is presented chronologically and juxtaposed with issue(s) mandated by state and federal statutes against irritated plaintiffs who see a Supreme Court resolution to the issue(s).

The concluding chapter contains a review and summary of information obtained from a review of the literature and from Supreme Court decisions. Finally, legally acceptable criteria for public funding of religious elementary and secondary schools are included.

Definition of Terms

Certiorari means a writ of review or inquiry.

Child-benefit theory means that the benefit is intended for the child, and any simultaneous benefit to a religious institution is incidental.

Concurring opinion means an opinion, separate from that which embodies the views and decisions of the majority of the court, prepared and filed by a judge who agrees in the general result of the decision, which either reinforces the majority opinion or voices disapproval of the grounds of the decision or the arguments on which it was based, though approving the final result.

General welfare theory is derived from the fact that Congress is constitutionally charged with maintaining the welfare of all citizens; therefore, aid may be extended under this theory, even though it incidentally aids a sectarian institution.

Public funds means federal or state revenues.

Public schools refers to schools established under state law (usually regulated in matters of detail by the local authorities) in various districts, counties, or towns, maintained at the public expense by taxation, and open with or without charge to the children of all the residents of the town or other district.

Religious schools means parochial, sectarian, or any school maintained by a religious group.

Independent school means a school other than public or religious.

Tripartite test refers to a constitutional test that was designed in arriving at a decision in *Lemon v. Kurtzman* (1971). The test consists of three measures of constitutionality:

1. Does the statute have a secular legislative purpose?
2. Is its primary effect neither to advance nor inhibit religion?
3. Does the statute foster an excessive government entanglement with religion?

Private school refers to any school that is neither sectarian nor public.

Chapter II

Review of the Literature

"History ... the eternal landscape of the past."
— Alfred Lord Tennyson, *In Memoriam,* 1850

Introduction

The American version of this church-state drama unfolds in the following manner. On Saturday, November 21, 1620, the *Mayflower* was anchored in Provincetown harbor. However, before the ship was anchored, William Brewster, John Carver, William Bradford and others, realizing they were somewhat north of Virginia and thus outside the jurisdiction of the London Company, agreed that some form of self-government compact was needed. The *Mayflower* pilgrims drew up the Mayflower Compact, and all men eligible (forty-one) signed it. One month later, December 21, 1620, after carefully exploring the coastal geography for the finest settlement site, the pilgrims landed at Plymouth.

In 1632, the Massachusetts Bay Company was chartered, with Boston as the capital, in 1632. In 1647 the General Court of the Massachusetts Bay Colony passed the Old Deluder Satan Act, the first public-funding act for education in America. Now both horns of the church-state dilemma have been identified — on the one horn a new theocratic political state and on the other, a public-funding act for education.

During the intervening 370 years, the ebb and flow of American church-state events, especially public support for religious elementary and secondary schools, have been omnipresent in American political and religious life. However, beginning with the decade of the 1970s, there was a flurry of state and federal legislative activities that necessitated Supreme Court attention to an extent unprecedented in the Supreme Court's history. From 1969 to 1986, the Supreme Court handed down more church-state decisions than in the entire 180-year history prior to 1969. There has in effect been a national public debate on public monies for religious elementary and

7

secondary schools for approximately 370 years. And to this date, the issue is like straws in the wind. Is there substance to the straws, and which way is the wind blowing?

The New England Colonies

In early autumn of 1620 in Plymouth, England, a strange human configuration gathered and began a journey that would ultimately change the direction of history. The *Mayflower's* human complement contained separatist pilgrims—Puritans and non–Puritans—"strangers." Led by William Brewster, the Puritans contracted with London merchants to form a joint economic venture (the Puritans' economic genesis and motivation should never be overlooked) in northern Virginia, around the Hudson River area.[1]

Already disillusioned by oppressive English laws that disallowed religious worship as they wished to practice it, and disenchanted with self-imposed religious exile in Leyden, Holland, because of cultural and economic deprivation, the Puritans sought an isolated sanctuary that would ensure religious freedom and economic opportunity.[2]

On September 16, 1620, the *Mayflower,* with more than a hundred passengers, set sail across the Atlantic and into American history. Rough weather, crowded living accommodations, and an improper diet made the crossing difficult. Sighting Cape Cod, the *Mayflower* pilgrims realized the ship was north of Virginia and outside the London Company's jurisdiction and thus had no legal authority for governance. It is at this point, especially when some of the non–Puritans began to discuss "their own liberty," that William Brewster, John Carver, William Bradford, and others insisted that some form of self-government compact (the first self-government compact in the New World) be agreed upon—the Mayflower Compact.[3] The Compact read:

> In ye name of God, Amen. We, whose names are underwritten, the loyal subjects of our dread soveraigne Lord, King James, by ye grace of God, of Great Britaine, Franc & Ireland king, Defender of ye faith, etc. Having undertaken for ye glorie of God, and advancements of ye Christian Faith and honour of our king and countrie, a Voyage to plant ye first Colonie in ye Northerne parts of Virginia, doe by these presents solomnly & mutually in ye presence of God, and one of another, covenant & combine ourselves together into a civill body politick; for our better ordering & preservation & furtherance of ye ends aforesaid; and by vertue hereof to enact, constitute, and frame such just & equall lawes, ordinances, acts, constitutions & offices, from time to time, as shall be thought most meet & convenient for ye generall good of ye colonie, unto which we promise all due submission and obedience.[4]

On Saturday, November 21, 1620, Captain John Jones sailed the *Mayflower* into Provincetown harbor and anchored. For the next month, the *Mayflower* pilgrims explored the countryside, seeking the best site for locating the settlement. On December 21, 1620, the pilgrims landed at a site they named Plymouth. At the conclusion of a difficult first year and with a bountiful harvest, the Plymouth Colony was a celebrated success. Over the next twenty years, because of religious oppression and economic opportunity, thousands of Puritans emigrated to New England, founding such towns as Salem, Dorchester, and Boston. Boston was chosen as the capital in 1632.[5]

Unlike the *Mayflower* pilgrims, the newly arriving Puritans were mainline English obsessed with the idea of purifying the Church of England. Specifically, the Puritans considered the English Reformation incomplete because (1) Roman Catholic ceremonial trappings permeated the Anglican church and worship services; (2) the Sabbath was secularized; (3) clergy education was inadequate; and (4) most important, the local church congregations needed greater autonomy.

With the formation of the Massachusetts Bay Company in 1629, the company's charter in effect established an autonomous Puritan society—"a city upon a hill"—a John Calvin theocratic republic had emerged.[6]

While the Puritans came to Massachusetts for freedom of worship, they allowed no religious freedom to others. Roger Williams, among the most celebrated religious dissidents, was banished by the General Court for insisting that church and state must be separate. Exiled from Massachusetts, Roger Williams founded Rhode Island, and included in the charter from Parliament were provisions for church-state separation and representative government.

Connecticut was founded by former Massachusetts Puritans with an announced purpose in the Fundamental Order of "purifying the gospel."[7] Both New Hampshire and Maine were settled by Puritans. New Hampshire was granted royal-province status in 1679, and Maine was claimed by Massachusetts.

The Puritan influence in America is pervasive. No other colonizing people dominated colonial culture as did the Puritans. The Catholics in Maryland, the Quakers in Pennsylvania, and the Baptists in Rhode Island, as important as those cultures were, were only marginal compared to the Puritans.

For purposes of this manuscript, we have focused on the dominating religious influence. The "City of God" was at hand—every fiber and sinew of Puritan society. Perhaps Nathaniel Hawthorne's magnificent novel *The Scarlet Letter* captures the Puritan theological imperative better than any other literary publication. In Chapter 2 Hawthorne described the Market Place (in Boston) in which Hester Prynne shortly would be forced to appear with her newborn baby, Pearl, and the scarlet letter embroidered on her breast:

> But, in that early severity of the Puritan character, an inference of this kind could not so indubitably be drawn. It might be that a sluggish bond-servant, or an undutiful child, whom his parents had given over to the civil authority, was to be corrected at the whipping-post. It might be, that an Antinomian, a Quaker, or other heterodox religionist was to be scourged out of town, or an idle and vagrant Indian, whom the white man's fire-stripes into the shadow of the forest. It might be, too, that a witch, like old Mistress Hibbins, the bitter-tempered widow of the magistrate, was to die upon the gallows. In either case, there was very much the same solemnity of demeanor on the part of the spectators; as befitted a people amongst whom religion and law were almost identical, and in whose character both were so thoroughly inferfused, that the mildest and the severest acts of public discipline were alike made venerable and awful.[8]

At the conclusion of Hawthorne's novel, the Reverend Arthur Dimmesdale (Pearl's father), after delivering his most brilliant sermon concerning the Deity and the community of mankind, especially related to New England, emerges from the church and begins the walk toward the town hall for a banquet. Dimmesdale, though walking feebly, resists all assistance. As he approaches the marketplace, he turns to the scaffold and calls Hester and Pearl to his side. Hester puts her arm around him and, with Pearl holding his hand, assists him up the scaffold. The crowd watches and listens in astonishment as he frees his sin-sick soul with the confession that he is Pearl's father:

> "I stand upon the spot where, seven years since, I should have stood; here with this woman...." With a convulsive motion, he tore away the ministerial band from before his breast. It was revealed!... Then, down he sank upon the scaffold![9]

The Reverend Dimmesdale, free at last, dies in Hester's arms.

Even the first public-funding act for education, the 1647 Old Deluder Satan Act, as the act's title implies, contained religious imperative; a chief purpose was to teach children to read the Bible. But one should understand that Calvinist theology was predicated upon the concept that piety grows from intelligence; education is an instrument of salvation. However, in time, the Puritan influence was diluted with the immigration of French Canadians and northern Europeans.[10]

The General Court of Massachusetts enacted four laws from 1634 to 1647 that are supremely important in establishing the direction of American public education. Two laws, in 1632 and 1637, established a general concept of a common property tax for town and colony benefit.[11] The 1642 enactment insisted that parents and guardians assume responsibility for their children's education, including ability to read and understand religion and Massachusetts law. And the fourth enactment, the 1647 Old Deluder Act, required a town with at least fifty families to

> appoint one within their towne to teach all such children as shall resort to him to write and read . . . wages shall be paid either by ye parents or masters of such children, or by ye inhabitants in general. . . .[12]

These four laws, in effect, established a cornerstone of the present American public education system.

Massachusetts's educational history is essentially the educational history of New England, including Maine and New Hampshire. Connecticut's educational history is similar to that of Massachusetts. Rhode Island's public education history begins in 1790. And Vermont, settled in 1724, was equally slow in developing public education.

In the middle Atlantic and southern states, education was almost entirely private. Indeed, there was no public-school system south of Connecticut before the Revolutionary War.[13] Middle Atlantic and southern education could best be characterized as localized religious schools with little lasting significance.

The War Years, 1776–1783

Education during the Revolution, because of general war conditions including finance, can best be described as almost nonexistent. While the majority of schools closed, some schools did operate intermittently; some city schools remained open. Charity schools suffered with many closings, and private schools managed better than most to surmount the wartime difficulties.

At the conclusion of the war, the federal government was bankrupt and struggling to survive. Moreover, apparently public education was never an important issue at the Constitutional Convention in 1787. For in the Constitution itself the word *education* is never mentioned. Among documents leading to the signing of the Constitution, the only educational item discussed concerned a national university. One must deduce that even though the founders of the American republic were supremely educated men, they must have concluded that education was a private function, by and large under control of the church.[14] However, there were some notable exceptions — Thomas Jefferson, George Washington, Francis Marion, John Jay, John Hancock, John Adams, and James Madison, to mention a few — who advocated a general education and promotion of science and literature.[15]

Even though the above national political leaders recognized and even promoted education — contending that education was critical for survival of the republic — there was no national groundswell for public education. Many Americans insisted that education should exist only for those who could pay for it. Many who supported free public education would limit attendance to poor children and the curriculum to basic rudiments of learning. Finally, others maintained that education should remain exclusively a church function.[16]

The eminent education historian Paul Monroe has suggested that

> No other single problem connected with education presented greater difficulties to our forefathers than that of its support. To begin with, most of them agreed with Jefferson that government is best which governs least. Certainly they believed that government to be best which taxes least. But they quite generally disagreed with Jefferson when he held that the support of education is one of the undoubted responsibilities of government.[17]

The Puritan public-education experience was a singular cultural expression that was not accepted outside New England.

The Nineteenth Century

Several significant activities launched the nineteenth-century American public-education experiment, an experiment that has never been duplicated in any other nation.

Public support was provided by national and state political leaders, such as Thomas Jefferson's admonition:

> If a nation expects to be ignorant and free in a state of civilization it expects what never was and never will be. . . . There is no safe deposit (for the functions of government), but with the people themselves; nor can they be safe with them without information.[18]

President George Washington's initial congressional address in 1790 insisted:

> There is nothing which can better deserve your patronage than the promotion of science and literature. Knowledge is in every country the surest basis of public happiness. In one in which the measure of government receives their impressions so immediately from the sense of the community as in ours, it is proportionally essential.[19]

Moreover, President Washington's farewell address in 1796 maintained:

Promote then, as an object of primary importance, institutions for the general diffusion of knowledge. In proportion as the structure of a government gives force to public opinion, it is essential that public opinion should be enlightened.[20]

General Francis Marion, seeking to promote free schools in South Carolina, admonished his political associates:

God preserve our legislature from penny wit and pound foolishness. What! Keep a nation in ignorance rather than vote a little of their own money for education! What signifies this government, divine as it is, if it be not known and prized as it deserves? This is best done by free schools. Men will always fight for their government according to their sense of its value. To value it aright they must understand it. This they cannot do without education.[21]

Chief Justice John Jay, writing to Dr. Benjamin Rush, maintained:

I consider knowledge to be the soul of a Republic, and as the weak and the wicked are generally in alliance, as much care should be taken to diminish the number of the former as of the latter. Education is the way to do this, and nothing should be left undone to afford all ranks of people the means of obtaining a proper degree of it at a cheap and easy rate.[22]

President James Madison insisted:

A satisfactory plan for primary education is certainly a vital desideratum in our republics.

A popular government without information or the means of acquiring it is but a prologue to a farce or a tragedy, or, perhaps both. Knowledge will forever govern ignorance; and a people who mean to be their own governors must arm themselves with the power which knowledge gives.[23]

Governor John Hancock, in his 1793 message to the General Assembly, declared:

Amongst the means by which our government has been raised to its present height of prosperity, that of education has been the most efficient; you will therefore encourage and support our Colleges and Academies; but more watchfully the Grammar and other town schools. These offer equal advantages to poor and rich, should the support of such institutions be neglected, the kind of education which a free government requires to maintain its force, would be very soon forgotten.[24]

President John Adams forcibly stated the motive for free public education:

> The instruction of the people in every kind of knowledge that can be of use to them in the practice of their moral duties as men, citizens, and Christians, and of their political and civil duties as members of society and free men, ought to be the care of the public and of all who have any share in the conduct of its affairs, in a manner that never yet has been practiced in any age or nation. The education here intended is not merely that of the children of the rich and noble, but of every rank and class of people, down to the lowest and the poorest. It is not too much to say that schools for the education of all should be placed at convenient distances and maintained at the public expense. The revenues of the State would be applied infinitely better, more charitably, wisely, usefully, and therefore politically in this way than even in maintaining the poor. This would be the best way of preventing the existence of the poor. . . . Laws for the liberal education of youth, especially of the lower classees of people, are so extremely wise and useful that, to a humane and generous mind, no expense for this purpose would be thought extravagant.[25]

The federal government's commitment to political stability and education was indicated in the Northwest Ordinance of 1784, Northwest Ordinance of 1785 (16th-township income was reserved for school support), and the Northwest Ordinance of 1787.[26] (When California was admitted into the Union, two townships, the 16th and 36th, were required.)

The influence of the New England states was significant — the Calvinist-Puritan educational imperatives encapsulating the New England states and subsequent New England influence on other geographical areas of the Union, especially settlers from New England settling the Northwest Territory.

Finally, there appeared an emerging political and social philosophy known as manifest destiny that encapsulated two attributes: (1) An idea the historians Charles and Mary Beard, in the *Rise of American Civilization,* call the idea of progress — that humankind can be made better by combining public institutions, schools, and material wealth for human betterment; (2) a spirit of self-government and local government association, and the general concept that self-government is the only political and social organization that offers a reasonable guarantee for liberty.

By 1820, thirteen of twenty-three states in the Union had constitutional recognition of education. Seven states — Massachusetts, Maine, Connecticut, New Hampshire, New York, Ohio, and Vermont — had statutes establishing school systems.[27] The schools were supported through an ingenious variety of school-finance schemes — property tax, education "fee" or tuition, fishing tax, salt-workings tax, lotteries, funds from congressional and state land grants, occupational tax, insurance-premium tax, bank tax, liquor; in 1836, federal Treasury surplus was distributed to the states for education purposes.[28]

The Union expanded dramatically during the second quarter of the nineteenth century—from coast to coast. Economic, social, political, and religious pressure made excessive demands on church-related education. National and state political, economic, educational, and religious leaders began clamoring for an education system—a free public-school system. Professor Ellwood Cubberley described the second quarter of the nineteenth century in the following manner:

> The second quarter of the nineteenth century may be said to have witnessed the battle for tax-supported, publically controlled and directed, and non-sectarian common schools. In 1825 such schools were the distant hope of statesmen and reformers; in 1850 they were becoming an actuality in almost every Northern State. The twenty-five years intervening marked a period of public agitation and educational propaganda; of many hard legislative fights. . . . Excepting the battle for abolition of slavery, perhaps no question has ever . . . caused so much feeling or aroused such bitter antagonisms. Old friends and business associates parted company, . . . lodges were forced to taboo the subject to avoid disruption, ministers and their congregations often quarreled over the question of free schools. . . .[29]

In 1927, the distinguished historians Charles and Mary Beard, writing in the *Rise of American Civilization,* said the "idea of progress" is the

> most dynamic social theory ever shaped in the history of thought—the idea of progress on the continual improvement in the lot of mankind on the earth by the attainment of knowledge and subjugation of the material world to the requirement of human welfare.[30]

The "idea of human progress" is a rather recent social and political concept. From Paleolithic hunter to Neolithic farmer and until the eighteenth century (some seeds of the "idea of human progress" were sown during the Renaissance and Reformation), the philosophical concept is absent. Even though Socrates, Plato, and Aristotle emphasized living "the good life" and pursuing wisdom, the concept of using human creative genius for continued human progress eludes their thinking. Plato's *Republic,* a brilliant philosophical treatise and certainly one of the most important published books on education, is a beautiful utopian testament to the status quo.

Early Christian theologians and philosophers mired in the quicksand of the human-depravity doctrine had no intellectual propensity for secular human eschatology. Medieval theologians, philosophers, politicans, and educational institutions maintained only survival intelligence. Some seeds of the "idea" were sown during the Renaissance. Such human developments as the printing press, published books, pamphlets, treatises, scientific inquiries, the religious revolution, changing political and economic conditions, and, in general, the spirit of humanism created an environment conducive to the "idea of progress"; yet the idea is elusive. Antiquated institutions and intelligence never surrender without a struggle. Both Copernicus and Galileo found the church dominant. Francis Bacon and Pascal, two philosophical luminaries, considered civilization old and dying—a perpetually held notion among philosophers and theologians. The eighteenth century, though, is a rather remarkable human century; the human condition made progress. Moreover, the idea of progress developed more fully in the American colonies and in France. On the European continent, French philosophers Abbe de Saint-Pierre, Condorcet, and Comte, along with the English philosopher Herbert Spencer, breathed life and intellectual direction into the "progress" concepts. But more important, American thinkers such as Thomas Paine, James Madison, John and Samuel Adams, Benjamin Franklin, and especially Thomas Jefferson (who forcefully and eloquently in the Declaration of Independence insisted that "life, liberty and the pursuit of happiness"—what a revolutionary idea: people are supposed to be happy) advanced the "progress" concept.

The transforming power of the "progress" philosophy became a dynamic instrument of American civilization. Moreover, the idea of progress and perfectibility of humankind and democratic institutions became the central theme for American public-education statesmen and philosophers. It is no mere accident that "progress" democracy and universal public education for all children, regardless of socioeconomic condition, met around the middle decade of the nineteenth century. The new democracy needed a dynamic political-social instrument that would ensure America's greatness through continued progress. Horace Mann (Massachusetts), Henry Barnard (Connecticut), John Pierce (Michigan), Samuel Lewis (Ohio), W.T. Harris (St. Louis), John Dewey, and associates forged the instrument: universal public education—America's greatest contribution to Western civilization.

Horace Mann, father of American public education and secretary of the Massachusetts State Board of Education, established the inescapable relationship between education and the progress of democracy. Like Jefferson, he believed that democracy's survival is in direct relationship to an intelligent, educated constituency. Horace Mann insisted that "never will wisdom preside in the halls of legislation ... until common schools ... create a more far-seeing intelligence and a purer morality than has ever existed among communities of men."[31]

For Mann, the public schools were social instruments shaping an emerging society of the new democracy. The goal of democratic education, therefore, must be "self-discipline, self-government and self-control."[32] Public education was the "great equalizer ... balance wheel of the social machinery ... creator of wealth undreamed of."[33]

William T. Harris, superintendent of schools, St. Louis, 1867, U.S. commissioner of education, publisher of America's first philosophical journal, *The Journal of Speculative Philosophy* (1867), and voluminous writer, compares favorably with Horace Mann and John Dewey in influencing universal public education. Dr. Harris's educational philosophy was centered on the idea of progress. In 1871, Dr. Harris maintained that "the spirit of American institutions is to be looked for in the public schools to a greater degree than anywhere else. . . . If the rising generation does not grow up with democratic principles the fault will be in the system of popular education."[34] On another occasion, Dr. Harris insisted, "An ignorant people can be governed, but only a wise people can govern itself."[35]

John Dewey, distinguished American philosopher and a dominating influence on American public education, addressed the idea of progress as the natural compelling attraction of democracy and education. Writing in *Democracy and Education,* his magnum opus, Professor Dewey maintained:

> The devotion of democracy to education is a familiar fact. The superficial explanation is that a government resting upon popular suffrage cannot be successful unless those who elect and who obey their governors are educated. Since a democratic society repudiates the principle of external authority, it must find a substitute in voluntary disposition and interest; these can be created only by education.[36]

Professor Dewey insisted the purpose of public schooling was to make society "more worthy, lovely and harmonious."[37]

By 1860, American public education was a qualified success. A majority of the states had public schools with at least one-half of the nation's children receiving a formal education. Thus, when President Abraham Lincoln gave his famous Gettysburg Address ("on this continent a new Nation, conceived in liberty, and dedicated to the proposition that all men are created equal"), he could point to the free public school that guaranteed educational opportunity on which liberty and political equality could be established.[38]

Yet there was a notable geographical character to American education. New England, for example, while pioneering public education, continued to have strong private schools. The Midwest had a much greater percentage of children attending public schools. The South, with North Carolina the single exception, lagged far behind the other regions. With the conclusion of the Civil War and as a condition for readmission into the Union, all southern states established public-school systems.[39]

Certainly with the 1874 decision in *Kalamazoo*[40] (that secondary schools are legitimate functions of public education and can be supported by a public tax), the American public-school system was firmly established and appeared to be irrevocable. P.A. Siljestrom, a Swedish historian who visited America in 1850 for the specific purpose of studying educational institutions, described the American enthusiasm for education in the following manner:

"Have you seen our popular schools?" is one of the first questions addressed to the stranger in the United States by young and old, by men and women, and this question in itself speaks volumes. But when the stranger finds, that in reality the popular schools are one of the most prominent subjects of national pride and satisfaction; that the question of popular education is not only of interest to some few philanthropists and thinkers, is not only discussed in legislative assemblies, but that it forms part of the national life, and is considered important, nay, the most important concern of the nation— then he feels that in the depths of American society there are forces at work, which in Europe have as yet produced but very mediocre results. That is, I think, the highest praise that can be bestowed on the United States. This constitutes the true greatness of the nation, and the best guarantee of its stability.[41]

And thus America developed fifty state public-education systems that provided true greatness, measured by any cosmic yardstick, and guaranteed stability.

The Fight for Public Funds for Religious Elementary and Secondary Schools

Four events both illustrated and shaped the direction of U.S. education. Each has been mentioned previously, but the importance of the sequence demands repetition. In 1642 the Massachusetts General Court enacted legislation mandating that parents and legal guardians assume responsibility for educating their children. In 1647, the Old Deluder Act required towns to establish schools and pay someone to teach the children. The Puritans established public-school systems financed with public monies that were pervasively religious. Good Calvinist theology insisted that education was an instrument of salvation.

Thus, early American public-education history, with New England's dominant influence plus continuing strings of European religious heritage, was simply public schools financed by public monies with a pervasively religious purpose. Moreover, public funds and other forms of public assistance were often made available to private agencies and religious groups for support of nonpublic education.[42] Apparently public assistance to nonpublic education was never predicated on private institutions (the old European habit) but on the thrust for an education and gratitude for any organization educating children.

Early in the nineteenth century, the public schools with a pervasively religious purpose collided with another religious institution, the Catholic Church. While public schools with a religious purpose were accepted in predominantly Protestant communities, the Protestant religion was anathema to Catholic parents. Indeed, Catholic religious leaders found public schools hostile to the Catholic church. And, of course, a solution to the problem was Catholic schools for Catholic children. But the perplexing public question was, At whose expense? Using New York City as an historical backdrop because of gravitational magnitude of political, social, religious, and educational issues, the story unfolds in the following manner.

The early English settlers in the colonies brought with them a heritage of English education that was centered around family, community, and church.[43] The American colonists sought a country where they could worship according to the dictates of conscience, a country yet unstained by state-established religions.[44] This desire for freedom of worship created conditions for a church-state battle that was beyond the perception of the earliest American colonists. The desire of the colonists to break the political bonds of an historical relationship with the Church of England eventually led the way to a well-defined separation of church and state.

Yet on the eve of the adoption of the federal Constitution, nine of the American states already had established churches.[45] Over the years three major developments eroded the state established church concept: (1) European immigration, especially large numbers of Irish and German Catholics; (2) developing schisms within established denominations; and (3) an emerging pragmatic political and religious philosophy best expressed in the opening words of the First Amendment to the Constitution—"Congress shall make no law respecting an establishment of religion or prohibiting the free exercise thereof."[46]

In the midst of spirited constitutional debates, James Madison had promised the opposition, led by Patrick Henry, that if Virginia ratified the Constitution, he would enthusiastically work for a constitutional amendment concerning individual rights. James Madison, early in life and as a student at Princeton, had rejected sectarianism with great concern for what he called the "hell-conceived principle of [religious] persecution" espoused by his Anglican colleagues.[47]

In his famous *Memorial and Remonstrance Against Religious Assessments* (Madison opposed a Virginia tax for support of Christian religion), Madison insisted:

> Who does not see that the same authority which can establish Christianity, in exclusion of all religions, may establish with the same ease any particular sect of Christians, in exclusion of all other sects? That the same authority which can force a citizen to contribute three pence only of his property for the support of any one establishment, may force him to conform to any other establishment in all cases whatever?"[48]

And no member of Congress was more influential in shaping the Bill of Rights, the first ten amendments to the Constitution, than James Madison, the father of the Constitution.

Patrick Henry, another Virginian, had vehemently argued against ratifying the Constitution, simply because of the absence of individual rights. Early in his political career, Patrick Henry had established his position with respect to religious liberty. The Virginia Assembly, during an economic crisis (1758), had temporarily suspended payment for church support required by English law. Anglican ministers sought judicial relief. Patrick Henry's legal counsel to the Virginia Assembly insisted

> that the Act of 1758 had every characteristic of a good law; . . . that a King, by disallowing acts of this salutary nature, from being the father of his people, degenerates into a tyrant, and forfeits all right to his subjects' obedience.
> [T]he only use of an established church and clergy in society, is to enforce obedience to civil sanctions . . . that when a clergy ceases to answer these ends, the community have no further need of their ministry, and may justly strip them of their appointments; that the clergy of Virginia, in this particular instance of their refusing to acquiesce in the law in question, had been so far from answering, that they had most notoriously counteracted, those great ends of their institution; that . . . instead of countenance, and protection and damages, (the clergy) very justly deserved to be punished with signal severity.[49]

Even though Virginia lost the decision, Patrick Henry's fame spread throughout colonial America and through the pages of history as a champion of religious liberty. He authored the Sixteenth Article of the Virginia bill of rights, which maintains

> that religion, or the duty we owe our Creator, and the manner of discharging it, can be directed only by reason and conviction, and not by force or violence; and, therefore, that all men should enjoy the fullest toleration in the exercise of religions, according to the dictates of conscience, unpunished and unrestrained by the magistrate, unless, under color of religion, any man disturb the peace, the happiness, or the safety of society; and that it is the mutual duty of all to practice Christian forbearance, love, and charity towards each other.[50]

Thomas Jefferson was a political colleague of James Madison, John Jay, and Alexander Hamilton in influencing the Constitution and especially the Bill of Rights' First Amendment. Writing to the Baptist Conference, Danbury, Connecticut, 1802, Thomas Jefferson insisted:

> Believing with you that religion is a matter which lies solely between man and his God: that he owes account to none other for his faith or his worship; that the legislative powers of the Government reach actions only, and not opinion, I contemplate with sovereign reverence that act of the whole American people which declared that their Legislature should "make no law respecting an establishment of religion or prohibiting the free exercise thereof, thus building a wall of separation between Church and State."[51]

Henry Steele Commanger, in *The American Mind,* describing nineteenth century America's pragmatic philosophy, observed that:

> (John) Locke rationalized a revolution and Jefferson inspired one.... For all practical purposes the warfare between Puritanism and the Enlightenment was as factitious in America as the later warfare between science and religion. Idealism was even more energetically Americanized, until in the end its spiritual ancestors could scarcely acknowledge its legitimacy. The American Transcendentalists subscribed sincerely to the metaphysics of Kant and Coleridge, but their busy emulation of the Utilitarians was a scandal.[52]

Alexis de Tocqueville, writing in early nineteenth century in *Democracy in America,* described religion in America:

> There is no country in the whole world in which the Christian religion retains a greater influence over the souls of men than in America, and there can be no greater proof of its utility, and of its conformity to human nature, that its influence is not powerfully felt over the most enlightened and free nation on earth.... In the United States religion exercises but little influence upon the laws and upon the details of public opinion, but it directs the manners of the community, and by regulating domestic life, it regulates the state.[53]

By 1840, church-state separation had occurred in every state in the Union. And because of the Protestant-Catholic schisms, church-state separation was becoming an important philosophical issue among leading education leaders. Horace Mann insisted the only religious instruction in public schools should be limited to teaching that offended no conscience.[54] Moreover, Mann maintained, public-education religious instruction should give to all "so much religious instruction as is compatible with the rights of others and with the genius of our government."[55] Samuel Lewis, Ohio's first state school superintendent, insisted in his *First Annual Report* to the General Assembly that public schools should establish a nondenominational stance. The Reverend Bushnell of New York maintained that "to insist that the state shall teach the rival opinions of sects and risk the loss of all instruction ... would be folly and wickedness together."[56]

W.T. Harris, superintendent of St. Louis Public Schools, divided the church-state educational question into two intellectual spheres: "the most fitting occasion for efficient instruction in religion on the one hand, and on the other hand the question of guarding the rights of private conscience and the separation of church and state."[57] In what is certainly the most important philosophical treatise ever written by an educator on church-state separation, Dr. Harris maintained that the principle of religious instruction is authority; that of secular instruction is demonstration and verification. It is obvious that these two principles should not be brought into the same school, but separated as widely as possible. Religious truth is revealed in allegoric and symbolic form, and is to be apprehended not merely by the intellect, but also by the imagination and the heart. The analytic understanding is necessarily hostile and skeptical in its attitude toward religious truth.[58]

Thus, the complete secularizing of public education was the only sensible and sane direction. Moreover, Dr. Harris insisted that Catholic parents would adopt public education if they could be ensured against proselytizing of their children by Protestant influences—a secular purity "where the Catholic may feel safe to leave his children."[59] But Dr. Harris insisted that church-state separation "does not make them godless nor the church less powerful, but quite the contrary."[60]

Meanwhile, by 1840, there were over two hundred Catholic schools in America. Moreover, in many school systems, public-school accommodations for Catholic children were established. Thus, in Lowell, Massachusetts, "Irish" schools existed for Catholic children only, and they were taught by Catholic teachers.[61] Even though the schools were public schools, at the conclusion of the school day and week, the schools were used by Catholics for religious purposes.[62] Yet where there was less predilection toward Catholic philosophy, many Americans feared a papist alliance with European Catholic monarchies to conquer America, subverting its free institutions. Catholic leadership—primarily the clergy—sought to neutralize the Protestant influence, thus making public schools more acceptable to Catholic children. Finally, Catholic bishops, realizing the futility of remaking the public schools in their image, met in Baltimore and acknowledged that a "separate system of education for the children of our communion" must be established.[63] But where should the financial support come from? In Europe, tax credits were granted to parents with children attending religious schools. Could not the same support come from the state?

The first and most significant religious-aid battle occurred in New York City in the early 1840s. On July 18, 1840, Bishop John Hughes returned from Europe and assumed leadership for what ultimately developed into major ideological warfare concerning public aid for religious elementary and secondary education. Two days later, July 20, 1840, in a speech in St. Patrick's Cathedral, he insisted that public schools were Protestant enclaves with Protestant religious practices and even a Protestant Bible (the King James Version), and in general anti–Catholic.[64] Moreover, Bishop Hughes rejected the general ideology that public schools were a harmonious social institution for democracy; he was an avowed separatist. In late August 1840, he wrote the bishop of New Orleans that the fight against public schools "will cause an entire separation of our children from those schools and excite greater zeal on the part of the people for Catholic education."[65] Bishop Hughes was a compelling speaker and imaginative leader, cajoling every human segment of the Catholic community to join the fight. Almost every fortnight over a period of months he spoke at St. James Church.[66] Continuously reiterating the themes indicated above, Bishop Hughes added one more theological imperative for education. Even if public education could guarantee a secular educational environment, secular education was never good enough. God and moral understanding were essential, and "the public school system in the City of New York is entirely favorable to the sectarianism of infidelity."[67] Thus, a public-school system fair to Catholics was essentially the same public-school system that existed in America during the first quarter of the nineteenth century—with public money for Catholic schools. Already approximately twenty thousand young religious contrarians were boycotting New York City schools. Governor William Seward urged that Catholic schools become an integral part of the New York City schools—Catholic schools at public expense. Governor Seward's exegesis suggested that

> the existing Catholic schools would become part of the state's common school system—Catholic public schools—even though they retained their private charters and religious affiliation. Public funds would thus be appropriated to finance denominational schools which Catholic children could attend without violating their religious convictions.[68]

History has a remarkable way of leveling politicians whose public policy is predicated on personal religious ideology. For at another time and place, Governor Seward challenged Abraham Lincoln for the Republican presidential nomination and lost to Lincoln simply because anti–Catholics in Indiana and Pennsylvania never forgot these policy recommendations.[69]

Armed with Governor Seward's plan, Catholic leaders wasted little time seeking their pro rata share of the common school fund. Moreover, Jewish and Presbyterian congregations demanded the same pro rata share(s) if the Catholic requests were honored:

> If your Honorable Body shall determine to grant their [Catholic] request, and thus establish the principle that this fund, though raised by general tax, may be appropriated to church or sectarian schools, then your memorialists respectfully but earnestly contend, that they are entitled to a rateable portion thereof....[70]

The New York Public School Society immediately challenged the Catholic request for public funds. Their argument was bitter but to the point: (1) public support for religious schools was "conclusively settled by the public and by law"; (2) Catholic clergy refused to cooperate in textbook revision; (3) Catholic clergy's public denunciations of the society indicated nothing would satisfy them; and (4) the society concluded the Catholic position was simply that "the teachings of Roman Catholicism were the truth, but the teachings of other religions were sectarianism."[71] Moreover, Bishop Hughes had advanced the argument to the society that if public funds were extended, religion would be excluded from the daily curriculum, that religious exercises would be deferred until after the normal school day. The Society concluded that a Catholic school day would be identical to a common school day, a distinction without a difference. Then why a Catholic school?

A three-person committee was appointed to study the public-aid issue and make recommendations to the New York City Board of Assistant Alderman. There was public debate on both sides of the issue, and finally the committee rejected Catholic claims, insisting that Catholics

> are taxed not as members of the Roman Catholic Church but as citizens of the State of New York; and not for the purposes of religion, but for the support of civil government. . . . Admit the correctness of the [Catholic] claim, that the Common Council of the City, or the Legislature of the State, may rightfully appropriate the Public Money to the purposes of religious instruction of any kind, in any school, and the consequence will be that the People may be taxed by law, for the support of some one or other of our numerous religious denominations. . . . By granting a portion of the School Fund to one sect, to the exclusion of others, a "preference" is at once created, a "discrimination" is made, and the object of this great Constitutional guarantee is defeated.[72]

During the 1842 election campaign, mobs of Catholics and anti-Catholics roamed New York streets fighting each other. The mayor called out the militia and police to protect St. Patrick's Cathedral. Bishop Hughes's home was stoned, and after failing to secure public funds, Bishop Hughes turned away from the political process, insisting that Catholics establish a separate school system. "Let parochial schools be established and maintained everywhere . . . proceed upon the principle that, in this age and country, the school is before the church."[73] In 1884, the Third Plenary Council of Baltimore mandated two important Catholic education objectives: (1) Catholic priests and bishops were to organize, erect, and maintain Catholic schools; (2) Catholic parents were obligated to send their children to religious schools.

In 1876, President Grant, reflecting on past conflicts and anticipating future church-state policy, insisted that no money be appropriated to religious schools:

Encourage free schools and resolve that not one dollar of the money appropriated to their support shall be appropriated to the support of any sectarian school; that neither the state or nation, nor both combined, shall support institutions of learning other than those sufficient to afford to every child in the land the opportunity of a good common-school education, unmixed with sectarian, pagan, or atheistical dogma.

Leave the matter of religion to the family altar, the church, and private school entirely supported by private contributions. Keep the church and state forever separate.[74]

Over the ensuing years, prime support for Catholic schools came from parish support, diocesan support, tuition, fees, fund-raising activities, contributed services of religious and lay school staff (especially relatively inexpensive services of teachers), and in recent years, indirect support from the federal and state governments. Catholic religious schools grew and flourished, and by 1900, some 5 percent of American elementary and secondary schoolchildren were enrolled in Catholic schools. By 1940, enrollment stood at 7 percent.[75] Indeed, Catholic school systems continued to increase until the mid–1960s and then, because of many financial and social difficulties, began to decline. One writer has estimated that one thousand Catholic schools closed between 1963 and 1969, with a 14 percent decline (5.9 to 4.8 million) in enrollment.[76]

As the decade of the 1970s approached, Catholic elementary and secondary schools were facing an uncertain future. Increasing costs and declining enrollments always chill school administrators. But there were already political, religious, social, and educational transitions blowing in the wind of American history. With the election of President Nixon, America began moving unmistakably in a conservative direction. During the 1970s, there was greater intensification of legislative church-state activities, thus greater judicial response. Moreover, the Supreme Court handed down more church-state decisions from 1969 to 1986 than in the entire 180 years prior to 1969.

Separation of Church and State

One definition of *religion* suggests that any "individual or group belief is religious if it occupies the same place in the lives of its adherents that orthodox beliefs occupy in the lives of their adherents."[77] Four characteristics should be present:

1. a belief regarding the meaning of life;
2. a psychological commitment by the individual adherent (or if a group, by the members generally) to this belief;

3. a system of moral practice resulting from adherence to this belief; and

4. an acknowledgment by its adherents that the belief (or belief system) is their exclusive or supreme system of ultimate beliefs.[78]

The *Random House College Dictionary* defines *religion* as

> a set of beliefs concerning the case, nature, and purpose of the universe; a specific and institutional set of beliefs and practices generally agreed upon by a number of persons or sects; a deep conviction of the validity of religious beliefs and practices. . . .[79]

Webster's Ninth New Collegiate Dictionary defines *religion* as

> the service and worship of God or the supernatural; commitment or devotion to religious faith or observance; a system of beliefs held to with an ardor and faith. . . .[80]

Justice John Paul Stevens has suggested that "religion begins where faith begins and intelligence leaves off."[81]

Discussing the subtleties and complexities of religion is a most difficult academic and intellectual task. There are literally thousands of publications dealing with the subject. We simply refer to William Blackstone's marvelous book *The Problem of Religious Knowledge,* Mortimer Adler's *How to Think About God,* Robert Jastrow's *God and the Astronomers,* and Carl Sagan's *The Dragons of Eden* as examples concerning the complexity of the subject.[82]

America was originally colonized by Europeans seeking an opportunity to worship freely. Although many countries function with a "state church" professing a reasonably uniform religious doctrine that can be a unifying force, the early settlers sought a land that did not have a "state church."[83]

In the United States, religious belief is provided an opportunity to flourish with no official government-sponsored religion encouraged. Moreover, church and state are separate; religions in America coexist with each other in a secular state. This is the American heritage, and while harmony usually prevails, it is sometimes a heritage of friction.[84]

The First Amendment

"Congress shall make no law respecting an establishment of religion, or prohibiting the free exercise thereof. . . ."[85] The First Amendment's purpose is not to strike merely at the official establishment but to create a complete and permanent separation of the spheres of religious activity and civil authority by comprehensively forbidding any form of public aid or support for religion.[86]

For James Madison and Thomas Jefferson, religious freedom was the crux of the struggle for freedom in general.[87] The First Amendment, so appropriately numbered, broadly forbids state support, financial or otherwise, of religion in any guise, form, or degree. The First Amendment disallows public funds for religious purposes. Throughout America's history, the Supreme Court has often and with a degree of specificity defined what First Amendment religious freedom means, as juxtaposed to a general definition of religion. The search for some national standard is very elusive. The Supreme Court often waffles. Consider the following as an example, which appeared in *Everson*:

> The "establishment of religion" clause of the First Amendment means at least this: Neither a state nor the Federal Government can set up a church. Neither can pass laws which aid one religion, aid all religions, or prefer one religion over another. Neither can force nor influence a person to go to or remain away from church against his will or force him to profess a belief or disbelief in any religion. No person can be punished for entertaining or professing religious beliefs or disbeliefs, for church attendance or nonattendance, no tax in any amount, large or small, can be levied to support any religious activities or institutions, whatever they may be called, or whatever form they may adopt to teach or practice religion. Neither a state nor the Federal Government can, openly or secretly, participate in the affairs of any religious organizations or groups and vice versa. In the words of Jefferson, the clause against establishment of religion by law was intended to erect "a wall of separation between church and state."[88]

This famous and often-quoted paragraph appears to be a sane, commonsense approach to the difficult church-state question — "a wall of separation between church and state." And even the *Everson* Court, armed with the above quote, managed to kick a sizable hole in Jefferson's "wall" by sustaining a New Jersey statute providing transportation for children attending religious schools. The Court predicated the judicial "hole" on the child-benefit theory. Thirty-three years later, the Supreme Court, in *Regan,* with Justice White writing the majority opinion, suggested the Court had never intended to establish "categorical imperatives and absolute approaches...."[89] And then Justice White's homily presents us with a sentence which begs for the standard that he suggests the Court has never intended to establish:

> This course sacrifices clarity and predictability, but this promises to be the case until the continuing interaction between the courts and the states — the former charged with interpreting and upholding the Constitution and the

latter seeking to provide education for their youth — produce a single, more encompassing construction of the Establishment Clause.[90]

From 1908, in *Quick Bear v. Leupp,*[91] the Supreme Court's first sectarian-schools decision, to 1985, in *Grand Rapids,*[92] the Supreme Court's most recent decision, the Court has presumably sought a "more encompassing construction of the Establishment Clause." To presume otherwise would condemn the Supreme Court to purposeless, mindless mediocrity, unworthy of "Supreme."

Prior to the 1970s, the Court developed two basic judicial church-state directions with respect to aid for religious schools: (1) the child-benefit theory, in general an accommodationist stance where public support is concerned; (2) the accommodationist pragmatism is absent in on-campus curriculum decisions. Moreover, in curriculum decisions, the Court began to develop the famous tripartite test that emerged finitely (many constitutional scholars perceived the tripartite *Lemon I* test as infinite) in *Lemon I.*[93]

The Supreme Court's involvement in education cases prior to the 1970s unfolded in the following manner. The 1908 *Quick Bear v. Leupp*[94] case focused on using federal money for contracting with sectarian schools to provide an education for Indian children on reservations. The practice continued for many years. In 1894, opposition developed, and Congress enacted legislation prohibiting sectarian education with the final appropriation in 1899.

Even though Commissioner of Indian Affairs Francis E. Leupp was effectively barred from using public funds for sectarian education, he was nonetheless petitioned by Sioux Indians, Rosebud Agency, South Dakota, to provide a pro rata share of an Indian trust fund to contract with the St. Francis Mission Roman Catholic School for an education for their children. The trust fund was established by Congress in an 1868 treaty with the Sioux Indians, and the requested pro rata share existed for "support and maintenance of day and industrial schools, including erection and repairs of school buildings...."[95] An injunction was sought on constitutional grounds by Reuben Quick Bear and Associates prohibiting using the funds; government "shall make no appropriation whatever for education in any sectarian schools."[96] The federal district court granted an injunction, and Commissioner Leupp appealed. The appeals court reversed, and Reuben Quick Bear and Associates appealed. The Supreme Court insisted that (1) the trust fund was private money, not public; (2) the Sioux Indians had requested a pro rata share for sectarian school support; and (3) this request was in reality a free exercise of religion, constitutionally protected. Chief Justice Fuller concluded:

[I]t seems inconceivable that Congress shall have intended to prohibit them from receiving religious education at their own cost if they desire it; such an intent would be one to prohibit the free exercise of religion amongst the Indians, and such would be the effect of the construction for which the complainants contend.[97]

As the chronology of Supreme Court landmark church-state decisions unfolds, the 1923 *Meyer v. Nebraska*[98] decision becomes supremely important. Even though the decision is barren of church-state terminology, the decision establishes the premise that a state's compelling interest in education may not encroach on parents' constitutional guarantees to direct their children's education.[99] And the chronology includes the 1923 *Frothingham v. Mellon*[100] decision, another non-church-state decision with imperative implications, which for the next forty-five years effectively precluded legal standing in federal courts to challenge federal money directed to religious schools. Justice Sutherland maintained that

his (the taxpayer's) interest in the moneys of the treasury — partly realized from taxation and partly from other sources — is shared with millions of others; is comparatively minute and indeterminable; and the effect upon future taxation of any payment out of the funds so remote, fluctuating, and uncertain that no basis is afforded for an appeal to the preventive powers of a court of equity.[101]

The 1925 *Pierce v. Society of Sisters*[102] case and its companion case, *Pierce v. Hill Military Academy,* did address a major church-state education issue. The Oregon law required that all children ages eight to sixteen years attend public schools.[103] The Supreme Court insisted, predicated on *Meyer,* that parents have the right to determine where their children will attend school. In affirming a lower-court decision, the Court concluded:

Under the doctrine of *Meyer v. Nebraska* ... we think it entirely plain that the Act of 1922 unreasonably interferes with the liberty of parents and guardians to direct the upbringing and education of children under their control. ... The child is not the mere creature of the state; those who nurture him and direct his destiny have the right, coupled with the high duty, to recognize and prepare him for additional obligations.[104]

Parents have a constitutional guarantee to determine placement of children in either public or nonpublic elementary schools.

In the 1930 *Cochran* decision,[105] the Supreme Court sustained a 1928 Louisiana statute compelling the state school board to provide "school books for school children free of cost" to all children in the state, including children attending private schools.[106] The state insisted the legislation was aid to children, not religious schools. The schools obtain nothing from them, nor are they relieved of a single obligation because of them. "The school children and the state alone are the beneficiaries."[107] Plaintiff Cochran protested on due-process grounds that his property was taxed for private-education purposes, which amounted to taxation without due process.[108] Chief Justice Hughes accepted the state rationale:

> Viewing the statute as having the effect thus attributed to it, we cannot doubt that the taxing power of the state is exerted for a public purpose. The legislature does not segregate private schools or their pupils, as its beneficiaries, or attempt to interfere with any matters of exclusively private concern. Its interest is education, broadly; its method, comprehensive. Individual interests are aided only as the common interest is safeguarded.[109]

The above Court homily effectively created the "child-benefit" theory: Religious schools may receive textbooks at public expense under the child-benefit theory.

The chronology of landmark church-state education cases includes another noneducation decision. *Cantwell v. Connecticut*[110] is important because the Supreme Court insisted that "the fundamental concept of liberty embodied in the Fourteenth Amendment embraces the liberties guaranteed by the First Amendment." In effect, the First Amendment religion clause is applicable to the states via the Fourteenth Amendment. The "absorption" theory was now complete, and the Supreme Court understood what it had been doing since the 1868 ratifiction of the Fourteenth Amendment.[111]

> The First Amendment declares that Congress shall make no law respecting an establishment of religion or prohibiting the free exercise thereof. The Fourteenth Amendment has rended the legislatures of the states as incompetent as Congress to enact such laws.[112]

The 1947 *Everson*[113] decision addressed the New Jersey legislative effort to provide transportation for children attending religious schools. Plaintiff Everson objected to the legislation on grounds that (1) taxation for private use without due process is a Fourteenth Amendment violation and (2) the First Amendment prohibits using tax money for religious schools. State courts were on opposite sides of the decision. Everson won in the lower court and lost in the New Jersey Court of Appeals. On appeal, the Supreme Court found that legislation was aid to children (the *Cochran* child-benefit theory) and satisfied a public need. Concerning Everson's second charge, the Court delivered perhaps its most celebrated description of what First Amendment establishment means (the full statement was quoted earlier in this chapter), including Jefferson's words: "In the words of Jefferson, the clause against establishment of religion by law was intended to erect 'a wall of separation between church and State.'"[114] The Court's majority (the decision was 5–4) maintained the New Jersey legislation had never made the slightest breach in the wall of separation. Moreover, the Court insisted, the First Amendment "requires the state to be neutral in its relations with groups of religious believers and non-believers; it does not require the state to be their adversary."[115]

In dissenting, Justice Jackson insisted the majority's logic contradicted its decision. He likened the Court's logic to Julia, who according to Byron, "While whispering, 'I will never consent,'—consented."[116] Justice Jackson also acknowledged the shallow logic upon which the child-benefit theory was predicated:

> Catholic education is the rock on which the whole structure rests, and to render tax aid to its Church school is indistinguishable to me from rendering the same aid to the Church itself.[117]

Justice Rutledge likewise chastened the majority, insisting the Court "sustained public payment for small concessions to religious schools while it made wholly private in character the larger things without which small could have no meaning or use."[118] Finally Justice Rutledge maintained the *Cochran* decision paved the way for this decision and that two decisions would create a rationale for a third. "Thus with time the most solid freedom steadily gives way before continuing corrosive decision."[119] How prophetic Justice Rutledge was.

The *Everson* decision signals the Court's accommodationist development. The judicial logic encapsulates the following antimonies. The Court's neutral position equates to an accommodationist position. The accommodationist pragmatism equals a positive response concerning tax funds for religious schools. The Court has raised an interesting provocative dichotomy, which logicians would call counter positive—that a "neutral" position must always be construed as favoring church-state legislation. For to construe "neutral" as opposing church-state legislation would be adversarial and not "neutral." But if the state general assemblies never promulgated church-state legislation, there would never be an adversarial response—which by the way is already forbidden by the judicial-accommodationist pragmatism. Of course the Court will seek a balance between accommodationist pragmatism and First Amendment establishment of religion. Pursuing such judicial logic in a simpler time—the child-benefit theory allowing transportation to religious schools—is one thing. But embracing the accommodationist pragmatism in *Regan*—the Court has never intended to establish "categorical imperatives and absolute approaches"—is indeed a judicial horse of another color.[120]

In the 1948 *McCollum*[121] case, the Court addressed the question of released time for on-campus religious instruction. Pupils choosing not to participate continued secular instruction. McCollum sought a court order forcing the school board to

> adopt and enforce rules and regulations prohibiting all instruction in and teaching of religious education in all public schools ... and in all public school houses and buildings in said district when occupied by public schools.[122]

McCollum argued that tax-supported schools were promoting religion. The Illinois state courts denied relief, and McCollum appealed to the Supreme Court. Justice Hugo Black, writing the Court's majority opinion, said, "This is beyond all question a utilization of the tax-established and tax-supported public school system to aid religious groups to spread their faith."[123] Justice Black once again expressed views announced by the majority and minority in *Everson* — even repeating *Everson*'s eloquent First Amendment definition. And then Justice Black acknowledged that

> the First Amendment rests upon the premise that both religion and government can best work to achieve their lofty aims if each is left free from the other within its respective sphere. Or, as we said in the *Everson* case, the First Amendment has erected a wall between Church and State which must be kept high and impregnable.[124]

The *McCollum* decision forbids released time for religious instruction on campus during the school day. Moreover, the accommodationist pragmatism expressed in *Cochran* and *Everson* is absent in *McCollum,* a curriculum case.

In *Zorach*[125] (1952) the Court addressed the issue of released time for off-campus religious instruction. Zorach and friends insisted that public schools manipulated schedules to accommodate religious activities. The Supreme Court, 6–3, rejected their arguments and sustained New York City's released time for an off-campus religious-instruction program. The three dissenting justices insisted the program used "a secular institution to force religion" on schoolchildren. Justice Jackson maintained that school "serves a temporary jail for a pupil who will not go to church. It takes more subtlety of mind than I possess to deny that this is governmental constraint in support of religion."[126]

Zorach sustains released time for off-campus religious instruction as constitutional. Moreover, the "neutral" accommodationist pragmatism is once again announced, this time in an off-campus curriculum case.

In the 1962 *Engel*[127] case the Supreme Court addressed the constitutionality of the New York State Board of Regents' mandated prayer: "Almighty God, we acknowledge our dependence upon Thee, and we beg

Thy blessings upon us, our parents, our teachers and our country."[128]
Plaintiffs claimed the prayer violated the First Amendment's establishment
clause. Plaintiffs were unsuccessful in the New York courts, but the
Supreme Court declared the Regents' prayer unconstitutional:

> When the power, prestige and financial support of government is placed
> behind a particular religious belief, the indirect coercive pressure upon
> religious minorities to conform to the prevailing officially approved religion
> is plain.[129]

Justice Douglas, in a concurring opinion, said:

> The point for decision is whether the Government can constitutionally
> finance a religious exercise. . . . I think it is an unconstitutional undertaking
> whatever form it takes.[130]

The "finance" issue Justice Douglas alludes to accrues from classroom
and teacher time reciting the prayer; there are no other "finance" issues in
the case. Moreover, Justice Douglas apparently realized the judicial
dichotomy in *Everson* and recanted his support of *Everson:*

> The *Everson* case seems in retrospect to be out of line with the First Amend-
> ment. Its result is appealing as it allows aid to be given to needy children.
> Yet by the same token, public funds could be used to satisfy other needs of
> children of parochial schools—lunches, books, and tuition being obvious
> examples.[131]

Thus the salient imperative of *Engel* is that prescribed prayer in public-
school classrooms, with teachers leading the recitation and children
reciting—religion in the curriculum decision—will fail constitutional
muster. The neutral accommodationist theory, even though expenditures
of tax dollars for classroom and teachers to administer the prayer were a
foregone conclusion, was never an issue. It is thus reasonable to assume
that whenever religious-curriculum issues are before the Supreme Court,
the neutral accommodationist theory will not be construed as favoring the
practice.

In 1963, *Abington School District*[132] extended the *Engel* rule. At issue
was a Pennsylvania statute requiring Bible reading without comment and
the Lord's Prayer recited at the beginning of each school day. The plaintiff
was successful in having the statute declared unconstitutional in the federal
district court, and on appeal by the Abington Township School Board, the
Supreme Court sustained.

Reviewing the past two decades of public-education church-state
history, the Court stated:

> The test may be stated as follows: What are the purpose and the primary effect of the enactment? If either is the advancement or inhibition of religion then the enactment exceeds the scope of legislative power as circumscribed by the Constitution. That is to say that to withstand the strictures of the Establishment Clause there must be a secular legislative purpose and a primary effect that neither advances nor inhibits religion.[133]

Continuing, the Court insisted that to allow encroachments even though minor would allow "the breach of neutrality that is today a trickling stream may all too soon become a raging torrent, and in the words of Madison, 'it is proper to take alarm at the first experiment on our liberties.'"[134]

Justice Douglas, in a separate concurring opinion, maintained that "through the mechanism of the State, all of the people are being required to finance a religious exercise that only some of the people want and that violates the sensibilities of others."[135] Finally Justice Douglas made his famous and often-quoted remarks with respect to public financing of religious schools:

> The most effective way to establish any institution is to finance it; and this truth is reflected in the appeals by church groups for public funds to finance their religious schools. Financing a church either in its strictly religious activities or in its other activities is equally unconstitutional, as I understand the Establishment Clause.
>
> Budgets for one activity may be technically separate from budgets for others. But the institution is an inseparable whole, a living organism, which is strengthened in proselytizing when it is strengthened in any department by contributions from other than its own members.
>
> Such contributions may not be made by the State even in a minor degree without violating the Establishment Clause. It is not the amount of public funds expended, as this case illustrates, it is the use to which public funds are put that is controlling. For the First Amendment does not say that some forms of establishment are allowed; it says that "no law respecting an establishment of religion" shall be made. What may not be done directly may not be done indirectly lest the Establishment Clause become a mockery.[136]

The *Schempp* decision reinforces *Engel* concerning prescribed Bible reading and the Lord's Prayer. Just as important, the Court is beginning to develop the tripartite test that will become fully developed in *Lemon I*[137] and remain the Court's primary First Amendment standard throughout the 1970s until 1986, the time frame for this book. The first two parts of the test are (1) there must be a secular legislative purpose, and (2) there must also be a primary effect that neither advances nor inhibits religion. Also, the neutral accommodationist theory is obviously silent in religious-curriculum decisions. It seems plausible to suggest that where public funds are used under the child-benefit theory (or incidental administrative costs in off-campus religious activities), there is no First Amendment religious advancement. However, where public funds are used for religious activities in public schools — a religious-curriculum case — the practice fails constitutional muster, as First Amendment religious advancement.

In 1968, *Allen*[138] again addressed the *Cochran* question, "apportioning state funds to school districts for the purchase of textbooks to be lent to parochial students."[139] Plaintiff insisted the practice failed constitutional muster, as First Amendment religious advancement. The New York trial court agreed but was reversed by the New York Court of Appeals. On appeal, the Supreme Court sustained, insisting the statutes had passed the *Schempp* test — "a secular legislative purpose and a primary effect that neither advances nor inhibits religion."[140] Moreover, the Court maintained that plaintiffs had never established that the "process of secular and religious training in religious schools are so intertwined that secular textbooks furnished to students by the public are in fact instrumental in the teaching of religion," a child benefit.[141] Justice Black, one of three dissenting justices (Justice Black also voted with the majority *Everson* Court), maintained:

> It requires no prophet to foresee that on the argument used to support this law others could be upheld providing for state or federal government funds to buy property on which to erect religious school buildings or to erect the buildings themselves, to pay the salaries of the religious school teachers, and finally to have the sectarian religious groups cease to rely on voluntary contributions of members of their sects while waiting for the Government to pick up all the bills for the religious schools.[142]

Even though Justice Black did not recant his *Everson* position, he did engage in fancy judicial tightrope walking by contending that books advance "ideologies," but school buses do not. Justice Black also knew that school buses transport pupils to religious schools where teachers and books advance "ideologies."

Justice Douglas noted that initial textbook selections were made by religious schools with local school-board approval. Since the school board is elected in New York, Justice Douglas insisted that "powerful religious-political pressures will therefore be on the state agencies to provide the books that are described."[143] Finally Justice Douglas acknowledged that even though he might be in error, the alternative was to introduce secularism into religious schools — state domination of religion; either way, "the principle of separation of church and state, inherent in the Establishment Clause of the First Amendment, is violated by what we today approve."[144]

The *Allen* decision reinforced the Court's decisions in *Cochran* and *Everson* — the child-benefit theory. Neutral accommodationist pragmatism means acceptance of legislation apportioning state funds to purchase textbooks for religious schools.

In *Flast v. Cohen*[145] (1968), the Court addressed the important issue concerning plaintiff's standing to litigate the Elementary and Secondary Education Act of 1965, especially the purchase of textbooks and other materials for religious schools. Relying on *Frothingham* (1923),[146] the District Court for the Southern District of New York held that plaintiff Flast lacked proper standing.

In *Frothingham,* the plaintiff was unsuccessful in challenging congressional action creating a maternity-care program increasing the plaintiff's tax because there is no federal statute or constitutional provision protecting citizens against tax increases, thus, no nexus between status and alleged infringement. Flast appealed, and the Supreme Court reversed the lower court's decision, holding that Flast had established a necessary connection between a tax used to support religious schools and the First Amendment guarantee of religious freedom:

> Consequently, we hold that a taxpayer will have standing ... to invoke federal judicial power when he alleges that congressional action under the taxing and spending clause is derogation of those constitutional provisions which operate to restrict the exercise of the taxing and spending power.[147]

The Court declined to provide judicial wisdom concerning federal expenditures for religious schools. Thus, the decision was limited to plaintiff's constitutional right to assert such a claim in federal courts. Justice Douglas, in a separate concurring opinion, waxed prophetic concerning the future of aid to religious schools. First, Justice Douglas acknowledged continuous efforts to stifle review of federal and state legislative efforts that aid religious schools. Second, he insisted, the Court should be readily available for citizens' redress in church-state cases, probably the only means of redress. Third, Justice Douglas recognized that "the mounting federal aid to sectarian schools is notorious and the subterfuges numerous."[148] Justice Douglas identified examples of subterfuges:

> Tuition grants to parents of students in church schools is considered by the clerics and their helpers to have possibilities. The idea here is that the parent receives the money, carries it down to the school, gives it to the priest. Since the money pauses a moment with the parent before going to the priest, it is argued that this evades the constitutional prohibition against government money for religion! This is a diaphanous trick which seeks to do indirectly what may not be done directly.
> Another one is the "authority." The state may not grant aid directly to church schools. But how about setting up an authority—like the Turnpike Authority? The state could give the money to the authority which, under one pretext or another, could channel it into the church schools. Yet another favorite of those who covet sectarian subsidies is "child benefit."

Government may not aid church schools, but it may aid the children in the schools. The trouble with this argument is that it proves too much. Anything that is done for a school would presumably be of some benefit to the children in it. Government could even build church school classrooms, under this theory, because it would benefit the children to have nice rooms to study in.[149]

With *Flast,* citizens have constitutional standing to challenge federal legislation aiding religious schools.

Summary

The *Flast* decision concludes the first seventy years of the twentieth century concerning aid to religious elementary and secondary schools. An analysis of decisions prior to the 1970s indicates (1) the child-benefit theory expressed in *Cochran, Everson,* and *Allen* is a viable constitutional route for legislatures seeking to aid religious schools; (2) the Court's "neutral" stance equates to an acoommodationist position pragmatically embracing the judicial ideology that a "neutral" position must always favor church-state legislation (the child-benefit theory as an example) concerning tax legislation for religious schools if at all possible. However, the neutral accommodationist pragmatism is absent in *McCollum, Engel,* and *Abington* — on campus-curriculum decisions. Yet in *Zorach,* regarding off-released time for religious worship, neutral accommodationist pragmatism is once again embraced. It is thus reasonable to assume that whenever there are on-campus religious-curriculum issues before the Supreme Court, neutral accommodationist pragmatism (at least prior to the 1970s) need not be construed as favoring either church-state legislation or school-board policies. Two parts of the Supreme Court tripartite test emerged during the decade of the 1960s: (1) there must be a secular legislative purpose; (2) the legislation must have a primary effect that neither advances nor inhibits religion. Chief Justice Warren Burger enunciated the third part of the tripartite test in *Walz* (1970)[150] (this decision upheld New York's religious-property-tax-exemption law) by stating that the test is whether the statute fosters "excessive entanglement" between government and religious institutions.

Thus at the threshold of the 1970s, it seems plausible to suggest that where public funds are used under the child-benefit theory for incidental administrative funds to administer off-campus released-time religious activities, as *Zorach* mandates, there is no First Amendment religious advancement. To the contrary, where public funds are used for religious activities on campus — religious-curriculum decisions — the practice fails constitutional muster, as religious advancement.

Finally, as the decade of the 1960s closed, Chief Justice Earl Warren retired and was replaced by Warren E. Burger. For the next seventeen years, Chief Justice Burger was America's senior jurist. Chapter 5 chronicles the Supreme Court activity applicable to public funds for religious schools during those seventeen years.

Federal and State Constitutional and Statutory Provisions for the Separation of Church and State

Introduction

Both federal and state governments have sought to maintain a wall of separation between church and state. Federal and state constitutional enactments vary in form but are explicit regarding separation.

Federal Provisions

The First Amendment of the Bill of Rights embodies two provisions for separation of church and state.

> Congress shall make no law respecting an establishment of religion, or prohibiting the free exercise thereof; or abridging the freedom of speech, or of the press; or the right of the people peaceably to assemble and to petition the Government for a redress of grievances.[1]

Questions concerning the relationship of church and state have perplexed Western civilization throughout human history. The establishment clause of the First Amendment was finally clarified in 1947 when the Supreme Court said:

> The "Establishment of Religion" clause of the First Amendment means at least this: neither a state nor a Federal Government can set up a church. Neither can pass laws which aid one religion, aid all religions, or prefer one religion over another. Neither can force nor influence a person to go to or remain away from church against his will or force him to profess a belief or disbelief in any religion. No person can be punished for entertaining or professing religious beliefs or disbeliefs, for church attendance or non-attendance. No tax in any amount, large or small, can be levied to support

any religious activities or instructions, whatever they may be called, or whatever form they may adopt to teach or practice religion. Neither a state nor the Federal Government can, openly or secretly, participate in the affairs of any religious organizations or groups and vice versa. In the words of Jefferson, the clause against establishment of religion by law was intended to erect "a wall of separation between church and state."[2]

The Fourteenth Amendment's absorption qualities ended all speculation that states' provisions varied from those of the federal government. Thus, through the Fourteenth Amendment, First Amendment freedom of religion is extended to all citizens. The Fourteenth Amendment states:

All persons born or naturalized in the United States, and subject to the jurisdiction thereof, are citizens of the United States and of the State wherein they reside. No state shall make or enforce any law which shall abridge privileges or immunities of citizens of the United States; nor shall any state deprive any person of life, liberty, or property, without due process of law; nor deny to any person within its jurisdiction the equal protection of the laws.[3]

There have been many constitutional "entanglement" decisions involving state and federal government. The basic argument, insists the Fourteenth Amendment, does not bind states to the establishment clause of the First Amendment. Finally, in the 1940 *Cantwell*[4] decision and with the absorption theory fully developed, the Supreme Court insisted that federal and state governments have the same religious relationship to American citizens.

State Provisions

"God and country" — the religious ethic of the land — testifies to the fact that America is a religious nation. Every national poll since the formation of America testifies to this statement. Moreover, nearly all state constitutions offer a reference to God and a request for the Almighty's consideration in the state's endeavors. Nowhere do states indicate hostility to religion. In the 1952 *Zorach* decision, the Supreme Court stated:

We are a religious people whose institutions presuppose a Supreme Being. We guarantee the freedom to worship as one chooses. We make room for as wide a variety of beliefs and creeds as the spiritual needs of men deem necessary.... We find no constitutional requirement which makes it necessary for government to be hostile to religion, and to throw its weight against efforts to widen the effective scope of religious influence.[5]

All but five states have preambles to their state constitutions that acknowledge God or a "Supreme Being." Only New Hampshire, Ohio, Oregon, Vermont, and Virginia have no such preamble. All fifty states express a reliance on God and acknowledge a "Supreme Being" (see Table 3.1). As an example, the bill of rights of Virginia's new constitution, adopted in 1971, reads:

> Article I–Section 16.   Free Exercise of Religion;
> No Establishment of Religion.
> That religion is the duty which we owe to our creator, and the manner of discharging it, can be directed only by reason and conviction, not by force or violence; and, therefore, all men are equally entitled to the free exercise of religion, according to the dictates of conscience; and that it is the mutual duty of all to practice Christian forbearance, love, and charity towards each other. No man shall be compelled to frequent or support any religious worship, place, or ministry whatsoever, nor shall be enforced, restrained, or molested, or burthened in his body or goods, nor shall otherwise suffer on account of his religious opinions or belief; but all men shall be free to profess and by argument to maintain their opinions in matter of religion, and the same shall in no wise diminish, enlarge, or affect their civil capacities. And the General Assembly shall not prescribe any religious test whatever, or confer any peculiar privileges or advantages on any sect or denomination, or pass any law requiring or authorizing any religious society, or the people of any district within this Commonwealth, to levy on themselves or others, any tax for the erection or repair of any house of public worship, or for the support of any church or ministry; but it shall be left free to every person to select his religious instructor, and to make for his support such private contract as he shall please.[6]

Virginia also incorporated into Section 16 of its bill of rights clear provisions concerning appropriations to religious or charitable bodies. The descriptive provisions establish greater clarity concerning church-state separation and acknowledge the duty of government to a Creator.[7]

The only other state to adopt a new constitution since 1970 is Montana. With less elaborate wording concerning a Creator or a wall of separation but with greater poetic beauty, Montana's preamble reads:

> We, the people of Montana grateful to God for the quiet beauty of our state, the grandeur of our mountains, the vastness of our rolling plains, and desiring to improve the quality of life, equality of opportunities and to secure the blessings of liberty for this and future generations, do ordain and establish this constitution.[8]

The Declaration of Rights of Montana, Article I, Section 5:

> Freedom of religion—The state shall make no law respecting an establishment of religion or prohibiting the free exercise thereof.[9]

Table 3.1

States with Preambles that Invoke God's Favor or Express Gratitude

States with Preambles	Invoke God's Favor	Express Gratitude
Alabama	X	
Alaska		X
Arizona		X
Arkansas	X	X
California	X	X
Colorado	X	X
Connecticut		X
Delaware		
Florida	X	X
Georgia		
Hawaii		X
Idaho	X	X
Illinois	X	X
Indiana		X
Iowa	X	X
Kansas		X
Kentucky	X	X
Louisiana	X	X
Maine	X	X
Maryland		X
Massachusetts	X	X
Michigan	X	X
Minnesota	X	X
Mississippi	X	X
Missouri		X
Montana		X
Nebraska		X
Nevada	X	X
New Jersey	X	X
New Mexico		X
New York	X	X
North Carolina	X	X
North Dakota		X
Oklahoma	X	
Pennsylvania	X	X
Rhode Island	X	X
South Carolina		X
South Dakota		X
Tennessee		X
Texas	X	
Utah		X
Washington		X
West Virginia		X
Wisconsin	X	X
Wyoming	X	X

The framers of the new Montana constitution describe an appreciation for God, but erect in Article I, Section 5, a wall of separation encompassing both the First and Fourteenth Amendments of the federal Bill of Rights.

Thus, while most states have clauses guaranteeing church-state separation, their constitutions reflect an acknowledgment of God. Table 3.1 (opposite) establishes that forty-five states have preambles that invoke God's favor or express gratitude to God (all state preambles are presented in Appendix A).

In addition, some preambles express hope for a more perfect government, recognize the privilege and freedom of forming their own government, express a desire to ensure tranquility, and acknowledge the willingness to transmit to posterity aspirations of the future.

All state constitutions provide for church-state separation. In recent years, many state legislators have felt pressures for constitutional revisions eliminating such separation.

Separation is accomplished in various ways. Prohibitions typically exist against one or more of the following: (1) required attendance at religious worship; (2) establishment of religion; (3) interference with freedom of worship or conscience; (4) religious tests as a qualification for holding public office, being a court witness, or being admitted to public school; (5) matters of religious beliefs in any judicial activity; (6) sectarian instruction in public schools; and (7) required support for religious or sectarian institutions, or religious and sectarian schools.

Table 3.2 (p. 44) indicates that thirty-eight states have constitutional prohibitions against religious qualifications for holding public office, being a witness, or being admitted to a public school (all fifty states' religious provisions are in Appendix A).

Alabama's constitutional prohibition against religious tests for holding public office is that "no religious test shall be required as a qualification to any office of public trust under this state."[10] Nebraska's constitution maintains in concise fashion that "no religious test shall be required as a qualification for office."[11]

Colorado's constitution is similar to other state constitutions in its prohibitions against religious tests for admittance to public schools: "No religious test or qualifications shall ever be required of any person as a condition of admission into any public educational institution of the state, either as teacher or student...."[12] Arizona's Article XI, Section 7, states:

> No sectarian instruction shall be imparted in any school or State educational institution that may be established under this Constitution, and no religious or political test or qualification shall be required as a condition of admission into any public educational institution of the State, as teacher, student, or pupil....[13]

Table 3.2

State Prohibitions Against Religious Tests as Qualifications for Holding a Public Office, Being a Witness, Being Admitted to a Public School

States	Holding Public Office	Being a Witness	Admission to a Public School
Alabama	X		
Arizona	X	X	X
Arkansas	X	X	
California		X	
Colorado	X		
Delaware	X		
Florida		X	
Georgia	X		
Idaho	X		X
Illinois	X		
Indiana	X	X	
Iowa	X	X	
Kansas	X	X	
Louisiana	X		
Maine	X		
Maryland	X		
Michigan	X		
Minnesota	X		
Mississippi	X		
Missouri	X		
Montana			X
Nebraska	X	X	X
Nevada		X	
New Jersey	X		
New Mexico			X
New York		X	
North Dakota		X	
Ohio	X	X	
Oklahoma	X		
Oregon	X	X	
Rhode Island	X		
South Dakota	X		
Tennessee	X		
Texas	X	X	
Utah	X	X	X
Washington	X	X	
Wisconsin	X	X	
Wyoming	X	X	

Table 3.3

State Prohibitions Against Interference with Freedom of Worship or Conscience

States	Freedom of Worship	Freedom of Conscience
Alabama		X
Arizona		X
Arkansas	X	X
California	X	
Colorado	X	
Connecticut	X	
Delaware	X	X
Florida	X	
Georgia	X	
Idaho	X	
Illinois	X	
Indiana	X	
Kansas	X	
Kentucky	X	
Louisiana	X	
Maine	X	
Maryland	X	
Massachusetts	X	
Michigan	X	
Minnesota	X	X
Mississippi	X	
Missouri	X	X
Montana	X	
Nebraska	X	X
Nevada	X	
New Hampshire	X	
New Jersey	X	
New Mexico	X	
New York	X	
North Carolina	X	X
North Dakota	X	
Ohio	X	X
Oklahoma	X	
Oregon	X	X
Pennsylvania	X	X
Rhode Island	X	
South Dakota	X	
Tennessee	X	X
Texas	X	X
Utah	X	
Vermont	X	X
Virginia		X
Washington	X	
West Virginia		X
Wisconsin	X	
Wyoming	X	

Table 3.4

State Prohibitions Against Requiring Church Attendance and State-Supported Establishment of Religion

States	Requiring Church Attendance	Establishment of Religion
Alabama	X	X
Alaska		X
Arkansas	X	X
California		X
Colorado	X	X
Connecticut	X	X
Delaware	X	X
Florida		X
Hawaii		X
Idaho	X	X
Illinois	X	X
Indiana	X	X
Iowa	X	X
Kansas	X	X
Kentucky	X	X
Louisiana		X
Maine		X
Maryland	X	
Michigan	X	
Minnesota	X	X
Missouri	X	X
Montana	X	X
Nebraska	X	X
New Hampshire		X
New Jersey	X	X
New Mexico	X	X
New York		X
North Dakota		X
Ohio	X	X
Pennsylvania	X	X
Rhode Island	X	
South Carolina		X
South Dakota	X	X
Tennessee	X	X
Texas	X	X
Utah		X
Vermont	X	
Virginia	X	X
West Virginia	X	
Wisconsin	X	X

Table 3.5

State Prohibitions Against Requiring Support for Religious or Sectarian Institutions and Religious or Sectarian Schools

States	Religious or Sectarian Institutions	Religious or Sectarian Schools
Alabama		X
Alaska	X	X
Arizona		X
Arkansas	X	X
California	X	X
Colorado	X	X
Connecticut	X	
Delaware	X	
Florida	X	
Georgia	X	
Hawaii	X	X
Idaho	X	X
Illinois	X	X
Indiana	X	
Iowa	X	
Kansas	X	
Kentucky	X	X
Louisiana	X	X
Maryland	X	
Massachusetts	X	X
Michigan	X	
Minnesota	X	X
Mississippi		X
Missouri	X	X
Montana	X	X
Nebraska	X	X
Nevada	X	
New Hampshire		X
New Jersey	X	
New Mexico	X	
New York		X
Ohio	X	
Oklahoma	X	
Oregon	X	
Pennsylvania	X	
Rhode Island	X	
South Carolina	X	X
South Dakota	X	
Tennessee	X	
Texas	X	
Utah	X	X
Vermont	X	
Virginia	X	X

Table 3.5 (cont.)

Washington	X	X
West Virginia	X	
Wisconsin	X	
Wyoming	X	X

Table 3.3 (p. 45) indicates that forty-six states prohibit interference with free exercise of worship or conscience. Most states equate freedom of worship with liberty of conscience.

Nineteen states have legislative enactments ensuring that freedom of religion is no justification for destruction of peace. For example, the Georgia Constitution: "The right of liberty of conscience shall not be so construed as to excuse acts of licentiousness, or justify practices inconsistent with the peace and safety of the State."[14] Twenty-nine states prohibit required church attendance. Thirty-six states have laws that prohibit the development of a state-supported religion, denomination, or form of worship.

Table 3.4 (p.46) presents a listing of states that have legislation restricting state-supported establishment of religion and abolishing required church attendance.

Table 3.5 (p. 47) indicates that five state constitutions prohibit sectarian instruction in the public schools: Alabama, Arizona, Mississippi, New Hampshire and New York. For example, Arizona's constitution states:

> No sectarian instruction shall be imparted in any school or state educational institution that may be established under this Constitution, and no religious or political test or qualification shall ever be required as a condition of admission into any public educational institution of the state, as teacher, student, or pupil; but the liberty of conscience hereby secured shall not be so construed as to justify practices or conduct inconsistent with the good order, peace, morality, or safety of the state, or with the rights of others.[15]

Table 3.5 (p. 47) also establishes that twenty-four states have constitutional provisions prohibiting support and/or denying payment of any tax monies for sectarian institutions. Massachusetts has a most elaborate and classic constitution concerning prohibition of public monies for education:

> No grant, appropriation or use of public money or property or loan of credit shall be made or authorized by the Commonwealth or any political subdivision thereof for the purpose of founding, maintaining or aiding any infirmary, hospital, institution, primary or secondary school, or charitable or religious undertaking which is not publicly owned and under exclusive control, order and supervision of public officers or public agents authorized by the Commonwealth....[16]

In addition to restricting use taxes for religious instruction, many states have restrictions against grants and/or donations of land for use by sectarian institutions. Montana's constitution:

> The legislature, counties, cities, towns, school districts, and public corporations shall not make any direct or indirect appropriation or payment from any public fund or monies, or any grant of lands or other property for any sectarian purpose or to aid any church, school, academy, seminary, college, university, or other literary or scientific institution, controlled in whole or in part by any church, sect, or denomination.[17]

Twenty-four states specifically prohibit the use of public funds to support religious schools.

As indicated, Virginia and Montana rewrote their constitutions during the 1970s, clearly reflecting denial of appropriations for religious schools and institutions. Reference has also been made to Montana's direct and indirect constitutional control of appropriations for religious activities. Virginia's new constitution maintains a firm perspective concerning appropriations to religious or charitable bodies:

> The General Assembly shall not make any appropriation of public funds, personal property, or real estate to any church or sectarian society, or any association or institution of any kind whatever which is entirely or partly, directly or indirectly, controlled by any church or sectarian society.[18]

Every state has some constitutional provision for church-state separation.

Federal and State Constitutional and Statutory Provisions Permitting the Use of Public Funds for Religious Schools

Introduction

Forty-two states now provide some public assistance to religious schools. Federal assistance, almost nil before 1965, totaled in excess of $41 million in 1984.[1] It is difficult to determine the amount of federal funds allocated to religious schools because the Education Consolidation and Improvement Act of 1981 indicates that public-school systems are to administer federal funds to private schools. Moreover, the block-grant and accounting procedures conceal actual dollar amounts granted to religious schools.

While this chapter examines federal and state constitutional and statutory codes, what never appears in school finance codes is income-tax enactments — the Minnesota type of legislation[2] — allowing parents a tax deduction for each child ($500 elementary, $700 secondary) enrolled in a tuition-charging elementary and secondary school. In addition, the Minnesota type of legislation allows deductions for textbooks, tennis shoes, sweatsuits, camera rental fees, calculator fees, home-economics fees, metal- and wood-shop costs, art supplies, music fees, transportation (school and field trips), and pencils and special notebooks required for class. As of March 1987, at least thirteen states had Minnesota-type legislation either in the discussion stage or pending. The Supreme Court, in *Mueller*[3] (1983) (see Chapter 5 for complete analysis), sustained the constitutionality of the statute.

Federal Aid to Religious Schools

The Smith-Hughes Act (1917) marks the beginning of direct federal cash grants to elementary and secondary schools. The act provided for annual appropriations allotted on the basis of rural population. The Smith-Hughes Act required the approval by federal authorities of state plans for courses of study, preparation of teachers, and even allocation of pupil time. The act required the state to provide at least 50 percent of the cost of the program. The Smith-Hughes Act provided aid to vocational programs.

In 1965, the Elementary and Secondary Education Act (ESEA) was enacted. The ESEA, the most massive aid bill affecting religious schools, provided assistance in numerous forms. Nowhere in the act were the words *parochial* or *church-related* mentioned. Over the years, the ESEA has continued to grow and undergo renovation. It seems likely that federal support for both public and nonpublic education will change drastically as a result of financial and political ideological considerations. Listed below are many federal programs that offer support for public and nonpublic schools.

The Education Consolidation and Improvement Act of 1981: effective July 1, 1982, the main purposes of this act are twofold.[4] First is the need to give state and local agencies responsibility for administering federal funds. Second is the consolidation of programs into block grants to reduce the administrative burden.

The act confers responsibility for administering public aid to private schools that qualify to local public-school systems. It is extremely difficult to determine actual costs of providing services to private schools because allocations to the public-school systems are block-granted, and accounting for exactly how much private schools receive is concealed in the overall grant.

Office of Compensatory Education. The Education for the Disadvantaged Act provides funding for programs meeting special needs of educationally disadvantaged children in low-income areas in public and nonpublic schools.[5]

Follow-Through is a program that provides comprehensive services to children from low-income families and strives to increase understanding about effective practices in educating these children.[6]

Follow-Through is an outgrowth of the Economic Opportunity Act of 1964.

Office of Educational Support. The Office of Education Support directly administers thirteen federal programs. Five programs provide opportunities for public and private nonprofit-organization participation.

The Law-Related Education Program provides for educating the public concerning the American legal system and principles of good citizenship.[7]

The Arts in Education Program brings together schools and community-arts resources.[8]

The Alcohol and Drug Abuse Program assists in the development of training programs for education personnel working in alcohol- and drug-prevention programs.[9]

The Inexpensive Book Distribution Program is channeled through Reading Is Fundamental, Inc., and aids in the distribution of inexpensive books to students from age three through high school, to increase the motivation to read.[10]

The Higher Education Act provides federal assistance to local education systems and to postsecondary educational institutions for planning and operating teacher centers.[11]

Special Programs. The Women's Educational Equity Act Program promotes educational equity for women through development and dissemination of model educational programs and materials.[12]

Office of Special Education. The Office of Special Education presently administers sixteen federal programs; six programs make funds available to nonpublic nonprofit organizations.

The Early Education for Handicapped Children program provides aid to public and private nonprofit agencies to build model programs for handicapped children from birth through age eight.[13]

Public and private nonprofit organizations may apply for funds through the Information and Recruitment Act. The specific purposes of this act are to provide funds to disseminate information, provide referral services for parents of handicapped children, and recruit educational personnel into hard-to-staff areas.[14]

The Media Services and Captioned Film Loan Program provides funds to establish and operate centers for materials for the handicapped. Program funding is through contracts.[15]

Model Programs for Severely Handicapped and Deaf-Blind Children and Youth provides funds for attaching innovative educational models or service-delivery components to ongoing educational services. This program is also funded through contracted arrangements.[16]

The Personnel Training for Education of the Handicapped Act provides funding for preparation of educators and other personnel who work with handicapped children, through preservice and in-service training.[17]

In addition to programs mentioned, federal funds are provided for various educational activities from a variety of departments in the Office of Education such as (1) Rehabilitation Services Administration, (2) Office of Student Financial Assistance, (3) Office of Higher and Continuing

Education, (4) Office of International Education, (5) Office of Vocational and Adult Education, (6) Youth Employment Program.

United States Department of Agriculture. The Department of Agriculture operates a reimbursement program designed to increase the consumption of fluid milk. Public Law 84-752 provides that milk may be distributed to "children in the United States in (1) nonprofit schools of high school grade and under, and (2) nonprofit nursery schools, childcare centers, settlement houses, summer camps, and similar nonprofit institutions devoted to the care and training of children."[18]

National School Lunch Act of 1946. This act provides, to the extent that funds are available, reimbursement for the cost of producing and serving lunch to pupils in public and/or nonpublic schools. The program also applies to residential child-care institutions for which applications have been approved.[19]

In conjunction with public law 85-478 and by amendment to the National School Lunch Act of 1946, a School Breakfast Program (Child Nutrition Act of 1966) provides breakfast-program reimbursement. It satisfies the same qualifying standards of the National School Lunch Program.[20]

State Aid to Religious Schools

Although all state constitutions provide for church-state separation and the majority of constitutions make direct statements prohibiting financial aid to sectarian institutions, public tax dollars are in fact flowing to religious schools through a variety of statutory mandates. In 1981, forty states made public assistance available to religious schools. By 1983, the number had increased to forty-two. In many instances, appropriations are made directly to students rather than schools (see Appendix B for a listing of state statutes applicable to this chapter).

Table 4.1 (p. 55) identifies states that have enacted into law either purchase-of-secular-educational services statutes or other statutes providing direct financial aid to elementary and secondary schools.

Transportation, textbooks and other materials, lunches, and health services are the most common forms of aid to religious schools. Most recently, legislative enactments receiving the greatest attention are tax-reduction or parental-reimbursement statutes, and near-direct aid to religious schools.

Purchase of Secular Educational Services. In 1970, six states had laws that allowed for purchase of secular educational services within guidelines as defined by state law. Table 4.1 (p. 55) indicates that in 1986 no state had a purchase-of-services act.

Table 4.1

States with Purchase of Secular Educational Services Laws and Other Direct Aid Laws

1986

States	Purchase of Services	Other Direct Aid
Arizona		X
Connecticut		X
Louisiana		X
Mississippi		X
New York		X
Ohio*		
Pennsylvania		X
Rhode Island		X
South Carolina*		X
Vermont		X

*New statutes effective 1983.

Other Direct-Aid Laws. Table 4.1 indicates that ten states have legislation appropriating direct aid to religious schools, including Connecticut's demonstration scholarship program, Mississippi's student-loan law, South Carolina's grants to students attending private schools, Vermont's law for the tuition of children in private schools, and Pennsylvania's parental reimbursement for nonpublic education. Rhode Island, New York, Louisiana, and Ohio reimburse nonpublic schools for the actual costs incurred due to state-required record keeping.

The Mississippi statute provides that private-school students can borrow up to $200 a year for a maximum amount of $2,400. If the recipient, upon high school graduation, continues to live in the state, the loan is forgiven at the rate of $200 per year.

Vermont's law pays for tuition of private-school pupils up to an amount equal to the average cost of a comparable year of public-school education if there is no public school available and the school board decides that is in the best interest of the pupils to do so.

South Carolina's law provides that

> every school child in the state who has not yet finished or graduated from high school and who desires to attend a private school located within the State shall be eligible for and entitled to receive a State scholarship grant in an amount equal to the per pupil cost to the State of public education as certified by the Governor.

The law is applicable only to those private schools that are independent and are not operated or controlled by any church, synagogue, sect, or other religious organization or institution.

The Connecticut demonstration scholarship program is a program for developing and testing the use of educational scholarships for all pupils eligible to attend school within the demonstration area. These scholarships are made available to parents or legal guardians of the recipient and may not be redeemed except for educational purposes at an approved school. An "approved school" is one that does not discriminate on the basis of race, color, or economic status and has filed a certificate with the State Board of Education that the school is in compliance with Title IV of the Civil Rights Act of 1964. Nor can the school require any fee above the amount of the scholarship.

Pennsylvania's reimbursement for nonpublic education is similar to Connecticut's act. Each approved school must meet the requirements of Title IV of the Civil Rights Act of 1964. Pennsylvania reimburses the parents of each elementary-age child attending nonpublic schools $75. Secondary students' parents are entitled to receive a $150 reimbursement.

The Louisiana legislative enactments are among the most inclusive for religious-school endeavors in America: state-mandated services such as required reports, records, testing, school lunchroom worker salary supplement, school lunch program, transportation reimbursements, special education for nonpublic-school students, textbooks, and tuition assistance (see Section 2990.3 Appendix B).

The Louisiana General Assembly apparently examines Supreme Court decisions, and when legislative enactments are sustained, adapts the successful legislative model to Louisiana's legislative language.[21]

Shared-Time and Driver-Education Laws. Table 4.2 (p. 57) indicates that fifteen states have laws providing for shared-time or driver-education courses to religious elementary and secondary schools.

Religious-school students (these are often Catholic schools) involved in shared-time activities attend public schools for specific courses, then return to their schools for the remaining hours of the school day. Often courses taken in the public schools are those that religious schools are ill equipped to provide.

Shared-time funds are normally disbursed on an average-daily-attendance basis. For example, Illinois law provides: "Pupils regularly enrolled in a public school for only a part of the school day may be counted on the basis of 1/6 day for every class hour of instruction of forty minutes or more attended pursuant to such enrollment."[22]

Colorado's shared-time statute utilizes federal funds for private schools. Pennsylvania's law, which provides for shared time, is unique:

Table 4.2

States That Make Shared-Time
or Driver Education Available to Elementary
and/or Secondary Religious Schools

States	Shared Time	Driver Education
California		X
Colorado	X	
Delaware		X
Hawaii		X
Idaho		X
Illinois	X	X
Iowa	X	X
Michigan*		X
Minnesota	X	X
Mississippi		X
New Hampshire	X	X
Oregon		X
Pennsylvania	X	X
Utah		X
Vermont		X

*See *Grand Rapids v. Ball,* 105 S. Ct. 3216 (1985). This is a major Supreme Court decision concerning shared-time activities. Chapter 5 provides a detailed analysis of *Grand Rapids.*

Section 5-502. Additional schools and departments. In addition to the elementary public schools, the board of school directors in any school district may establish, equip, furnish, and maintain the following additional schools or departments for the education and recreation of persons residing in said district, and for the proper operation of its schools, namely: —

High schools	Museums
Vocational schools	Reading rooms
Trade schools	Playgrounds
Cafeterias	Schools for physically
Agricultural schools	and mentally handicapped
Evening schools	Truant schools
Kindergartens	Parental schools
Libraries	Schools for adults
Public lectures	

Such other schools or departments, when established, shall be an integral part of the public school system in such school district and shall be so administered.

No pupil shall be refused admission to the courses in these additional schools or departments, by reason of the fact that his elementary or academic education is being or has been received in a school other than a public school.[23]

Often driver education is provided for in public high schools when not available to students at private-school campuses. California's law concerning driver education:

> *Section 41902.* Allowances by the Superintendent of Public Instruction shall be made only for driver training classes maintained in accordance with the rules and regulations as set forth by the State Board of Education.
>
> Driver training shall be available without tuition to eligible students commencing on July 1, 1969. The governing board of a district may make driver training available during school hours, or at other times, or any combination thereof.[24]

Transportation and Textbooks. Table 4.3 (p. 59) indicates that there are thirty states providing transportation and/or textbooks to religious schools.

Seventeen states lend textbooks to nonpublic-school students. Since 1980, several states have expanded the textbook statutes to include educational media and instructional materials. Six states now have statutes providing for a variety of media and materials.

California's law concerning loans of state-adopted instructional materials to nonpublic pupils is typical of textbook and materials laws:

> *Section 60315.* Loan of state-adopted instructional materials to nonpublic school pupils. The Superintendent of Public Instruction shall lend to pupils entitled to attend the public elementary schools of the district, in attendance at a school other than a public school under the provisions of Section 48222, instructional materials adopted by the state board for use in the public elementary schools. No charge shall be made to any pupil for the use of such adopted materials.
>
> Materials shall be loaned pursuant to this section only after, and to the same extent that, materials are made available to students in attendance in public elementary schools. However, no cash allotment may be made to any nonpublic school.
>
> Materials shall be loaned for the use of nonpublic elementary school students after the nonpublic school student certifies to the State Superintendent of Public Instruction that student materials are desired and will be used in a nonpublic elementary school by the nonpublic elementary school student. Enacted Stats 1976 ch 1010 Section 2, operative April 30, 1977.[25]

Section 123.932 of the Minnesota statutes defines instructional materials to be provided to private schools to include

Table 4.3

States That Make Transportation and/or Textbooks, Educational Media, and Instructional Materials Available to Religious Elementary and/or Secondary Schools

States	Transportation	Textbooks	Educational Media and Instructional Materials
Alaska	X		
California	X	X	X
Colorado			X
Connecticut	X	X	
Delaware	X		
Illinois	X		
Indiana	X		
Iowa	X	X	X
Kentucky	X		
Louisiana	X	X	
Maine	X	X	X
Maryland	X	X	
Massachusetts	X	X	
Michigan	X		
Minnesota	X	X	X
Mississippi		X	
Montana	X		
Nebraska	X		
Nevada	X		
New Hampshire	X	X	X
New Jersey	X	X	
New Mexico		X	
New York	X	X	
North Dakota	X		
Ohio	X	X	
Oregon	X		
Pennsylvania	X	X	
Rhode Island	X	X	
South Dakota		X	
Washington	X		
Wisconsin	X		

documents, pamphlets, photographs, reproductions, pictorial or graphic work; filmstrips, prepared slides; prerecorded video programs; prerecorded tapes; cassettes and other sound recordings; manipulative materials; desk charts, games, study prints and pictures; desk maps; models; learning kits; blocks or cubes; flash cards; individualized multimedia systems; prepared instructional computer software programs; and prerecorded film cartridges.[26]

It should be noted that emphasis in the California law is placed on the term *loaned* and requires that no cash grant to nonpublic schools be allowed. Minnesota's statute acknowledges that materials must first be available to public schools.

Twenty-seven states have statutes requiring school boards to provide transportation for religious-school students. Many of the statutes providing transportation for nonpublic students are designed in a delimiting fashion such as providing for no greater transportation service than approved for public-school students. Massachusetts has a simple transportation statute that is comprehensive yet concise:

> *Chapter 76, Section 1.* School attendance regulated. Pupils who, in the fulfillment of the compulsory attendance requirements of this section, attend private schools of elementary and high school grades so approved shall be entitled to the same rights and privileges as to transportation to and from school as are provided by law for pupils of public schools and shall not be denied such transportation because their attendance is in a school which is conducted under religious auspices or includes religious instruction in its curriculum, nor because pupils of the public schools in a particular city or town are not actually receiving such transportation.[27]

In 1947, the Supreme Court, in *Everson,* upheld New Jersey's transportation law, which allows parents to be reimbursed by tax money for the cost of transporting pupils to religious schools. New Jersey's law differs from many in allowing for a tax reimbursement for the cost of transportation.[28]

Lunches and Health Services. Table 4.4 (opposite) lists states having statutes that provide lunches and health services for nonpublic students. Only nine states make any reference to lunch assistance for nonpublic students. In most cases, these state statutes are really enabling legislation for the use of federal funds in feeding programs. Connecticut's Health and Sanitation Act:

> *Section 10-215a.* Nonpublic school participation in feeding programs. Nonpublic schools may participate in the school breakfast, lunch, and other feeding programs provided in section 10-215 to 10-215c under regulations promulgated by the state board of education in conformance with said sections and the federal laws governing said programs. [29]

Thirteen states provide some type of health services to students in nonpublic schools. These services are usually offered to nonpublic schools on the same basis as public schools. Typical of these statutes is the Kansas law:

Table 4.4

States That Make Lunches and/or Health Services Available to Elementary and/or Secondary Religious Schools

States	Lunches	Health Services
Arizona		X
California	X	
Connecticut	X	X
Hawaii		X
Illinois	X	
Iowa	X	X
Kansas		X
Louisiana	X	
Maine		X
Maryland		X
Michigan		X
Mississippi		X
Missouri	X	
New Hampshire		X
New York		X
Ohio		X
Oregon	X	
Pennsylvania	X	X
Rhode Island	X	

Section 72-5939. Any school district which provides auxiliary school services to pupils attending its schools shall provide on an equal basis the same auxiliary school services to every pupil, whose parent or guardian makes a request therefore, residing in the school district and attending a private, nonprofit elementary or secondary school.... Speech and hearing diagnostic services and diagnostic psychological service, if provided in the public schools of the school district, shall be provided in any private, nonprofit elementary or secondary school which is located in the school district. Therapeutic psychological and speech and hearing services and programs and services for exceptional children, which cannot be practically provided in any private, nonprofit elementary or secondaray school which is located in the school district, shall be provided in the public schools of the district, in a public center, or in mobile units located off the private, nonprofit elementary or secondary school premises ... and, if so provided in the public schools of the school district or in a public center, transportation to and from such public school or public center shall be provided by the school district.[30]

Miscellaneous Assistance. Table 4.5 (p. 63) indicates that there are thirteen states with miscellaneous religious-aid statutes that would not fit neatly into any of the preceding categories.

1. Alaska has a statute oriented exclusively toward eighth-grade pupils in private schols. The law provides for the furnishing of final-examination questions and the granting of eighth-grade diplomas in the same manner as in the public schools.
2. Arizona has a statute exempting from weight fees motor vehicles owned and operated by nonprofit schools and used exclusively for transporting pupils.
3. California's statute enables visually handicapped students in non-public schools to have access to specialized books, equipment, and materials without cost.
4. Florida's statute allows nonpublic school pupils to use the diagnostic and resources centers available to public-school children for a fee.
5. Private and religious schools in Maryland may connect television facilities to a closed-circuit educational-television system maintained for the public-school system.
6. Iowa had a statute that prohibited loans of public money to private schools. This statute was repealed in 1981.
7. Nevada has statutes providing for the procurement and distribution of federal surplus property to nonprofit schools and other eligible institutions.
8. New Hampshire has a permissive act enabling school districts to provide private schools, at state expense, with such benefits as educational testing, school guidance, and psychologists' services.
9. New Jersey provides for special classes and other facilities for all, including religious handicapped students.
10. Ohio allows school boards to purchase from private agencies or from any private individual services designed to promote vocational education or vocational rehabilitation.
11. South Carolina provides for itinerant teachers to assist in schools of any description where there are visually handicapped students in attendance.
12. North Carolina has a statute providing transportation for children with special needs to the nearest appropriate private school having a special-education program approved by the state board of education. Another statute provides for local boards of education to bear the cost of educating children with special needs who are assigned to group homes, foster homes, or similar facilities. The North Carolina statutes also provide for voluntary participation in any state-operated or state-sponsored program that would otherwise be available to such school, including but not limited to the high school competency-testing and statewide testing programs.

Table 4.5

States with Assistance to Religious Elementary and Secondary Schools
1984

States	Transportation	Textbooks and/or Educational Media Instructional Materials	Lunches	Health Services and/or Equal Basis Auxiliary Services	Shared Time	Driver Education	Other Direct Aid	Miscellaneous
				Types of Assistance				
Alaska	X		X					X
Arizona				X			X	X
California	X	X	X			X		X
Colorado		X			X			
Connecticut	X	X	X	X		X	X	X
Delaware	X					X		
Florida						X		X
Hawaii				X		X		
Idaho						X		
Illinois	X		X		X	X		
Indiana	X							
Iowa	X	X	X	X	X	X		X
Kansas				X				
Kentucky	X				X			
Louisiana	X	X	X			X	X	X
Maine	X	X		X				
Maryland	X			X				X
Massachusetts	X	X		X				
Michigan	X			X		X		
Minnesota	X	X		X	X	X		
Mississippi		X		X		X	X	
Missouri			X					
Montana	X							
Nebraska	X							
Nevada	X		X					X
New Hampshire	X	X	X	X	X	X		X
New Jersey	X	X	X	X				X
New Mexico		X						
New York	X	X		X			X	
North Carolina								X
North Dakota	X							
Ohio	X	X		X		X	X	X
Oregon	X		X			X		
Pennsylvania	X	X	X	X	X	X	X	
Rhode Island	X	X	X		X		X	
South Carolina							X	
South Dakota		X				X		
Utah						X		
Vermont						X	X	
Washington					X			
West Virginia	X	X						
Wisconsin	X					X		

13. West Virginia allows any private school to participate voluntarily in any state-operated or state-sponsored programs that are available to such schools by law.

Table 4.5 (p. 63) presents a composite listing of all states' religious elementary and secondary legislation as of 1985. Undoubtedly, other legislative activities will harden into statutes providing tax funds for private and religious schools.

From 1980 to 1986, the trend was to expand legislative enactments providing more and more assistance to religious schools. The latter four years gave private schools an even firmer grasp on public purse strings. Moreover, with the Supreme Court's *Mueller* decision, sustaining the Minnesota parent-reimbursement statute, there came a flurry of legislative enactments replicating Minnesota's statute.

Chapter V

The Supreme Court and the Legality of Using Tax Funds for Religious Elementary and Secondary Schools: 1969–1986 – The Burger Years

Overview

There is an old adage that the Supreme Court follows public opinion. At another point in this book we indicated that for approximately twenty years (beginning in 1965) America has been moving unmistakably in a conservative direction. And indeed, throughout American history, the body politic is always moving either right or left – conservative or liberal – with the broad mainstream of the body politic remaining somewhere in the middle. But the middle standard is continuously changing. While the conservative mood was flowing almost imperceptibly in the late 1960s and early 1970s, a perspicuous conservative pall spread over the 1976 presidential race. By the 1980 presidential race, the conservative mood, which had been gathering momentum since 1965, emerged as a political force and created an atmosphere conducive to the election of a conservative president.

Does the Supreme Court really respond to public opinion? We will not answer that question but we will seek to chronicle judicial history, and the reader must pursue that question.[1]

If, as historical wisdom suggests, presidents often appoint Supreme Court justices according to their own political ideology, clearly presidential appointments can signal a Court's new directions. President Nixon inherited a "liberal" Court, the Warren Court.[2]

The Court's vote in the 1971 *Lemon I*[3] decision was 8–0, declaring Pennsylvania's Non-Public Elementary and Secondary Education Act unconstitutional: the statute "excessively entangles" government and religion. (Justice Thurgood Marshall did not participate in the decision.) In a companion case, *DiCenso,*[4] the Court voted 8–1 (Justice White dissenting), holding Rhode Island's Salary Supplement Act unconstitutional ("excessively entangles" government and religion). Over the years covered in this book (1969–1986) the Court's personnel were gradually changed because of death and retirement. Of course, the new appointments presumably reflected the political ideology of the president who did the appointing. In the 1968 presidential election, President Nixon promised that if elected he would appoint justices in his judicial image—strict constitutional constructionists. President Nixon appointed four justices: Chief Justice Burger; Justices Blackmun, Powell, and Rehnquist. President Gerald Ford appointed Justice John Paul Stevens. In 1981, President Ronald Reagan appointed Justice Sandra Day O'Connor. In 1986, with the retirement of Chief Justice Burger, President Reagan appointed Justice Rehnquist as chief justice and Antonia Scalia as associate justice. On June 26, 1987, Justice Lewis F. Powell, Jr., announced his retirement. President Reagan nominated Judge Robert H. Bork, of the United States Court of Appeals for the D.C. Circuit, as Justice Powell's successor.

As already indicated, the Court was almost unanimous in *Lemon I* (8–0) and *DiCenso* (8–1). In the 1980 *Regan* decision,[5] that almost unanimous Court was now split 5–4, declaring a New York statute appropriating public money to private and religious schools for state-mandated testing and reporting services constitutional. Moreover, that same 5–4 split remained in the 1983 *Mueller* decision.[6] We will describe the Court's gradual personnel and judicial changes over the years.

Finally, at the threshold of the 1970s, the Court had insisted that where public funds were used under the child-benefit theory as in *Cochran, Everson,* and *Allen* or incidental administrative funds to administer off-campus religious activities as *Zorach* mandates, there was no First Amendment religious advancement. The neutral accommodationist theory that emerges from the above cases simply means that "neutral" must always be construed as favoring church-state legislation; for to construe "neutral" as opposing church-state legislation would be adversarial. To the contrary, the Court maintained that where there were religious-curriculum decisions, as described in *McCollum, Engel* and *Schempp,* and where incidental money to administer an on-campus program, the practice failed to pass constitutional muster. Also, the Court had the tripartite test in place. The tripartite test was predicated on seventy years of litigation and quasi-legislative (school-board policies) activities. The tripartite test: (1) Does the statute have a secular legislative purpose? (2) Does the statute effectively neither advance nor inhibit religion? (3) Does the statute "excessively entangle" government and religion? A de facto fourth point almost emerged and has been a continuous issue in many cases throughout the sixteen years: Does the statute have potential for "political fragmentation and divisiveness"?

1970–1975

Cochran, Everson, and *Allen,* all landmark cases, demonstrated the child-benefit theory: Such aid benefits the child, not the church. However, beginning with the 1970s, a hybrid judicial-political-religious concept emerged in the Supreme Court — *excessive entanglement* — that dramatically affected legislative activity concerning public funds for religious schools. Child benefits, textbooks, bus transportation have at times been questionable church-state activities. Nonetheless, child-benefit activities are innocent and pale beside purchase of auxiliary services, tax credits, parent reimbursement, and other legislative activities funneling millions of public dollars into religious schools.

Beginning the late 1960s and early 1970s, state legislative activities escalating public funds for religious schools burst on the American society. Within this political-religious environment, the Supreme Court was mandated to find new directions, constitutional interpretations, and clarifications. Time and time again, the Supreme Court would declare a particular enactment unconstitutional as religious advancement, only to have the state legislature rework the defective legislation, re-fund the new enactment, only to have the new enactment challenged all over again. Thus by the midway point of the 1970s, the Supreme Court had already handed down more church-state decisions than in any other period of Supreme Court history.

Such were the conditions on June 28, 1971, when the Supreme Court, in an 8–0 decision in *Lemon I* (Justice Marshall did not participate), declared Pennsylvania's Non-Public Secondary and Elementary Education Act unconstitutional and by an 8–1 vote in *DiCenso* (Justice White dissenting) declared Rhode Island's Salary Act unconstitutional. In a third related case, largely unnoticed at the time, *Tilton v. Richardson,* the Court in a 5–4 decision upheld the constitutionality of the Higher Education Facilities Act of 1963, which provides construction grants for religious colleges and universities as well as for public institutions.

Chief Justice Burger, delivering the majority opinion, maintained that analysis of such cases hinged on the following factors: (1) Does the statute have a secular legislative purpose? (2) Does the statute advance or inhibit religion? (3) Does the statute "excessively entangle" government and religion?[7]

In the Pennsylvania and Rhode Island cases, investigative efforts failed to establish legislative intent to advance religion. Therefore, "excessive entanglement" becomes the judicial focus. Justice Burger found that "the accumulative impact of the entire relationship arising under the statute in each state involves excessive entanglement between government and religion."[8]

In analyzing the Rhode Island plan, Justice Burger maintained that salaries to religious school teachers brought "excessive entanglement" into action. "The teacher is employed by religious organization, subject to the direction and discipline of religious authorities . . . most of the lay teachers are of the Catholic faith."[9] Justice Burger did not question the good faith of religious school teachers; however, he did recognize the extreme difficulty of "remaining religiously neutral."[10] Religious schoolteachers with the best professional intentions would find circumstances in teaching activities for which complete separation of secular teaching and religious dogma would prove impossible. Moreover, the Rhode Island legislature fashioned comprehensive controls (insuring First Amendment constitutionality) that required continued state surveillance. Because of the "ideological character" of books and teachers, Justice Burger found that "unlike a book, a teacher cannot be inspected once so as to determine the extent and intent of his or her professional beliefs . . . these prophylactic contacts will involve excessive and enduring entanglement between state and church."[11] Teaching surveillance and inspecting school records and religious content of programs are "fraught with a sort of entanglement that the Constitution forbids."[12]

The Pennsylvania statute has the same constitutional flaws as Rhode Island's statute: (1) salaries to religious schoolteachers; (2) continuous teacher surveillance and monitoring of school programs; and (3) direct financial aid to religious schools. It is intuitively obvious, said Justice Burger, that cash grants requiring continuous surveillance and monitoring of religious-school programs create "an intimate and continuing relationship between church and state."[13]

Justice Burger, calling attention to a "broader base of entanglement," emphasized "the divisive political potential" of the statutes. Religious-aid partisans will promote and champion "political activities to achieve their goals."[14] Political candidates will be forced to choose which side to join, and voters will enlist according to religious convictions. Moreover, Justice Burger maintained, the potential for "political fragmentation and divisiveness on religious lines is thus likely to be intensified."[15]

Continuing, Chief Justice Burger said:

> Taxpayers generally have been spared vast sums by the maintenance of these educational institutions by religious organizations, largely by gifts of faithful adherents. The merits and benefits of these schools, however, are not the issue before us in these cases. The sole question is whether state aid to those schools can be squared with the dictates of the Religious clause.[16]

The great strength of these cases, as indicated in future Supreme Court decisions, is found in the concurring opinions of Justices Brennan and

Douglas, joined by Justice Black with Justice Marshall concurring. Justices Brennan, Douglas, and Black took exceptional care to explain their rationale on four imperative issues:

1. Difference between direct aid to religious organizations and tax exemptions for churches;
2. Difference between aid and child benefits;
3. Why direct aid cannot be allowed under public-relief theory;
4. Why the state through direct aid cannot claim to assist the secular as opposed to the sectarian function of a religious body.

Direct Aid and Tax Exemptions

Justice Brennan illuminates this issue by quoting from *Walz v. Tax Commission*:

> The symbolism of tax exemption is significant as a manifestation that organized religion is not expected to support the state; by the same token, the state is not expected to support the church.[17]

Direct Aid and Child Benefit

Justice Brennan first reviewed the judicial theory and historical practice of the child-benefit concept — aid goes to children and not to religious institutions. Secondly, he introduced the district court's contention that in Roman Catholic schools, secular and sectarian education in both theory and practice are "inextricably intertwined." Finally, Justice Brennan explained that direct subsidies, unlike child benefits, go to religious schools, "thus perpetuating the church-school body *en masse* to insure the existence of a religion. We cannot blink the fact that the secular education those schools provide goes hand in hand with religious mission which is the only reason for the school's existence."[18]

Direct Aid and the Public-Relief Theory

Quoting from *Cook County v. Chicago Industrial School,* Justice Brennan asserted:

> The recurrent argument, consistently rejected in the past, has been that government grants to sectarian schools are not to be viewed as impressible subsidies "because (the school) relieves the state of a burden which it would otherwise be itself required to bear ... they will render a service to the state by performing for it its duty of educating the children of its people."[19]

While acknowledging that church schools have a valid educational purpose, Justice Brennan maintained that this consideration was not the issue. The central issue is that "in using sectarian institutions to further goals in secular education, the three statutes do violence to the principle that 'government may not employ religious means to serve secular interests, however legitimate they may be, at least without a clearest demonstration that non-religious means will not suffice.'"[20]

Direct Aid and Secular Function of a Religious Body

Justice Douglas's insight is of considerable importance at this point. After reviewing Supreme Court history concerning financial support for religious activities, Justice Douglas stated:

> [I]n spite of this long and constant history there are those who have the courage to announce that a state may nonetheless finance the secular part of a sectarian school's educational program. That, however, makes a grave constitutional decision turn merely on cost accounting and bookkeeping entries. A history class, a literature class, a science class in a religious school is not a separate institute; it is part of the organic whole which the state subsidizes.... What the taxpayers give for salaries of those who teach only the humanities or science without any trace of proselytizing enables the school to use all of its own funds for religious training. And sophisticated attempts to avoid the Constitution are just as invalid as simple minded ones.[21]

Justice Brennan, examining verifiable state control of tax funds, conjured images of the Grand Inquisitor in reverse: "The picture of state inspector prowling the halls of religious schools and auditing classroom instruction surely raises more than an imagined spectre of governmental secularization of a creed."[22] Acknowledging that the state had an undisputed interest in maintaining minimal education quality, Justice Brennan said that "the state has no proper interest in prescribing the precise forums in which such skills and knowledge are learned."[23]

Finally, Justice Douglas acknowledged difficulties with the curriculum:

> The curriculum presents subtle and difficult problems. The Contitutional mandate can in part be carried out by censoring the curricula. What is palpably a sectarian course can be marked for deletion. But the problem only starts there. No matter what the curriculum offers, the question is, what is taught?[24]

Justice White's dissenting opinion contained a paradigm of his position in future church-state cases. Moreover, in the immediate future Justice White would attract two allies, Chief Justice Burger and Justice Rehnquist. Justice White's dissent was based on two major considerations:

(1) The Court's decision was simply theoretical; there was no actual proof that tax-supported nonpublic teachers of secular subjects would insert religious dogma into nonreligious subjects. (2) The Court had created an "insoluble paradox." Justice White's reasoning was that if religion is taught, no taxes may be used; if taxes are used, religion may not be taught. Moreover, when the state extracts a promise of "no religion" and establishes legislative controls to audit compliance, the Court is creating "excessive entanglement"—"an insoluble paradox."

Two days later, June 30, 1971, the Supreme Court sustained a federal district court's decision in *Johnson v. Sanders,*[25] declaring Connecticut's Non-Public School Secular Education Act unconstitutional as First Amendment establishment. The enactment would have paid 20 percent of teachers of secular subjects in nonpublic schools.

At the conclusion of 1971, the direct purchase of secular educational services in religious schools described in *Lemon I, DiCenso,* and *Saunders* was unconstitutional. Justice White was the lone dissenter in *DiCenso.*

The year 1972 was significant for five reasons: (1) the October 10, 1972, *Essex v. Wolman*[26] "parent-reimbursement" decision; (2) the December 29, 1972, *Kosydar v. Wolman*[27] "tax-credit" relief for parents with children in private elementary and secondary schools; (3) *Johnson v. New York State Education Department;*[28] (4) Justice Powell and Justice Rehnquist, President Nixon's new appointments to the Supreme Court; and (5) intensification in church-state legislation and litigation.

As for the litigation, we turn first to the Ohio story. On October 10, 1972, the Supreme Court, in *Essex v. Wolman,*[29] affirmed without written opinion a three-judge federal district-court decision declaring that Ohio's parent-reimbursement statute "fosters an excessive government entanglement with religion by transferring public funds to religiously oriented private schools in violation of establishment clause."[30]

Approximately two months later, the Ohio General Assembly enacted a tax-credit statute, litigated as *Kosydar v. Wolman.*[31] In *Johnson*[32] the Supreme Court never really addressed the issue—a state enactment providing free textbooks for children grades seven through twelve (including private schools), free textbooks for grades one through six contingent upon a taxpayer vote. In school districts where plaintiffs resided, the school district had not elected to provide free textbooks for grades one through six. Plaintiffs insisted the enactment created a wealth classification, thus denying them equal protection. Before the Court could review the question, a tax was levied, so the case was remanded to determine if the book issue was moot. And it was.

As the year 1972 closed, church-state legislative activity and litigation pace were intensive. Voluminous church-state legislation was in the making.[33]

The year 1973 has often been referred to as the watershed year in church-state education litigation. On April 2, 1973, in *Lemon II*,[34] the Supreme Court, in a 5–3 decision (Justice Marshall did not participate), sustained the concept of payment to religious schools for services rendered prior to the date when the legislative enactment was declared unconstitutional. Chief Justice Burger, writing the majority opinion, found no bad faith in payment for expenses incurred before the Court's decision. Justice Douglas, joined by Brennan and Stewart, maintained that allowing payment "under the program, even for past services, violated the establishment clause of the First Amendment."[35]

June 25, 1973, was a "cataclysmic" day in the history of church-state activities. The Supreme Court handed down eight significant decisions.[36] While there may have been a more significant church-state case decided on a particular day in Supreme Court history, never has the Court been involved with as many important decisions with such devastating church-state results. The Supreme Court mandated three major and five lesser decisions that have had significant impact on recent church-state judicial history and legislative enactments.

The Supreme Court considered *Nyquist*[37] as the command case. The *Nyquist* case developed on appeal from the federal District Court, Southern District, New York. The central question was New York legislative activities establishing three financial-grant programs for private and religious schools: (1) Section I provided money grants to "qualifying"[38] private and religious nonpublic schools for "maintenance" and for "repair" of school facilities and equipment, thereby insuring students' health, safety, and welfare. The legislative formula provided $30 per pupil annually; $40 was provided if the school facilities were twenty-five years old. (2) Section II developed a tuition-reimbursement plan ($50 per pupil for elementary schools and $100 for secondary schools — no grant to exceed 50 percent of actual tuition) for parents whose children attended private or religious schools with annual incomes of less than $5,000. (3) Sections III, IV, and V provided tax relief for parents unable to qualify under Section II (this section allowed parents to deduct a fixed amount from adjusted gross income for each child attending nonpublic schools).

The New York legislature maintained that the statute was (1) secular, neutral, and nonideological; (2) necessary for providing alternative education systems for a pluralistic society; (3) necessary because a sharp decline in nonpublic schools would create educational chaos caused by swelling enrollments and affecting the quality of public education.

Justice Powell, writing the majority opinion, employed the tripartite test: Does the statute (1) have a secular legislative purpose, (2) effectively advance or prohibit religion, and (3) excessively entangle government and religion? Justice Powell acknowledged the legislature's genuine concern for health, safety, welfare, and quality education for all children. However, regardless of these concerns, the legislative enactments must pass constitutional tests of (1) religious advancement and (2) excessive entanglement of government in religion.

Virtually all schools receiving payment under Section I (maintenance and repair) were Roman Catholic schools. Moreover, religious schools might conceivably finance the entire maintenance and repair budget from state funds. Justice Powell found that there were no statutory controls restricting state funds for general secular purposes. Funds might be used for personnel maintaining a school chapel and other rooms where religious dogma was taught.[39] Therefore, Justice Powell continued, "it simply cannot be denied that this action has a primary effect that advances religion in that it subsidizes directly the religious activities of sectarian elementary and secondary schools."[40]

In responding to judicial philosophical questions raised by defendants comparing the aid allowed in *Everson, Allen,* and *Tilton,* Justice Powell said these cases recognized that religious schools often performed secular-education functions and that aid (presumably child-benefit type) may be "channeled through the secular without providing direct aid to the sectarian."[41] Justice Powell delineated how narrow the channel really was and suggested that often financial aid "directly and indirectly" promotes religious functions by freeing funds of sectarian institutions for other purposes. Yet, such "indirect and incidental" religious benefits are not sufficient constitutional deficiencies to invalidate state law. Finally, Justice Powell pointed to the Court's dicta in *Tilton* as the clearest example of Section I's constitutional flaw: "If the state may not erect buildings in which religious activities are to take place, it may not maintain such buildings or renovate them when they fall into disrepair."[42] Therefore, said Justice Powell, the maintenance-and-repair section clearly violates the establishment clause.[43]

Section II (involving tuition-reimbursement credits), Justice Powell insisted, also fails the "effect" test for the same constitutional reasons that invalidate maintenance-and-repair grants. In absence of effective governmental accounting safeguards confirming state aid for secular, neutral, and nonideological purposes, "it is clear from our cases that direct aid, in whatever form, is invalid."[44] The constitutional issue is clear: whether grants to parents instead of sectarian schools can sufficiently transcend the establishment clause.

Appellants, drawing extensively upon *Everson* and *Allen,* suggested that parental grants did not breach the "wall of separation." Justice Powell elaborated on differences between citizen benefits (transportation and textbooks were analogous to police and fire protection) and religious benefits and indicated that "aid to parents was one of many factors considered."[45]

Justice Powell recognized Justice Black's classic dissent in *Allen* concerning fears of ingenious religious-aid legislation. Justice Powell insisted that while Justice Black's fear of massive legislative activities paying the entire religious school bill was not yet realized, "the ingenious plans for channeling state aid to sectarian schools that periodically reached the Court abundantly support the wisdom of Justice Black."[46]

The state pressed two other basic arguments: (1) Tuition reimbursement to parents was constitutionally permissible. (2) The plan made it possible for low-income parents to exercise their First Amendment rights to provide a religious education for their children. However, regardless of legislative human considerations and constitutional explanations, Justice Powell maintained, "The state has taken a step which can only be regarded as one 'advancing' religion."[47]

Sections III, IV, and V also provide tax credits for parents not included in Section II. Justice Powell found that Sections III, IV, and V were not different from Section II. Justice Powell said:

> The qualifying parent under either program receives the same form of encouragement and reward for sending his children to non-public schools. The only difference is that one parent receives an actual cash payment while the other is allowed to reduce by an arbitrary amount the sum he would otherwise be obliged to pay over to the state.[48]

Justice Powell's opinion cut at the legislative matrix:

> We know of no historical precedent for New York's recently promulgated tax relief program. Indeed it seems clear that tax benefits for parents whose children attend religious schools are a recent innovation.... Special tax funds, however, cannot be squared with a principle of neutrality established by the decision of this Court. To the contrary, insofar as such benefits render assistance to parents who send their children to sectarian schools, their purpose and inevitable effect are to aid and advance those religious institutions.[49]

Chief Justice Burger, in what appeared to be a judicial paradox, joined the Court's majority in Section I (maintenance-and-repair provision) but dissented in Sections II, III, IV, and V (tuition reimbursement and tax credits). Burger, citing historical precedents in *Everson, Allen,* and *Walz,* suggested his associates had ignored the Court's mandates and direction. (Justice White and Justice Rehnquist joined Chief Justice Burger in dissent.)

The *Levitt*[50] case (the second of eight cases) on appeal from a federal district court in New York (three-judge court declared the statute unconstitutional as "establishment"), concerns legislative appropriation of

$28 million for reimbursement to nonpublic schools for "mandated services," specifically,

> for expenses of services for examinations and inspection in connection with administration, grading and the compiling and reporting of the results of tests and examinations, maintenance of pupil health records, recording of personnel qualifications and characteristics and the preparation and submission to the state of various other reports as provided for or required by law.[51]

State "mandated services" encapsulate a multitude of administration activities such as grading, compiling, and reporting results of tests and examinations, primarily two types: (1) state-prepared examinations administered statewide (such as "Regents Examinations" and "Pupil Examination Program Test"); (2) traditional teacher-made "paper and pencil tests" for assessing student progress. Qualifying schools with grades 7–12 received $45 per student. Schools were not financially accountable for tax money.

Again reasoning per *Nyquist,* the New York General Assembly insisted that tax grants should not under any stretch of the imagination be construed as payment for religious instruction or worship. However, Chief Justice Burger, writing the majority opinion (Justice White dissented), found that the statute contained essentially the same constitutional issue as *Nyquist*[52] — the primary effect of advancing religion. While not questioning teachers' integrity, the statute provided no accountability that teacher-prepared tests would be free of religious instruction. Moreover, the statute contained a "substantial risk" and "potential for conflict."[53] Chief Justice Burger said:

> [W]e are left with no choice under *Nyquist* but to hold that Chapter 138 constitutes an impermissible aid to religion; this is so because the aid that will be devoted to secular functions is not identifiable and separate from the sectarian activities.[54]

Chief Justice Burger rejected arguments that the statute was within the spirit and limits of *Everson* and *Allen,* and that "mandated services" should have state assistance. Chief Justice Burger implied that (1) bus rides and textbooks were substantially different from teacher tests, which were "an integrated part of the teaching process,"[55] and (2) the state may mandate lighting and sanitary facilities with no compulsion for financial assistance. Continuing, Chief Justice Burger said that "lump sum payments under Chapter 138 violate the establishment clause."[56]

The *Lemon III*[57] case (the third of eight cases) came on appeal from a lower court that declared a statute unconstitutional as "establishment"

(Pennsylvania's controversial parent-reimbursement act for nonpublic education). The statute provided partial payment ($75 for elementary-school children, $150 for secondary-school children) to parents whose children attended nonpublic schools. The statute was funded from the state "cigarette tax" and was administered by a five-member Pennsylvania Parent Assistance Authority.

The enactment, to avoid the constitutional strangulation of *Lemon I,* provided no "administrative" or "accountable" features in curriculum-development, personnel, and instruction policies in nonpublic schools. Moreover, Pennsylvania's legislature cloaked the statute in general secular splendor (1) nonpublic schoolchildren reduce cost of public schools; (2) there is a severe hardship on parents of nonpublic schoolchildren; and (3) if Pennsylvania's 500,000 nonpublic schoolchildren were to be "dumped" in public schools, annual operating costs would be extreme. Pennsylvania's legislature acknowledged that parents of nonpublic schoolchildren provided a vital educational service to the state and prevented "an otherwise intolerable public burden."[58]

Justice Powell, writing the majority opinion (6–3 decision with Burger, White, and Rehnquist dissenting) pointed specifically to *Lemon I.* Just two months later, the Pennsylvania legislature had created the parent-reimbursement statute.

Powell acknowledged the legitimacy of a legislative secular purpose, but concluded the Court was interested in the total effect. The statute's characteristics, said Powell, are almost identical to New York's statutes in *Nyquist* in that 90 percent of children in nonpublic schools were in religious schools with imperative religious purposes.

> For purposes of determining where the Pennsylvania tuition reimbursement program has impermissible effect of advancing religion, we find no constitutionally significant distinctions between this law and the one declared invalid today in *Nyquist.*[59]

Regardless of the statute's secular purpose, Powell insisted, "the state has singled out a class of its citizens for a special benefit."[60] The constitutional issue is

> Whether that benefit be viewed as a simple tuition subsidy, as an incentive to parents to send their children to sectarian schools, or as a reward for having done so, at bottom its intended consequence is to preserve and support religious-oriented institutions.[61]

The Pennsylvania statute, Powell maintained, is "financial support of religion," therefore unconstitutional.

Parents of secular nonpublic schoolchildren asked the Court to make a distinction between secular and sectarian schools, and to declare Pennsylvania's enactment constitutional concerning private secular schools. Justice Powell insisted that there was no distinction; secular and sectarian are distinctions without a difference insofar as Pennsylvania's statute is concerned.

Finally, Powell pointed to the "insoluble paradox" that Justice White recognized in *Lemon I.* Lamenting the Court's anguish, Justice Powell insisted that "the problem rests not with doctrines or theories of the Supreme Court, but within the establishment clause—'Congress' and the states by virtue of the Fourteenth Amendment, shall make no law respecting the establishment of religion."[62]

Chief Justice Burger filed a dissenting opinion in which White and Rehnquist joined.

In *Marburger v. Public Funds for Public Schools of New Jersey* (the fourth of eight cases),[63] the Supreme Court reinstated an injunction mandated by the federal District Court for New Jersey declaring New Jersey's "auxiliary-service" enactment unconstitutional. Justice Brennan temporarily set the lower court's decision aside until the entire Court could address the issue.[64]

The New Jersey legislation established two programs to aid nonpublic schools: (1) reimbursement to parents with children in nonpublic schools of the cost of "secular, non-ideological textbooks, instructional materials and supplies ... ten dollars for elementary children and twenty dollars for secondary children,"[65] and (2) excess money from the above reimbursements appropriated to qualifying schools, predicated on total student enrollment to acquire secular supplies, equipment, and auxiliary services (equipment included such items as projectors, viewers, recorders, cameras, typewriters, and other apparatuses used for instruction in science, math, music, and art).

In *Hunt v. McNair* (the fifth of eight cases),[66] a higher-education case, the Supreme Court (6–3, Justices Brennan, Douglas, and Marshall dissenting) sustained the South Carolina Educational Facilities Act as constitutionally permissible, in substance authorizing a financial arrangement between the Education Facilities Authority and the Baptist College at Charleston (operated by the Southern Baptist Convention). The arrangement provided for the Baptist College to transfer part of the campus to the authority, which would lease back the transferred property to the college at a rental price. The authority would then issue revenue bonds ($3.5 million) for use by the college to pay off indebtedness and build new buildings; the bonds would be retired from rents paid by the college under terms of the lease. At final payment, the authority would transfer the property back to the college.

Justice Powell, writing the majority opinion, held that the legislative enactment did not violate the First Amendment establishment clause: (1) the legislation had a secular purpose; (2) the bond issue's primary effect neither advanced nor inhibited religion; and (3) there was no excessive entanglement between the authority and religion.[67]

Justices Brennan, Douglas, and Marshall found that the enactment involved the authority "to an unconstitutional degree in policing the college's affairs, and thus violated the First Amendment's establishment clause."[68]

The sixth case, *Essex v. Wolman*,[69] was discussed earlier in this chapter. And the seventh decision, *Kosydar v. Wolman*,[70] *Grit v. Wolman* at the Supreme Court level,[71] logically follows *Essex v. Wolman*. As already indicated, this district-court decision is layered on the earlier spring 1972 *Essex v. Wolman* parent-reimbursement case. We belabor *Kosydar* somewhat because of the apparent political-judicial intrigue between the Ohio General Assembly, the Ohio governor, and the federal court. Approximately two months from the declaration of the parent-reimbursement enactment as unconstitutional, the Ohio General Assembly enacted the tax-credit statute that accommodated the same political ideology already declared unconstitutional. Moreover, *Kosydar* is much broader based than *Essex v. Wolman*.

After the parent-reimbursement statute was declared unconstitutional, the Ohio General Assembly quickly enacted tax-credit relief for parents whose children attended private and religious schools, and the provision was signed into law by Ohio's governor June 21, 1972 (approximately two months had elapsed since the declaration as unconstitutional of the parent-reimbursement statute). The statute provides, for parents and children enrolled in private and religious nonpublic schools, a graduated tax credit with a maximum of $90 per child attending nonpublic schools. A parent (taxpayer) could claim the maximum $90 per child against liability to the state or be reimbursed a maximum of $90 per child if overpayment had been made. The overpayment refund reserve came from a "rotary fund" funded by the state treasurer.

Ohio's tax-credit statute was considerably broader in scope and sequence than the parent-reimbursement statute. However, while the statute was broader based, the sectarian nature was essentially the same. Ohio's nonpublic student population was approximately 13 percent of the state's total school population. Of those who attended religious schools, approximately 95 percent attended Catholic schools. The Court found that the only novel question in the case was whether a state using taxing machinery can confer benefits, in this instance tax credits, on a particular class of people who send their children to nonpublic schools and whether such a statute violates the First Amendment establishment clause.[72] The lower court concluded that it was an impermissible constitutional violation; the statute aided religion.

The district court applied the *Lemon I* tripartite test. The statute strangled on "neither advances nor inhibits religion."[73] The district court did not question the general wisdom or imperative social purposes of the statute. The court insisted it was concerned not with "improper motivation" but with the effect the statute had on constitutional rights.

The district court elaborated on general secular services available to all schools, such as fire and police protection, and bus service. Such general secular benefits accruing to religious schools are "remote, minimal and incidental and not different from the benefits flowing generally to society."[74] However, where the effective class (as a result of legislation) is predominately religious and the rewards provided are not ideologically neutral, in substance the statute advances religion, and such an enactment becomes highly suspect.[75] Thus, said the district court, when the state transfers financial rewards to a class of people that is overwhelmingly sectarian, without adequate accounting controls, the likelihood arises that state is assisting religion.[76]

The district court insisted that to reward through tax credits parents who forego use of public schools in order to send their children to non-public schools "is to grant that taxpayer a relevant economic advantage when compared to the taxpayers generally."[77] In responding to appellant's arguments, the district court said:

> The State does not have an affirmative duty to sustain all religion, like flies in amber, for the pluralistic interest of society. The adoption of such a view would mark a profound and radical departure from the philosophy of separation of church and state which has characterized this country from its very inception.[78]

The district court held:

> We hold that where, as here, the recipient of state ... benefits is a predominantly sectarian class of schools and, therefore, as a matter of law the primary effect of such benefits is to advance religion, then the form of these benefits, whether by tax credits, exemption or deductions, cannot alone insulate them from First Amendment infirmity.[79]

The district court quoted Justice Douglas in *Abingdon:* "What may not be done directly may not be done indirectly lest the establishment clause becomes a mockery."[80]

On January 22, 1973, the Supreme Court denied a stay of judgment of the district court.[81] And on June 25, 1973, the Court affirmed the district court's judgment without written opinion. Justice White would have reversed the judgment of the district court.

The eighth and final Supreme Court decision on June 25, 1973, was *Cathedral Academy.*[82] This case challenged New York's Chapter 138 providing for state reimbursement to private elementary and secondary schools for state-mandated services—in this case certain testing and record keeping. A three-judge federal district court had declared Chapter 138 unconstitutional as First Amendment establishment. On direct appeal, the Supreme Court, with Chief Justice Burger writing the majority opinion, affirmed the lower court's decision. Burger, expressing five members' views (Justices Douglas, Brennan, and Marshall insisted their affirmance was delineated in *Nyquist* and *Lemon III,* and Justice White dissented), maintained that Chapter 138 was unconstitutional aid to religion because there was no provision to identify and separate the secular functions from the sectarian.

At the conclusion of 1973, the pace of church-state legislation and litigation was intensive. The Supreme Court more clearly defined permissible constitutional guidelines. (1) In light of *Lemon I, DiCenso, Johnson,* and other cases, purchases of "auxiliary services" and "general secular services activities" were constitutionally impermissible as "entanglement" or establishment of religion. (2) In light of *Nyquist, Lemon III, Essex, Kosydar,* and *Marburger,* parent-reimbursement and/or tax-credit enactments were constitutionally impermissible as establishment of religion (Burger, White, and Rehnquist disagreed). (3) In light of *Levitt,* state-mandated-service statutes were constitutionally impermissible as establishment of religion. (4) Based on *Tilton* and *Hunt v. McNair,* higher-education enactments pass constitutional muster for two reasons: first, the neutral accommodationist pragmatism employed by the Court favors such legislation; second, according to the majority, college and university students are older, more mature, and less impressionable than elementary and secondary children—bad theology makes bad law. (5) Based on *Cochran, Everson,* and *Allen,* the Court continued to allow general secular services to all child benefits such as transportation and textbooks.

The year 1974 had four church-state decisions: (1) *Franchise Tax Board of California v. United Americans for Public Schools;*[83] (2) *Luetkemeyer v. Kaufmann;*[84] (3) *Marburger v. Public Funds for Public Schools of New Jersey;*[85] and (4) *Wheeler v. Barrera.*[86]

In *Franchise Tax Board of California,*[87] the Supreme Court affirmed, without written opinion, a federal district court decision (also without written opinion) declaring a California enactment providing state income-tax reductions for parents who send children to private elementary and secondary schools unconstitutional as religious advancement. Justice White, joined by Chief Justice Burger and Justice Rehnquist dissented: "For the reasons stated in my dissent in *Committee for Public Education and Religious Liberty v. Nyquist,* 413 U.S. 756 813-824, 93 S. Ct. 2955, 37 L. Ed. 2d 948 (1973), I disagree and respectfully dissent."[88]

In *Luetkemeyer v. Kaufmann,*[89] the Supreme Court (6–3) affirmed the judgment of a federal district court that Missouri's providing transportation for students to public schools but disallowing transportation to sectarian elementary and secondary schools was constitutional. Justice White, joined by Chief Justice Burger, filed a dissenting opinion. Before addressing Justice White's dissenting opinion, a closer examination of the district court's judgment is imperative.

Urban Luetkemeyer's two children attended St. Martin's Parochial School. The public school bus passed within two hundred yards of Mr. Luetkemeyer's house and enroute to the public schools, passed right by St. Martin's. Mr. Luetkemeyer brought legal action, claiming that the state must provide bus transportation to St. Martin's. Specifically, Mr. Luetkemeyer contended that (1) bus transportation to school was a public service that should be available to all, if available to any, regardless of school description; (2) Missouri bus-transportation statutes were "arbitrary and capricious"; and (3) the statutes denied the plaintiffs equal protection and due process of law — giving up a religious right to secure a public benefit.[90] Thus, the compelling constitutional question was whether Missouri had to extend bus transportation to religious schools, whether a statute creating an exclusively public-school transportation service was constitutional.

District Judge John W. Oliver (writing the majority opinion) rejected the child-benefit theory on which plaintiffs relied heavily by maintaining that "principles which state what a State may do may not properly be read as a command to what a State must do."[91]

Mr. Luetkemeyer insisted that bus transportation to schools was a vital part of the state's education scheme and was especially important to the safety and welfare of children, that absence of bus transportation to religious schools was lack of equal protection and due process. Judge Oliver concluded that if a student had no constitutional right to a public education, then surely a student had no constitutional right to a parochial education nor a constitutional right to "receive free public transportation to and from parochial schools."[92]

Thus, continued Judge Oliver, Missouri statutes are not "arbitrary and capricious." The statutes promote the legitimate state action "of maintaining a very high wall between church and state."

In conclusion, Judge Oliver said:

> We find and conclude that the Constitution of the United States does not compel the state of Missouri to provide equal transportation services to private and church-sponsored schools and that it may, as it has, elect to provide such service only for its public schools.[93]

Justice White's dissenting opinion focused on (1) the child-benefit theory — that after *Everson,* the Missouri enactment "seems to be denied because certain students are seeking religious training";[94] (2) federal equal-protection principles, violated unless there was a "valid interest supporting ... different treatment accorded public school and parochial school students";[95] and (3) denial of transportation, creating arbitrariness and raising questions "whether the State has not become the 'adversary' of the religion and has placed burdens on appellant's free exercise rights."[96]

In summary, the Supreme Court simply affirmed Missouri legislative enactment that provided public transportation to public schools and disallowed public transportation to private or religious schools.

In *Marburger,*[97] the Court, without written opinion, affirmed the judgment of the federal district court declaring New Jersey's parent-reimbursement and purchase-of-auxiliary-service enactment unconstitutional. *Marburger* (1973) was detailed earlier in this chapter, but judicial procedure provided another appeal before the Court. Again, Burger, White, and Rehnquist noted probable jurisdiction and would have scheduled the case for oral argument.

Perhaps *Wheeler v. Barrera*[98] was the most important 1974 church-state case, and the Court addressed an issue never before addressed by the Court—Title I of the 1965 Elementary and Secondary Education Act (ESEA).

This case came initially from the federal District Court, Western District, Missouri, through the Eighth Circuit Court of Appeals, which reversed. The case concerns Title I of the ESEA, specifically aid to education of deprived children in nonpublic schools. Title I of ESEA provides federal funds for special-education programs for deprived children in public and nonpublic schools.

Parents of children in nonpublic schools demanded that the Kansas City School Board provide "in-kind" Title I programs comparable to Title I programs in public schools. The Kansas City School Board (also the Missouri State School Board) maintained that Title I programs demanded by parents (1) violated the state constitution and (2) exceeded imperatives of Title I.

Historically, Title I was the first federal enactment providing education programs for children in both private and public schools. Specifically, Title I provides Federal funds for educationally deprived children "who are handicapped or whose needs ... result from poverty, neglect, delinquency, or cultural linguistic isolation from the community at large."[99]

The Supreme Court was confronted with three significant constitutional issues: (1) did Title I mandate "on-the-premises" instruction for religious schools similar in substance to public-school programs? (2) Would Title I-funded teachers providing instruction in on-the-premises religious schools breach the establishment clause? (3) What types of "comparable" Title I services are religious schools entitled to?

To answer the first question, Justice Blackmun, writing the Court's majority opinion, acknowledged that Title I–funded teachers providing remedial instruction established the conflict of the case. Plaintiffs (parents) and defendants (school board) had refused to move from positions apparently limited from religious, emotional, and political motivation. Plaintiffs maintained that "comparable" Title I programs simply meant classroom instruction in religious schools and refused to accept or recognize other educational alternatives. However, the school board insisted that the state constitution prohibited using public funds for religious-schoolteachers and refused to compromise their position. It is proper to note that the Missouri attorney general in an advisory opinion disagreed with the school board and did not participate in the state's defense.

Justice Blackmun insisted that Kansas City's school board "had failed to meet their statutory commitment to provide comparable services to children in non-public schools."[100] Moreover, instructional programs provided children in religious schools "were plainly inferior both qualitatively and quantitatively."[101] However, Justice Blackmun cautioned, "the opinion of the Court of Appeals is not to be read to the effect that petitioners must submit an approved plan that employs the use of Title I teachers on private school premises during regular hours."[102]

Justice Blackmun held that the court of appeals erred in holding that federal statutes superseded the Missouri Constitution.[103] Justice Blackmun said, "Title I evinces a clear intention that state constitutional spending proscriptions not be preempted as a condition for accepting federal funds."[104] Examining the historical intent of the act, Justice Blackmun acknowledged that guidelines governing expenditures of federal funds are "purely a question of State and not Federal law" and that "Federal law under Title I is to the effect that State law should not be disturbed."[105] Moreover, Justice Blackmun continued, Missouri has no obligation under Title I to provide on-premises instruction in religious schools, and the court of appeals decision in this area was unnecessary—the decision was an "advisory opinion." However, Justice Blackmun continued, what Title I mandates is "comparable" services, "the choice of programs is left to the State with a proviso that comparable (not identical) programs are also made available to eligible private school children."[106] While recognizing that state school systems might still opt for on-premises instruction as a plausible direction, Justice Blackmun insisted that if educational and constitutional circumstances mandated otherwise, he would recommend three broad alternatives. (1) Comparable instruction programs that effectively exclude on-premises instruction; here, Blackmun alluded to an extensive listing of educational possibilities in the footnotes. Even though plaintiffs maintained that "comparable" meant on-premises instruction and nothing else, Title I programs could not be defeated "simply because private schools refused to participate unless aid offered in the particular form it requested ... the Act does not give the private schools a veto power...."[107] (2) If state school systems were unable to develop "comparable" Title I programs for religious schools, then eliminate on-premises public-schoolteachers and relegate all Title I programs "to other means, such as a neutral site or summer program that are less likely to give rise to the gross disparity present in this case."[108] (3) The last alternative suggested by Blackmun, and perhaps the least attractive, was nonparticipation in the program.[109] The logic here is simple enough: If public schools do not participate, religious schools cannot participate.

In responding to the second question regarding Title I teachers providing instruction in religious schools, Blackmun suggested that this significant constitutional issue was not "ripe" for decision: "[A]t this time, we intimate no view as to the establishment effect of any particular program"[110] Moreover, Justice Blackmun acknowledged that the establishment clause has been historically a delicate issue for the Supreme Court. Likewise, Title I on-premises instruction could offer a variety of educational programs and directions; each case must require "a careful evaluation of the facts."[111]

In response to the third question—what types of Title I services are religious schools entitled to?—Blackmun, while insisting that relief was imperative, maintained that religious schools "are not entitled to any particular form of service, and it is the role of the State and local agencies and not of the Federal Courts, at least at this stage, to formulate suitable plan."[112]

This case contains many serious constitutional implications concerning future litigation (even inviting litigation). Justice Powell, writing a brief concurring opinion, acknowledged serious constitutional entanglement when he said, "I would have serious misgivings about the constitutionality of a statute that required the utilization of public school teachers in sectarian schools."[113] Moreover, Justice White (who had dissented with the majority in recent cases) recognized the same imperative issues, especially "on the premises instruction ... I would have thought that any such arrangement would be impermissible under the Court's recent cases construing the establishment clause."[114] Likewise, Justice Douglas, in a dissenting opinion, acknowledged significant constitutional questions. Douglas suggested the judiciary "had been seduced" by cosmetic education institutions, public and nonpublic, educating disadvantaged children. Douglas reviewed briefly the Court's historical position on church-state activities, especially in recent years, and found that the decision conflicted with recent decisions. Moreover Douglas said:

> The present case is plainly not moot; a case of controversy exists; and it is clear that if the traditional First Amendment barriers are to be maintained, no program serving students in religious schools could be designed under

this act—whether regular school hours are used, or after school hours, or weekend hours. The plain truth is that under the First Amendment, as construed to this day, the Act is unconstitutional to the extent it supports sectarian schools, whether directly or through its students.

We should say so now and save the endless hours and efforts which hopeful people will expend in an effort to constitutionalize what is impossible without constitutional amendment.[115]

The case was finally decided in 1976 by the Missouri Supreme Court. The case was remanded to the federal district court and subsequently on appeal again to the circuit court of appeals, and finally the case appeared on the Missouri Supreme Court docket. In 1976, the Missouri Supreme Court declared that (1) Title I funds are "public" funds, not "federal funds"—a distinction without a difference; (2) Title I funds deposited with the state treasury are "money donated" for public-school purposes as decided by the Missouri Constitution and statutes; and (3) use of Title I money for teachers and services (including textbooks and transportation) in parochial schools is aid to religion and constitutionally impermissible.[116]

In light of the Supreme Court decisions in *Franchise Tax Board of California* and *Marburger,* parent-reimbursement and/or tax-credit enactments to aid religious schools continued to be constitutionally impermissible, as establishment of religion. Chief Justice Burger, Justice White, and Justice Rehnquist disagreed. The child-benefit theory promoted in *Cochran, Everson,* and *Allen* suffered little if any in *Luetkemeyer.* In reality, *Wheeler* did little to settle compelling Title I (as of 1982, Chapter I) constitutional questions; the constitutional issues raised were considerably more important than constitutional questions answered. Finally, the year 1974 saw a continuing increase in church-state legislative and judicial activities.[117]

The year 1975 had three significant events: (1) *Meek v. Pittenger,*[118] a Supreme Court decision of principal importance; (2) armed with the tripartite test, the Court appeared to reach a constitutional plateau concerning impermissible aid to religious schools, as demonstrated in *Meek;* and (3) Justice William O. Douglas retired from the Court on November 13, 1975.

On May 19, 1975, the Supreme Court decided a most important religious-aid case in *Meek v. Pittenger.* And in retrospect, the Burger Court appeared to reach a constitutional plateau concerning public funds for religious schools. The *Meek* circumstances were construed as devastating to political and religious leaders seeking legislative enactments supporting public funds for religious schools. The Court appeared to truncate almost every conceivable possibility of "auxiliary services." Yet that appearance was deceiving, as the record indicates.

The *Meek* case came on appeal from the Federal District Court for the

Eastern District, Pennsylvania (same route of *Lemon I* and *Lemon III*), concerning Pennsylvania's legislative efforts to aid religious and private schools. The district court (always consistent in church-state decisions) denied relief. Plaintiffs appealed. The Supreme Court, in a 6–3 decision, affirmed in part ("textbook" provision of Act 195), and reversed as "establishment," Act 194 and remaining parts of Act 195.

The facts of the case are as follows: The Commonwealth of Pennsylvania, through genuine concern for all children in elementary and secondary schools, had continuously made an effort to aid sectarian and private schools. This was especially true in the early 1970s, as witnessed by legislative and judicial efforts that produced the three *Lemon* cases. The pattern is one of legislative simplicity. The Pennsylvania General Assembly enacted legislation aiding religious schools, and the Supreme Court declared the legislation unconstitutional (*Lemon I*, 1971). The General Assembly returned to the sectarian-aid drawing board and enacted new legislation. Again, the Supreme Court declared the action unconstitutional (*Lemon III*, 1973). The General Assembly, with a concern for religion and all of Pennsylvania's elementary and secondary children, initiated new action. And once again the Supreme Court invalidated all but the "textbook" portion (*Meek*, 1975). Thus, continuous legislative and judicial confrontation provided an interesting prelude to this church-state decision.

In 1972, the Pennsylvania legislature established Acts 194 and 195. Act 194 was a general "auxiliary-service" statute providing counseling, testing, psychological services, and speech and hearing therapy. Moreover, the act provided for teachers and other related services for exceptional children, for remedial students, and for educationally disadvantaged students. Finally, Act 194 provided for "secular" services currently enjoyed by all public-schoolchildren.

Act 195 provided that textbooks, instructional materials, and instructional equipment be loaned to sectarian and private schools.

In February 1973, plaintiffs sought relief from legislative imperatives. With the exception of the restrictive instructional-equipment provision, injunctive relief was denied by the federal district court.

Justice Stewart, writing for the Court, reviewed recent church-state history. He called attention to the tripartite test and considered the test a "convenient, accurate distillation of this Court's effort over the pat decade" to bring understanding and continuity to the evaluation of constitutionality of government action. However, continued Stewart, one must not consider the test as "setting precise limits."[119]

Justice Stewart dealt with the textbook issue first, calling attention to *Allen* (1968). He found that "financial benefit of Pennsylvania's textbook program, like New York's, is to parents and children, not to the non-public schools."[120] Moreover, said Stewart, books that were loaned to religious schools were usable and "acceptable" for public-school use. There was no suggestion that "religious" books be used.

In handling the remaining elements of Act 195 — instructional material and instructional equipment — Stewart acknowledged the sincerity and legitimacy of concern of the Pennsylvania General Assembly for all children. But, said Justice Stewart, "direct loan of instructional materials and equipment has the unconstitutional effect of advancing religion because of the predominantly religious character of the schools benefiting from the Act."[121] Some instructional material and equipment, such as maps, charts, globes, and laboratory equipment, might be secular "self-policing." Yet, "it would simply ignore reality to attempt to separate secular education functions from the predominantly religious role."[122] Moreover, it is impossible to "characterize Act 195 as channeling aid to the secular without providing direct aid to the sectarian."[123] And even though state aid was earmarked for secular use only when utilized by an institution whose primary function was religion, "this constitutes an impermissible establishment of religion."[124]

Act 194 provided for professional teachers and therapists on religious-school premises, and this complicated the issue constitutionally. Recounting the Court's thinking in *Lemon I* and *DiCenso,* Justice Stewart emphasized that teachers must "play a strictly non-ideological role."[125] And for Pennsylvania to guarantee that Act 194 personnel did not advance religion would "give rise to a(n) intolerable degree of entanglement between church and state."[126]

Proponents of Act 194 argued that personnel worked outside the academic mainstream with remedial and/or exceptional students and that this differed considerably from *Lemon I* and *DiCenso*. To that fundamental position, Stewart replied that teachers were teachers, whether remedial or otherwise, "and a state-subsidized guidance counselor is surely as likely as a state-subsidized chemistry teacher to fail on occasion to separate religious instruction and the advancement of religious beliefs from his secular educational responsibilities."[127]

Finally, Stewart, like Burger in *Lemon I* and *DiCenso,* called attention to the political divisiveness of the statute. The acts created a serious potential for "conflict and provide[d] successive opportunities for political fragmentation and diversion along religious lines."[128]

The 6–3 decisions regarding both acts did not include the same lineup of justices. For instance, Stewart, Blackmun, Powell, Douglas, Brennan, and Marshall were in the majority in declaring Acts 194 and 195 unconstitutional as establishment of religion. Burger, Rehnquist, and White were in the minority on the same issue. However, the "textbook provision" found Burger, White, Rehnquist, Stewart, Blackmun, and Powell in the majority, with Douglas, Brennan, and Marshall dissenting.

Brennan (with whom Douglas and Marshall concurred) filed a blistering opinion on the textbook provision of Act 195. To Justice Brennan the imperative question was simply how could instructional material be aid to religious institutions and textbooks not be aid? Moreover, if Act 194 and the instructional materials and equipment elements of Act 195 were divisive, surely the "textbook provision" was also.

Burger also filed a noteworthy dissent concerning every element of Acts 194 and 195 excepting the textbook provision. Indicating his disbelief of the majority decision, Burger called his fellow justices' position "crabbed" and their logic distorted. Rehnquist, with whom Justice White concurred, filed a dissenting opinion in which he delineated his established position (see Table 5.1, opposite).

As indicated earlier, the Court appeared to reach a plateau in *Meek,* more clearly defining permissible constitutional limitations. Based on the first five years of the 1970s' decisions, auxiliary services and general secular services were constitutionally impermissible as "entanglement" or "establishment." Theoretically, the *Meek* decision truncated almost every conceivable possibility of "auxiliary service."

In the light of *Essex, Kosydar, Lemon III, Marburger,* and *Franchise Tax Board of California,* parent-reimbursement and tax-credit enactments were constitutionally impermissible as "establishment" of religion.

The child-benefit theory developed in *Cochran, Everson,* and *Allen* received an additional boost in *Meek.* Douglas, Brennan, and Marshall now dissented at least on the textbook provision of the child benefits.

Finally, it should be noted that Justice William O. Douglas retired on November 14, 1975, after serving on the Court for thirty-six years, longer than any justice in Supreme Court history.

At the conclusion of 1975, the Court was philosophically split 6–3 on church-state issues, with Burger, White and Rehnquist dissenting.

1976–1980

The Burger Court activities regarding church-state legislation during the last five years of the 1970s were just as voluminous and precedent-setting as the previous five years. The five years from 1976 to 1980 focused on (1) sectarian higher-education-aid cases, with *Roemer v. Board of Education*[129] the imperative decision; (2) two major sectarian-school-aid decisions; (3) what appeared to be a philosophical plateau, as expressed in *Meek,* of virtually eliminating public funds for the purchase of "auxiliary services" and "general secular services"—a new judicial course in *Wolman v. Walters* (1977)[130] and *Committee for Public Education and Religious Liberty v. Regan* (1980);[131] (4) the tripartite test first expressed in *Lemon I*

Table 5.1

Meek v. Pittenger
Breakdown of Voting on the Statutes

Justices	*Act 194* (auxiliary services)	*Act 195* (instruction materials and equipment)	*Act 195* (textbook loan))
Justice Burger	D	D	C
Justice Blackmun	C	C	C
Justice Brennan	C	C	D
Justice Douglas	C	C	D
Justice Marshall	C	C	D
Justice Powell	C	C	C
Justice Stewart	C	C	C
Justice Rehnquist	D	D	C
Justice White	D	D	C

Legend: C = Concur
          D = Dissent

became no "litmus-paper test" and no "categorical imperatives and absolute approaches";[132] (5) President Gerald Ford appointed Justice John Paul Stevens to the Supreme Court; and (6) the retirement of Justice William O. Douglas, especially his leadership, his vote, and personal influence in shaping the Court's church-state decisions for thirty-six years. His dissenting opinion in *Wheeler v. Barrera* challenged his associates to a more demanding intellectual and scholarly judicial pursuit when less effort seemed to be the order of the day. In historical retrospect, Douglas's intellectual capacity and human integrity have been sorely missed.

In 1976, *Roemer*,[133] a sectarian higher-education decision, was the Court's first church-state case following Justice Douglas's retirement. *Roemer* is germane to this study from an ideological and an education-finance standpoint.

Roemer began in 1971 when the Maryland General Assembly legislated subsidy payments to higher education institutions (1) based on the number of students—15 percent of the state cost per pupil; and (2) excluding religious programs—seminary or theological academic programs.[134] Moreover, the subsidy was noncategorical. However, in 1972, the legislature added a provision that grants could not be used for sectarian purposes. The grant program, administered by the Maryland Council for Higher Education, established compliance procedures: (1) to determine eligible institutions; (2) to insure that institutions do not use grant money for sectarian purposes; and (3) to establish a fiscal-year report concerning grant expenditures. Also, the council insisted on on-site investigation of expenditures if necessary.

This action was initiated by four Maryland citizens and taxpayers challenging the constitutionality, under the First Amendment establishment clause, of the statute as applied to four Roman Catholic colleges (a Methodist-affiliated institution was originally involved and later dropped). As three-judge federal district court (2–1 decision), applying the tripartite test of *Lemon I*, held initially that the statute was unconstitutional. However, the statute passed constitutional muster when amended, generally disallowing expenditure of public funds for sectarian purposes. The district court decision was appealed to the Supreme Court.

On June 21, 1976, the Supreme Court (5–4 decision), with Justice Blackmun writing the majority opinion, sustained the district court's decision (Burger, Powell, White and Rehnquist made up the majority; Marshall, Brennan, Stewart, and Stevens composed the minority). Blackmun briefly reviewed Supreme Court church-state history, particularly those cases that supported aid—*Bradfield*, 125 U.S. 291 (1891), *Everson*, 330 U.S. 1 (1947), and *Allen*, 397 U.S. 236 (1968). While insisting that the Court "has not been blind to the fact that in aiding a religious institution to perform a secular task, the state frees the institution's resources to be put to sectarian ends,"[135] Blackmun acknowledged "a hermetic separation of the two is an impossibility it has never required."[136] Moreover, "Neutrality is what is required."[137] The state must neither discriminate against nor aid religion.

With the historical bases established, Blackmun responded to plaintiff's concern—the *Lemon I* three-part test. With the first part of *Lemon I* test no factor, Justice Blackmun turned to parts two and three—plus "political divisiveness."

Thus, in response to the advancing-religion question Blackmun detailed religious aspects of the four colleges involved. They were (1) "formal affiliation with the Roman Catholic Church,"[138]nonetheless "characterized by high degree of an institutional autonomy";[139] (2) "Roman Catholic chaplains ... hold Roman Catholic religious exercises on campus"— attendance was not mandatory, and spiritual development was a secondary characteristic of the institution; also "religious indoctrination was not a substantial purpose";[140] (3) while theology and religious courses are part of the mandatory curriculum and taught by Roman Catholic clerics, they are simply part of the "liberal arts program; moreover, the courses have no 'religious pressures'";[141] (4) while many classes at the four colleges begin with prayer, there was no official policy, and the institutions indicate such practice was part of the individual professor's academic freedom;[142] (5) while "academic quality," not religious consideration, was important in faculty hiring, the Court noted that "budgetary considerations lead the colleges generally to favor members of religious orders, who often receive less than a full salary";[143] (6) while the majority of students were Roman Catholic, students "are chosen without regard to religion."[144]

Justice Blackmun recognized there was a "role of religion" apparent in the institutions. Nonetheless, the secular can be separated from the sectarian. Moreover, "We must assume that the colleges and the Council, will exercise their delegated control"[145] to an extent satisfying both the statute and the constitution.

Concerning the excessive-entanglement question, Blackmun recognized the difficulty that "primary effect" had on "excessive entanglement," and reviewed excessive entanglement of the Maryland statute in great detail. The statute (1) clearly prohibited sectarian use; (2) provided for annual funding with the possibility of greater demand for money; (3) provided for annual proposal and approval of expenditures (even to the extent of a special bank deposit) by the administrative council; and (4) provided for the establishment of fiscal credibility, including on-site investigation by the Council.[146] While recognizing there was no "exact science in gauging the entanglement," Blackmun found that the Maryland statute was sufficiently free from excessive entanglement.[147]

As for the political-divisiveness question, Blackmun acknowledged that the annual funding with the possibility of increased funding demands "aggravated the danger of political fragmentation ... on religious lines."[148] Yet Blackmun insisted there was no danger of substantial political divisiveness: "[T]he danger of political divisiveness is substantially less when the aided institution is not an elementary or secondary school but a college...."[149]

White, along with Rehnquist, filed a concurring opinion. For White, the three-part test established in *Lemon I* was still unreconcilable; the "insoluble paradox" is apparent, and this decision sheds no new light.[150]

Brennan, Stewart, and Stevens filed dissenting opinions. Brennan insisted the Maryland statute "offended the constitution" as an advancement of religion; the evidence overwhelmingly established the colleges to be church-related with a religious mission permeating every element. Brennan suggested that he would not only declare the statute unconstitutional as advancement of religion but would order the colleges to refund money already expended.[151]

Stewart was greatly concerned with the compelling difference between compulsory theological and religious courses taught as part of the curriculum as compared with religious courses taught as an academic discipline in *Tilton*. Here the theological and religious courses were taught by Roman Catholic clerics who may be "devoted to deepening religious experiences."[152]

Stevens indicated that "the pernicious tendency of a state subsidy to tempt religious schools to compromise their religious mission without wholly abandoning" it is certainly apparent.[153]

Even though *Roemer* was a higher-education case, the decision signaled cataclysmic possibilities. (1) The 5–4 lineup of justices on higher-education matters departed from the 6–3 lineup since *Lemon I*. (2) The logic enunciated in the *Lemon I* tripartite test provided such a clear philosophical statement for legislative evaluation that Blackmun insisted that *Lemon I*, Part II — "primary effect of advancing religion" — was so substantive as to complicate Part III — "excessive entanglement"; in essence, the tripartite standard appeared to lose favor because the "standard" demanded simple answers. (3) For the first time in the 1970s the neutral accommodationist theory becomes important in a majority opinion — "neutrality is what is required." The state must neither aid nor discriminate against religion. Once again, "neutral" must be construed as favoring church-state enactments providing public funds for sectarian institutions. (4) Justice Stevens apparently aligned with the *Lemon I* majority, replacing Justice Douglas. Theoretically the Court should have continued to divide 6–3 on public funds for religious schools. (5) Perhaps the Court placed elementary and secondary issues in one category and higher education in another; "the danger of political divisiveness is 'substantially less' when the aided institution is not an elementary or secondary school."[154] "Our holdings are better reconciled in terms of the character of the aided institutions, found to be so dissimilar as between those considered in *Tilton*, and *Hunt*, on the one hand, and those considered in *Lemon I, Nyquist*, and *Levitt* on the other."[155]

During 1977, church-state issues, both legislative and judicial, continued at a frenzied pace. In January 1977, there were forty-seven church-state cases pending in federal courts. The cases were wide-ranging, involving religious practices in schools, the teaching of transcendental meditation, the distribution of Bibles on public-school campuses, school boards' observance of religious holidays of employees, and, of course, public aid to religious schools.[156]

Wolman v. Walters[157] was the major 1977 decision. This case, decided June 24, 1977, arrived on appeal from the federal District Court for the Southern District of Ohio challenging the constitutionality of the Ohio statute authorizing financial aid to sectarian schools. The statute specifically authorized (1) the purchase of secular textbooks that were used in public schools and approved by the school superintendent for loans to pupils or parents on request made to the nonpublic school;[158] (2) standardized tests and scoring services for sectarian schools;[159] (3) speech and hearing diagnostic services, diagnostic psychological services (by local school-board employees), and physician's services, with all treatment administered at sectarian schools' direction;[160] (4) specialized therapeutic, guidance, and remedial services by employees of local school boards and/or state department of health, administered in public schools, public centers, or secular mobile units located off sectarian-school premises;[161] (5) loans to pupils or parents of instructional material and equipment, incapable of diversion to religious use;[162] (6) transportation for field trips;[163] and (7) public-funded physician, nursing, dental, and optometric services (not challenged).

The district court approved the constitutionality of textbooks; standardized testing and scoring services; and diagnostic, therapeutic, and remedial services. The court adjudged provisions for instructional materials, equipment, and field trips unconstitutional.

The district court had temporarily restrained the expenditure of any funds. However, by consent of all parties, the three-judge court modified the restraining order to permit expenditure of funds to purchase textbooks and lend them to pupils or their parents. The Supreme Court reversed the district court decision in part and affirmed in part (see Table 5.2 for a breakdown of the voting on each provision).

Justice Blackmun, writing for the Court, briefly examined the history of the statute in view of *Meek v. Pittenger*.[164] Initial biennial funding was $80 million. Ohio has 720 chartered nonpublic schools. Of these, twenty-nine schools are secular (4 percent of the school population). Of 96 percent of the school population attending 691 sectarian schools, 92 percent attend Catholic schools.

Blackmun again recognized the historical tripartite test. He dismissed the "first prong," secular legislative purpose, as not applicable. "We are satisfied that the challenged statute reflects Ohio's legitimate interest in protecting the health of its young and in providing a fertile educational environment for all school children of the State."[165] However, "effect and entanglement" are the difficult properties.[166] Moreover, each mandate of the statute must be examined against "firmly rooted" precedents.[167]

Table 5.2

Wolman v. Walter
Voting Breakdown on the Statute

Justices	PART I General History Review concerning church-state	PART II Establishment Clause—Secular purpose	PART III Textbooks Section 3317.06(H)	PART IV Testing & Scoring Section 3317.06(J)	PART V Diagnostic Services, Hearing, & Psychology Section 3317.06(D), (F)	PART VI Therapeutic Services—Guidance & Remedial Section 3317.06(H), (I), (K)	PART VI (G) Therapeutic Services—Guidance & Remedial Section(G), 3317.06	PART VII Instruction Materials & Equipment Section 3317.06(B), (C)	PART VIII Field Trips Section 3317.06(L)
Burger	Yes	Yes	Yes	Yes	Yes	Yes	Yes	Yes	Yes
Blackmun	Yes	Yes	No	No	Yes	Yes	Yes	No	No
Brennan	Yes	No	No	No	No	No	No	No	No
Marshall	Yes	No	No	No	Yes	No	Yes	No	No
Powell	Yes	Yes	Yes	Yes	Yes	Yes	Yes	No	Yes
Stevens	Yes	No	No	No	Yes	Yes	Yes	No	No
Stewart	Yes	Yes	Yes	Yes	Yes	Yes	Yes	No	No
Rehnquist	Yes	Yes	Yes	Yes	Yes	Yes	Yes	Yes	Yes
White	Yes	Yes	Yes	Yes	Yes	Yes	Yes	Yes	Yes
	9–0	6–3 that the statute Section 3317.06 has a secular legislative purpose	5–4 for textbooks as constitutional	5–4 for testing & scoring as administered content are constitutional	8–1 for diagnostic services as administered are constitutional	7–2 for therapeutic services as administered are constitutional	8–1 for therapeutic services as administered are constitutional	6–3 against instruction materials & equipment unconstitutional as advancing religion	5–4 against field trips are unconstitutional as advancing religion

(Justice Marshall separated Part VI (G) from Part VI (H), (I), and (K). In setting up the table, we followed his directive.)

§3317.06(A)—Purchase of Secular Textbooks

Blackmun recognized the "striking resemblance" of the statute to systems already approved in *Board of Education v. Allen*[168] and *Meek v. Pittenger.*[169] Thus, "§ 3317.06 (A) is constitutional."[170]

§ 3317.06 (J)—Testing and Scoring

This section passes constitutional muster because (1) no money flows either to the sectarian school or the parents; (2) the tests are commercial standardized achievement tests and are graded by the commercial firm, so that no sectarian schoolteachers are involved, and tests are free of religious instruction; and (3) the state has a legitimate concern with quality and standards of instruction.[171]

§ 3317.06 (D), (F)—Diagnostic Services

Both (D), concerning speech and hearing diagnostic services, and (F), concerning diagnostic psychological services, were constitutionally permissible. Such services are general health services to the child, which are constitutionally permissible; moreover, diagnostic services differ considerably from teaching and counseling in that they have very little educational substance.[172] Finally, limited contact with children in a diagnostic relationship simply did not provide much opportunity to espouse sectarian views. Thus, (D) and (F) "will not be impermissible entanglement."[173]

§ 3317.06 (G), (H), (I), (K)—Therapeutic, Guidance, and Remedial Services

The above services were provided in public schools, public centers, or mobile units located off nonpublic-school premises. Transportation was provided where needed to appropriate diagnostic sites. Personnel providing services were school-board employees. Appellants specifically worried about the "situation where a facility is used to service only non-public school students."[174] Again, Justice Blackmun called attention to the differences between *Meek*[175] and *Lemon I*[176] and the present circumstances. Blackmun concluded "that providing therapeutic and remedial services at neutral sites" off nonpublic-school premises does not either advance religion or create excessive entanglement between church and state. Thus, "sections 3317.06 (G), (H), (I), and (K) are constitutional."[177]

§ 3317.06 (B), (C) — Instructional Materials and Equipment

These sections provide instructional materials and equipment loans directly to pupils or parents instead of directly to sectarian or nonpublic schools, which was the focus of *Meek*. However, Blackmun, after a brief historical review of the Ohio General Assembly's efforts to aid nonpublic schools and a review of *Meek* concerning this issue, said that "(d)espite technical changes in legal bailee, the program and substance is the same as before.... In view of the impossibility of separating the secular education function from the sectarian, the state aid inevitably flows in part in support of the religious role of the schools."[178] Thus (B) and (C) advance the sectarian enterprise and therefore are unconstitutional.[179]

§ 3317.06 (L) — Field Trips

This section sought to provide field-trip transportation for sectarian schools similar to that provided to public schools. No restrictions (except similarity to public-school field trips) were established, and nonpublic school teachers made the decisions concerning destination, frequency, and timing. Justice Blackmun reviewed *Everson*[180] and suggested that travel in *Everson* "was unrelated to any aspect of the curriculum."[181] Field trips "are [an] integral part of the education experience . . . [and] must be treated as was the funding of maps and charts in *Meek* . . . the funding of buildings and tuition in . . . *Nyquist* . . . and the funding of teacher prepared tests in *Levitt*. . . ."[182] Thus (L) advances religion and is therefore constitutionally impermissible.

Brennan, Marshall, Powell, and Stevens filed opinions concurring in part and dissenting in part. (Table 5.2 precisely delineates how the individual justices decided particulars of the statute.) A drift in judicial philosophy concerning church and state appeared to be developing among some members of the Court.

Justice Brennan

Brennan insisted that the entire statute entangled the "establishment clause." While recognizing the Ohio General Assembly's efforts to fashion a statute that avoided conflict, Justice Brennan maintained:

> The [First] Amendment nullifies sophisticated as well as simpleminded . . . attempts to avoid its prohibitions . . . and, in any event, ingenuity in draftsmanship cannot obscure the fact that this subsidy to sectarian schools amounts to $88,800,000 (less) now the sums appropriated to finance § 3317.06 (B) and (C) which today are invalidated just for the initial biennium.[183]

Justice Marshall

Table 5.2 indicates that Marshall joined the Court's majority on Parts
I, V, VII, VIII, and (G) only in Part VI. The Court had lumped (G), (H),
(I), and (K) under the broad rubric of the therapeutic services in Part VI.
We have acceded to Justice Marshall's distinction concerning (G) in Part
VI in establishing Table 5.2. Therefore, Part VI (G), (H), (I), and (K) are
set up separately. The (G) section provides therapeutic, psychological,
speech and hearing services. Such services differ, insisted Marshall, from
those authorized under (H), (I), and (K) providing guidance and counseling
services directly to support programs of sectarian schools and providing
specialized teachers for disabled children. The therapeutic services under
(H), (I), and (K), said Marshall, "are clearly intended to aid the sectarian
schools. ..."[184] Moreover, Marshall indicated that he was now ready to
reverse *Allen*.[185] Calling attention to Blackmun's remark that tension existed between *Allen* and *Meek,* Marshall maintained that he would "resolve
that tension by overruling *Allen*."[186]

> I am now convinced that *Allen* is largely responsible for reducing the "high
> and impregnable" wall between church and state.... By overruling *Allen,*
> we could free ourselves to draw a line between acceptable and unacceptable
> forms of aid ... that line ... should be placed between general welfare pro-
> grams ... and programs of educational assistance.[187]

If such imperatives develop, political disputes that divide people along
religious lines would disappear.

Justice Powell

Powell, concurring in part and dissenting in part (see Table 5.2), appeared to be drifting toward a different philosophical direction than in
earlier decisions.[188] Perhaps Chief Justice Burger's influence was becoming
heavy. Powell was concerned with state funds finding appropriate methods
to aid children in sectarian settings without violating the establishment
clause. He considered such aid "in the public interest." He implied that
American children should have some alternatives to public education, and
religious schools provide such opportunities. Moreover, public schools
should have competition, and religious schools provide competition. Also
a religious school "relieves substantially the tax burden incidental to the
operation of public schools."[189] He did not feel that at that point in the
twentieth century "there are significant dangers to the establishment
clause." Finally, he perceived that "deep political divisions along religious
lines [are] remote. ..."[190]

Justice Stevens

Stevens also concurred in part and dissented in part (see Table 5.2). Quoting from Clarence Darrow's argument in *Scopes*, [191] Justice Stevens said:

> The realm of religion ... is where knowledge leaves off, and where faith begins, and it never has needed the arm of the State for support, and wherever it has received it, it has harmed both the public and the religion that it would pretend to serve.[192]

Moreover, said Stevens, there is no fundamental difference between direct and indirect aid, and no difference between textbooks and instructional materials like maps and globes. For that reason, Stevens would reject the "tripartite test" and adopt Justice Black's test enunciated in *Everson:*

> No tax in any amount, large or small, can be levied to support any religious activity or institutions, whatever they may be called, by whatever form they may adopt to teach or practice religion.[193]

Furthermore, "This Court's efforts to improve on the *Everson* test have not proven successful. 'Corrosive precedents' have left us without firm principles on which to decide these cases.... States have been encouraged to search for new ways of achieving forbidden ends."[194] Finally, the "high and impregnable" wall "had been reduced to a blurred, indistinct, and variable barrier" and served neither the church nor the public.[195]

The *Wolman* decision was a landmark case. *Wolman* was Blackmun's third major church-state decision and was as difficult as *Roemer*. In reality, though, the Ohio statute was complex, and the Court's justices lined up on many sides of the issues. *Wolman* signaled a new direction. The clear position of *Lemon I,* that "red letter day" June 25, 1973 (*Nyquist, Levitt, Lemon III*), and the imperative of *Meek* gave way to the judicial quicksand of *Wolman*.

The dissenting opinions in *Wolman* are important. Justice Marshall was ready to reverse *Allen* and *Cochran*. Justice Stevens (Justice Douglas's replacement) would replace the tripartite test with Black's enunciation in *Everson* of "no tax in any amount" for religious schools. Justice Brennan's position was certainly clear: the entire Ohio statute was "entanglement." Justice Powell seemed caught in the vortex of indecision and change; his colloquy—alternatives to public education, public schools should have competition, virtues of religious schools, and absence of political divisiveness—smacked of neutral accommodationist pragmatism and cannot be squared with his position expressed in previous decisions.

At the conclusion of 1977 and as the result of *Wolman,* legislative enactment may fund the following religious elementary and secondary educational activities:

1. Textbooks (5–4 vote);
2. Testing and scoring;
3. Diagnostic services (8–1);
4. Therapeutic services: psychological, speech, and hearing services (7–2); and
5. Therapeutic services: guidance and counseling.

Under *Wolman,* legislative enactments may not fund the following religious elementary and secondary educational activities:

1. Instructional materials and equipment (6–3);
2. Field trips (5–4).

During the years 1978, 1979, and 1980, church-state legislative and judicial activities at both state and federal levels continued. As an example, in 1979, the Supreme Court, in *Byrne v. Public Funds for Public Schools of New Jersey*[196] found (6–3) a New Jersey enactment that provided parents with children in religious schools on a full-time basis a $1,000-per-child personal tax deduction unconstitutional as religious advancement. Burger, White, and Rehnquist would have voted probable jurisdiction and set the case for oral argument.

And the Court, in *Meltzer v. Board of Public Instruction of Orange County,*[197] reaffirmed (7–2) the landmark *Engel, Schempp,* and *Murray* decisions concerning public-school-sponsored devotional activities. The Court sustained a 1978 decision of the Fifth Circuit Court of Appeals holding that required daily Bible reading and prayer in public schools and permitting distribution of Bibles in classrooms by the Gideons were unconstitutional as religious advancement. Also, the Court, in *Flory v. Sioux Falls School District,*[198] refused (7–2) to hear an Eighth Circuit Court of Appeals decision sustaining school-board policy concerning religious elements in Christmas programs and activities in the Sioux Falls school system. The Eighth Circuit Court of Appeals found that "much of the art, literature and music associated with traditional holidays particularly Christmas had 'acquired a significance which is no longer confirmed to the religious sphere of life.'"[199] The court matched school-board policy against the *Lemon I* tripartite test and held that school-board policy was constitutional:

> We simply hold, on the basis of the record before us, that the policy and rules adopted. . . . When read in the light of the district court's holding that

segments of the 1977 Christmas program at one of the elementary schools were impermissible are not violative of the First Amendment.[200]

And finally the Supreme Court, in *Stone v. Graham* (1980),[201] by a 5–2 vote without oral argument, struck down a Kentucky statute that required posting in public classrooms the Ten Commandments. The Court insisted the statute violated the Constitution as First Amendment establishment; the statute's purpose was not a secular one. Kentucky's efforts to satisfy the first element of the tripartite test included (1) the Ten Commandments display was funded through private contributions; (2) on each posted display in small print was the notation "The secular application of the Ten Commandment is clearly seen in its adoption as the fundamental legal code of Western Civilization and the Common Law of the United States."[202] The Supreme Court, in reversing the Kentucky Supreme Court (the Kentucky Supreme Court was equally divided), maintained that the Ten Commandments constituted "a sacred text in the Jewish and Christian faiths and no legislative recitation of a supposed secular purpose can blind us to that fact."[203]

The most important 1980 decision, at least from the standpoint of public funds for religious schools, was *Committee for Public Education and Religious Liberty v. Regan*.[204]

This case was a legislative response to the Supreme Court's *Levitt*[205] decision in 1973, which struck down a New York statute appropriating public money to private and religious schools for state-mandated testing and reporting services. The new statute sought to remove the unconstitutional provision. Thus, the new statute provided no general reimbursement for preparation, administration, or grading of teacher-prepared tests. The new statute provided only for actual costs of providing secular services, including school enrollment and attendance data and administration of state-prepared examinations. Moreover, the statute provided for auditing payments and verifying services. the district court in New York initially declared the statute unconstitutional, and the Supreme Court on appeal remanded the case in light of *Wolman*. On remand, the district court held the statute constitutional.

The Supreme Court, with Justice White writing the majority opinion (Burger, Stewart, Powell, and Rehnquist joined to make the majority) insisted the statute arrangement did not violate the First Amendment establishment clause. The statute, said White, was "purely secular" for the purpose of preparing New York citizens "for the challenge of American life in the last decades of the twentieth century."[206] Moreover, there was no excessive government entanglement because (1) private and religious schools had no control over test content and test outcome—thus, there was no "substantial risk the test could advance religion"; (2) test reporting for which reimbursement was provided contained no religious support — thus no primary religious effect; and (3) the statute reimbursement and audit provisions provided ample safeguards against excessive entanglement.

Justices Blackman, Brennan, and Marshall dissented, insisting that while the statute had manifested a "clear secular purpose, it had a primary effect of advancing religion and also fostered excessive government entanglement with religion."[207] Justice Stevens maintained that the statute in every element violated the First Amendment establishment clause.[208]

The central issue in this case has whether or not lump-sum payments could be made to private and religious schools without violating the First Amendment "advancement" and the excessive-government-entanglement provision of the Court's tripartite test. The answer was that New York may do so.

A sense of prophetic justice pervaded Justice White's majority opinion. He had waited nine years to write this decision. In the 1971 *DiCenso* case,[209] White was the lone dissenting justice in a case that struck down Rhode Island's Salary Supplement Act as unconstitutional on the basis of First Amendment advancement of religion and excessive government entanglement. In *DiCenso,* Chief Justice Warren Burger said:

> Obviously a direct money subsidy would be a relationship pregnant with involvement and, as with most government grant programs, could encompass sustained and detailed administrative relationship for enforcement of statutory or administrative standards. . . . [210]

In *DiCenso,* direct money grants created excessive government entanglement. In historical retrospect, how clear, simple, and innocent, the *DiCenso* case was — an 8-1 majority at the beginning of the 1970s. But Justice White had insisted the decision was predicated on a false hypothesis — that nonpublic teachers (paid with public money) teaching secular subjects might insert religious dogma into the secular courses.

White's second and more important criticism was that the Court had created "an insoluble paradox." Justice White reasoned that the Court had held, in effect, that if religion was taught, no tax could be used. The opposite logic would suggest that if religion was not taught, public taxes could be used. Yet, acknowledged White, while the state expected a promise from the church-sponsored schools that no religion could be taught and established auditing procedures to validate that promise, the state then became entangled in the no-entanglement aspect of the Court's establishment-clause jurisprudence.

In 1973, Justice White was still very much concerned about the "insoluble paradox" in *Nyquist,*[211] *Levitt,*[212] and *Lemon III.*[213] The Court's solid 6-3 majority held through *Meek*[214] in 1975. However, in 1976, *Roemer*[215] (a higher-education case) found Justice White with the majority — the insoluble paradox was a phantom in higher-education cases. That is, the insoluble paradox existed but could not be seen. The 1977 *Wolman* case[216] found White voting yes for all nine parts of the Ohio statute, and with the majority in seven parts. The insoluble paradox still applied to elementary and secondary school cases, but the imperative of *Lemon I, Lemon III, Meek* and other cases had given way to the quicksand of *Wolman*. Thus, after almost a decade of dissenting, White found himself with a majority and designated by Chief Justice Burger to write the majority opinion. The insoluble paradox of 1971 ceased to exist in 1980.

Justice White insisted that the law "provided ample safeguards against excessive or misdirective reimbursement."[217] Calling attention to the district court's description of the audit procedure, he held that (1) the private and/or religious schools must maintain separate accounting for expenses incurred, and make application for reimbursement with the necessary reports and documents required by the state commissioner of education; (2) the commissioner must audit all reports, vouchers, and all other documents; (3) the state Department of Audit must inspect documents occasionally; and (4) if schools are overpaid as determined by audits, "the excess must be returned to the state immediately."[218] Finally, in response to the political-divisiveness issue, Justice White in the footnotes suggested there was "no merit whatsover" in the plaintiffs' argument.

With the basic tripartite-test issue settled, Justice White turned to the Court's recent record. The plaintiff had argued that *Levitt II* (as the case was often called) could not be squared with *Meek*. White pointed out that a majority (including *Meek*'s author) had upheld in *Wolman* provisions of a state statute that provided payment for preparation and grading of tests in secular subjects. Thus, the *Meek* opinion was never an issue in *Levitt II*, or else

> the majority in *Wolman* was silently disavowing *Meek*, in whole or in part, that case was simply not understood by this court to stand for the broad proposition urged by appellants and espoused by the District Court in *Levitt II*.[219]

Finally, White pointed out the difficulty in the establishment clause cases, lamenting that they are "not easy; they stir deep feelings; and we're divided among ourselves, perhaps reflecting the different views on this subject of the people of this country."[220] (Perhaps White should have examined footnote 8 of this case.) Anyway, White, while acknowledging that this decision was no "litmus-paper test," suggested the Court had never intended to establish "categorical imperatives and absolute approaches"[221] And then he presented a sentence that described the last five years of the 1970s concerning aid to religious elementary and secondary schools:

This course sacrifices clarity and predictability, but this promises to be the case until the continuing interaction between the courts and the states – the former charged with interpreting and upholding the Constitution and the latter seeking to provide education for their youth – produce a single, more encompassing construction of the Establishment Clause.[222]

Perhaps Justice White was suggesting a new church-state standard such as the one that Justice Stevens affirmed in *Wolman.* At any rate, footnote 8 should somehow be squared with the tripartite test, for the obvious political divisiveness along religious lines was becoming a major national issue.

Justice Blackmun (with whom Brennan and Marshall joined) began the dissent:

> The Court . . . takes a long step backward in the inevitable controversy that emerges when a state legislature continues to insist on providing aid to parochial schools.[223]

Blackmun then ran the litany of church-state religious-aid cases, insisting the issue had been clarified in *Meek* and *Wolman,* while acknowledging that "the line, wavering through it may be" was nonetheless drawn. Blackman discussed the lineups of justices at the beginning of the 1970s and at the end.

> Now, some of those who joined in *Lemon, Levitt, Meek,* and *Wolman* in invalidating, depart and validate. I am able to attribute this defection only to a concern about the continuing and emotional controversy and to a persuasion that a good-faith attempt on the part of a state legislature is worth a nod of approval.[224]

Blackmun found that the New York statute passed the first part of the tripartite test (the secular purpose) but was flawed with respect to the second and third parts. By providing direct financial aid, the statute thus advanced religion in violation of the establishment clause.[225] Moreover, the statute's auditing procedure – certifying secular expenditures only – was "excessive entanglement that the Establishment Clause forbids."[226]

Justice Stevens filed an interesting dissenting opinion. While agreeing with Blackmun that the New York statute was constitutionall flawed, Stevens once again called for a new standard, which, as he had already suggested in *Wolman,* would abandon the effort to subsidize nonpublic schools, and "I would resurrect the 'high and impregnable' wall between the church and state constructed by the Framers of the First Amendment."[227]

So *Regan* (or as Justice White fondly referred to the case, *Levitt II*) allowed lump-sum payments to private or religious schools for the actual cost of state-mandated testing and reporting services, including school-enrollment and attendance data and adminstration of state-prepared examinations. The statute also provided for auditing payments and verifying services. The Court divided 6–3 in *Levitt I* (1973), banishing the legislative enactment as First Amendment establishment, and in *Levitt II* (1980) divided 5–4, finding essentially the same statute constitutional. Justice White acknowledged that *Levitt II* was no "litmus-paper test" and suggested the Court had in reality never intended to establish "categorical imperatives and absolute approaches."

Thus the tripartite test first expressed in *Lemon I* (1970) that appeared to provide a judicial standard establishing a degree of uniformity throughout federal and state judicial systems became in 1980 an elusive standard—no "litmus-paper test" and no "categorical imperatives and absolute approaches." The neutral accommodationist pragmatism was expressed again where public funds are ued in legislative enactments. Finally, while Justice White acknowledged the political-divisiveness issue in footnote 8, otherwise he never addressed the issue. Yet in 1980, political divisiveness along religious lines was becoming a major national issue. How else could the enormous number of cases be explained?

1981–1985

Church-state legislation and litigation during the first five years of the 1980s was just as voluminous and precedent-setting as those of the previous eleven years. The Burger Court over the five years 1981–1985 focused on (1) *Bob Jones University v. United States, Goldsboro Christian Schools v. United States*[228] (*Bob Jones University* was a higher-education case and *Goldsboro* a religious-school case); (2) the landmark *Mueller v. Allen* (1983),[229] regarding a "tuition, textbooks, and transportation" tax credit for children attending religious schools; (3) *Grand Rapids v. Ball*[230] (1985), shared-time instructors teaching academic subjects within religious schools; and (4) *Aquilar v. Felton,*[231] a Chapter I case with the same ideological properties as *Grand Rapids*.

Finally, President Reagan's initial imprimatur on the Supreme Court occurred as the result of Justice Stewart's retirement (1981) and the appointment of Justice Sandra Day O'Connor.

In 1983, the Supreme Court addressed the issue of tax-exempt statute for *Bob Jones University* and *Goldsboro Christian Schools*.[232] Bob Jones University is located in South Carolina where the Internal Revenue Service denied tax-exempt status because of the university's racially discriminatory admission policy. A federal district court in South Carolina found for Bob Jones University, and on appeal the Fourth Circuit Court of Appeals reversed; certiorari was granted by the Supreme Court. Meanwhile, in eastern North Carolina, the Goldsboro Christian Schools were seeking refund of social-security and unemployment taxes, and the Internal Revenue Service filed a counterclaim for unpaid taxes. The federal district court found for the Internal Revenue Service, and on appeal the Fourth Circuit Court of Appeals sustained. Certiorari was granted by the Supreme Court. Both Bob Jones University and Goldsboro Christian Schools insisted their First Amendment religious freedom was violated.

Chief Justice Burger, writing for an almost unanimous Court (Justice Rehnquist dissented), maintained that

> non-profit private schools that prescribed and enforced racially discrimina-
> tory admission standards on the basis of religious doctrine do not qualify
> as tax exempt organizations under the Internal Revenue Code, nor are con-
> tributions to such schools deductible as charitable contributions.[233]

And Chief Justice Burger insisted that both Bob Jones University and Goldsboro Christian Schools enforced racially discriminatory admission policies.

The flawed Bob Jones University admission policy encapsulates: (1) while since 1975 black unmarried students were allowed to enroll, there was a University polcity that prohibited interracial dating and marriage; (2) interracial married students would be expelled; (3) students with membership in organizations advocating interracial marriage would be expelled, interracial-dating students dismissed; and (4) students subverting university interracial policies would be expelled.[234]

Bob Jones University and the Internal Revenue Service had been at odds with each other since 1970 when the Internal Revenue Service formally notified the university of its intention to change the tax-exempt status because of racial discrimination in university admission policies. Of course, Bob Jones University sought an administrative resolution to the developing crisis. Unsuccessful, Bob Jones University in 1971 instituted legal action,[235] seeking an injunction against the Internal Revenue Service's revoking the tax-exempt status. Bob Jones was denied injunctive relilef because the Internal Revenue Service had not yet assessed or collected any tax. In April 1975, the Internal Revenue Service notified the university of its intent to change the university's tax-exempt status. In January 1976, the Internal Revenue Service kept that promise and revoked the university's tax-exempt status, effective December 1970. The university subsequently filed returns for the period December 1, 1970–December 31, 1975, paid a total tax of $21 on a single employee for 1975, and filed for a refund. The Internal Revenue Service denied the refund.

Bob Jones University then initiated the present case, seeking to recover the $21, and the Internal Revenue Service countersued, seeking an unpaid federal unemployment tax totaling $489,675.59 plus interest for 1971-1975.[236] The federal district court found for Bob Jones University and insisted the Internal Revenue Service had exceeded delegated powers. Moreover, the Internal Revenue Service had violated the university's First

Amendment religious freedoms.[237] The Fourth Circuit Court of Appeals reversed, insisting that Bob Jones University did not meet the common-law sense of "charitable" and that Bob Jones University's racial policies "violated the clearly defined public policy, rooted in our Constitutions, condemning racial discrimination and, more specifically, the government policy against subsidizing racial discrimination in education, public or private."[238] Thus, the Internal Revenue Service action was not constitutionally flawed.

The Goldsboro Christian Schools (Goldsboro, N.C.) was established in 1963 and has since maintained a racially discriminatory admission policy predicated on biblical interpretation. Children of mixed race (one parent Caucasian) were occasionally admitted. After auditing Goldsboro Christian Schools' records for 1969–1972, the Internal Revenue Service denied tax-exempt status and required Goldsboro Christian Schools to pay taxes under both the Federal Insurance Contributions Act and the Federal Unemployment Tax Act.[239] Goldsboro paid social-security and unemployment tax for a single employee for 1969–1972, totaling $3,459.93, then filed suit seeking refund of that payment. The Internal Revenue Service countersued, seeking refund of that payment. The Internal Revenue Service countersued, seeking $160,073.96 in unpaid social-security and unemployment taxes for 1969–1972. The federal district court found for the Internal Revenue Service, stating that even though Goldsboro's admission policies were predicated on a sincerely held religious conviction, tax-exempt status could not be allowed for a "private school maintaining racially discriminatory admission policies."[240] Moreover, the Internal Revenue Service's decision did not violate the First Amendment free exercise or establishment clause. On appeal, the Fourth Circuit Court of Appeals affirmed. Both *Bob Jones University* and *Goldsboro Christian Schools* came through the Fourth Circuit Court of Appeals, and both were granted certiorari by the Supreme Court.

Chief Justice Burger first reviewed Internal Revenue Service policy, specifically §170 and §501(c)(3) concerning the common-law "charity" concept: (1) whether the educational institutions fell within one of eight categories of "charitable" nature and (2) whether the educational institutions' activities (discriminatory admission policies) were contrary to established national policy.

After reviewing the historical record concerning the Internal Revenue Service and the entire concept of "charitable exemption," Burger concluded:

> History buttresses logic to make clear that, to warrant exemption under §501(c)(3), an institution must fall within a category specified in that section and must demonstrably serve and be in harmony with the public interest. The institution's purpose must not be so at odds with the common community conscience as to undermine any public benefit that might otherwise be conferred.[241]

There "can no longer be any doubt that racial discrimination in education violates deeply and widely accepted views of elementary justice."[242] After a brief revew of American desegregation history, Burger said that "racial discrimination in education violates a most fundamental national public policy, as well as rights of individuals."[243] Thus, maintained Burger, the Internal Revenue Servce "did not exceed its authority."[244]

As to the second question, whether the educational institutions' admission policies were discriminatory and contrary to established policy: (1) the record admitted that Goldsboro Christian Schools "maintained racially discriminatory policies";[245] and (2) even though Bob Jones University maintained that the university "allows all races to enroll," subject only to a policy concerning intermarriage and interracial dating,[246] "decisions of this Court firmly establish that discrimination on the basis of racial affiliation and association is a form of discrimination."[247]

Justice Rehnquist filed an exhaustive and detailed dissenting opinion. He insisted that Congress had never granted the Internal Revenue Service such power. Moreover, Congress has never established national policy concerning tax-exempt status for religious schools with racially discriminatory admission polcies. "But as of yet, Congress has failed to do so. Whatever the reason for the failure, this Court should not legislate for Congress."[248]

Predicated on *Bob Jones University* and *Goldsboro Christian Schools,* religious schools, colleges, and universities with discriminatory admission policies as determined by the Internal Revenue Service will be denied tax-exempt status.

The last 1983 Supreme Court decision, *Mueller v. Allen,*[249] perhaps the most important decision since *Brown I,* 74 S. Ct. 686 (1954), addressed an ideological issue previously settled in *Essex v. Wolman* (1972, 1973), *Kosydar v. Wolman* (1972), *Grit v. Wolman* (1973), *Marburger v. Public Funds for Public Schools of New Jersey* (1973, 1974), *Lemon III* (1973), *Nyquist* (1973), *Franchise Tax Board of California v. United Americans for Public Schools* (1974), and *Byran v. Public Funds for Public Schools of New Jersey* (1979) — tax deduction for expenses incurred by parents in sending their children to religious schools.

The *Mueller* case came on appeal from the Eighth Circuit Court of Appeals where plaintiff taxpayers challenged a Minnesota statute allowing all parents with children attending tuition-charging elementary and secondary schools to deduct expenses accrued for "tuition, textbooks, and transportation."[250] The Minnesota statute provided "tuition, textbooks, and transportation" for *all* parents, not just parents with children in private or religious schools. The statute's delimiting factor is that schools must be tuition-charging schools. With minor exceptions (usually when children cross attendance lines) public schools charge no tuition. The enactment (amended 1978 statute) allowed a tax deduction not exceeding $500 per pupil (grades K through six) and $700 per pupil (grades seven through twelve).

The plaintiff-taxpayers were unsuccessful in the federal district court, and on appeal, the Eighth Circuit Court of Appeals sustained, holding that the Minnesota enactment "substantially benefited a 'broad class of Minnesota citizens'"[251]

Justice Rehnquist, writing for the 5–4 majority (Stevens, Brennan, Marshall, and Blackmun made up the minority) acknowledged the difficulty of the case, stating that the Court was asked to decide "whether Minnesota's tax deduction bears greater resemblance to those types of assistance to parochial schools we have approved, or to those we have struck down."[252] Proceeding immediately to the *Lemon I* tripartite test (which Justice Rehnquist suggested had provided guidance but "no more than (a) helpful signpost"), the majority addressed the issue of secular purpose.[253] Rehnquist, often using *Nyquist* (1973) as the appropriate foil, insisted that little time need be spent in addressing the secular-purpose heading:

> A state's decision to defray the cost of education expense incurred by parents—regardless of the type of school their children attend—evidences a purpose that is both secular and understandable.[254]

Moreover, an educated constituency is important to the "political and economic health" of a community, and there may be states, such as Minnesota, with a strong interest in guaranteeing the financial stability of nonpublic education. Justsice Rehnquist never addressed an apparent dichotomy of whether Point A, "political and economic health," achieved congruence with Point B, "financial stability of nonpublic elementary and secondary schools," and what and where is the ideological relationship.[255] Moreover, nonpublic elementary and secondary schools provide a substantial tax relief for the general public. Finally, Justice Rehnquist (alluding to Justice Powell's remarks in *Wolman*) suggested that "private schools may serve as a benchmark for public schools, in a manner analogous to the 'TVA yardstick' for private power companies."[256]

With the first part of the *Lemon I* test settled, Rehnquist addressed the second part of the tripartite test (as he indicated, the more difficult question, whether the statute had the primary effect of advancing religion).[257] Rehnquist concluded the statute was not constitutionally flawed, for the following reasons: (1) The questionable legislative enactment, §290.09 (22), was just one of many justifiable tax deductions, "such as those for medical expenses . . . and charitable contributions."[258] And Rehnquist insisted that predicated on past Court decisions,

> the Minnesota legislature's judgment that a deduction for education expenses fairly equalizes the tax burden of its citizens and encourages

desirable expenditures for education purpose is entitled to substantial deference.[259]

(2) But the enactment's most attractive feature was that the deduction was "available" for *all* parents, parents with children in nonpublic and public schools, "open to a broad class of nonreligious as well as religious," and "the provision of benefits to so broad a spectrum of groups is an important index of secular effect."[260] In reality, the Minnesota statute, suggested Rehnquist, was "more similar" to *Allen* and *Everson,* which permitted *all* parents, "whether their children attend public school or private — to deduct their children's educational expenses."[261] (3) The Minnesota statute contained an establishment-clause-sanctifying element, in that whatever aid Minnesota wished to "provide parochial schools" Minnesota did through individual deductions, thus reducing "the Establishment Clause objections."[262] Even though Rehnquist raised the question of how public funds flow to religious schools,

as here, aid to parochial schools is available only as a result of decisions of individual parents no 'imprimatur of state approval,' . . . can be deemed to have been conferred on any particular religion, or on religion generally.[263]

(4) In 1983, America suffers no deep political division along religious lines that the establishment clause was promulgated to protect against. Moreover, the establishment clause does not "encompass the sort of attenuated financial benefit" that the Minnesota enactment gave to parochial schools because the financial benefits are "ultimately controlled by the private choices of individual parents."[264]

Plaintiff argued that the enactment's primary effect was aid to religious schools. A statistical analysis of tax deductions was presented to the Court. Moreover, plaintiff suggested that parents of public-schoolchildren, with exceptions, could claim no tuition deduction. Finally, plaintiff pointed out that 96 percent of all children in Minnesota private schools attend religious schools — religious extent but not religious intent.[265] Respondents countered that plaintiff failed to include such items as (1) transportation, summer-school tuition, tuition paid by parents when their children attend schools outside their school district, equipment rental or purchase, and tuition for education not provided by the public schools.[266]

Justice Rehnquist found that plaintiff's empirical data was flawed; "we fail to see the significance of the report."[267] Plaintiff's analysis of 1976 data — revenue analysis — did not square with 1979 revenue analysis; and "the 1976 Memorandum was not intended as any comprehensive or binding agency."[268] Thus there was no need to consider plaintiffs' reasoning — that is, "the extent to which various classes of private citizens claimed benefits under the law." Furthermore, such data

> would scarcely provide the certainty that this field stands in need of, nor can we perceive principled standards by which such statistical evidence might be evaluated ... we believe it wiser to decline to engage in the type of empirical inquiry into these persons benefitted by state law which petitioners urge.[269]

Thus, found Rehnquist, the Minnesota enactment satisfied the primary-effect test.

In addressing the third part of the tripartite test, excessive entanglement of the state with religion, Rehnquist stated that the only probable possibility concerned "comprehensive, discriminating, and continuing state surveillance"[270] of textbooks that otherwise qualify for a deduction. State officials "must disallow deductions taken from 'instructional books and materials used in the teaching of religious tenets doctrines or worship, the purpose of which is to inculcate such tenets doctrines of worship.'"[271] Yet secular-textbook selection should not prove difficult for state officials. After all, *Allen, Meek* and *Wolman* passed constitutional muster in secular-textbook selection,[272] so the "excessive entanglement" does not constitutionally flaw the Minnesota enactment. All three parts of the tripartite test have been addressed, so the court of appeals judgment is affirmed.

Justice Marshall, with whom Brennan, Blackmun, and Stevens filed a dissenting opinion, wasted little time on judicial polemics by insisting that the Minnesota statute "subsidizes tuition payment to sectarian schools," which the establishment clause prohibits.[273] And the issue, suggested Marshall, is not whether the legislative enactment provides a direct or indirect formula, a distinction without a difference.

> It is equally irrelevant whether a reduction in taxes takes the form of a tax 'credit,' a tax 'modification,' or a tax 'deduction.' ... What is of controlling significance is not the form but the 'substantive impact' of the financial aid.[274]

Moreover, the Minnesota statute was further flawed by allowing tax deductions "for cost of books and other instructional materials used for sectarian purposes ... pencils and notebooks — are severable from the other deductions."[275] Finally, Marshall indicated he would limit deductions for educational transportation "as it relates to the cost of traveling between home and school."[276]

In light of the fact we believe this is the most important Supreme Court decision affecting public education since *Brown I* (it is also the most important nonpublic education decision, especially concerning religious schools, since *Pierce,* 1925), we present Marshall's dissenting opinion in detail.

Marshall acknowledged that the majority did not question the judicial vitality of *Nyquist* — a state may not aid religious schools either through a direct grant or aid to parents in religious schools, whether in the form of cash payments or tax credits. The Minnesota enactment is not significantly different from the New York statute, which *Nyquist* invalidated — "it has a direct and immediate effect of advancing religion."[277] And even though the Minnesota statute applies to all parents with children attending elementary and secondary schools that charge tuition, (1) during the 1978–1979 academic year, 90,000 children were enrolled in nonpublic schools chargin tuition; (2) 95 percent of the 90,000 children attended religious schools; and (3) during the 1978–1979 academic year, of the 815,000 children attending Minnesota's public schools, only 79 students made their parents eligible for tuition tax deductions — "Minnesota's public schools are generally prohibited by law from charging tuition."[278]

Thus, in answer to the first part of the tripartite test, Marshall insisted that even though the Minnesota legislation had a secular purpose, "promoting pluralism and diversity" among schools, the establishment clause required more. Legislation cannot immunize from "further scrutiny a law which ... has a primary effect that advances religion."[279] Moreover, continued Marshall:

> By ensuring that parents will be reimbursed for tuition payments they make, the Minnesota statute requires that taxpayers in general pay for the cost of parochial education and extends a financial "incentive to parents to send their children to sectarian schools."[280]

Thus, the Minnesota legislative enactment does not pass the secular-purpose part of the tripartite test.

In response to part two of the tripartite test, whether the statute has a primary effect of promoting religion, Marshall insisted that the Minnesota statute's primary effect was advancing religion:

> The statute is little more than a subsidy of tuition masquerading as a subsidy of general educational expenses. The other deductible expenses are *de minimis* in comparison to tuition expenses.[281]

In response to the majority's assertion that the statute was constitutionally sanitized because the statute included the adjective *all*, Marshall once again recited the quantitative data ("statistical evidence that the majority fears would lead to constitutional undertainty") and insisted the actual analysis necessary was the same judicial standard applied in similar cases, *Nyquist* and *Lemon III* — "what the statute on its face purports to do."[282] And in Minnesota over 90 percent of the children affected by the legislation attend religious schools. Furthermore, historical experience compels the Court to acknowledge that general state financial assistance to religious schools "will further religious education because the majority of the schools which charge tuition are sectarian."[283]

To the "look-alike" scenario that Rehnquist developed (*Nyquist* [1973], *Allen* [1968], and *Everson* [1947]), Marshall indicated, "One might as well say that a tangerine bears less resemblance to an orange than to an apple."[284] For Marshall, *Allen* and *Everson* "are inapposite today for precisely the same reason that they were inapposite in *Nyquist*."[285]

Another Minnesota enactment (Minn. Stat. §290.09 22) authorized the state school board to provide public-school textbooks to nonpublic schools. The challenged Minnesota statute in this case provided that particular textbooks (books and instructional materials pervasively religious are disallowed for deduction) qualify for a deduction. Justice Rehnquist, addressing this issue under the third part of the tripartite test, excessive government entanglement, indicated this legislative element was not constitutionally flawed.

What is presented here (from Marshall's viewpoint) are two statutes providing textbooks. Minnesota's statute authorizing the state school board to provide textbooks used in the public schools to nonpublic schools is synonymous with *Allen* and *Meek*. But the challenged statute in this case "permits a deduction for books that are chosen by the parochial schools themselves."[286] Otherwise, "parents have little reason to purchase textbooks that can be borrowed under this provision."[287] Thus, the textbook provision, along with the transportation expenses (except cost of traveling between home and school), is First Amendment establishment.

Finally, Marshall insisted,

> In focusing upon the contribuitons made by church related schools, the majority has lost sight of the issue before us in this case. . . . For the first time, the Court has upheld financial support for religious schools without any reason at all to assume that the support will be restricted to the secular functions of those schools and will not be used to support religious instruction.[288]

So, predicated on *Mueller,* an enactment providing tuition and other educational deductions including the adjective *all—all* meaning all parents with children in tuition-charging elementary and secondary schools—will pass First Amendment establishment muster. Parent reimbursements, tax credits, and tuition grants provided only to parents with children in nonpublic schools will fail constitutional muster. But why sould any state general assembly make a silly mistake and not include the adjective *all,* which has constitutional properties? When the adjective *all* is included, a state general assembly may then aid religious schools without fear of constitutional difficulty.

And legislative controls concerning revenue reduction can be reasonably computed because the majority of schools charging tuition are religious schools. With exceptions, the only public schoolchildren paying tuition are children attending schools outside their school districts. Over the United States one can reasonably predict that less that 1 percent would include public schoolchildren. Approximately 95 percent would accrue to parents with children in religious schools. Already there are thirteen states with Minnesota-type legislation pending.

Moreover, for the second time in the history of the Supreme Court, an associate justice, in this case Justice Rehnquist, suggested that public schools need competition. Competition presumably would improve the public schools—"private schools may serve as a bench mark for public schools, in a manner analogous to the 'TVA yardstick.'"[289] Public education is a governmental creation—a creature of the state within fifty states.

As Chapter 2 indicates, the American public school is a uniquely American institution. No other nation on the face of the earth has tried such an experiment and been as successful. And many believe the American public school to be America's greatest contribution to Western civilization. American public schools became great not because of competition with religious schools but because public schools became the instrument of American democracy, is the only philosophical rationale for creating a public-school system in a democracy. The history of American public education is one of pride and growth. Chapter 2 indicates that religious education over the nation was in a state of steady decline through the 1960s—until *Brown I* and *II,* the Civil Rights Act of 1964, and subsequent federal decisions forced integration. And the result was white flight—white flight to suburban and rural schools, but more important, white flight to nonpublic schools, especially religious schools. We suggest that the Supreme Court of *Brown I* is not the Supreme Court of *Mueller.*

And yet the single most important stress of American public education today is racial desegregation. And *Mueller* is the most important Supreme Court public-education decision since *Brown I.* As already indicated, public education is a state governmental creation. So are police departments, fire departments, state courts, county government, and municipalities. Would the same competition logic apply to governmental creations mentioned above? Is there some plausible logic to suggest that if the "TVA yardstick" logic is really applicable to the above governmental creations, a competitive "TVA yardstick" would be good for government and, yes, even the Supreme Court itself? But then, it is difficult to apply logic to the Court's *Mueller* decision.

In 1984, the Supreme Court handed down two decisions: (1) a financial decision, *Allen v. Wright,*[290] concerning legal standing of citizens to litigate the Internal Revenue Service's seeking more aggressive action denying tax-exempt status to private schools that racially discriminate against black students; (2) a church-state curriculum decision, *Wallace v. Jaffree,*[291] invalidating Alabama's statute authorizing teachers to lead "willing students" in a prescribed prayer to "Almighty God."

The 1984 school-finance decision, *Allen v. Wright,*[292] concerns legal standing by black Americans to sue the Internal Revenue Service when those citizens perceive the Internal Revenue Service has not adopted sufficient standards and procedures in denying tax-exempt status to racially discriminatory private schools. The Court's majority opinion (5–3, Justices Brennan, Blackmun, and Stevens dissenting) was written by Justice Sandra O'Connor. Plaintiffs, parents of black children (whose children never applied for admission to a racially discriminatory private school or any other private school), sought declaratory and injunctive relief. The federal district court dismissed plaintiffs' action for lack of standing. The District of Columbia Court of Appeals reversed.[293]

Justice O'Connor found that the doctrine of *standing* requires that "a plaintiff must allege personal injury fairly traceable to the defendant's allegedly unlawful conduct and likely to be redressed by the requested relief."[294] Neither plaintiff described injury sufficient to justify standing. First, Justice O'Connor stated, the plaintiffs' argument that "they are harmed directly by the mere fact of government financial aid to discriminatory private schools . . . is not a judicially cignizable injury."[295] Second, even though plaintiffs complained that their children's ability to receive an education in a racially integrated school was a judicially cognizable and a serious recognized legal issue, "the injury cannot support standing because the injury alleged is not fairly traceable to the government conduct respondents challenge as unlawful."[296]

In dissent, Justice Brennan maintained that the Court "uses standing to slam the courthouse door against plaintiffs who are entitled to full consideration of their claims on the merits."[297] And thus Justice Brennan would have allowed "respondents a chance to prove their case on the merits."[298]

Justice Stevens, with whom Justice Blackmun joines, filed a lengthy dissenting opinion. Justice Stevens framed his dissent in three propositions:

1. respondents have adequately alleged "injury in fact";
2. their injury is fairly traceable to the conduct they claim to be unlawful; and
3. the "separation of powers" principle does not create a jurisdictional obstacle to the consideration of the merits of their claim.[299]

In *Wallace v. Jaffree* and *Smith v. Jaffree,*[300] the Court declared that Alabama's "James Law" authorizing teacher-conducted prayer activities was unconstitutional. The Court agreed to consider Alabama's enactment requiring public schools to "observe up to one minute of non-activity for meditation or silent prayer."[301]

The Alabama enactment provided that any teacher or professor in any public-education institution

> may pray, may lead willing students in prayer, or may lead willing students in the following prayer: Almighty God, You alone are our God. We acknowledge You as the Creator and Supreme Judge of the world. May Your justice, Your truth, and Your peace abound this day in the hearts of our country- ment, in the counsels of our government, in the sanctity of our homes and in the classrooms of our schools in the name of our Lord. Amen.[302]

The cost for teacher's time administering the "James Prayer" was never an issue. Moreover, the Supreme Court continued to be absoslutely consistent in church-state school-curriculum matters.

In 1985, the Court decided three major cases: (1) *Grand Rapids School District v. Ball*[303] — public tax resources for shared-time and community-education programs in religious schools; (2) *Aquilar v. Felton*[304] — federal financing of educational programs in religious elementary schools; and (3) *Wallace v. Jaffree*[305] — Alabama's legislative enactment requiring public schools to observe a minute for meditation or silent prayer.

In *Grand Rapids,*[306] the Court, in a 5–4 decision (Burger and O'Connor concurred in part and dissented in part; Rehnquist and White dissented), held that the Grand Rapids shared-time and community-education program (providing classes to religious schools in religious school buildings but leased by the school district) was First Amendment religious establishment, thus unconstitutional.[307] Both the federal district court and court of appeals had declared the school-board practice unconstitutional (the circuit court was split –1). The issues before the circuit court were

> 1. The school board leased for both the shared-time and community-education programs through a standard lease from nonpublic school classroom and other facilities. The lease stipulated $6.00 per elementary schoolroom per week and $10.00 for secondary rooms per week.
> 2. The leased facilities were "'desanctified'" of religious symbols, crucifixes, or artifacts. However, often religious symbols or artifacts abounded in adjoining corridors, surrounding rooms, and connecting buildings.[308]
> 3. School-board policy required teachers to post signs where public school classes convened "designataing it as a public school classroom." One teacher indicated she carried her "public school" sign with her as she convened classes throughout the religious building.

Moreover, there were no outside signs indicating public-school activities were convened inside.[309]

4. The record indicates that with exceptions, the children attending public-school classes were the same children attending religious classes—the same children in the same building with an identical schedule, except that if a public-school teacher taught the class, a public-school sign appeared and that space momentarily was sterilized of religious trappings. Even though the shared-time program was available to all public-school students (the adjective *all,* as in *Mueller,* is present again), "the record is abundantly clear that only non-public school students wearing the cloak of a 'public school student' can enroll in it."[310] In effect, there was a public school buried deep in the bowels of a religious school, the only entrance being admission as a religious-school student.

5. A significant number of shared-time teachers, always employed within school-board policy guidelines, formally taught in religious schools (often teaching in the same religious school where public-school classes were now convened). A majority of community education classes were taught by teachers who held dual employment by both public and religious schools.[311] The record does not indicate proportional salary accruing to either school-board or religious schools.

6. Shared-time education programs in Michigan are more than sixty years old. The standard shared-time program represents non-public students enrolled in religious schools for content classes and in public schools for more secular classes such as physical education, shorthand, typing, reading, math, etc. However, in the Grand Rapids prototypical program, both religious and public-education activities occur within the same building—a religious building leased by the school board—"with the exception of physical education, industrial arts, music, and art, the educational opportunities offered through the program are, in the main, supplementary to the core curriculum of the public schools."[312] A secondary student would spend approximately 10 percent of an academic year in public-school classes. Physical education, a prerequisite for high school graduation, is taught only by public schoolteachers.

7. Community-education classes were taught at the conclusion of the regular school day. Secondary-school courses were often substantive—astronomy, computer programming, typing, bookkeeping. Each Community-education class must enroll students for the class to make; thus popularity of the instructor becomes important. And thus the reason the school-board employs teachers already employed by the religious schools—a ready following.

8. The public- and religious-school calendars were often not coterminous. Thus, the school board "attempted to accommodate the non-public schools."³¹³

Justice Brennan, writing for the Court's majority, reviewed briefly the history of the First Amendment religious clause and decided that the Grand Rapids policy should be measured against the *Lemon I* criteria; after all, the *Lemon I* test focuses on "purposes, effect, entanglement—that determine whether a particular state action is an improper 'law respecting an establishment of religion.'"³¹⁴ And there is no dispute concerning the first part of the *Lemon I* tripartite test. The shared-time and community-education programs are "'manifestly secular.'"³¹⁵

Concerning *Lemon I*'s second test—religious advancement—Justice Brennan insisted that the programs in "pervasively sectarian" schools impermissibly advanced religion in three ways:

1. Teachers participating in the program(s) "may become involved in intentionally or inadvertently inculcating particular religious tenets or beliefs."³¹⁶
2. The impressionable eyes of young children may perceive "a crucial symbolic link between government and religion."³¹⁷
3. The public-financed programs may provide a subsidy to the "primary religious mission" of the religious schools.³¹⁸

Community-Education and Shared-Time Teachers

Justice Brennan acknowledged that almost every teacher in the community-education program was employed by the religious schools. And even though the school board employed all teachers in the shared-time program, "'a significant portion'" were previously employed in the religious schools.³¹⁹ Further complicating the constitutional question, teachers were expected to serve their religious schools "zealously" while employed by the religious schools, then jettison religious activities when the secular classes began. Moreover, teachers were expected to perform the split sectarian-secular activities with the same students and in the same schoolrooms. There is no question of good faith, said Brennan. Yet, maintained Brennan,

> There is a substantial risk that overtly or subtly the religious message they are expected to convey during the regular school day will infuse the supposedly secular classes they teach after school.³²⁰

The Impressionable Eyes and Ears of Young People

Even though most of the teachers in the shared-time program were full-time public-school teachers, "a significant portion ... previously worked in the religious schools."[321] Moreover, shared-time teachers were performing an "even more" important education service than community-education program teachers:

> Shared Time instructors are teaching academic subjects in religious schools in courses virtually indistinguishable from the other courses offered during the regular religious-school day.[322]

Finally, Brennan considered the "substantial risk" that both programs carried. While a teacher may unwillingly or knowingly direct a course toward the religious schools' mission, it was unlikely that either students or parents would detect the ideological direction. After all, if children were in religious schools throughout the day, "they would have little motivation or ability to discern improper ideological cotent...."[323] In such an atmosphere,

> Government promotes religion as effectively when it fosters a close iden-tification of its powers and responsibilities with those of any—or all—religious denominations as when it attempts to inculcate specific religious doctrines.[324]

Brennan found that the symbolic union of church and state is "most likely to influence children of tender years" and "is an impermissible effect under the Establishment Clause."[325]

The Public Subsidy to Religious Schools

First Justice Brennan ran the litany of church-state finance cases delineating those cases that allowed indirect public aid and those denying public aid: "the Establishment Clause prohibition of forms of aid that pro-vide 'direct and substantial advancement of the sectarian enterprise.'"[326] And then the question emerges: Is public aid in this case forbidden, in effect advancing religion? Justice Brennan insisted that public assistance to both community-education and shared-time programs were like cash grants to religious schools, thus religious advancement:

> The programs challenged here, which provide teachers in addition to the in-structional equipment and materials, have a similar—and forbidden—effect of advancing religion. This kind of direct aid to the educational function of the religious school is indistinguished from the provision of a direct cash subsidy to the religious school that is most clearly prohibited under the Establishment Clause.[327]

In rejecting petitioners' claim that public aid in *Grand Rapids* was similar to aid allowed in *Allen, Meek,* and *Wolman* — as aid to children, not religious schools — Justice Brennan acknowledged that in effect, "all aid to religious schools ultimately 'flows' to the students."[328] Yet, maintained Justice Brennan, as the Court has explained many times: "Where, as here, no meaningful distinction can be made between aid to the students and aid to the school, the concept of a loan to individuals is a transparent fiction."[329] Moreover, if petitioners' argument that both programs only "supplemented the curriculum" were accepted, then a circuitous series of events could occur, allowing school-board discretion gradually to

> take over the entire secular curriculum of the religious schools, for the latter could surely discontinue existing courses so that they might be replaced a year or two later by a Community Education or Shared Time course with the same time content.[330]

Brennan acknowledged that shared-time programs occupied only 10 percent of the religious-schoolchildren's time, but the Court could not fix the percentage of time students could participate in the secular classes while in the sectarian school. What would the percentage formula be?

> To let the genie out of the bottle in this case would be to permit ever larger segments of the religious school curriculum be turned over to the public school system, thus violating the cardinal principle that the state may not in effect become the prime supporter of the religious school system.[331]

Thus, concluded Brennan, both the community-education and shared-time programs have the primary effect of religious advancement in three ways: (1) public-provided teachers in a pervasively religious influence "may subtly or overtly indoctrinate . . . students in particular religious tenets";[332] (2) the symbolic union of church and state — public-funded instruction within a religious school — "threatens to convey a message of state support for religion to students and to the general public";[333] and (3) the public-funded programs "in effect subsidize the religious functions "in effect subsidize the religious functions of a parochial school. . . ."[334]

Chief Justice Burger, concurring in part and dissenting in part, concluded that the community-education program violated the establishment clause, while the shared-time program did not.[335]

Justice O'Connor, also concurring in part and dissenting in part, concluded that the community-education program violated the establishment clause": [T]he program has the perceived and actual effect of advancing the religious aim of the church-related schools."[336] Yet the shared-time program was not constitutionally flawed; the record did not indicate that shared-time teachers attempted to proselytize students. Moreover, only a small fraction of shared-time teachers were formally employed by the religious schools, and there was no evidence to indicate "that the perceived or actual effect of the Shared Time program will be to inculcate religion at public expense."[337]

Justice Rehnquist dissented, primarily on his perception of the "faulty-wall" premise stated in his dissenting opinion in *Wallace v. Jaffree*: "[T]he Court blinds itself to the first 150 years' history of the Establishment Clause."[338] How could teaching Spanish, math, and gymnastices create "a greater 'symbolic line' than the municipal creche upheld in *Lynch v. Donnelly. . . .*"[339] Moreover, the majority had impugned public-schoolteachers' integrity. "Not one instance of attempted religious inculcating exists in the records. . . ."[340]

In summary, *Grand Rapids* holds that a school-board policy expending public funds for schoolteachers teaching within the environs of religious schools is constitutionally flawed as religious advancement.

The final 1985 school-finance decision, *Aquilar v. Felton,*[341] was an appeal from the Second Circuit Court of Appeals addressing the issue of federal funds received under Title I of the 1965 Elementary and Secondary Education Act to pay salaries of public employees who taught in religious schools. (A unanimous court of appeals declared the practice unconstitutional as religious establishment.) In 1981, the act became known as The Education Consolidation and Improvement Act of 1981, and Title I became known as Chapter I (see Chapter IV of the present work). Even though the Court recognized the official change to Chapter I, the Court continued to refer to Chapter I as Title I.

Readers may remember that the 1974 *Wheeler*[342] case addressed Title I issues of "in-kind" programs—on-premises instruction for religious schools similar in substance to public-school programs. Justice Blackmun wrote the majority opinion (8–1 decision, Justice Douglas dissenting) and made recommendations concerning "comparable instructional programs" not "on the premises instruction." Blackmun's *Wheeler* decision speaks for itself, but in the final analysis, this case was settled in the Missouri Supreme Court in *Mallory v. Barrera*[343] (1976). The Missouri Supreme Court insisted that Title I funds were "public" funds, not "federal" funds, and when Title I funds were deposited with the state treasury, the funds were "money donated" for public-school purposes as provided by the Missouri Constitution and statutes. Moreover, use of Title I funds for teachers and related services (including textbooks and transportation) in religious schools violated the Missouri Constitution as religious advancement.[344]

Justice Brennan, writing majority opinion in *Aquilar* (the Court split 5–4 with Powell, Stevens, Marshall, and Blackmun joining Brennan, held that New York policy using Title I federal funds for public teachers to teach in parochial school was unconstitutional as First Amendment establishment.[345]

Title I of the 1965 Elementary and Secondary Education Act authorized the Secretary of education to provide financial assistance to school districts (including private schools) throughout the United States for low-socioeconomic-status children. Title I programs were designed to supplement existing programs, not create new ones. In early 1966, the New York City School Board initiated Title I programs, with public-funded teachers, on the premises of parochial schools, the majority (82 percent) of children enrolled in Roman Catholic schools.[346] The programs included reading, math, English (as a second language), and guidance programs. Teachers, guidance counselors, psychologists, psychiatrists, and social workers composed the professional cohort. The Title I programs in religious schools were supervised by the school board's Bureau of Nonpublic Schools including unannounced supervisory visits. All professional personnel were directed to avoid religious activities and to exclude religious materials from their classrooms. Moreover, they were encouraged to keep contact with religious-school personnel to a minimum.[347] Also, religious-school administrators were "required to clear the classrooms used by the public school personnel of all religious symbols."[348]

In 1978, plaintiffs (taxpayers) initiated action in the federal district court, claiming that the Title I program violated the establishment clause. The district court—with the companion case, *National Coalition for Public Education and Religious Liberty v. Harris*[349] (*PEARL*) involving an identical Title I issue, already decided, affirming Title I constitutionality—granted summary judgment predicated on the decision in *PEARL*. The Second Circuit Appeals Court reversed, holding the Title I practice religious advancement.[350] The Supreme Court granted certiorari.

Justice Brennan began by noting similarities with programs declared unconstitutional in *Ball:* publicly funded teachers teaching in religious schools; supplies and materials provided to students; the schools were religious; and instructors "are told that they are public school employees under the sole control of the public school system."[351] The New York School Board distinguished *Ball* because New York had adopted a "system for monitoring the religion content of publicly funded Title I classes in the religious schools."[352]

Brennan found that established monitoring activities resulted in "excessive entanglement of church and state."[353] There are two concerns: (1) nonadherents to the religious doctrine suffer, even when the government activity is "largely secular"; (2) even adherents receiving financial benefits suffer because they are limited by government intrusion. Quoting from *McCollum,*

> The First Amendment rests upon the premise that both religion and govern-
> ment can best work to achieve their lofty aims if each is left free from the
> other within its respective sphere.[354]

Brennan cited decisions addressing the excessive-entanglement doctrine — *Lemon I, Meek,* and *Marburger.* He compared *Roemer, Hunt,* and
Tilton, higher-education cases, with the elementary and secondary schools
receiving Title I funds were pervasively sectarian, which had "as a substantial purpose the inculcation of religious values."[355] Moreover, many schools
began the school day, and often classes, with prayers; the schools often
reported to their affiliated churches, and finally, the vast majority of religious
schools receiving funds were Catholic, administered by the local parish.
Thus, there were two elements involving the excessive-entanglement doctrine: (1) public aid was provided to schools that were pervasively religious;
(2) because the aid was in human form, teachers, there must be continuous
monitoring to "ensure absense of a religious message."[356] Finally, Brennan,
describing the "Grand Inquisitor" in reverse (state agencies stalking the
religious schools' hallways, inspecting teachers, students, and religious
symbols — "secularization of a creed" — and coalescing administrative decisions and personnel (schedules, classroom assignments, services, dissemination of information, and student problems) held that the program, despite
being well intentioned, "remained constitutionally flawed."[357]

It is worth noting that Brennan raised the political-divisiveness issue,
first announced in *Lemon I,* then buried by Powell's dissenting opinion in
the 1977 *Wolman* decision:

> As government agencies must make these judgments, the dangers of
> political divisiveness along religious lines increase.[358]

Justice Powell's concurring opinion is significant for two reasons:

1. In the early 1970s, the Supreme Court was split 6–3 on public
funds for religious elementary schools, and Justice Powell had allied
himself with the majority. Beginning with the 1977 *Wolman* decision
(Justice Powell concurred in part and dissented in part), Justice Powell
began to defect form the solid six. In the 1980 *Regan* (state-mandated
services) and the 1983 *Mueller* (tax-credit) decisions, Justice Powell
allied himself with the old minority and with Justice O'Connor helped
establish a new majority five, permitting public aid under the above-
described conditions to religious schools. However, Justice Powell
promised in the 1974 *Wheeler* decision (a Title I case) that if Title I
meant public-funded teachers on a religious-school campus, he would
be opposed to such a practice. Justice Powell kept that 1974 promise
in this 1985 case.

2. In the 1977 *Wolman* decision, Justice Powell suggested that "deep political divisions along religious lines [are] remote...." In 1985, Justice Powell acknowledged that "this risk of entanglement is compounded by the additional risk of political divisiveness stemming from aid to religion at issue here."[359]

Powell began his concurring opinion by recognizing that both programs (Grand Rapids's and New York's) had created much good with little harm. Yet, insisted Justice Powell, "there is too great a risk of government entanglement in the administration of religious schools. ..."[360] Moreover, "this risk of entanglement is compounded by the additional risk of political divisiveness stemming from the aid to religion at issue here."[361] And while Powell did not really think there would be religious dominance of the American democratic process,

> nonetheless, there remains a considerable risk of continuing political strife over the propriety of direct aid to religious schools and the proper allocation of limited governmental resources.... Thus, any proposal to extend direct governmental aid to parochial schools alone is likely to spark political disagreement from taxpayers who support the public schools ... the potential for such divisiveness is a strong additional reason for holding that Title I and Grand Rapids programs are invalid on entanglement grounds.[362]

Finally, Powell found that the Title I program violated the effects prong of the tripartite test:

> The constitutional defect in the Title I program as indicated above, is that it provides a direct financial subsidy to be administered in significant part by public school teachers within parochial schools—resulting in both the advancement of religion and forbidden entanglement.[363]

Chief Justice Burger, dissenting, said that the Court's decision "exhibits nothing less than hostility toward religion and the children who attend church sponsored schools."[364]

Justice Rehnquist, dissenting, maintained that the Court took "advantage of the 'Catch 22' paradox of its own creation whereby aid must be supervised to ensure no entanglement but the supervision itself is held to cause an entanglement."[365]

Justice O'Connor, dissenting, developed a lengthy analysis of New York's nineteen-year-old Title I program and juxtaposed that analysis against the Court's 1975 *Meek* decision.[366]

O'Connor first addressed the "effect" test. Direct state aid to parochial schools that advanced the schools' religious mission was unconstitutional. The New York program served a secular purpose of aiding needy children;

there was no program "to advance or endorse religion."[367] Indeed, the New York program was nineteen years old, and there "has never been a single incident in which a Title I instructor ... attempted to 'indoctrinate' the students in particular religious tenets at public expense."[368] And the reason for such an "unblemished" record was the professional nature of Title I teachers who obey instructions not to inculcate religion in the classroom. Concerning the questions of Title I funds subsidizing the religious function of parochial schools by assuming responsibilty for the secular curriculum, the effect was "tenuous" because Title I funds could be used only for programs and services not otherwise available to children. And even if there were duplication of programs and services, the majority position was flawed:

> Our Establishment Clause decisions have not barred remedial assistance to parochial school children, but rather remedial assistance *on the premises of the parochial school.*[369]

O'Connor questioned the difference between a remedial class offered in a parochial school and one offered in a portable classroom immediately off the school campus. Justice O'Connor then suggested that *Wolman* had been "wrongly decided."[370]

Concerning the entanglement prong of *Lemon I,* O'Connor simply could not accept the majority's analysis of entanglement as established in *Meek,* "the *Meek* opinion was flawed."[371] Moreover, *Meek*'s "thoughtful dissents" (Burger, Rehnquist, and White were the dissents in *Meek*) had insisted that Act 194 of the Pennsylvania enactment, providing teachers to religious schools, was constitutional. Moreover, there was no record indicating peripatetic public-schoolteachers attempting to inculcate religion in religious schools' classrooms. Finally, O'Connor lamented that the "risk identified in *Meek* was greatly exaggerated."[372]

Concerning the political-divisiveness issue, O'Connor suggested there had been little controversy over the Title I program, except for the litigants in this case. O'Connor concluded:

> I reject this theory and the analysis in *Meek v. Pittenger* on which it is based. I cannot close my eyes to the fact that, over almost two decades, New York's public school teachers have helped thousands of impoverished, parochial school children. ... Their praiseworthy efforts have not eroded and do not threaten the religious liberty assured by the Establishment Clause.[373]

Justice White dissented for the same reasons indicated in *Lemon I* and other decisions. "I am satisfied that what the states have sought to do in these cases is well within their authority and is not forbidden by the Establishment Clause."[374]

The final 1985 decision, *Wallace v. Jaffree,*[375] is a nonfinance decision but a major curriculum decision with important implications for this study. As indicated earlier, the cost of implementing an enactment mandating religion in the curriculum (i.e., teacher and administrative cost) is never the issue. Nonetheless, there is cost — enormous cost.

The *Wallace* case came on appeal from alabama. Justice Stevens, writing the majority opinion (the Court split 6–3, Burger, White and Rehnquist dissenting), held the Alabama enactment (authorizing in public schools a moment of silence for "meditation or voluntary prayer") and endorsement of religion, unconstitutional as religious establishment.[376]

In 1981, the Alabama General Assembly enacted legislation authorizing a one-minute period of silence "for meditation or voluntary prayer" in all public schools. There were three parts to the Alabama legislation:

1. Section 16-1-20 simply provided that a child had a right to meditate in silence. The federal district court discovered no constitutional flaws with 16-1-20. Moreover, there was no challenge.
2. Section 16-1-20.1 authorized a period of silence for "meditation or voluntary prayer."
3. Section 16-1-20.2 authorized teachers to lead willing students in the following prayer:

   Almighty God, You alone are God. We acknowledge You as the Creator and Supreme Judge of the World. May Your justice, Your truth, and Your peace abound this day in the hearts of our countrymen, in the counsels of our government, the sanctity of our homes and in the classrooms of our schools in the name of our Lord. Amen.[377]

The district court found that Sections 16-1-20.1 and 16-1-10.1 were a legislative effort to encourage religion but insisted that "Alabama has the power to establish a state religion if it chooses to do so."[378]

In 1983, Justice Powell, as Circuit Judge, entered an order staying the district court decision concerning Section 16-1-20.2 (that Supreme Court decision has been chronicled in the 1984 section of this chapter). Thus Section 16-1-20.1 — the minute of silence for meditation or voluntary prayer — was the remaining issue.

Justice Stevens began with a historical review of the First Amendment religious freedom made applicable to the states by the Fourteenth Amendment. He directed his analysis especially to the assertion that Alabama had the power to establish a state religion. Stevens decided that this case turned on the first part of the tripartite test: Does the statute have a secular purpose? Stevens found that "the statute had no secular purpose."[379] Section 16-1-20.1 sponsor state Senatory Donald Holmes inserted in the legislative record a statement maintaining that the legislation "was an effort to return voluntary prayer to the public schools"[380] Moreover, Senator Holmes indicated in testimony before the district court that he had "no other purpose in mind."[381] The state offered no evidence of secular purpose. Thus the legislative intent was to return prayer to the public schools. [W]e conclude that §16-1-20.1 violates the First Amendment."[382]

Justice Powell filed a concurring opinion, finding that the enactment's "purpose was solely religious in character. . . . Nothing in the record . . . identifies a clear secular purpose . . . the State also failed to identify any non-religious reason for the statute's enactment."[383] Finally, Powell stated that a pure moment-of-silence statute would likely pass constitutional muster.[384]

Justice O'Connor filed a concurring opinion. O'Connor's opinion is important because, as she indicated, "I am new to the struggle, I am not ready to abandon all aspects of the *Lemon* test. I do believe . . . the standards . . . in *Lemon* should be reexamined. . . ."[385] Thus, fresh judicial intelligence joined America's supreme tribunal in addressing church-state issues, the most important question in Western civilization.

Justice O'Connor first found that

> nothing in the United States Constitution as interpreted by this Court or in the laws of the State of Alabama prohibits public school children from voluntarily praying at any time before, during, or after the school day.[386]

However, that is not the issue; the issue is that Alabama's legislative enactment "intentionally crossed the line between creating a quiet moment during which those so inclined may pray, and affirmatively endorsing the particular religious practice of prayer."[387]

She continued:

> However deferentially one examines its text and legislative history, however objectively one views the message attempted to be conveyed to the public, the conclusion is unavoidable that the purpose of the statute is to endorse prayer in public schools . . . which is in violation of the Establishment Clause, and cannot be upheld.[388]

Finally, O'Connor decided that "moment of silence statutes of many states should satisfy the Establishment Clause standards we have here applied."[389]

Chief Justice Burger, dissenting, maintained that "to suggest that a moment-of-silence statute that includes the word 'prayer' unconstitutionally endorses religion, while one that simply provides for a moment of silence does not, manifests not neutrality but hostility toward religion."[390] "The mountains have labored and brought forth a mouse."[391]

Justice White, dissenting, recognized his continually being "out of step with many of the Court's decisions dealing with this subject matter," but did not believe the enactment infirm.[392]

Justice Rehnquist, in a lengthy dissenting opinion, recommended a basic reconsidertion of church-state precedents and the establishment clause. Beginning with *Everson,* Rehnquist considered the establishment clause. The *Everson* Court had quoted President Jefferson's "wall of separation between church and state," which appeared in his 1802 letter to the Danbury Baptist Association. The *Everson* Court had quoted from the 1879 *Reynolds* decision (a Mormon's free-exercises-clause challenge to a federal polygamy law): "In the words of Jefferson, the clause against establishment of religion by law was intended to erect 'a wall of separation between church and state'" (see *Reynolds v. United States,* 98 U.S. 145, 164 [1879]). The *Reynolds* decision, maintained Rehnquist, was the only direct liaison to Jefferson's historical metaphor, "the only authority cited as direct precedent for the 'wall of separation theory.'"[393] Rehnquist proceeded in three historical directions regarding the establishment clause:

1. Concerning Jefferson's 1802 letter, Rehnquist suggested that Jefferson's letter was nothing more than "a short note of courtesy, written fourteen years after the amendments were passed by Congress."[394]

   Moreover, Jefferson was Ambassador to France at the time the Bill of Rights was passed by Congress; thus, he was not present at the debate. Finally,

   it is impossible to build sound constitutional doctrine upon a mistaken understanding of constitutional history, but unfortunately, the Establishment Clause has been expressly freighted with Jefferson's misleading metaphor for nearly forty years.[395]

2. Next, Rehnquist recognized Jefferson's fellow Virginian James Madison, who played a significant role drafting the Bill of Rights. Rehnquist suggested that Madison's involvement could best be described as activities that "were less those of a dedicated advocate of the wisdom of such measures than those of a prudent statesman...."[396] Continuing, Rehnquist maintained "his sponsorship of the Amendment in the House was obviously not that of a zealous believer...."[397]

3. Having described Jefferson's and Madison's First Amendment church-state activities, Rehnquist proceeded with a snippet analysis of congressional debate of the First Amendment. Rehnquist concluded:

one would have to say that the First Amendment Clause should be read no more broadly than to prevent the establishment of a national religion or the governmental preference of one religious sect over another.[398]

Finally, Rehnquist found:

The 'wall of separation between church and state' is a metaphor based on bad history, a metaphor which has proved useless as a guide to judging. It should be frankly and explicitly abandoned.[399]

In 1986, Chief Justice Burger submitted his resignation to President Reagan. President Reagan nominated Associate Justice William H. Rehnquist to become the nation's sixteenth chief justice and Antonia Scalia to become an associate justice. On September 17, 1986, the Senate confirmed Justice Rehnquist by a 65–53 vote, bringing to a close a tumultuous period in the Court's history.

Summary

Beginning early in the 1970s, the Court, aided by a judicial ideology deduced over decades of Supreme Court church-state decisions, the *Lemon I* tripartite test, was a virtually unanimous Court in *Lemon I* and *DiCenso*. The Court's direction was clear, and its decisions were firm. A relative certainty permeated Court decisions concerning public aid to religious schools throughout the first seven years.

In late 1972 and early 1973, the court divided ideologically 6–3 concerning public funds for religious schools. Burger, White, and Rehnquist formed the omnipresent dissent.

The 1970s experienced an intensive pace in church-state legislation and resulting litigious activities. The emotional involvement of some state legislatures, religious leaders, and lay citizens encapsulating the New-Right religious fundamentalist and right-wing political groups was unprecedented in American history. And often there was open defiance of Supreme Court decisions, some state legislatures promulgating statutes that clearly violated the Court's decisions. The reasoning apparently was to funnel funds into religious schools until the statutes were declared unconstitutional, as in *Lemon I* (1971), *Lemon II* (1972), *Lemon III* (1973), and *Meek* (1975). Perhaps another motivation for state legislatures was to find constitutionally acceptable legislation aiding religious schools.

While the child-benefit theory allowed textbooks (*Cochran, Allen*) and transportation (*Everson*) state enactments continuously ran into the judicial ideological juggernaut, the *Lemon I* tripartite test.

In time, though, with a change in court personnel and ideology, the *Lemon I* tripartite test diminshed as an absolute: "no litmus-paper test . . . and no categorical imperatives and absolute approaches." The tripartite test was too inclusive and demanded serious judicial scholarship — a standard mirror, reflecting flawed enactments and illogical judicial decisions.

The Court signaled a new direction in *Wolman* (1977). Justice Powell was the first Supreme Court justice in American history to suggest that non-public schools "often afforded wholesome competition with our public schools. . . ." To continue Powell's logic as applicable to governmental creations (and that is what public school systems are in a democracy) staggers the imagination.

In *Regan* (1980), the Court reversed *Levitt I* (1973) concerning state-mandated testing and reporting services. And in *Mueller* (1983), the Court reversed more than a decade of identical decisions regarding tax credits, parent reimbursements, and parent deductions, and sustained Minnesota's deduction legislation simply because the statute included the adjective *all*. *Mueller,* said Justice Rehnquist, was more like *Allen* (1968) and *Cochran* (1930), using the child-benefit theory.

Mueller is the most important decision affecting public education since *Brown I* and *II*. Also, *Mueller* is the most important religious-school decision since *Pierce* (1925). *Mueller* has the potential to establish two public-funded school systems in America: (1) a public-education system, with unchurched, minority, handicapped, and indigent students enrolled; (2) a religious-schools system, with almost all white students.

Already there are thirteen states with "Minnesota" legislation pending. And Justice Rehnquist was the second justice to suggest that public education would benefit from nonpublic schools: "[P]rivate schools may serve as a benchmark for public schools, in a manner analogous to the 'TVA yardstick' for private power companies." Moreover, the judicial theory of "intent" versus "extent," a concept applied by the Court in de facto segregated school-system cases surfaced for the first time in church-state litigation. Plaintiffs argued that the Minnesota legislation intended to provide direct public aid to religious schools.

Justice Rehnquist rejected these data: "[W]e believe it wiser to decline to engage in the type of empirical inquiry into these persons benefited by state law which petitioners urge." Moreover, once again the Court adopted neutral accommodationist pragmatism.

Predicated on Court decisions from 1969 to 1986, legislative enactments containing the following elements were declared unconstitutional: (1) tuition grants, (2) tax credits, parent reimbursements, tuition deduction (unless the award is available for all), (3) religious teachers' salary supplements, (4) provision of instructional or therapeutic personnel to religious schools, (5) public funds for repair and maintenance of religious schools, (6) payment for teacher-prepared tests, (7) transportation for field trips, (8) provisions for instructional equipment other than textbooks, (9) textbook loans to schools that racially discriminate, and (10) shared-time academic instruction (at public expense) within religious schools.

The Court has held constitutional the following legislative enactments: (1) textbook loans (except as explained in 9 above), (2) transportation to religious schools, (3) state-mandated testing and reporting services, (4) medical and therapeutic services, and (5) tax deductions (included in the legislation must be the adjective *all*) for all parents with children attending a tuition-charging school. The Minnesota statute includes provision for books, supplies, equipment, and transportation. Moreover, the books may be required textbooks, and the transportation may include field trips.

Chapter VI

Summary and Conclusions

The Supreme Court during the Burger years decided more church-state cases than in the 180 years prior to 1969. Many of those decisions have had far-reaching implications with a decided effect on staunch sectarian legislative supporters. Dozens of religious enactments were caught in the vortex of religious and political activities. Moreover, the Supreme Court's church-state decisions from 1969–1986 were characterized by both quality and quantity.

Summary

The American version of this church-state drama began the day the *Mayflower* anchored in Provincetown harbor, November 21, 1620, with the Mayflower Compact signed by forty-one eligible signers. The *Mayflower* pilgrims, one month later, December 21, 1620, settled at Plymouth with the Mayflower Compact, a God-centered civil-government document.

In 1629, the Massachusetts Bay Company was chartered, Boston being chosen as the capital in 1632. The Massachusetts Bay Company Charter in effect established a sectarian autonomous Puritan society, and a theocratic republic emerged. Even though the Puritans came to Massachusetts for religious freedom, they did not come for freedom of religion; they allowed no religious freedom for others. The Puritan influence in America was pervasive, no other colonizing people dominating colonial culture.

From 1634 to 1647, the Massachusetts General Court enacted four laws that became the cornerstones of American public educaton: (1) the 1632 and 1637 enactments established the general concept of a common property tax for general benefit; (2) the 1642 enactment mandated parental responsibility for education, including reading, religion, and Massachusetts law; (3) in

1647, the first public-education finance act (Old Deluder Satan Act) was passed. The first public-education finance law financed public education with pervasive religious influence—a Protestant public school.

In due time, other New England states followed. And after the Revolutionary War, the Northwest Ordinances of 1784, 1785, and 1787 indicated the new federal government's commitment to public education on the frontier. The New England states' educational imperatives on other geographical areas were absolutely important.

The new nation and a new educational concept—public education and democracy—emerged together.

From 1825 to 1850, the Union expanded dramatically, and so did public education. Social, political, and religious pressures made excessive demands on church-related schools. National and state political, economic, educational, and religious leaders clamored for a public-education system, a free public-education system. By 1850, public schools existed in almost every northern state. And by 1860, American education was a qualified success, a majority of states having public schools. Americans' enthusiasm for public education was often expressed to foreign visitors: "Have you seen our public schools?"

The fight for public funds for religious schools began in 1647 with the Old Deluder Act. What the Puritans did was simply to establish public-school systems, financed with public monies, that were pervasively religious. Good Calvinist theology insisted that education was an instrument of salvation. Moreover, public funds were often made available to private agencies and religious organizations for nonpublic education. There was such a thirst for education that gratitude for any organization educating children suggested public support.

Early in the nineteenth century, public schools with a pervasively Protestant religious purpose collided with another emerging American religious institution—the Catholic Church. Catholic leaders viewed Protestant public schools as hostile to the Catholic Church. The solution to the problem was public finance for Catholic public schools. Juxtaposed with the sectarian-school-finance struggle was the church-state-separation concept emerging with the Constitution, especially the Bill of Rights. The American concept of church-state separation had become a political reality.

By 1840, church-state separation had occurred in every state in the Union. Moreover, because of the Protestant-Catholic schisms, church-state separation was becoming an imporant philosophical issue for leading education statesmen.

The secularization of public schools included two distinct directions: (1) public funds for public schools only; (2) the secularization of curricular and noncurricular activities. The religious confrontation was bitter, and in time the Catholic church established a religious-school system. President

Grant, in 1876, reflecting on past conflict and future national church-state policy, insisted that "not one dollar of money appropriated for public schools ever go to support religious schools." Over the years, the American public schools grew and flourished as a uniquely American institution. Moreover, Catholic religious schools from the 1884 Third Plenary mandate flourished with 5 percent enrollment in 1900, 9 percent in 1940, and continued to increase until the mid-1960s.

As the 1970s approached, Catholic schools (with over one thousand schools closed from 1963–1969) faced an uncertain future. But there were political, religious, social, and educational transitions in American history—almost imperceptible, but nonetheless, change was occurring. President Nixon was elected; America was moving unmistakably in a conservative direction.

At the threshold of the 1970s, the Supreme Court held that public funds under the child-benefit theory (as in *Cochran, Everson,* and *Allen*) and incidental administrative costs for off-campus religious activities (as *Zorach* mandates) constituted no First Amendment religious advancement. On the other hand, where there were on-campus religious-curriculum programs (as described in *McCollum, Engel* and *Schempp*), these programs failed to pass constitutional muster.

Moreover, the Court, after seventy years of litigation, developed a national church-state standard for federal and state courts—the *Lemon I* tripartite test: (1) Does the statute have a secular legislative purpose? (2) Does the statute effectively advance or inhibit religion? (3) Does the statute excessively entangle government and religion? In the early 1970s, the Burger Court moved with authority and clarity (*Lemon I* and *DiCenso*). With *Meek* (1975), the Court closed off all public funds to religious schools except child-benefit resources. However, *Wolman* (1977) signaled a new direction. Moreover, state assemblies were promulgating church-state enactments at a record pace. And with *Regan* (1980) and *Mueller* (1983), the Court's new majority (5–4) began to erase the 1970s decisions. Yet the 1985 *Grand Rapids* and *Felton* cases, reestablishing the former coalition of justices, declared the Grand Rapids and New York City school boards' practices unconstitutional. The Burger years concluded on May 27, 1986, when Chief Justice Burger submitted his resignation. President Reagan nominated Justice Rehnquist to become chief justice, and he was confirmed on September 17, 1986.

In Chapter I, some basic questions relating to the topic of this study were proposed. Discussions developed around those six questions provide insight concerning church-state legislative enactments and Supreme Court decisive litigation.

What are the major legal issues regarding public funding for religious schools? The major legal issues concerning public funds for religious schools are those questions enunciated in the *Lemon I* tripartite test. A fourth category — political divisiveness — was raised in *Lemon I.* On one occasion, the Fourteenth Amendment's equal-protection and due-process issues were raised.

From an analysis of Supreme Court decisions, the following conclusions are drawn:

1. The first part of the tripartite test — does the statute or policy or action have a secular purpose? — does not emerge as a major constitutional question. The statute is "facially neutral"; in *Grand Rapids,* school-board policy was secular on its face. There is no way to determine legislative or school-board intent except through analysis of the extent of the action. Thus, the first part of the tripartite test is relatively uneventful where sophisticated legislative and school-board politicians practice. However, in *Wallace v. Jaffree* — a moment-of-silence case — the Court insisted the statute lacked any clear secular purpose.

2. The second and third parts of the tripartite test — does the statute advance or inhibit religion? and does the statute excessively entangle government and religion? — are inevitable constitutional issues — the "insoluble paradox," the most controversial of constitutional relationships — and most difficult to square with the establishment clause.

3. The political-divisive issue is almost always presented, beginning with *Lemon I,* but rejected as Justice Powell suggested in *Wolman:* "deep political divisions along religious lines (are) remote"; Justice White, in *Regan,* though acknowledging that the Court was divided, suggested in footnote 8 there was no merit "sufficient to raise the danger of future political divisiveness along religious lines"; and Justice Rehnquist in *Mueller* did not find the Minnesota statute with attenuated financial resources for religious schools "is apt to lead to strife and frequently strain a political system to the breaking point." However, Justice Powell, who in *Wolman* insisted that "deep political divisions along religious lines (are) remote," maintained in *Grand Rapids* (1985): "This risk of entanglement is compounded by the additional risk of political divisiveness...." At another point, Powell acknowledged that "there remains a considerable risk of continuing political strife over the propriety of direct aid to religious schools...."

4. Finally, the tripartite test is no longer the absolute test envisioned in *Lemon I.* Justice White indicated in *Regan* the tripartite test was no "litmus-paper test" and there were no "categorical imperatives and no absolute approaches." Justice Rehnquist in *Mueller*

suggested the *Lemon I* test was "no more than [a] helpful signpost," and in *Wallace v. Jaffree* Justice Rehnquist suggested that *Lemon I* was flawed because it was predicated upon an unsound analysis and understanding of constitutional history; Justice Stevens maintained in *Wolman* that he was ready to adopt Justice Black's test enunciated in *Everson* (1947): "no tax in any amount, large or small, can be levied to support any religious activity or institutions, whatever they may be called, by whatever form they may adopt to teach or practice religion." Justice O'Connor, a fresh voice in the 1985 *Grand Rapids, Felton,* and *Wallace* decisions insisted that she was not "ready to abandon all aspects of the *Lemon* Test."

5. The Fourteenth Amendment's equal-protection and due-process clauses, with the exception of *Leutkemeyer* (1974), has not been a major constitutional question.

Which of these issues are likely to be included in court cases related to public funds for religious schools? From *Lemon I* (1971) until *Regan* (1980), the tripartite test carried a solid measure of constitutional validity. And today all three parts of the *Lemon I* test are still very important in federal and state courts of limited jurisdiction. Moreover, the *Lemon I* test is compellingly important to the Supreme Court to the extent that in every church-state case, the majority follows the *Lemon I* format. The *Lemon I* test appears to be a compulsory table of contents, an imperative outline worth exploring. Even though some justices have suggested the *Lemon I* test is no longer absolute — Justice Rehnquist adopted the "look alike test" in *Mueller* (Does the case look more like *Allen* (1968) or *Nyquist* (1973)? — no justice feels compelled to abandon the tripartite test. The test is a helpful signpost. Moreover, as educators throughout the centuries have known concerning any test, justices have learned to use the *Lemon I* test to anchor their differing judicial ideologies.

We presume that constitutional issues concerning public funds for religious schools will continue into the 1990s. The debate will be vigorous and often hostile. And the judicial, religious, and political debate concerning constitutionality of metaphysical questions — what is God's? and what is Caesar's? — begs for some definitive standard. Human history and the American experience suggest that the "high and impregnable" wall of separation of church and state be maintained. And yet with *Mueller* there is potential for a publicly funded national religious-school system.

Which of the legal principles established by the landmark decisions are applicable to the states' constitutional and statutory provisions? All church-state issues are judicially answered, as those questions relate to the First Amendment made applicable to the fifty states by the Fourteenth

Amendment. The Fourteenth Amendment extends to citizens of the states equal protection and due process of the United States Constitution and its amendments. Moreover, the federal judiciary supersedes state courts. Thus all lesser courts respond to the Constitution as determined by the Supreme Court.

From an analysis of Supreme Court decisions from 1969 to 1986, legislative enactments must satisfy the following legal principles:

1. have a secular purpose;
2. neither inhibit nor advance a religion;
3. not create excessive government entanglement;
4. not create political divisiveness;
5. not violate equal-protection considerations of any group;
6. "generally" benefit children;
7. not involve indirect aid that can be converted to direct aid for a sectarian purpose;
8. allow services that provide for the general welfare of the population in a secular fashion;
9. where tax-deduction, parent-reimbursement, and other enactments address cost relief for parents with children in religious schools, the legislation must include the adjective *all*.

What specific issues related to public funds for religious schools are being litigated? Assuming judicially acceptable enactments from many general assemblies, *Wolman, Regan,* and *Mueller* are reasonably clear examples of future litigation. It is reasonable to assume that given the nature of the educational and political process, creative litigious questions have not been exhausted. In recent years, as *Lemon I* (1971), *Lemon III* (1973), *Meek* (1975), *Levitt I* (1973), and *Regan* (1980) indicate, state legislatures simply launder the constitutionally flawed process and present another statute providing public funding to religious schools, searching for judicial acceptance at some level. And as *Wolman* (1977), *Regan* (1980), and *Mueller* (1983) indicate, those statutes may pass constitutional muster. The school-board policy in *Grand Rapids* raised the age-old concept of publicly funded religious schools. As indicated in Chapter 2, in 1840, over two hundred Catholic schools existed in America. Moreover, many public-school systems accommodated Catholic parents and children. In Lowell, Massachusetts, "Irish" schools were established for Catholic children only and were taught by Catholic teachers. Even though the schools were public schools at the conclusion of the school day, the schools were used by Catholics for religious purposes. Moreover, in 1986, the New-Right fundamentalists were establishing Christian academies at a rate unprecedented in American history and may rival Catholic religious schools—two major religious school systems with different religious ideologies seeking public funds.

Early in the nineteenth century, as Chapter II indicates, America had publicly funded Protestant schools and some publicly funded Catholic schools. The two school systems were ideologically hostile and boded no goodwill for the American democracy. But America was a struggling young nation. Later, America jettisoned the religious albatross secularizing the public schools, and both America and religion have been well served by that decision. And even though *Grand Rapids* and *Felton* were major Supreme Court decisions, the 5-4 split represents a fragile alliance that could be destroyed with new appointments to the Court or sanitized legislative enactments.

Finally, a federal tax deduction (the Minnesota type) and perhaps even a voucher system hang omnipresent before the United States Congress. The tax deduction could cost the federal Treasury an estimated $5–$25 billion.

Can any trends be determined from analysis of the Court decisions? Analysis of these could best be classified as a *Tale of Two Cities:* "For it was the best of times and it was the worst of times...." The pattern was often change, reversal, confusion, and at times some justices were unpredictable.

The *Lemon I* Court was a virtually unanimous Court with clarity of purpose and direction. By 1973, the Court divided ideologically 6-3. The Court signaled a new direction in *Wolman* (1977). In time, with a change in Court personnel and ideology reflecting the political conservative direction, the *Lemon I* tripartite test diminished in importance. And in *Regan* (1980) the Court, with a new majority (5-4) reversed *Levitt I* (1973). Moreover, in *Mueller* (1983), the Court (5-4) reversed more than a decade of tax-credit, parent-reimbursement, and tax-deduction decisions because Minnesota's statute contained the adjective *all.* And yet in the 1985 *Grand Rapids* and *Felton* cases, the Court (5-4) insisted that public-funded teachers may not teach in religious schools.

Based on the legal precedents, what are the acceptable criteria for using public funds for religious schools? Based on an analysis of Supreme Court decisions from 1969 to 1986, legislative enactments encapsulating the following attributes will be declared unconstitutional:

1. tuition grants;
2. tax credits, parent reimbursement, tuition deduction (unless the award is available for *all*);
3. elementary and secondary teachers' salary supplement;

4. provisions of instructional or therapeutic personnel to religious schools;
5. public funds for repair and maintenance of religious schools;
6. payment for teacher-prepared tests;
7. transportation for field trips;
8. provisions for instructional equipment other than textbooks;
9. textbook loans to schools that racially discriminate;
10. shared-time instructors at public expense teaching academic subjects in religious schools.

The following legislative enactments will pass constitutional muster:

1. textbook loans (except as explained in 9 above);
2. transportation to religious schools;
3. state-mandated testing and reporting services;
4. medical and therapeutic services;
5. tax deductions — the statute must include the adjective *all,* as in "all parents with children in tuition charging schools." The tax deduction (as Minnesota's enactment indicates) can include provision for books (these books can be textbooks determined by religious schools), supplies, equipment, and transportation (transportation includes scheduled field trips).

Conclusions

The legality of using public funds for religious schools is a heavily litigated activity in recent years. The Burger Court decided more church-state cases than in the Court's entire history prior to 1969. The judicial activity reflected the urgency of competing groups for financial aid for education. Based on an analysis of Supreme Court judicial decisions, the following conclusions can be made:

1. Every indication — political, legislative, social, religious, and educational — suggests there will be continuous church-state judicial activity in both public funds for religious schools and curricular and extracurricular areas.
2. The *Lemon I* tripartite test is still a compelling judicial standard against which the constitutionality of church-state cases can be evaluated. However, the First Amendment establishment clause — the "insoluble paradox" between separation and entanglement — begs judicial measurement without qualification.

3. Even though the *Lemon I* tripartite test remains a compelling measure of constitutionality, a more sophisticated and refined standard, probably encapsulating the *Lemon I* test, will emerge. And at least one justice — Justice Stevens — has suggested a more simple test: "No tax ... can be levied to support any religious activity. ..."

4. Many state assemblies will continue to promulgate statutes providing public funds for religious schools, insisting the legislation should pass constitutional muster.

5. The decisions in *Wolman* (1977), *Regan* (1980), and *Mueller* (1983) acknowledged model legislative enactments that will pass constitutional muster.

6. The Supreme Court will continue to sustain constitutionality of child-benefit enactments.

7. The Supreme Court will continue to declare unconstitutional enactments containing religious curricular and extracurricular imperatives (i.e., prayer, Bible reading, Genesis statutes, including the new balanced-treatment scientific-creation statutes). However, there is every reason to suggest that legislative imperatives requiring "one moment for silent meditation" will pass constitutional muster.

8. The Congress will continue discussion concerning a voucher system and a national "tax-deduction" (the Minnesota model) plan for parents with children in religious schools. Passage would necessitate constitutional-validity litigation. Moreover, assuming passage of a Minnesota-type national "tax-deduction" would in time suggest a different state public-education funding formula, requiring tuition payment by all taxpayers with school-age children to the extent allowable by the national "tax-deduction" statute. Taxpayers then would simply claim the tax deduction from federal income tax. In effect, the United States government would be supporting the states' public education systems, and the states would be relieved, to the extent allowable, of the financial burden.

9. The *Mueller* decision has potential to establish two publicly funded school systems in America: a public-education system and a public-funded religious-school system.

10. The decisions in *Grand Rapids* and *Felton* have for the moment effectively precluded states from publicly funding instructors to teach academic subjects in religious schools.

For over 340 years, the American system of public funds for religious schools has developed. Early in the nineteenth century, two religious organizations, Protestant and Catholic, competed for public funds. Political divisiveness existed to such an extent that religious contrarians boycotted public schools and a dangerous condition prevailed. Jews and Presbyterians demanded pro rata shares if Catholic requests were honored. The major conflicting religious ideologies were a foreboding parasite to the American democracy. In 1840, America was a struggling young nation seeking an identity. And church-state relationship, often cluttered with European heritage, conflicted with the First Amendment establishment clause; the relationship of both to the new national institution, public education, provided difficult moments. In time, America jettisoned the religious albatross securalizing the public school, including curricular and extracurricular programs and delimiting public funds for public schools.

On the eve of America's centennial, the securalizing process permeated the nation to such an extent that President Grant insisted that not one tax cent be used for sectarian educational institutions. Oregon even enacted legislation requiring all children to attend public schools. Of course, the Supreme Court, in *Pierce* (1925), declared that statute unconstitutional.

During the early 1970s, the *Lemon I* tripartite test provided certainty. By the 1975 *Meek* decision, the Court had virtually closed the conduit pumping public funds to religious schools by state legislative *fiat*.

In time, though, with Supreme Court personnel and ideological change mingling with the new conservatism the Court signaled a new direction with *Wolman* (1977), *Regan* (1980), and *Mueller* (1983). And now *Mueller* has created a national condition that has potential for establishing two publicly funded school systems: (1) a public-education system with unchurched minority, handicapped, and indigent students enrolled; (2) a religious-school system with almost all white students.

The publicly funded religious-school systems will be composed of two major religious institutions: (1) the long-established Catholic parochial-school system; (2) the newly emerging New Right fundamentalist Christian academies; and (3) many lesser ones. There are over one thousand religious denominations in America. Perhaps in time, the New Right fundamentalist academies will rival the Catholic parochial-school system in religious importance and political power.

Schools are instruments of organizations, and as such are good only if they serve their ends effectively. The ends are determined by each organization's philosophy. Schools are never commensurate, and as the ends vary, so do schools.

The American public-school system, America's greatest contribution to Western civilization, exists to satisfy the state's compelling interest in education, which in a democracy is to provide an enlightened citizenry to participate effectively in and perpetuate the democracy.

The first part of the tripartite test concerning secular purpose should not be lost. Simply examine the purposes and objectives of religious schools, and the answer will ring clear.

Throughout America's history, religious schools have made a significant contribution to elementary and secondary education. But the difficult question is What is Caesar's, and what is God's? And how does the establishment clause respond to each question? In a democracy, surely there is a better standard than the *Mueller* "look-alike" test.

State Constitutional and Statutory Provisions Related to the Prohibition of Using Public Funds for Religious Schools

Alabama

Preamble

We the people of the State of Alabama, in order to establish justice, insure domestic tranquility and secure the blessings of liberty to ourselves and our posterity, invoking the favor and guidance of Almighty God, do ordain and establish the following Constitution and form of government for the State of Alabama.

Article I

Declaration of Rights

3. That no religion shall be established by law; that no preference shall be given by law to any religious sect, society, denomination or mode of worship; that no one shall be compelled by law to attend any place of worship; nor to pay tithes, taxes or other rates for building or repairing any place of worship, or for maintaining any minister or ministry; that no religious test shall be required as a qualification to any office of public trust under this State; and that the civil rights, privileges and capacities of any citizen shall not be in any manner affected by his religious principles.

Article XIV

Education

263. No money raised for the support of the public schools shall be

appropriated to or used for the support of any sectarian or denominational school.

Alaska

Preamble

We the people of Alaska, grateful to God and to those who founded our nation and pioneered this great land, in order to secure and transmit to succeeding generations our heritage of political, civil, and religious liberty within the Union of States, do ordain and establish this constitution for the State of Alaska.

Article IX

Public Debt, Revenue, and Taxation

Section 10. No tax shall be laid or appropriation of public money made in aid of any church, or sectarian school, or any public service corporation.

Article XI

Education

Section 7. No sectarian instruction shall be imparted in any school or State educational institution that may be established under this Constitution, and no religious or political test or qualification shall ever be required as a condition of admission into any public educational institution of the State, as teacher, student, or pupil; but the liberty of conscience hereby secured shall not be so construed as to justify practices or conduct inconsistent with the good order, peace, morality, or safety of the State, or with the rights of others.

Article XX

Ordinance

The following ordinance shall be irrevocable without the consent of the United States and the people of this State:

First. Perfect toleration of religious sentiment shall be secured to every inhabitant of this State, and no inhabitant of this State shall ever be molested in person or property on account of his or her mode of religious worship, or lack of the same.

Seventh. Provisions shall be made by law for the establishment and maintenance of a system of public schools which shall be open to all the children of the State and be free from sectarian control, and said schools shall always be conducted in English.

The State shall never enact any law restricting or abridging the right of suffrage on account of race, color, or previous condition of servitude.

Arkansas

Preamble

We, the people of the State of Arkansas, grateful to Almighty God for the privilege of choosing our own form of government, for our civil and religious liberty, and desiring to perpetuate its blessings and secure the same to ourselves and posterity, do ordain and establish this Constitution.

Article II

Declaration of Rights

Section 24. All men have a natural and indefeasible right to worship Almighty God according to the dictates of their own consciences; no man can, of right, be compelled to attend, erect or support any place of worship; or to maintain any ministry against his consent. No human authority can, in any case or manner whatsoever, control or interfere with the right of conscience; and no preference shall ever be given, by law, to any religious establishment, denomination or mode of worship above any other.

Section 25. Religion, morality and knowledge being essential to good government, the General Assembly shall enact suitable laws to protect every religious denomination in the peaceable enjoyment of its own mode of public worship.

Section 26. No religious test shall ever be required of any person as a qualification to vote or hold office, nor shall any person be rendered incompetent to be a witness on account of his religious belief; but nothing herein shall be construed to dispense with oaths or affirmations.

Article XIV

Education

Section 1. *Free School System.* — Intelligence and virtue being the safeguards of liberty and the bulwark of a free and good government, the State shall ever maintain a general, suitable and efficient system of free public schools and shall adopt all suitable means to secure to the people the advantages and opportunities of education. The specific intention of this amendment is to authorize that in addition to existing constitutional or statutory provisions the General Assembly and/or public school districts may spend public funds for the education of persons over twenty-one (21) years of age and under six (6) years of age, as may be provided by law, and no other interpretation shall be given to it.

Section 2. No money or property belonging to public school fund, or to this State for the benefit of schools or universities, shall ever be used for any other than the respective purposes to which it belongs.

California

Preamble

We, the people of the State of California, grateful to Almighty God for our freedom, in order to secure and perpetuate its blessings, do establish this Constitution.

Article I

Declaration of Rights

Freedom of Religion

Section 4. Free exercise and enjoyment of religion without discrimination or preference are guaranteed. This liberty of conscience does not excuse acts that are licentious or inconsistent with the peace or safety of the State. The Legislature shall make no law respecting an establishment of religion.

Article XIII

Legislative Department

Public Aid for Sectarian Purposes Prohibited

Section 24. Neither the Legislature, nor any county, city and county, township, school district or other municipal corporation, shall ever make an appropriation, or pay from any public fund whatever, or grant anything to or in aid of any religious sect, church, creed, or sectarian purpose or help to support or sustain any school, college, university, hospital, or other institution controlled by any religious creed, church, or sectarian denomination whatever; nor shall any grant or donation of personal property or real estate ever be made by the State, or any city, city and county, town or other municipal corporation for any religious creed, church, or sectarian purpose whatever. . . .

Article IX

Education

No Public Money for Sectarian Schools

Section 8. No public money shall ever be appropriated for the support of any sectarian or denominational school, or any school not under the exclusive control of the officers of the public schools; nor shall any sectarian or denominational doctrine be taught, or instruction thereon be permitted, directly or indirectly, in any of the common schools of this State.

Colorado

Preamble

We, the people of Colorado, with profound reverence for the Supreme Ruler of the Universe, in order to form a more independent and perfect government; establish justice; insure tranquility; provide for the common defense; promote the general welfare and secure the blessings of liberty to ourselves and our posterity, do ordain and establish this constitution for the "State of Colorado."

Article II

Bill of Rights

Section 4. Religious freedom. — That the free exercise and enjoyment of religious profession and worship, without discrimination, shall forever hereafter be guaranteed; and no person shall be denied any civil or political right, privilege or capacity, on account of his opinions concerning religion; but the liberty of conscience hereby secured shall not be construed to dispense with oaths or affirmations, excuse acts of licentiousness or justify practices inconsistent with the good order, peace or safety of the state. No person shall be required to attend or support any ministry or place of worship, religious sect or denomination against his consent. Nor shall any preference be given by law to any religious denomination or mode of worship.

Article V

Legislative Department

Section 34. Appropriations to private institutions forbidden. — No appropriation shall be made for charitable, industrial, educational or benevolent purposes to any person, corporation or community not under the absolute control of the state, nor to any denominational or sectarian institution or association.

Article IX

Education

Section 7. Aid to private schools, churches, etc., forbidden. — Neither the general assembly, nor any county, city, town, township, school district or other public corporation, shall ever make any appropriation, or pay from any public fund or monies whatever, anything in aid of any church or sectarian society, or for any sectarian purpose, or to help support or sustain any school, academy, seminary, college, university or other literary or scientific institution, controlled by any church or sectarian denomination whatsoever; nor shall any grant or donation of land, money or other personal property, ever be made by the state, or any such public corporation, to any church, or for any sectarian purpose.

Section 8. Religious test and race discrimination forbidden. — Sectarian tenets. — No religious test or qualification shall ever be required of any person as a condition of admission into any public educational institution of the state, either as a teacher or student; and no teacher or student of any such institution shall ever be required to attend or participate in any religious service whatever. No sectarian tenets or doctrines shall ever be taught in the public schools, nor shall any distinction or classification of pupils be made on account of race or color, nor shall any pupil be assigned or transported to any public educational institution for the purpose of achieving racial balance.

Connecticut

Preamble

The People of Connecticut acknowledging with gratitude, the good providence of God, in having permitted them to enjoy a free government; do, in order more effectually to define, secure, and perpetuate the liberties, rights and privileges which they have derived from their ancestors; hereby, after a careful consideration and revision, ordain and establish the following constitution and form of civil government.

Article First

Declaration of Rights

Section 3. The exercise and enjoyment of religious profession and worship, without discrimination, shall forever be free to all persons in the state; provided, that the right hereby declared and established, shall not be so construed as to excuse acts of licentiousness, or to justify practices inconsistent with the peace and safety of the state.

Article Seventh

Of Religion

It being the right of all men to worship the Supreme Being, the Great Creator and Preserver of the Universe, and to render that worship in a mode consistent with the dictates of their consciences, no person shall by law be compelled to join or support, nor be classed or associated with, any congregation, church or religious association. No preference shall be given by law to any religious society or denomination in the state. Each shall have and enjoy the same and equal powers, rights and privileges, and may support and maintain the ministers and teachers of its society or denomination, and may build and repair houses for public worship.

Article Eighth

Of Education

Section 4. The fund, called the SCHOOL FUND, shall remain a perpetual fund, the interest of which shall be inviolably appropriated to the support and encouragement of the public schools throughout the state, and for the equal benefit of all the people thereof. The value and amount of said fund shall be ascertained in such manner as the general assembly may prescribe, published, and recorded in the comptroller's office; and no law shall ever be made, authorizing such fund to be diverted to any other use than the encouragement and support of public schools, among the several school societies, as justice and equity shall require.

Delaware

Preamble

Through Divine goodness, all men have by nature the rights of worshipping and serving their Creator according to the dictates of their consciences, of enjoying and defending life and liberty, of acquiring and protecting reputation and property, and in general of obtaining objects suitable to their condition, without injury by one to another; and as these rights are essential to their welfare, for due exercise thereof, power is inherent in them; and therefore all just authority in the institutions of political society is derived from the people, and established with their consent, to advance their happiness; and they may for this end, as circumstances require, from time to time, alter their Constitution of government.

Article I

Bill of Rights

1. Freedom of Religion

Section I. Although it is the duty of all men frequently to assemble together for the public worship of Almighty God; and piety and morality, on which the prosperity of communities depends are hereby promoted; yet no man shall or ought to be compelled to attend any religious worship, to contribute to the erection or support of any place of worship, or to the maintenance of any ministry, against his own free will and consent; and no power shall or ought to be vested in or assumed by any magistrate that shall in any case interfere with, or in any manner control the rights of conscience, in the free exercise of religious worship, nor a preference given by law to any religious societies, denominations, or modes of worship.

Article X

Education

3. Use of educational funds by religious schools; exemption of school property from taxation.

Section 3. No portion of any fund now existing or which may hereafter be appropriated, or raised by tax, for educational purposes, shall be appropriated to, or used by, or in aid of any sectarian, church or denominational school; provided, that all real or personal property used for school purposes, where the tuition is free, shall be exempt from taxation and assessment for public purposes.

4. Use of Public School Fund

Section 4. No part of the principal or income of the Public School Fund, now or hereafter existing, shall be used for any other purpose than the support of free public schools.

5. Transportation of Nonpublic School Students

Section 5. The General Assembly, notwithstanding any other provision of this Constitution, may provide by an Act of the General Assembly, passed with the concurrence of a majority of all the members elected to each House, for the transportation of students of non-public elementary and high schools.

Florida

Preamble

We, the people of the State of Florida, being grateful to Almighty God for our constitutional liberty, in order to secure its benefits, perfect our government, insure domestic tranquility, maintain public order, and guarantee equal civil and political rights to all, do ordain and establish this constitution.

Article I

Section 3. There shall be no law respecting the establishment of religion or prohibiting or penalizing the free exercise thereof. Religious freedom shall not justify practices inconsistent with public morals, peace or safety. No revenue of the state or any political subdivision or agency thereof shall ever be taken from the public treasury directly or indirectly in aid of any church, sect, or religious denomination or in aid of any sectarian institution.

Article IX

Section 6. The income derived from the state school fund shall, and the principal of the fund may, be appropriated, but only to the support and maintenance of free public schools.

Georgia

Preamble

To perpetuate the principles of free government, insure justice to all, preserve peace, promote the interest and happiness of the citizen, and transmit to posterity the enjoyment of liberty, we, the people of Georgia, relying upon the protection and guidance of Almighty God, do ordain and establish this Constitution.

Article I

Bill of Rights

Section I

Section 2-102, Paragraph XII. Freedom of conscience. All men have the natural and inalienable right to worship God, each according to the dictates of his own conscience, and no human authority should, in any case, control or interfere with such right of conscience.

Section 2-103, Paragraph XIII. Religious opinions; liberty of conscience. No inhabitant of this State shall be molested in person or property, or prohibited from holding any public office, or trust, on account of his religious opinions; but the right of liberty of conscience shall not be so construed as to excuse acts of licentiousness, or justify practices inconsistent with the peace and safety of the State.

Hawaii

Preamble

We, the people of the State of Hawaii, grateful for Divine Guidance, and mindful of our Hawaiian heritage, reaffirm our belief in a government of the people, by the people, and with an understanding heart toward all the peoples of the earth, do hereby ordain and establish this constitution for the State of Hawaii.

Article I

Bill of Rights

Freedom of Religion, Speech, Press, Assembly and Petition

Section 3. No law shall be enacted respecting an establishment of religion or prohibiting the free exercise thereof, or abridging the freedom of speech or of the press, or the right of the people peaceably to assemble and to petition the government for a redress of grievances.

Article VI

Taxation and Finance

Appropriations for Private Purposes Prohibited

Section 2. No tax shall be levied or appropriation of public money or property made, nor shall the public credit be used, directly or indirectly, except for a public purpose. No grant shall be made in violation of Section 3 of Article I of this constitution.

Article IX

Education

Public Education

Section 1. The State shall provide for the establishment, support and control of a statewide system of public schools free from sectarian control, a state university, public libraries and such other educational institutions as may be deemed desirable, including physical facilities therefor. There shall be no segregation in public educational institutions because of race, religion or ancestry; nor shall public funds be appropriated for the support or benefit of any sectarian or private educational institution.

Idaho

Preamble

We, the people of the state of Idaho, grateful to Almighty God for our freedom, to secure its blessings and promote our common welfare do establish this Constitution.

Article IX

Education and School Lands

5. Sectarian appropriations prohibited. — Neither the legislature nor any county, city, town, township, school district, or other public corporation, shall ever make any appropriation, or pay from any public fund or monies whatever, anything in aid of any church or sectarian or religious society, or for any sectarian or religious purpose, or to help support or sustain any school, academy, seminary, college, university, or other literary or scientific institution, controlled by any church, sectarian or religious denomination whatsoever; nor shall any grant or donation of land, money or other personal property ever be made by the state, or any such public corporation, to any church or for any sectarian or religious purpose.

6. Religious test and teaching school prohibited. — No religious test or qualification shall ever be required of any person as a condition of admission into any public educational institution of the state, either as teacher or student; and no teacher or student of any such institution shall ever be required to attend or participate in any religious service whatever. No sectarian or religious tenets or doctrines shall ever be taught in the public schools, nor shall any distinction or classification of pupils be made on

account of race or color. No books, papers, tracts or documents of a political, sectarian or denominational character shall be used or introduced in any schools established under the provisions of this article, nor shall any teacher or any district receive any of the public school monies in which the schools have not been taught in accordance with the provisions of this article.

Illinois

Preamble

We, the People of the State of Illinois grateful to Almighty God for the civil, political and religious liberty which He has permitted us to enjoy and seeking His blessing upon our endeavors, in order to provide for the health, safety and welfare of the people; maintain a representative and orderly government; eliminate poverty and inequality; assure legal, social and economic justice; provide opportunity for the fullest development of the individual; insure domestic tranquility; provide for the common defense; and secure the blessings of freedom and liberty to ourselves and our posterity, do ordain and establish this constitution for the State of Illinois.

Article I

Bill of Rights

Inherent and Inalienable Rights.

Religious Freedom.

Section 3. The free exercise and enjoyment of religious profession and worship, without discrimination, shall forever be guaranteed; and no person shall be denied any civil or political right, privilege or capacity, on account of his religious opinions; but the liberty of the conscience hereby secured shall not be construed to dispense with oaths or affirmations, excuse acts of licentiousness, or justify practices inconsistent with the peace or safety of the State. No person shall be required to attend or support any ministry or place of worship against his consent, nor shall any preference be given by law to any religious denomination or mode of worship.

Article X

Education

Goal—Free Schools

Section 1. A fundamental goal of the People of the State is the educational development of all persons to the limits of their capacities.

The State shall provide for an efficient system of high quality public educational institutions and services. Education in public schools through the secondary level shall be free. There may be such other free education as the General Assembly provides by law.

The State has the primary responsibility for financing the system of public education.

Public Funds for Sectarian Purposes Forbidden.

Section 3. Neither the General Assembly nor any county, city, town, township, school district, or other public corporation, shall ever make any appropriation or pay from any public fund whatever, anything in aid of any church or sectarian purpose, or to help support or sustain any school, academy, seminary, college, university, or other literary or scientific institution, controlled by any church or sectarian denomination whatever; nor shall any grant or donation of land, money, or other personal property ever be made by the State, or any such public corporation, to any church or for any sectarian purpose.

Indiana

Preamble

To the end that justice be established, public order maintained, and liberty perpetuated: We, the people of the State of Indiana, grateful to Almighty God for the free exercise of the right to choose our own form of government, do ordain this Constitution.

Article I

Bill of Rights

Section 2. All men shall be secured in the natural right to worship Almighty God, according to the dictates of their own consciences.

Section 3. No law shall, in any case whatever, control the free exercise and enjoyment of religious opinions, or interfere with the rights of conscience.

Section 4. No preference shall be given, by law, to any creed, religious society, or mode of worship; and no man shall be compelled to attend, erect, or support, any place of worship, or to maintain any ministry, against his consent.

Section 5. No religious test shall be required, as a qualification for any office of trust or profit.

Section 6. No money shall be drawn from the treasury, for the benefit of any religious or theological institution.

Section 7. No person shall be rendered incompetent as a witness, in consequence of his opinions on matters of religion.

Article 8

Education

Section 3. The principal of the Common School fund shall remain a perpetual fund, which may be increased, but shall never be diminished; and the income thereof shall be inviolably appropriated to the support of Common Schools, and to no other purpose whatever.

Iowa

Preamble

WE, THE PEOPLE OF THE STATE OF IOWA, grateful to the Supreme Being for the blessings hitherto enjoyed, and feeling our dependence on Him for a continuation of those blessings, do ordain and establish a free and independent government, by the name of the STATE OF IOWA, the boundaries whereof shall be as follows: ...

Article I

Bill of Rights

Section 3. The General Assembly shall make no law respecting an establishment of religion, or prohibiting the free exercise thereof; nor shall any person be compelled to attend any place of worship, pay tithes, taxes or other rates for building or repairing places of worship, or the maintenance of any minister, or ministry.

Section 4. No religious test shall be required as a qualification for any office or public trust, and no person shall be deprived of any of his rights, privileges, or capacities, or disqualified from the performance of any of his public or private duties, or rendered incompetent to give evidence in any court of law or equity, in consequence of his opinions on the subject of religion; and any part of any judicial proceedings shall have the right to use a witness, or take the testimony of any other person not disqualified on account of interest, who may be cognizant of any fact material to the case; and parties to suits may be witnesses, as provided by law.

Kansas

Preamble

We, the people of Kansas, grateful to Almighty God for our civil and religious privileges, in order to insure the full enjoyment of our rights as American citizens, do ordain and establish this constitution of the State of Kansas, with the following boundaries, to wit: ...

Bill of Rights

7. Religious liberty. The right to worship God according to the dictates of conscience shall never be infringed; nor shall any control of or interference with the rights of conscience be permitted, not any preference be given by law to any religious establishment or mode of worship. No religious test or property qualification shall be required for any office of public trust, nor for any vote at any election, nor shall any person be incompetent to testify on account of religious belief.

Article VI

Education

6. (c). No religious sect or sects shall control any part of the public educational funds.

Kentucky

Preamble

We, the people of the Commonwealth of Kentucky, grateful to Almighty God for the civil, political and religious liberties we enjoy, and invoking the continuance of these blessings, do ordain and establish this Constitution.

Bill of Rights

That the great and essential principles of liberty and free government may be recognized and established, we declare that:

Section 1. Right of life, liberty, worship, pursuit of safety and happiness, free speech, acquiring and protecting property, peaceable assembly, redress of grievances, bearing arms. All men are, by nature, free and equal, and have certain inherent and inalienable rights, among which may be reckoned:

First: The right of enjoying and defending their lives and liberties.

Second: The right of worshiping Almighty God according to the dictates of their consciences.

Section 5. Right of religious freedom. No preference shall ever be given by law to any religious sect, society or denomination; nor to any particular creed, mode of worship or system of ecclesiastical polity; nor shall any person be compelled to attend any place of worship, to contribute to the erection or maintenance of any such place, or to the salary or support of any minister of religion; nor shall any man be compelled to send his child to any school to which he may be conscientiously opposed; and the civil rights, privileges or capacities of no person shall be taken away, or in anywise diminished or enlarged, on account of his belief or disbelief of any religious tenet, dogma or teaching. No human authority shall in any case whatever, control or interfere with the rights of conscience.

Education

157.330 (2). The resources of the public school foundation program fund shall be paid into the State Treasury, and shall be drawn out or appropriated only in aid of public schools as provided by statute.

Louisiana

Preamble

We, the people of the State of Louisiana, grateful to Almighty God for the civil, political and religious liberties we enjoy, and desiring to secure the continuance of these blessings, do ordain and establish this Constitution.

Bill of Rights

4. Freedom of Religion

Section 4. Every person has the natural right to worship God according to the dictates of his own conscience. No law shall be passed respecting an establishment of religion, nor prohibiting the free exercise thereof; nor shall any preference ever be given to, nor any discrimination be made against, any church, sect, or creed of religion, or any form of religious faith or worship.

Article IV

Section 8. Public funds; prohibited expenditure for sectarian, private, charitable or benevolent purposes; state charities; religious discrimination.

Section 8. No money shall ever be taken from the public treasury, directly or indirectly, in aid of any church, sect or denomination of religion, or in aid of any priest, preacher, minister or teacher thereof, as such, and no preference shall ever be given to, nor any discrimination made against, any church, sect or creed of religion, or any form of religious faith or worship. No appropriation from the State treasury shall be made for private, charitable or benevolent purposes to any person or community; provided, this shall not apply to the State Asylums for the Insane, and State Schools for the Deaf and Dumb, and the Blind, and the Charity Hospitals, and public charitable institutions conducted under state authority.

Article XII

12. No appropriation of public funds for private or sectarian schools.

Section 13. No appropriation of public funds shall be made to any private or sectarian school. The Legislature may enact appropriate legislation to permit institutions of higher learning which receive all or part of their support from the State of Louisiana to engage in interstate and intrastate education agreements with other state governments, agencies of other state governments, institutions of higher learning of other state governments, and private institutions of higher learning within or outside state boundaries.

Article XIV

15. Civil service system; state; cities

Section 15 (A) (1). Appointments and promotions; examination; discriminations. (As amended Acts 1952, No. 18) ... No person in the "State" or "City Classified Service," having gained civil service status shall be discriminated against or subjected to any disciplinary action except for cause, and no person in the State or City Classified Service shall be discriminated against or subjected to any disciplinary action for political or religious reasons, and all such persons shall have the right of appeal from such action.

Maine

Preamble

Objects of government.

We the people of Maine, in order to establish justice, insure tranquility, provide for our mutual defense, promote our common welfare, and secure to ourselves and our posterity the blessings of liberty, acknowledging with grateful hearts the goodness of the Soverign Ruler of the Universe in affording us an opportunity, so favorable to the design; and imploring His aid and direction in its accomplishment agree to form ourselves into a free and independent State, by the style and title of the State of Maine, and do ordain and establish the following Constitution for the government of the same.

Article I

Declaration of Rights

Religious freedom.

Section 3. All men have a natural and unalienable right to worship Almighty God according to the dictates of their own consciences, and no one shall be hurt, molested or restrained in his person, liberty or estate for worshiping God in the manner and season most agreeable to the dictates of his own conscience, nor for his religious professions or sentiments, provided he does not disturb the public peace, nor obstruct others in their religious worship; — and all persons demeaning themselves peaceably, as good members of the state, shall be equally under the protection of the laws, and no subordination nor preference of any one sect or denomination to another shall ever be established by law, "nor shall any religious test be required as a qualification for any office or trust," under this State; and all religious societies in this State, whether incorporate or unincorporate, shall at all times have the exclusive right of electing their public teachers, and contracting with them for their support and maintenance.

Maryland

Declaration of Rights

We the People of the State of Maryland, grateful to Almighty God for our civil and religious liberty, and taking into our serious consideration the best means of establishing a good Constitution in the State for the sure foundation and more permanent security thereof, declare:

Article 36. That as it is the duty of every man to worship God in such a manner as he thinks most acceptable to Him, all persons are equally entitled to protection in their religious liberty; wherefore, no person ought by any law to be molested in his person or estate, on account of his religious persuasion, or profession, or for his religious practice, unless, under the color of religion, he shall disturb the good order, peace or safety of the State, or shall infringe the laws of morality, or injure others in their natural, civil or religious rights; nor ought any person to be compelled to frequent, or maintain, or contribute, unless on contract, to maintain any place of worship, or any ministry; nor shall any person, otherwise competent, be deemed incompetent as a witness, or juror, on account of his religious belief; provided, he believes in the existence of God, and that under His dispensation such person will be held morally accountable for his acts, and be rewarded or punished therefor either in this world or in the world to come.

Nothing shall prohibit or require the making reference to belief in, reliance upon, or invoking the aid of God or a Supreme Being in any governmental or public document, proceeding, activity, ceremony, school institution, or place.

Nothing in this article shall constitute an establishment of religion.

Article 37. That religious test ought never to be required as a qualification for any office of profit or trust in this State, other than a declaration of belief in the existence of God, nor shall the Legislature prescribe any other oath of office than the oath prescribed by this Constitution.

Article 38. That every gift, sale or devise of land to any Minister, Public Teacher, or Preacher of the Gospel, as such, or to any Religious Sect, Order or Denomination, or to, or for the support, use or benefit of, or in trust for, any Minister, Public Teacher, or Preacher of the Gospel, as such, or any Religious Sect, Order or Denomination, without the prior or subsequent sanction of the Legislature, shall be void; except always, any sale, gift, lease or devise of any quantity of land, not exceeding five acres, for a church, meeting-house, or other house of worship, or parsonage, or for a burying ground, which shall be improved, enjoyed or used only for such purpose; or such sale, gift, lease or devise shall be void. Provided, however, that except in so far as the General Assembly shall hereafter by law otherwise enact, the consent of the Legislature shall not be required to any gift, grant, deed, or conveyance executed after the 2nd day of November, 1948, or to any devise or bequest contained in the will of any person dying after said 2nd day of November, 1948, for any of the purposes hereinabove in this Article mentioned.

Article VIII

Section 3. School Fund.

The School Fund of the State shall be kept inviolate and appropriated only to the purposes of education.

Massachusetts

Preamble

1. Objects of Government; Body Politic, How Formed, Its Nature.

The end of the institution, maintenance, and administration of government is to secure the existence of the body politic, to protect it, and to furnish the individuals who compose it with the power of enjoying in safety and tranquility their natural rights, and the blessings of life; and whenever these great objects are not obtained, the people have a right to alter the government, and to take measures necessary for their safety, prosperity and happiness.

The body politic is formed by a voluntary association of individuals: it is a social compact, by which the whole people covenants with each citizen, and each citizen with the whole people, that all shall be governed by certain laws for the common good. It is the duty of the people, therefore, in framing a constitution of government, to provide for an equitable mode of making laws, as well as for an impartial interpretation, and a faithful execution of them; that every man may, at all times, find his security in them.

We, therefore, the people of Massachusetts, acknowledging with grateful hearts, the goodness of the great Legislator of the universe, in affording us, in the course of His providence, an opportunity, deliberately and peaceably, without fraud, violence or surprises, of entering into an original, explicit, and solemn compact with each other; and of forming a new constitution of civil government, for ourselves and posterity; and devoutly imploring His direction in so interesting a design, do agree upon, ordain and establish the following DECLARATION OF RIGHTS, AND FRAME OF GOVERNMENT, AS THE CONSTITUTION OF THE COMMONWEALTH OF MASSACHUSETTS.

Part of the First

A Declaration of the Rights of the Inhabitants of the Commonwealth of Massachusetts

Right and duty of public religious worship. Protection therein.

II. It is the right as well as the Duty of all men in society, publicly, and at stated seasons to worship the SUPREME BEING, the great Creator and preserver of the Universe, And no Subject shall be hurt, molested, or restrained, in his person, Liberty, or Estate, for worshipping God in the manner and season most agreeable to the Dictates of his own conscience, or for his religious beliefs.

Religious Societies.

Article III. Instead of the Third Article of the Bill of Rights, the following Modification and Amendment thereof is substituted.

As the public worship of GOD and instructions in piety, religion and morality, promote the happiness and prosperity of a people and the security of a Republican Government; — Therefore, the several religious societies of this Commonwealth, whether corporate or unincorporate, at any meeting legally warned and holden for that purpose, shall ever have the right to elect their pastors or religious teachers, to contract with them for their support to raise money for erecting and repairing houses for public worship, for the maintenance of religious instruction and for the payment of necessary expenses; And all persons belonging to any religious society shall be taken and held to be members, until they shall file with the Clerk of such society, a written notice, declaring the dissolution of their membership and thenceforth shall not be liable for any grant or contract, which may be thereafter made, or entered into by such society: — And all religious sects and denominations demeaning themselves peaceably and as good citizens of the Commonwealth, shall be equally under the protection of the law; and no subordination of any one sect or denomination to another shall ever be established by law.

Article XVIII

Religious Freedom; Expenditure of Public Money for Certain Institution Prohibited, Exceptions.

Section 1. No law shall be passed prohibiting the free exercise of religion.

Section 2. No grant, appropriation of the use of public money or property or loan of credit shall be made or authorized by the Commonwealth or any political subdivision thereof for the purpose of founding, maintaining or aiding any infirmary, hospital, institution, primary or secondary school, or charitable or religious undertaking which is not publicly owned and under the exclusive control, order and supervision of public officers or public agents authorized by the Commonwealth or federal authority or both, except that appropriations may be made for the Soldier's Home in Massachusetts and for free public libraries in any city or town and to carry out legal obligations, if any, already entered into; and no such grant, appropriation or use of public money or property or loan of public credit shall be made or authorized for the purpose of founding, maintaining or aiding any church, religious denomination or society. Nothing herein contained shall be construed to prevent the Commonwealth from making grants-in-aid to private higher educational institutions or to students or parents or guardians of students attending such institutions.

Section 3. Nothing herein contained shall be construed to prevent the commonwealth, or any political division thereof, from paying to privately controlled hospitals, infirmaries, or institutions for the deaf, dumb, or blind not more than the ordinary and reasonable compensation for the care or support actually rendered or furnished by such hospitals, infirmaries, or institutions to such persons as may be in whole or in part unable to support or care for themselves.

Section 4. Nothing herein contained shall be construed to deprive any inmate of a publicly controlled reformatory, penal or charitable institution of the opportunity of religious exercises therein of his own faith; but no inmate of such institution shall be compelled to attend religious services or receive religious instruction against his will, or, if a minor, without the consent of his parent or guardian.

Section 5. This amendment shall not take effect until the October first next succeeding its ratification and adoption by the People.

Michigan

Preamble

We, the people of the state of Michigan, grateful to Almighty God for the blessings of freedom, and earnestly desiring to secure these blessings undiminished to ourselves and our posterity do ordain and establish this constitution.

Article I

Declaration of Rights

Equal protection; discrimination.

Section 2. No person shall be denied the equal protection of the laws; nor shall any person be denied the enjoyment of his civil or political rights or be discriminated against in the exercise thereof because of religion, race, color or national origin. The legislature shall implement this section by appropriate legislation. Freedom of worship and religious belief; appropriations.

Section 4. Every person shall be at liberty to worship God according to the dictates of his own conscience. No person shall be compelled to attend, or, against his consent, to contribute to the erection or support of any place of religious worship, or to pay tithes, taxes or other rates for the support of any minister of the gospel or teacher of religion. No money shall be appropriated or drawn from the treasury for the benefit of any religious sect or society, theological or religious seminary; nor shall property belonging to the state be appropriated for any such purpose. The civil and political rights, privileges and capacities of no person shall be diminished or enlarged on account of his religious belief.

Article VIII

Education

Free public elementary and secondary schools; discrimination.

Section 2. The legislature shall maintain and support a system of free public elementary and secondary schools as defined by law. Every school district shall provide for the education of its pupils without discrimination as to religion, creed, race, color or national origin.

No public monies or property shall be appropriated or paid or any public credit utilized, by the legislature or any other political subdivision or agency of the state directly or indirectly to aid or maintain any private, denominational or other nonpublic preelementary, elementary, or secondary school. No payment, credit, tax benefit, exemption of deductions, tuition voucher, subsidy, grant or loan of public monies or property shall be provided, directly or indirectly, to support the attendance of any student or the employment of any person at any such nonpublic school or at any location or institution where instruction is offered in whole or in part to such nonpublic school students. The legislature may provide for the transportation of students to and from any school.

Article IX

Finance and Taxation

State, school aid fund, source and distribution.

Section 11. There shall be established a state school aid fund which shall be used exclusively for aid to school districts, higher education and school employees' retirement systems, as provided by law. One-half of all taxes imposed on retailers on taxable sales at retail of tangible personal property, and other tax revenues provided by law, shall be dedicated to this fund. Payments from this fund shall be made in full on a scheduled basis, as provided by law.

Minnesota

Preamble

We, the people of the state of Minnesota, grateful to God for our civil and religious liberty, and desiring to perpetuate its blessings and secure the same to ourselves and our posterity, do ordain and establish this Constitution:

Article I

Bill of Rights

Freedom of conscience; no preference to be given to any religious establishment or mode of worship.

Section 16. The enumeration of rights in this constitution shall not be construed to deny or impair others retained by and inherent in the people. The right of every man to worship God according to the dictates of his own conscience shall never be infringed, nor shall any man be compelled to attend, erect or support any place of worship, or to maintain any religious or ecclesiastical ministry, against his consent; nor shall any control of or interference with the rights of conscience be permitted or any preference be given by law to any religious establishment or mode of worship; but the liberty of conscience hereby secured shall not be so construed as to excuse acts of licentiousness, or justify practices inconsistent with the peace or safety of the State, nor shall any money be drawn from the treasury for the benefit of any religious societies or religious or theological seminaries.

No religious test or property qualifications to be required.

Section 17. No religious test or amount of property shall ever be required as a qualification for any office of public trust under the State. No religious test or amount of property shall ever be required as a qualification of any voter at any election in this State; nor shall any person be rendered incompetent to give evidence in any court of law or equity in consequence of his opinion upon the subject of religion.

Article XIII

Miscellaneous Subjects

Uniform system of public schools

Section 1. The stability of a republican form of government depending mainly upon the intelligence of the people, it is the duty of the legislature to establish a general and uniform system of public schools. The legislature shall make such provisions by taxation or otherwise as will secure a thorough and efficient system of public schools throughout the state.

Prohibition as to aiding sectarian school

Section 2. In no case shall any public money or property be appropriated or used for the support of schools wherein the distinctive doctrines, creeds or tenets of any particular Christian or other religious sect are promulgated or taught.

Mississippi

Preamble

We, the people of Mississippi in convention assembled, grateful to Almighty God, and invoking his blessing on our work, do ordain and establish this constitution.

Article III

Section 18. No religious test as a qualification for office shall be required; and no preference shall be given by law to any religious sect or mode of worship; but the free enjoyment of all religious sentiments and the different modes of worship shall be held sacred. The rights hereby secured shall not be construed to justify acts of licentiousness injurious to morals or dangerous to the peace and safety of the state, or to exclude the Holy Bible from use in any public school of this state.

Article VIII

Section 208. No religious or other sect or sects shall ever control any part of the school or other educational funds of this state; nor shall any funds be appropriated toward the support of any sectarian school, or to any school that at the time of receiving such appropriation is not conducted as a free school.

Missouri

Preamble

We, the people of Missouri, with profound reverence for the Supreme Ruler of the Universe, and grateful for His goodness, do establish this constitution for the better government of the State.

Article I

Bill of Rights

Section 5. Religious freedom — liberty of conscience and belief — limitations. — That all men have a natural and indefeasible right to worship Almighty God according to the dictates of their own consciences; that no human authority can control or interfere with the rights of conscience; that no person shall, on account of his religious persuasion or belief, be rendered ineligible to any public office or trust or profit in this state, be disqualified from testifying or serving as a juror, or be molested in his person or estate; but this section shall not be construed to excuse acts of licentiousness, nor to justify practices inconsistent with the good order, peace or safety of the state, or with the right of others.

Section 6. Practice and support of religion not compulsory — contracts therefor enforcible. — That no person can be compelled to erect, support or attend any place or system of worship, or to maintain or support any priest, minister, preacher or teacher of any sect, church, creed or denomination of religion; but if any person shall voluntarily make a contract for any such object, he shall be held to the performance of the same.

Section 7. Public aid for religious purposes — preferences and discriminations on religious grounds. — That no money shall ever be taken from the public treasury, directly or indirectly, in aid of any church, sect or denomination of religion, or in aid of any priest, preacher, minister or teacher thereof, as such; and that no preference shall be given to nor any discrimination made against any church, sect or creed of religion, or any form of religious faith or worship.

Article IX

Education

Section 8. Prohibition of public aid for religious purposes and institutions. — Neither the general assembly, nor any county, city, town, township, school district or other municipal corporation, shall ever make an appropriation or pay from any public fund whatever, anything in aid of any religious creed, church or sectarian purpose or to help to support or sustain any private or public school, academy, seminary, college, university, or other institution of learning controlled by any religious creed, church or sectarian denomination whatever; nor shall any grant of donation personal property or real estate ever be made by the state, or any county, city, town, or other municipal corporation, for any religious creed, church, or sectarian purpose whatever.

Montana

Preamble

We, the people of Montana grateful to God for the quiet beauty of our state, the grandeur of our mountains, the vastness of our rolling plains, and desiring to improve the quality of life, equality of opportunities and to secure the blessings of liberty for this and future generations, do ordain and establish this constitution.

Article I

Declaration of Rights

Section 5. Freedom of religion. — The state shall make no law respecting an establishment of religion or prohibiting the free exercise thereof.

Article X

Education and Public Lands

Section 6. Aid prohibited to sectarian schools.

(1) The legislature, counties, cities, towns, school districts, and public corporations shall not make any direct or indirect appropriation or payment from any public fund or monies, or any grant of lands or other property for any sectarian purpose or to aid any church, school, academy, seminary, college, university, or other literary or scientific institution, controlled in whole or in part by any church, sect, or denomination.

(2) This section shall not apply to funds from federal sources provided to the state for the express purpose of distribution to non-public education.

Section 7. Non-discrimination in education. No religious or partisan test or qualification shall be required of any teacher or student as a condition of admission into any public educational institution. Attendance shall not be required at any religious service. No sectarian tenets shall be advocated in any public educational institution of the state. No person shall be refused admission to any public educational institution on account of sex, race, creed, religion, political beliefs, or national origin.

Nebraska

Preamble

We, the people, grateful to Almighty God for our freedom, do ordain and establish the following declaration of rights and frame of government, as the Constitution of the State of Nebraska.

Article I

Bill of Rights

Section 4. All persons have a natural and indefeasible right to worship Almighty God according to the dictates of their own consciences. No person shall be compelled to attend, erect or support any place of worship against his consent, and no preference shall be given by law to any religious society, nor shall any interference with the rights of conscience be permitted. No religious test shall be required as a qualification for office, nor shall any person be incompetent to be a witness on account of his religious beliefs; but nothing herein shall be construed to dispense with oaths and affirmations. Religion, morality, and knowledge, however, being essential to good government, it shall be the duty of the Legislature to pass suitable laws to protect every religious denomination in the peaceable enjoyment of its own mode of public worship, and to encourage schools and the means of instruction.

Article VII

Education

Section 11. Appropriation of public funds; handicapped children; sectarian instruction; religious test of teacher or student. Not withstanding any other provision in the Constitution, appropriation of public funds shall not be made to any school or institution of learning now owned or exclusively controlled by the state or a political subdivision thereof; PROVIDED, that the Legislature may provide that the state or any political subdivision thereof may contract with institutions not wholly owned or controlled by the state or any political subdivision to provide for educational or other services for the benefit of children under the age of twenty-one years who are handicapped, as that term is from time to time defined by the Legislature, if such services are nonsectarian in nature.

All public schools shall be free of sectarian instruction.

A religious test or qualification shall not be required of any teacher or student for admission or continuance in any school or institution supported in whole or in part by public funds or taxation.

Nevada

Preamble

We, the people of the State of Nevada, Grateful to Almighty God for our freedom in order to secure its blessings, insure domestic tranquility, and form a more perfect Government, do establish this CONSTITUTION.

Article I

Declaration of Rights

Section 4. The free exercise and enjoyment of religious profession and worship, without discrimination or preference, shall forever be allowed this state; and no person shall be rendered incompetent to be a witness on account of his opinions on matters of his religious belief; but the liberty of conscience hereby secured shall not be so construed as to excuse acts of licentiousness, or justify practices inconsistent with the peace, or safety of this state.

Article XI

Education

Section 2. The legislature shall provide for a uniform system of common schools, by which school shall be established and maintained in each school district at least six months in every year, and any school district which shall allow instruction of a sectarian character therein may be deprived of its proportion of the interest of the public school fund during such neglect or infraction, and the legislature may pass such laws as will tend to secure a general attendance of the children in each school district upon said public schools.

Section 9. No sectarian instruction shall be imparted or tolerated in any school or university that may be established under this constitution.

Section 10. No public funds of any kind or character whatever, state, county, or municipal, shall be used for sectarian purposes.

New Hampshire

Bill of Rights

5th. Every individual has a natural and unalienable right to worship God according to the dictates of his own conscience, and reason; and no subject shall be hurt, molested or restrained, in his person, liberty, or estate, for worshipping God in the manner and season most agreeable to the dictates of his own conscience, or for his religious profession, sentiments, or persuasion; provided he doth not disturb the public peace or disturb others in their religious worship.

6th. As morality and piety, rightly grounded on evangelical principles, will give the best and greatest security to government, and will lay, in the hearts of men, the strongest obligations to due subjection; and as the knowledge of these is most likely to be propagated through a society, therefore, the several parishes, bodies corporate, or religious societies shall at all times have the right of electing their own teachers, and of contracting with them for their support or maintenance, or both. But no person shall ever be compelled to pay towards the support of the schools of any sect or denomination. And every person, denomination or sect shall be equally under the protection of the law and no subordination of any one sect, denomination or persuasion to another shall ever be established.

Article 83

Privided, nevertheless, that no money raised by taxation shall ever be granted or applied for the use of the schools or institutions of any religious sect or denomination.

New Jersey

Preamble

We, the people of the State of New Jersey, grateful to Almighty God for the civil and religious liberty which He hath so long permitted us to enjoy, and looking to Him for a blessing upon our endeavors to secure and transmit the same unimpaired to succeeding generations, do ordain and establish this Constitution.

Article I

Rights and Privileges

3. No person shall be deprived of the inestimable privilege of worshipping Almighty God in a manner agreeable to the dictates of his own conscience; nor under any pretense whatever be compelled to attend any place of worship contrary to his faith and judgment; nor shall any person be obliged to pay tithes, taxes, or other rates for building or repairing any church or churches, place or places of worship, or for the maintenance of any minister or ministry, contrary to what he believes to be right or has deliberately and voluntarily engaged to perform.

4. There shall be no establishment of one religious sect in preference to another; no religious or racial test shall be required as a qualification for any office or public trust.

5. No person shall be denied the enjoyment of any civil or military right, nor be discriminated against in the exercise of any civil or military right, nor be segregated in the militia or in the public schools, because of religious principles, race, color, ancestry or national origin.

New Mexico

Preamble

We, the people of New Mexico, grateful to Almighty God for the blessings of liberty, in order to secure the advantages of a state government, do ordain and establish this constitution.

Article II

Bill of Rights

Section 11. Every man shall be free to worship God to the dictates of his own conscience, and no person shall ever be molested or denied any civil or political right or privilege on account of his religious opinion or mode of religious worship. No person shall be required to attend any place of worship or support any religious sect or denomination; nor shall any preference be given by law to any religious denomination or mode of worship.

Article IV

Section 31. No appropriation shall be made for charitable, educational or other benevolent purposes to any person, corporation, association, institution or community, not under the absolute control of the state. . . .

Article XII

Education

Section 3. The schools, colleges, universities and other educational institutions provided for by this Constitution shall forever remain under the exclusive control of the State, and no part of the proceeds arising from the sale or disposal of any lands granted to the State by Congress, or any other funds appropriated, levied or collected for educational purposes, shall be used for the support of any sectarian, denominational or private school, college or university.

Section 9. No religious test shall ever be required as a condition of admission into the public schools or any educational institution of this State, either as a teacher or student and no teacher or students of such school or institution shall ever be required to attend or participate in any religious service whatsoever.

Article XXI

Compact With the United States

Section 1. Religious toleration — Polygamy. — Perfect toleration of religious sentiment shall be secured, and no inhabitant of this state shall ever be molested in person or property on account of his or her mode of religious worship. Polygamous or plural marriages and polygamous cohabitation are forever prohibited.

Section 4. Provision shall be made for the establishment and maintenance of a system of public schools which shall be open to all the children of the State and free from sectarian control, and said schools shall always be conducted in English.

New York

Preamble

We the People of the State of New York, grateful to Almighty God for our Freedom, in order to secure its blessings, DO ESTABLISH THIS CONSTITUTION.

Article I

Bill of Rights

(Freedom of worship; religious liberty.) Section 3.

The free exercise and enjoyment of religious professions and worship, without discrimination or preference, shall forever be allowed in this state to all mankind; and no person shall be rendered incompetent to be a witness on account of his opinions on matters of religious belief; but the liberty of conscience hereby secured shall not be so construed as to excuse acts of licentiousness, or justify practices inconsistent with the peace or safety of this state.

Article VII

State Finances

(Gift or loan of state credit or money prohibited; exceptions for enumerated purposes.) Section 8.1. The money of the state shall not be given or loaned to or in aid of any private corporation or association, or private undertaking; nor shall the credit of the state be given or loaned to or in aid of any individual, or public or private corporation or association, or private undertaking, but the foregoing provisions shall not apply to any fund or property now held or which may hereafter be held by the state for educational purposes.

Article XI

Education

(Use of public property or money in aid of denominational schools prohibited; transportation of children authorized.)

Section 3. Neither the state nor any subdivision thereof shall use its property or credit or any public money, or authorize or permit either to be used, directly or indirectly, in aid or maintenance, other than for examination or inspection, of any school or institution of learning wholly or in part under the control or direction of any religious denomination, or in which any denominational tenet or doctrine is taught, but the legislature may provide for the transportation of children to and from any school or institution of learning.

North Carolina

Preamble

We, the people of the State of North Carolina, grateful to Almighty God, the Sovereign Ruler of Nations for the preservation of the American Union and the existence of our civil, political or religious liberties, and acknowledging our dependence upon Him for the continuance of those blessings to us and our posterity, do, for the more certain security thereof, and for the better government of this State, ordain and establish this Constitution.

Article I

Declaration of Rights

Section 13. Religious liberty. All persons have a natural and inalienable right to worship Almighty God according to the dictates of their own consciences, and no human authority should, in any case whatever, control or interfere with the rights on conscience.

Article IX

Education

Section 6. State School Fund. The proceeds of all lands that have been or hereafter may be granted by the United States to this State, and not otherwise appropriated by this State or the United States; all moneys, stocks, bonds, and other property belonging to the State for purposes of public education; the net proceeds of all sales of the swamp lands belonging to the State, and all other grants, gifts and devises that have been or hereafter may be made to the State, and not otherwise appropriated by the State, or by the terms of the grant, gift, or devise, shall be paid into the State Treasury and, together with so much of the revenue of the State as may be set apart for that purpose, shall be faithfully appropriated and used exclusively for establishing and maintaining a uniform system of free public schools.

North Dakota

Preamble

We, the people of North Dakota, grateful to Almighty God for the blessings of civil and religious liberty, do ordain and establish this constitution.

Article I

Declaration of Rights

Section 4. The free exercise and enjoyment of religious profession and worship, without discrimination or preference, shall be forever guaranteed in this state, and no person shall be rendered incompetent to be a witness or juror on account of his opinion on matters of religious belief; but the liberty of conscience hereby secured shall not be so construed as to excuse acts of licentiousness, or justify practices inconsistent with the peace or safety of this state.

Article VIII

Education

Section 147. A high degree of intelligence, patriotism, integrity and morality on the part of every voter in a government by the people being necessary in order to insure the continuance of that government and the prosperity and happiness of the people, the legislative assembly shall make provision for the establishment and maintenance of a system of public schools which shall be open to all children of the state of North Dakota and free from sectarian control. This legislative requirement shall be irrevocable without the consent of the United States and the people of North Dakota.

Section 152. All colleges, universities, and other educational institutions, for the support of which lands have been granted to this state, or which are supported by a public tax, shall remain under the absolute and exclusive control of the state. No money raised for the support of the public school of the state shall be appropriated to or used for support of any sectarian school.

Article XVI

Compact with the United States

The following article shall be irrevocable without the consent of the United States and the people of this state:

Section 203. First. Perfect toleration of religious sentiment shall be secured, no inhabitant of this state shall ever be molested in person or property on account of his or her mode of religious worship.

Ohio

Article I

Bill of Rights

7. Rights of conscience; the necessity of religion and knowledge.

All men have a natural and indefeasible right to worship Almighty God according to the dictates of their own conscience. No person shall be compelled to attend, erect, or support any place of worship, or maintain any form of worship, against his consent; and no preference shall be given, by law, to any religious society; nor shall any interference with the rights of conscience be permitted. No religious test shall be required, as a qualification for office, nor shall any person be incompetent to be a witness on account of his religious belief; but nothing herein shall be construed to dispense with oaths and affirmations. Religion, morality, and knowledge, however, being essential to good government, it shall be the duty of the General Assembly to pass suitable laws, to protect every religious denomination in the peaceable enjoyment of its own mode of public worship, and to encourage schools and the means of instruction.

Article VI

Education

2. Common school fund to be raised; how controlled.

The General Assembly shall make such provisions, by taxation, or otherwise, as, with the income arising from the school trust fund, will secure a thorough and efficient system of common schools throughout the State; but, no religious or other sect, or sects, shall ever have any exclusive right to, or control of, any part of the school funds of this State.

Oklahoma

Preamble

Invoking the guidance of Almighty God, in order to secure and perpetuate the blessing of liberty; to secure just and rightful government; to promote our mutual welfare and happiness, we, the people of the State of Oklahoma, do ordain and establish this Constitution.

Article I

Federal Relations

2. Religious liberty—Polygamous or plural marriages.

Perfect toleration of religious sentiment shall be secured, and no inhabitant of the State shall ever be molested in person or property on account of his or her mode of religious worship, and no religious test shall be required for the exercise of civil or political rights, polygamous or plural marriages are forever prohibited.

5. Public schools—Separate Schools

Provisions shall be made for the establishment and maintenance of a system of public schools, which shall be open to all the children of the State and free from sectarian control; and said schools shall always be conducted in English: Provided, that nothing herein shall preclude the teaching of other languages in said public schools: And Provided, further, that this shall not be construed to prevent the establishment and maintenance of separate schools for white and colored children.

Article II

Bill of Rights

5. Public money or property — Use for sectarian purposes.

No public money or property shall ever be appropriated, applied, donated, or used, directly or indirectly, for the use, benefit or support of any sect, church, denomination, or system of religion, or for the use, benefit or support of any priest, preacher, minister, or other religious teacher or dignitary, or sectarian institution as such.

Oregon

Article I

Section 2. Freedom of worship. All men shall be secure in the Natural right, to worship Almighty God according to the dictates of their own consciences.

Section 3. Freedom of religious opinion. No law shall in any case whatever control the free exercise, and enjoyment of religious (*sic*) opinions, or interfere with the rights of conscience.

Section 4. No religious qualification for office. No religious test shall be required as a qualification for any office of trust or profit.

Section 5. No money to be appropriated for religion. No money shall be drawn from the Treasury for the benefit of any religious, or theological institution, nor shall any money be appropriated for the payment of any religious services in either house of the Legislative Assembly.

Section 6. No religious test for witnesses or jurors. No person shall be rendered incompetent as a witness, or juror in consequence of his opinions on matters of religion; nor be questioned in any Court of Justice touching his religious belief to affect the weight of his testimony.

Pennsylvania

Preamble

We, the people of the Commonwealth of Pennsylvania, grateful to Almighty God for the blessings of civil and religious liberty, and humbly invoking His guidance, do ordain and establish this Constitution.

Article I

Declaration of Rights

Religious Freedom

Section 3. All men have a natural and indefeasible right to worship Almighty God according to the dictates of their own consciences; no man can of right be compelled to attend, erect or support any place of worship, or to maintain any ministry against his consent; no human authority can, in any case whatever, control or interfere with the rights of conscience, and no preference shall ever be given by law to any religious establishments or modes of worship.

Religion

Section 4. No person who acknowledges the being of a God and a future state of rewards and punishments shall, on account of his religious sentiments, be disqualified to hold any office or place of trust or profit under this Commonwealth.

Article III

Legislation

Section 15. Public school money not available to sectarian schools.

No money raised for support of the public schools for the Commonwealth shall be appropriated to or used for the support of any sectarian school.

Appropriations for Public Assistance, Military Service Scholarships

Section 29. No appropriation shall be made for charitable, educational and benevolent purposes to any person or community nor to any denominational and sectarian institution, corporation or association: Provided, that appropriations may be made for pensions or gratuities for military service and to blind persons twenty-one years of age and upwards and for assistance to mothers having dependent children and to aged persons without adequate means of support and in the form of scholarship grants or loans for higher educational purposes to residents of the Commonwealth enrolled in institutions of higher learning except that no scholarship, grants or loans for higher educational purposes shall be given to persons enrolled in a theological seminary or school of theology.

Section 30. Charitable and Educational Appropriations. No appropriation shall be made to any charitable or educational institution not under the absolute control of the Commonwealth, other than normal schools of the State, established by law for the professional training of teachers, except by a vote of two-thirds of all the members elected to each House.

Rhode Island

Preamble

We, the people of the State of Rhode Island and Providence Plantations, grateful to Almighty God for the civil and religious liberty which He hath so long permitted us to enjoy, and looking to Him for a blessing upon our endeavors to secure and to transmit the same unimpaired to succeeding generations, do ordain and establish this constitution of government....

Article I

Declaration of Certain Constitutional Rights and Principles

In order effectually to secure the religious and political freedom established by our venerated ancestors, and to preserve the same for our posterity, we do declare that the essential and unquestionable rights and principles hereinafter mentioned shall be established, maintained, and preserved, and shall be of paramount obligation in all legislative, judicial, and executive proceedings.

Section 3. Whereas Almighty God hath created the mind free; and all attempts to influence it by temporal punishments or burdens, or by civil incapacitations, tend to beget habits of hypocrisy and meanness; and whereas a principal object of our venerable ancestors, in their migration to this country and their settlement of this state, was, as they expressed it, to hold forth a lively experiment, that a flourishing civil state may stand and be best maintained with full liberty in religious concernments: We, therefore, declare that no man shall be compelled to frequent or to support any religious worship, place, or ministry whatever, except in fulfillment of his own voluntary contract; nor enforced, restrained, molested, or burdened in his body or goods; nor disqualified from holding any office; nor otherwise suffer on account of his religious belief; and that every man shall be free to worship God according to the dictates of his own conscience, and to profess and by argument to maintain his opinion in matters of religion; and that the same shall in no wise diminish, enlarge, or affect his civil capacity.

Article XII

Of Education

Section 2. The money which now is or which may hereafter be appropriated by law for the establishment of a permanent fund for the support of public schools, shall be securely invested, and remain in perpetual fund for that purpose.

Section 4. The general assembly shall make all necessary provisions by law for carrying this article into effect. They shall not divert said money or fund from the aforesaid uses, nor borrow, appropriate, or use the same, or any part thereof, for any other purpose, under any pretense whatsoever.

South Carolina

Constitution of the State of South Carolina

We, the people of the State of South Carolina, in Convention assembled, grateful to God for our liberties, do ordain and establish this Constitution for the preservation and perpetuation of the same.

Article I

Declaration of Rights

Section 2. Religious worship — freedom of speech — petition. — The General Assembly shall make no law respecting an establishment of religion or prohibiting the free exercise thereof, or abridging the freedom of speech or of the press; or the right of the people peaceably to assemble and to petition the Government or any department thereof for a redress of grievances.

Article XI

Public Education

Section 4. Direct aid to religious or other private educational institutions prohibited.

No money shall be paid from public funds nor shall the credit of the State or any of its political subdivisions be used for the direct benefit of any religious or other private educational institution.

Article XVII

Miscellaneous Matters

Section 4. Supreme Being—No person who denies the existence of a Supreme Being shall hold any office under this Constitution.

South Dakota

Preamble

We, the people of South Dakota, grateful to Almighty God for our civil and religious liberties, in order to form a more perfect and independent government, establish justice, insure tranquility, provide for the common defense, promote the general welfare and preserve to ourselves and to our posterity the blessing of liberty, do ordain and establish this constitution for the State of South Dakota.

Article VI

Bill of Rights

Section 3. The right to worship God according to the dictates of conscience shall never be infringed. No person shall be denied any civil or political right, privilege or position on account of his religion but the liberty of conscience hereby secured shall not be so construed as to excuse licentiousness, the invasion of the rights of others, or justify practices inconsistent with the peace or safety of the state.

No person shall be compelled to attend or support any ministry or place of worship against his consent nor shall any preference be given by law to any religious establishment or mode of worship. No money or property of the state shall be given or appropriated for the benefit of any sectarian or religious society or institution.

Article VIII

Education and School Lands

Section 16. No appropriation of lands, money or other property or credits to aid any sectarian school shall ever be made by the state, or any county or municipality within the state, nor shall the state or any county or municipality within the state accept any grant, conveyance, gift, or bequest, of lands, money or other property to be used for sectarian purposes, and no sectarian instruction shall be allowed in any school or institution aided or supported by the state.

Article XXII

Compact with the United States

Fourth. That provision shall be made for the establishment and maintenance of systems of public schools, which shall be open for all the children of this state, and free from sectarian control.

Tennessee

Preamble

We, the delegates and representatives of the people of the State of Tennessee, duly elected, and in Convention assembled, in pursuance of said Act of Assembly, have ordained and established the following Constitution and form of government for this State, which we recommend to the people of Tennessee for their ratification: That is to say—

Article I

Declaration of Rights

Section 3. Freedom of Worship. — That all men have a natural and indefeasible right to worship Almighty God according to the dictates of their own conscience; that no man can of right be compelled to attend, erect, or support any place of worship, or to maintain any minister against his consent; that no human authority can, in any case whatever control or interfere with the rights of conscience; and that no preference shall ever be given, by law to any religious establishment or mode of worship.

Section 4. No religious or political test. — That no political or religious test, other than an oath to support the Constitution of the United States and of this State, shall ever be required as a qualification to any office or public trust under this state.

Article IX

Disqualifications

Section 2. No atheist shall hold a civic office. — No person who denies the being of God, or a future state of rewards and punishments, shall hold any office in the civil department of the State.

Article XI
Miscellaneous Provisions

Section 12. Education's inherent value — Public Schools — Support of higher education. The State of Tennessee recognizes the inherent value of education and encourages its support. The General Assembly shall provide for the maintenance, support and eligibility standards of a system of free public schools. The General Assembly may establish and support such post-secondary educational institutions, including public institutions of higher learning, as it determines.

Section 15. Religious holidays. — No person shall in time of peace be required to perform any service to the public on any day set apart by his religion as a day of rest.

Texas

Preamble

Humbly invoking the blessings of Almighty God, the people of the State of Texas do ordain and establish this Constitution.

Article I

Bill of Rights

That the general, great and essential principles of liberty and free government may be recognized and established, we declare:

Section 4. There Shall Be No Religious Test for Office. — No religious test shall ever be required as a qualification to any office or public trust in this State; nor shall anyone be excluded from holding office on account of his religious sentiments, provided he acknowledge the existence of a Supreme Being.

Section 5. How Oaths Shall Be Administered. — No person shall be disqualified to give evidence in any of the courts of this State on account of his religious opinions, or for want of any religious belief, but all oaths or affirmations shall be administered in the mode most binding upon the conscience, and shall be taken subject to the pains and penalties of perjury.

Section 6. Freedom in Religious Worship Guaranteed. — All men have a natural and indefeasible right to worship Almighty God according to the dicates of their own consciences. No man shall be compelled to attend, erect or support any place of worship, or to maintain any ministry against his consent. No human authority ought, in any case whatever, to control or interfere with the rights of conscience in matters of religion, and no preference shall ever be given by law to any religious society or mode of worship. But it shall be the duty of the Legislature to pass such laws as may be necessary to protect equally every religious denomination in the peaceable enjoyment of its own mode of public worship.

Section 7. No appropriation for Sectarian Purposes. — No money shall be appropriated or drawn from the Treasury for the benefit of any sect, or religious society, theological or religious seminary, nor shall property belonging to the State be appropriated for any such purposes.

Article VII

Education

The Public Free Schools

Section 5. The principal of all bonds and other funds, and the principal arising from the sale of the lands hereinbefore set apart to said school fund, shall be the permanent school fund, and all the interest derivable therefrom and the taxes herein authorized and levied shall be the available school fund. The available school fund shall be applied annualiy to the support of the public free schools. And no law shall ever be enacted appropriating any part of the permanent or available school fund to any other purpose whatever; nor shall the same, or any part thereof ever be appropriated to or used for the support of any sectarian school; and the available school fund herein provided shall be distributed to the several counties according to their scholastic population and applied in such manner as may be provided by law.

Section 3 of Article VIII. Taxes to Be Collected for Public Purposes Only. — Taxes shall be levied and collected by general laws and for public purposes only.

Utah

Preamble

Grateful to Almighty God for life and liberty, we, the people of Utah, in order to secure and perpetuate the Principles of free government, do ordain and establish this CONSTITUTION.

Article I

Declaration of Rights

Section 1. (Inherent and inalienable rights.)

All men have the inherent and inalienable right to enjoy and defend their lives and liberties; to acquire, possess and protect property; to worship according to the dictates of their consciences; to assemble peaceably, protest against wrongs, and petition for redress of grievances; to communicate freely their thoughts and opinions, being responsible for the abuse of that right.

Section 4. (Religious liberty)

The rights of conscience shall never be infringed. The State shall make no law respecting an establishment of religion or prohibiting the free exercise therof; no religious test shall be required as a qualification for any office of public trust or for any vote at any election; nor shall any person be incompetent as a witness or juror on account of religious belief or the absence thereof. There shall be no union of Church and State, nor shall any church dominate the State or interfere with its functions. No public money or property shall be appropriated for or applied to any religious worship, exercise or instruction, or for the support of any ecclesiastical establishment. No property qualification shall be required of any person to vote, or hold office, except as provided in this Constitution.

Article III

Ordinance

(Religious toleration. Polygamy forbidden.)

First: — Perfect toleration of religious sentiment is guaranteed. No inhabitant of this State shall ever be molested in person or property on account of his or her mode of religious worship; but polygamous or plural marriages are forever prohibited.

(Free, nonsectarian schools)

Fourth: — The Legislature shall make laws for the establishment and maintenance of a system of public schools, which shall be open to all the children of the State and be free from sectarian control.

Article X

Education

Section 2. (Free nonsectarian schools.)

The Legislature shall provide for the establishment and maintenance of a uniform system of public schools, which shall be open to all children of the State, and be free from sectarian control.

Section 12. (No religious or partisan tests in schools.)

Neither religious nor partisan test or qualification shall be required of any person as a condition of admission, as teacher or student, into any public institution of the State.

Section 13. (Public aid to church schools forbidden.)

Neither the Legislature nor any county, city, town, school district or other public corporation, shall make any appropriation to aid in the support of any school, seminary, academy, college, university or other institution, controlled in whole, or in part, by any church sect or denomination whatever.

Vermont

Chapter I

A Declaration of the Rights of the Inhabitants of the State of Vermont

Religious freedom and worship

Article 3rd. That all men have a natural and unalienable right, to worship Almighty God, according to the dictates of their own consciences and understandings, as in their opinion shall be regulated by the word of God; and that no man ought to, or of right can be compelled to attend any religious worship, or erect or support any place of worship, or maintain any minister, contrary to the dictates of his conscience nor can any man be justly deprived or abridged of any civil right as a citizen, on account of his religious sentiments, or peculiar mode of religious worship; and that no authority can, or ought to be vested in, or assumed by, any power whatever, that shall in any case interfere with, or in any manner control the rights of conscience, in the free exercise of religious worship. Nevertheless, every sect or denomination of Christians ought to observe the sabbath or Lord's day, and keep up some sort of religious worship, which to them shall seem most agreeable to the revealed will of God.

Chapter II

(Section 68. Laws to encourage virtue and prevent vice; schools; religious societies)

Section 68. Laws for the encouragement of virtue and prevention of vice and immorality ought to be constantly kept in force, and duly executed; and a competent number of schools ought to be maintained in each town unless the general assembly permits other provisions for the convenient instruction of youth. All religious societies, or bodies of men that may be united or incorporated for the advancement of religion and learning, or for other pious and charitable purposes, shall be encouraged and protected in the enjoyment of the privileges, immunities, and estates, which they in justice ought to enjoy, under such regulations as the general assembly of this state shall direct.

Virginia

Bill of Rights

A DECLARATION of rights by the good people of Virginia in the exercise of their sovereign powers, which rights do pertain to them and their posterity, as the basis and foundation of government.

Article I

Section 16. Free exercise of religion; no establishment of religion. That religion or the duty which we owe to our Creator, and the manner of discharging it, can be directed only by reason and conviction, not by force or violence; and, therefore, all men are equally entitled to the free exercise of religion, according to the dictates of conscience; and that it is the mutual duty of all to practice Christian forbearance, love, and charity towards each other. No man shall be compelled to frequent or support any religious worship, place, or ministry whatsoever, nor shall be enforced, restrained, molested, or burthened in his body or goods, nor shall otherwise suffer on account of his religious opinions or belief; but all men shall be free to profess and by argument to maintain their opinions in matters of religion, and the same shall in nowise diminish, enlarge, or affect their civil capacities. And the General Assembly shall not prescribe any religious test whatever, or confer any peculiar privileges or advantages on any sect or denomination, or pass any law requiring or authorizing any religious society, or the people of any district within the Commonwealth, to levy on themselves or others, any tax for the erection or repair of any house of public worship, or for the support of any church or ministry; but it shall be left free to every person to select his religious instructor, and to make for his support such private contract as he shall please.

Article IV

Section 16. Appropriations to religious or charitable bodies. The General Assembly shall not make any appropriation of public funds, personal property, or real estate to any church or sectarian society, or any association or institution of any kind whatever which is entirely or partly, directly or indirectly, controlled by any church or sectarian society. Nor shall the General Assembly make any like appropriation to any charitable institution which is not owned or controlled by the Commonwealth; the General Assembly may, however, make appropriations to nonsectarian institutions for the reform of youthful criminals and may also authorize counties, cities, or towns to make such appropriations to any charitable institution or association.

Article VIII

Education and Public Instruction

Section 10. State appropriations prohibited to schools or institutions of learning not owned or exclusively controlled by the State or some subdivision thereof; exceptions to rule.

No appropriation of public funds shall be made to any school or institution of learning not owned or exclusively controlled by the State or some political subdivision thereof; provided, first, that the General Assembly may, and the governing bodies of the several counties, cities and towns may, subject to such limitations as may be imposed by the General Assembly, appropriate funds for educational purposes which may be expended in furtherance of elementary, secondary, collegiate or graduate education of Virginia students in public and nonsectarian private schools and institutions of learning, in addition to those owned or exclusively controlled by the State of any such county, city, or town; second, that the General Assembly may appropriate funds to an agency or to a school or institution of learning owned or controlled by an agency, created and established by two or more States under a joint agreement to which this State is a party for the purpose of providing educational facilities for the several States joining in such agreement; third, that counties, cities, towns and districts may make appropriations to nonsectarian schools of manual, industrial or technical training and also to any school or institution owned or exclusively controlled by such county, city, town, or school district.

Washington

Preamble

We, the people of the State of Washington, grateful to the Supreme Ruler of the Universe for our liberties, do ordain this constitution.

Declaration of Rights

Article I

Section 11. Religious Freedom. Absolute freedom of conscience in all matters of religious sentiment, belief and worship, shall be guaranteed to every individual, and no one shall be molested or disturbed in person or property on account of religion; but the liberty of conscience hereby secured shall not be so construed as to excuse acts of licentiousness or justify practices inconsistent with the peace and safety of the state. No public money or property shall be appropriated for or applied to any religious worship, exercise or instruction, or the support of any religious establishment: *Provided, however,* That this article shall not be so construed as to forbid the employment by the state of a chaplain for such of the state custodial, correctional and mental institutions as in the discretion of the legislature may seem justified. No religious qualification shall be required for any public office or employment, nor shall any person be incompetent as a witness or juror, in consequence of his opinion on matters of religion, nor be questioned in any court of justice touching his religious belief to affect the weight of his testimony.

Article IX

Education

Section 2. Public School System. The legislature shall provide for a general and uniform system of public schools. The public school system shall include common schools, and such high schools, normal schools, and technical schools as may hereafter be established. But the entire revenue derived from the common school fund and the state tax for common schools shall be exclusively applied to the support of the common schools.

Section 4. Sectarian Control of Influence Prohibited. All schools maintained or supported wholly or in part by the public funds shall be forever free from sectarian control or influence.

Article XXVI

Compact with the United States

The following ordinance shall be irrevocable without the consent of the United States and the people of this state:

First: That perfect toleration of religious sentiment shall be secured and that no inhabitant of this State shall ever be molested in person or property on account of his or her mode of religious worship.

West Virginia

Preamble

Since through Divine Providence we enjoy the blessings of civil, political and religious liberty, we, the people of West Virginia, in and through the provisions of this Constitution, reaffirm our faith in and constant reliance upon God and seek diligently to promote, preserve and perpetuate good government in the State of West Virginia for the common welfare, freedom and security of ourselves and our posterity.

Article III

Bill of Rights

Religious Freedom Guaranteed

15. No man shall be compelled to frequent or support any religious worship, place or ministry whatsoever; nor shall any man be enforced, restrained, or molested or burthened, in his body or goods, or otherwise suffer, on account of his religious opinions or belief, but all men shall be free to profess, and, by argument, to maintain their opinions in matters of religion; and the same shall, in no wise, affect, diminish or enlarge their civil capacities; and the Legislature shall not prescribe any religious test whatever, or confer any peculiar privileges or advantages on any sect or denomination, or pass any law requiring or authorizing any religious society, or the people of any district within this State, to levy on themselves, or others, any tax for the erection or repair of any house of public worship, or for the support of any church or ministry, but it shall be left free for every person to select his religious instructor, and to make for his support such private contracts as he shall please.

Wisconsin

Preamble

We, the people of Wisconsin, grateful to Almighty God for our freedom, in order to secure its blessings, form a more perfect government, insure domestic tranquility and promote the general welfare, do establish this constitution.

Article I

Bill of Rights

Freedom of worship; liberty of conscience; state religion; public funds.

Section 18. The right of every man to worship Almighty God according to the dictates of his own conscience shall never be infringed; nor shall any man be compelled to attend, erect or support any place of worship, or to maintain any ministry, against his consent; nor shall any control of, or interference with, the rights of conscience be permitted, or any preference be given by law to any religious establishments or modes of worship; nor shall any money be drawn from the treasury for the benefit of religious or theological seminaries.

Religious tests prohibited.

Section 19. No religious tests shall ever be required as a qualification for any office of public trust under the state, and no person shall be rendered incompetent to give evidence in any court of law or equity in consequence of his opinions on the subject of religion.

Article X

Education

District schools; tuition; sectarian instruction.

Section 3. The legislature shall provide by law for the establishment of district schools, which shall be as nearly uniform as practicable; and such schools shall be free and without charge for tuition to all children between the ages of four and twenty years; and no sectarian instruction shall be allowed there; but the legislature by law may, for the purpose of religious instruction outside the district schools, authorize the release of students during regular school hours.

Wyoming

Preamble

We, the people of the state of Wyoming, grateful to God for our civil, political and religious liberties, and desiring to secure them to ourselves and perpetuate them to our posterity, do ordain and establish this constitution.

Article I

Declaration of Rights

Section 18. Religious Liberty. The free exercise and enjoyment of religious profession and worship without discrimination or preference shall be forever guaranteed in this state, and no person shall be rendered incompetent to hold any office of trust or profit, or to serve as a witness or juror, because of his opinion on any matter of religious belief whatever; but the liberty of conscience hereby secured shall not be so construed as to excuse acts of licentiousness or justify practices inconsistent with the peace or safety of the state.

Section 19. Appropriations for religion prohibited. No money of the state shall ever be given or appropriated to any sectarian or religious society or institution.

Article III

Legislative Department

Section 36. Prohibited appropriations. No appropriation shall be made for charitable, industrial, educational or benevolent purposes to any person, corporation or community not under the absolute control of the state, nor to any denominational or sectarian institution or association.

Article VII

Education

Section 8. Distribution of school funds. Provision shall be made by general law for the equitable allocation of such income among all the school districts in the state. But no appropriation shall be made from said fund to any district for the year in which a school has not been maintained for at least three (3) months; nor shall any portion of any public school fund ever be used to support or assist any private school, or any school, academy, seminary, college or other institution of learning controlled by any church or sectarian organization or religious denomination whatever.

Section 12. Sectarianism prohibited. No sectarian instruction, qualifications or tests shall be imparted, exacted, applied or in any manner tolerated in the schools of any grade or character controlled by the state, nor shall attendance be required at any religious service therein, nor shall any sectarian tenets or doctrines be taught or favored in any public school or institution that may be established under this constitution.

Appendix B

State Acts Providing Assistance to Religious Elementary and Secondary Schools

Alaska

Section 14.45.020. The commissioner may furnish final examination questions for the eighth grade pupils in private and denominational schools and grant eighth grade diplomas in the same manner as in the public schools.

Section 14.09.020. In those places in the state where the department or a school district provides transportation for children attending public schools, the department shall also provide transportation for children who, in compliance with the provisions of ch. 30 of this title, attend nonpublic schools which are administered in compliance with state law where the children, in order to reach the nonpublic schools, must travel distances comparable to, and over routes the same as, the distances and routes over which the children attending public school are transported. The commissioner shall administer this nonpublic school student transportation program, integrating it into existing systems as much as feasible, and the cost of the program shall be paid from funds appropriated for that purpose by the legislature.

Section 14.52.130. Assistance to nonprofit private schools.
(a) Federal assistance for food service to nonprofit private schools shall be provided by the department either in form of direct payments or by payments made through the school district in which the nonprofit private school is geographically located.

(b) If the department is precluded by law from making direct or indirect payments to these schools, the commissioner shall withhold funds from the apportionments to schools or districts for the purpose of making direct payments to these schools. Withholding of these funds shall be based on the rate of federal assistance per child per year for the schools or districts as determined by federal law or regulation and the number of children attending nonprofit private schools in the state.

Section 14.07.020 (8). In cooperation with the Department of Health and Social Services, Department of Education shall exercise general supervision over public and private pre-elementary schools (3–5 years) and over the educational nurseries.

Arizona

Exemption from payment of weight fees; religious institutions; non-profit schools; disaster assistance organizations; government entities

Section 28-207.

A. Motor vehicles, trailers or semitrailers owned and operated by religious institutions and used exclusively for the transportation of property produced and distributed for charitable purposes without compensation are exempt from the weight fee provided by Section 28-206.

B. For the purposes of subsection A of this section, "religious institution" means a recognized organization having an established place of meeting for religious worship which holds regular meetings for that purpose at least once each week in not less than five cities or towns in the state.

C. Motor vehicles owned and operated by nonprofit schools recognized as being tax exempt by the federal government and used exclusively for the transportation of pupils in connection with the school curriculum are exempt from the weight fee provided by Section 28-206.

D. Motor vehicles, trailers and semitrailers owned by any nonprofit organization in this state which presents to the motor vehicle division a form approved by the director of the division of emergency services pursuant to Section 26-318 are exempt from the weight fee provided by Section 28-206.

E. A vehicle owned and operated by a foreign government, a consul or other official representative of a foreign government, by the United States, by a state or political subdivision of a state or by an Indian tribal government is exempt from the weight fee provided by Section 28-206.

As amended Laws 1980, Ch. 24, Section 2; Laws 1980, Ch. 100, Section 1.

Definitions

Section 36-899. In this chapter, unless the context otherwise requires:

1. "Department" means the department of health services.

2. "Director" means the director of the department of health services.

3. "Hearing evaluation services" means services which include the identification, testing, evaluation and initiation of follow-up services as defined in the rules and regulations of the department, as provided by Section 36-899.03.

4. "Hearing screening evaluation" means the evaluation of the ability to hear certain frequencies at a consistent loudness.

5. "Private education program" means all programs of private education offering courses of study for grades kindergarten through the twelfth grade of high school.

6. "Public education program" means all kindergarten, primary and secondary programs of education within the public school system, including but not beyond the twelfth grade of common or high school.

Added Laws 1971, Ch. 76, Section 1. As amended Laws 1973, Ch. 158, Section 164.

Program for all school children; administration

Section 36-899.01.

A. A program of hearing evaluation services is established by the department. Such services shall be administered to all children as early as possible, but in no event later than the first year of attendance in any public or private education program, or residential facility for handicapped children, and thereafter as circumstances permit until the child has attained the age of sixteen years or is no longer enrolled in a public or private education program.

B. The program of hearing evaluation services for children in a public education program shall be administered by the department with the aid of the department of education.

Added Laws 1971, Ch. 76, Section 1.

Powers of the department; limitations

Section 36-899.02.

A. The department may, in administering the program of hearing evaluation services:

1. Provide consulting services, establish or supplement hearing evaluation services in local health department, public or private education programs or other community agencies.

2. Provide for the training of personnel to administer hearing screening evaluations.

3. Delegate powers and duties to other state agencies, county and local health departments, county and local boards of education or boards of trustees of private education programs or other community agencies to develop and maintain periodic hearing evaluation services.

4. Provide services by contractual arrangement for the development and maintenance of periodic hearing evaluation services.

5. Accept reports of hearing evaluation from qualified medical or other professional specialists employed by parents or guardians for hearing evaluation when such reports are submitted to the department.

B. The department shall not replace any qualified existing service.

Added Laws 1971, Ch. 77, Section 1.

Special Education Voucher Fund for Private Education.
Section 15-1181. *Definitions.*

In this article, unless the context otherwise requires:

1. "Fund" means the state permanent special education voucher fund.

2. "Place" or "placement" means placement of a person in a private institution, as defined in this article, for special education only or for special education and residential and custodial care.

3. "Placing agency" means the department of corrections, the department of economic security or the juvenile courts.

4. "Private institution" means a child welfare agency which is licensed and supervised by the department of economic security and which also has been approved by the division of special education pursuant to Section 15-765 (C) for the purpose of providing special education.

5. "Special education" means the adjustment of the environmental factors, modification of school curricula and adaptation of teaching methods, materials and techniques to provide educationally for those children who are gifted or handicapped to such an extent that they do not profit from the regular school curricula or need special education services in order to profit. Difficulty in writing, speaking or understanding the English language due to environmental background in which a language other than English is spoken primarily or exclusively shall not be considered a sufficient handicap to require special education.

Added Laws 1981, Ch. 1, Sec. 2. Amended by Laws 1981, Ch. 314, Sec. 17.

Section 15-1182. *Permanent special education voucher fund; administration.*

A. There is established a permanent special education voucher fund which shall consist of legislative appropriations.

B. The fund shall be administered by the superintendent of public instruction for the purposes provided in this article.

C. Each fiscal year the state board of education shall include in its budget request for assistance to schools a separate line item for the permanent special education voucher fund.

Added Laws 1981, Ch. 1, Sec. 2.

Section 15-1184. *Voucher; application, approval; requirements; budgets: prohibited uses.*

A. When a placing agency has determined to place a person in a private institution to receive special education, the placing agency, upon application to and approval by the division of special education, shall have a voucher issued as provided in this article to pay the special educational institutional costs of the person at the private institution.

B. The director of the division of special education shall develop requirements for the approval of vouchers, as provided in this section, including the requirement that the person be educationally evaluated and that specific placement be recommended by the placing agency as provided in Section 15-1185 before an application can be made.

C. If a placing agency makes a diagnostic placement of a person in a private institution, the placing agency shall notify the director of the division of special education of the date of initial placement.

D. If approved, the voucher, in an amount not exceeding the sum of the following, shall be paid directly to the private institution in a manner prescribed by the superintendent of public instruction:

    1. For group A, the base level multiplied by two.

    2. For group B, the sum of the base for kindergarten through eight and the support level weight for the category, multiplied by the base level.

    3. For both group A and B, one hundred dollars for the capital outlay costs and fifty dollars for transportation costs.

E. When a diagnostic placement is terminated within thirty days of the initial placement and when a specific placement for special education purposes is made, the voucher, if approved, shall be paid directly to the private institution from the date of initial placement.

F. For the purpose of this article, the chief official of each placing agency and the superintendent of public instruction shall jointly prescribe a uniform budgeting format to be submitted by each private institution and to be used in determining special educational instructional costs and residential costs of persons placed.

G. Any special education voucher issued pursuant to this article shall not be used in any school or institution that discriminates on the basis of race, religion, creed, color or national origin.

Added Laws 1981, Ch. 1, Sec. 2. Amended Laws 1982, Ch. 28, Sec. 2.

Section 15-1186. *School District Responsibility.*

For the purpose of this section, the school district of residence of a person who is placed in a private institution and who is receiving a voucher pursuant to this article shall be considered the school district in which the private institution is located. The school district in which the person is placed shall be responsible for reviewing educational progress of such person and integrating the person into the school as soon as feasible, but the school district shall not be financially responsible for such person while the person remains in the custody of the placing agency. The person shall remain a resident of the school district in which he is placed only as long as he remains in the custody of the placing agency.

Added Laws 1981, Ch. 1, Sec. 2.

California

Transportation—Supplementary Services

Section 39808. Transportation of pupils attending other than public school. The governing board of any school district may allow pupils entitled to attend the school of the district, but in attendance at a school other than a public school, under the provisions of Section 48222, transportation upon the same terms and in the same manner and over the same routes of travel as is permitted pupils attending the district school.

The allowance of this section shall be restricted to actual transportation when furnished by the district to children attending the district school, and nothing in this section shall be construed to authorize or permit in lieu of transportation payments of money to parents or guardians of children attending private schools.

The Education Code provides that the governing board of a school district may allow pupils entitled to attend the school of the district, but actually in attendance at a private school, transportation on the same terms and in the same manner and over the same routes of travel as is permitted pupils attending district schools. But only the furnishing of actual transportation is authorized by this provision, not the payment, in lieu thereof, of money to parents or guardians of children attending private schools. This provision is applicable to pupils attending any private school that qualifies, including one operated by a religious denomination; and is not in contravention of either the federal or state constitution. It does not violate the constitutional prohibition against public aid for sectarian purposes, since the purpose of the statute is to promote the public welfare by aiding in practical ways the education of the young, and the pupils transported are its true beneficiaries. Any advantages received therefrom by a private or parochial school are merely incidental and thus immaterial in determining the validity of the statute. Moreover, the protection of children from the hazards of traffic is justifiable under the same considerations that support police and fire protection and other governmental services. (*California Jurisprudence,* Sec. 344, 3d. ed.)

Section 60313. Central clearinghouse-depository and duplication center re specialized books, etc. The Superintendent of Public Instruction shall establish and maintain a central clearinghouse-depository and duplication center for specialized textbooks, reference books, recordings, study materials, tangible apparatus, equipment and other similar items for the use of visually handicapped students enrolled in the public schools of California who may require their use as shall be determined by the state board.

Such instructional materials in specialized media shall be available to other handicapped minors enrolled in the public schools of California who are unable to benefit from the use of conventional print copies of textbooks, reference books, and other study materials in a manner determined by the state board.

The specialized textbooks, reference books, recordings, study materials, tangible apparatus, equipment and other similar items shall be available for use by visually handicapped students enrolled in the public community colleges, California State University and Colleges, and the University of California.

Enacted Stats 1976 Ch. 1010, Section 2, operative April 30, 1977.

Section 60314. Loan of specialized books, etc. to nonpublic school pupils. The Superintendent of Public Instruction shall loan to pupils entitled to attend the public schools of California, but in attendance at a school other than a public school under the provisions of Section 48222, the items specified in Section 60313, without cost to the pupils or to the nonpublic school which they attend.

Section 60315. Loan of state-adopted instructional materials to nonpublic pupils. The Superintendent of Public Instruction shall lend to pupils entitled to attend public elementary schools of the district, but in attendance at a school other than a public school under the provisions of Section 48222, the following items adopted by the state board for use in the public elementary schools:

(a) Textbooks and textbook substitutes for pupil use.
(b) Educational materials for pupil use.
(c) Tests for pupil use.
(d) Instructional materials systems for pupil use.
(e) Instructional materials sets for pupil use.

No charge shall be made to any pupil for the use of such adopted materials.

Items shall be loaned pursuant to this section only after, and to the same extent that, items are made available to students in public elementary schools. However, no cash allotment may be made to any nonpublic school.

Items shall be loaned for the use of nonpublic elementary school students after the nonpublic school student certifies to the State Superintendent of Public Instruction that such items are desired and will be used in a nonpublic elementary school by the nonpublic elementary school student.

Amendments:

A 1978 amendment: (1) amended the first paragraph by designating the first sentence to be the introductory clause and the second sentence to be the second paragraph; (2) substituted "the following items" for "Instructional materials" in the introductory clause; (3) said specifically what those items were; and (4) substituted "items" for "materials" wherever it appears in the third and fourth paragraphs.

Court Action:

In a taxpayers' action challenging the constitutionality of Section 60315, which authorized the Superintendent of Public Instruction to lend, without charge, textbooks used in the public schools, and which provided funds for that purpose, the trial court committed reversible error in concluding the program was constitutional, with a clearly secular legislative purpose not involving the expenditure of public money for the direct benefit of sectarian schools, and that any benefit to such schools, though substantial, was only indirect and incidental.

The program relieved the private schools which received books from the state of the necessity to include those books in their budgets and thus reduced the rental fee charged to parents by the private schools, and therefore the benefit to religious schools provided by the statute was neither indirect nor remote. Moreover the character of the benefit provided by the textbook loan program resulted in the appropriation of money to advance the educational function of the schools.

Accordingly, the statute was unconstitutional because it violated the prohibition of Cal. Const., art. IX, sec. 8 and Cal. Const., art. XVI, sec. 5, which prohibit the appropriation of money for the support of sectarian schools. If the fact that a child is aided by an expenditure of public money ("child benefit" theory) insulates a statute from challenge, constitutional proscriptions against state aid to sectarian schools would be virtually eliminated.

California Teachers Assoc. v. Riles (1981) 29 Cal. 3d 794, 176 Cal. Rptr. 300, 632 P.2d 953.

Section 41311. State child nutrition fund. There is hereby created in the State Treasury the State Child Nutrition Fund which is continuously appropriated to the Department of Education without regard to fiscal years to carry out the purposes of Article 10 (commencing with Section 49530) of Chapter 9 of Part 27 of Division 4 of this title and of Article 3.5 (commencing with Section 41350) of this chapter.

The State Child Nutrition Fund shall be administered by the State Department of Education under policies established by the State Board of Education. It is the intent of the Legislature that the fund shall provide permanent financial assistance to eligible school districts, county superintendents of schools, local agencies, private schools, parochial schools, and child development programs, for implementing the school meal program. The fund shall be used to reimburse the cafeteria account of school districts, county superintendents of schools, local agencies, private schools, parochial schools, and child development programs, based upon the number of qualifying meals served to students.

Driver Education — Allowance
by Superintendent of Public Instruction

Section 41902. Allowances by the Superintendent of Public Instruction shall be made only for driver training classes maintained in accordance with the rules and regulations as set forth by the State Board of Education.

Driver training shall be available without tuition to all eligible students commencing on July 1, 1969. The governing board of a district may make driver training available during school hours, or at other times, or any combination thereof.

Lunches — Specific Provisions — Surplus Property

Section 12110. Designation. The State Department of Education is hereby designated as the California State Agency for Surplus Property.

Section 12111. Cooperation with Federal Government. Said agency is authorized and directed to cooperate with the Federal Government and its agencies in securing the expeditious and equitable distribution of surplus personal property and food commodities donated by the Federal Government to public agencies, institutions and organizations in California, to assist such agencies, institutions and organizations in securing such property or food commodities and to do all things necessary to the execution of its powers and duties.

The state agency may enter into cooperative agreements with federal agencies to assist it in carrying out the purposes of this article.

Section 12112. Acquisition and disposition of property from Federal Government. Whenever by the provisions of any act of Congress or any rule or regulation adopted thereunder the agency is authorized to accept, receive, or purchase for resale from the Federal Government or any agency thereof, and with the approval of the Department of General Services, any property or food commodities and to provide for its disposition or resale, it is authorized to do so and is vested with all necessary power and authority to accomplish such acceptance, purchase, receipt, disposition and resale. The agency is hereby exempted from the provisions of Article 2, Chapter 6, Part 5.5, Division 3, Title 2 of the Government code.

Colorado

Use of Federal Funds

Section 22-32-110 (cc). To provide, in the discretion of the local board, out of federal grants made available specifically for this purpose, special educational services and arrangements, such as dual enrollment, educational radio and television, and mobile educational services, for the benefit of educationally deprived children in the district who attend nonpublic schools, without the requirement of full time public school attendance, and without discrimination on the grounds of race, color, religion, or national origin.

(dd) To provide, in the discretion of the local board, out of federal grants made available specifically for this purpose, library resources, which for the purposes of this title shall mean books, periodicals, documents, magnetic tapes, films, phonograph records, and other related library materials, and printed and published instructional materials for the use and benefit of all children in the district, both in public and nonpublic schools, without charge and without discrimination on the grounds of race, color, religion, or national origin.

Connecticut

Section 10-215a. Nonpublic school and nonprofit agency participation in feeding programs. Nonpublic schools and nonprofit agencies may participate in the school breakfast, lunch and other feeding programs provided in sections 10-215 to 10-215c under such regulations as may be promulgated by the state board of education in conformance with said sections and the federal laws governing said programs.

Section 10-217a. Health and welfare services for children in nonprofit private schools. State aid.

(a) Each town which provides health and welfare services for children attending its public schools shall provide the same health and welfare services for children attending private schools therein, not conducted for profit, when a majority of the children attending such schools are from the state of Connecticut. Such determination shall be made by adding the number of all pupils enrolled in such school on October first and May first, or the full school days immediately preceding such dates, during the school year next prior to that in which the health and welfare services are to be provided, and dividing by two. Such health and welfare services shall include the services of a school physician, school nurse and dental hygienist, school psychologist, speech remedial services, school social worker's services, special language teachers for non–English-speaking students and such clerical, supervisory and administrative services necessary to the provision of the services enumerated in this section.

(b) Any town providing such services for children attending such private schools shall be reimbursed by the state for the amount paid for such services. At the close of each school year any town which provides such services shall file an application for such reimbursement on a form to be provided by the state board of education. Payment shall be made as soon as possible after the close of each fiscal year.

(c) The pay of certificated personnel shall be subject to the rules and regulations providing for the state teacher's retirement fund by the board of education of such town applicable to certificated teaching personnel in the public schools of such town. This subsection (c) shall be retroactive to July 1, 1968.

Section 10-228a. Free textbook loans to pupils attending nonpublic schools. Each local and regional board of education may, at the request of any nonpublic elementary or secondary school pupil, including kindergarten pupil, residing in and attending a nonpublic school in such district, or at the request of the parent or guardian of such pupil, arrange for a loan of textbooks currently in use in the public schools of such district to such pupil free of charge, provided the loan of any such textbook shall be requested for not less than one semester's use.

Section 10-239a. Demonstration scholarship program. Short title. Legislative intent. Sections 10-239a to 10-239h, inclusive, shall be known and may be cited as the demonstration scholarship program authorization act of 1972. It is the intent of the legislature to enable up to six local or regional boards of education to participate in the demonstration program designed to develop and test the use of education scholarships for school children. The purpose of this demonstration scholarship program is to develop and test education scholarships as a way to improve the quality of education by making schools, both public and private, more responsive to the needs of children and parents, to provide greater parental choice, and to determine the extent to which the quality and delivery of educational services are affected by economic incentives. The demonstration scholarship program authorized by Sections 10-239a to 10-239h, inclusive, shall aid students and shall not be used to support or to benefit any particular schools.

Section 10-239b. Definitions. As used in sections 10-239a to 10-239h, inclusive:

(1) "Demonstration area" means the area designated by the participating local or regional board of education for the purposes of a demonstration scholarship program defined in subsection (2) of this section, which area shall include a substantial number of needy or disadvantaged students.

(2) "Demonstration scholarship program" means a program for developing and testing the use of educational scholarships for all pupils eligible to attend public or private schools within the demonstration area, which scholarships shall be made available to the parents or legal guardians of a scholarship recipient in the form of a drawing right, negotiable certificate or other document which may not be redeemed except for educational purposes at schools fulfilling the requirements of subsection (a) of Section 10-239e.

(3) "Demonstration board" means a board established by the local or regional board of education to conduct the demonstration scholarship program.

(4) "Contract" means the agreement entered into by the local or regional board of education and a federal governmental agency for the purpose of conducting a demonstration scholarship program.

Section 10-239c. Contract with federal agency for funds. The local or regional board of education may contract with a federal governmental agency for funds to establish a demonstration scholarship program to exist for a period of up to five years, such board to receive such state and local aid for any of its students as would otherwise be provided by law regardless of whether or not such students participate in a demonstration scholarship program, which funds may be expended under the demonstration scholarship program as the demonstration contract shall provide and within the demonstration area.

Section 10-239d. Demonstration board and staff. Scholarships. The local or regional board of education may establish a demonstration board and staff and may authorize it to administer the demonstration project authorized by Sections 10-239a to 10-239h, inclusive, provided the costs of such organization shall be borne by the contracting federal agency. The members of the demonstration board, if it is not the local or regional board of education itself, shall serve for the terms established by the appointing board.

(1) The demonstration board may: (a) Employ a staff for the demonstration board, (b) receive and expend funds to support the demonstration board and scholarships for children in the demonstration area, (c) contract with other government agencies and private persons or organizations to provide or receive services, supplies, facilities and equipment, (d) determine rules and regulations for use of scholarships in the demonstration area, (e) adopt rules and regulations for its own government, (f) receive and expend funds from the federal governmental agency necessary to pay for the costs incurred in administering the program, (g) otherwise provide the specified programs, services and activities.

(2) The demonstration board shall award a scholarship to each school child residing in the demonstration area, subject only to such age and grade restrictions which it may establish. The scholarship funds shall be made available to the parents or legal guardian of a scholarship recipient in the form of a drawing right, certificate or other document which may not be redeemed except for educational purposes.

(3) The demonstration board shall establish the amount of the scholarship in a fair and impartial manner as follows: There shall be a basic scholarship equal in amount to every other basic scholarship for every eligible student

in the demonstration area. In no case shall the amount of the basic scholarship fall below the level of average current expense per pupil for corresponding grade levels in the public schools in the demonstration area in the year immediately preceding the demonstration program.

(4) In addition to each base scholarship, compensatory scholarships shall be given to disadvantaged children. The amount of such compensatory scholarships and the manner by which children may qualify for them shall be established by the demonstration board.

(5) Adequate provision for the pro rata or incremental redemption of scholarships shall be made.

(6) The contract shall provide sufficient money to pay all actual and necessary transportation costs incurred by parents in sending their children to the school of their choice within the demonstration area, subject to distance limitations imposed by existing law.

(7) The contract shall specify that the contracting federal governmental agency shall hold harmless the participating board from any possible decreased economies of scale or increased costs per pupil caused by the transition to a demonstration program.

Section 10-239e. Use of scholarships. Eligibility of schools. (a) The demonstration board shall authorize the parents or legal guardian of scholarship recipients to use the demonstration scholarships at any public or private school in which the scholarship recipient is enrolled provided such public or private school:

(1) meets all educational, fiscal, health and safety standards required by law.

(2) does not discriminate against the admission of students and the hiring of teachers on the basis of race, color or economic status and has filed a certificate with the state board of education that the school is in compliance with Title VI of the Civil Rights Act of 1964.

(3) in no case levies or requires any tuition, fee or charge above the value of the education scholarship.

(4) is free from sectarian control or influence except as provided in subsection (b) of this section.

(5) provides public access to all financial and administrative records and provides to the parent or guardian of each eligible child in the demonstration area comprehensive information in written form, on the courses of study offered, curriculum, materials and textbooks, the qualifications of teachers, administrators, and paraprofessionals, the minimum school day,

the salary schedules, financial reports of money spent per pupil and such other information as may be required by the demonstration board.

(6) provides periodic reports to the parents on the average progress of the pupils enrolled.

(7) meets any additional requirements established for all participating schools by the demonstration board.

(b) In compliance with the constitutional guarantee of free exercise of religion, schools may be exempted from subdivision (4) of subsection (a) of this section if they meet all other requirements of eligibility.

Section 10-239f. Collective bargaining by teachers. Nothing contained in Sections 10-239a to 10-239h, inclusive, shall be construed to interfere in any way with the rights of teachers of participating local or regional boards of education to organize and to bargain collectively regarding the terms and conditions of their employment. Teachers employed in the demonstration area shall be bound by the terms of such bargaining in the same way and to the same extent as if there were no demonstration area.

Section 10-277. (Reimbursement for transportation of high school pupils from towns or regional school districts not maintaining high schools. Transportation to non-public schools. Suspension of services.)

(a) For the purposes of this section, "high school" means any public high school or public junior high school approved by the state board of education.

(b) Any town or regional school district which does not maintain a high school shall pay the reasonable and necessary cost of transportation of any pupil under twenty-one years of age who resides with such pupil's parents or guardian in such school district and who, with the written consent of the board of education, attends any high school approved by the state board of education. The town or regional board of education may, upon request, enter into a written agreement with the parents of any high school pupil permitting such pupil to attend an approved public high school other than that to which transportation is furnished by the school district and each may pay such costs of transportation as may be agreed upon. Such necessary and reasonable cost of transportation shall be paid by the town treasurer or the regional school district treasurer upon order of the superintendent of schools, as authorized by the board of education. The board of education may also, at its discretion, provide additional transportation for any pupil attending such high school to and from the point of embarkation in the town in which the pupil resides. Annually, before August first, the superintendent of schools of each school district so transportating pupils to high school shall certify under oath to the state board of education the names of the high schools to which such pupils were transported and the number of pupils so transported to each school together with the total cost to the town of such transportation. Upon application to the state board of education, any town or regional school district which so provides transportation for high school pupils enrolled in a school not maintained by such district pursuant to this section shall, annually, be reimbursed by the state for such transportation in accordance with the provisions of sections 10-266 and 10-266n.

(c) Any town or regional school district which is transporting students to a high school, shall have the authority, at its discretion, to furnish similar transportation to nonpublic high schools or junior high schools located within the same town to which the town or regional school district is transporting students in accordance with subsection (b) of this section, or to nonpublic high schools or junior high schools located in a town adjacent to the transporting town or regional school district, or to a town adjacent to the town in which is located the public high school or junior high school to which the students are transported. If such town or regional school district does provide such transportation, it shall be reimbursed in the same manner and amounts as provided in subsection (b) of this section.

(d) Any town or regional school district which provides transportation services pursuant to the provisions of this section may suspend such services in accordance with the provisions of section 10-233c.

Section 10-280a. Transportation for pupils in nonprofit private schools outside school district. Any local or regional board of education may provide transportation to a student attending an elementary or secondary nonpublic school, not conducted for profit and approved by the state board of education, outside the school district wherein such student resides with a parent or guardian, provided that no grant shall be provided for any costs incurred by such board for transportation beyond a contiguous school district, and provided further that such elementary or secondary nonpublic school is located within the state of Connecticut. Any local or regional board of education which provides transportation services pursuant to this section may suspend such services in accordance with the provisions of Section 10-233c. Upon application to the state board of education, any local or regional board of education which so provides such transportation shall annually be reimbursed by the state for such pupil transportation in accordance with the provisions of Sections 23 and 24, provided the maximum amount appropriated by the state in any fiscal year, for the purposes of this section, shall not exceed one hundred fifty thousand dollars. If in any fiscal year applications for reimbursement pursuant to this section total an amount in excess of one hundred fifty thousand dollars, each local and regional board of education shall be reimbursed in an amount equal to its proportionate share of the funds appropriated for such fiscal year.

Section 10-281. Transportation for pupils in nonprofit nonpublic schools. Any municipality or school district shall provide, for its children attending nonpublic schools therein, not conducted for profit, the same kind of transportation services provided for its children attending public schools when a majority of the children attending such a nonpublic school is from the state of Connecticut. Such determination shall be made by adding the number of all pupils enrolled in each such school on October first and May first, or the full school days immediately preceding such dates, during the school year next preceding that in which the transportation services are to be provided, and dividing by two. In no case shall a municipality or school district be required to expend for transportation to any nonpublic school in any one school year, a per pupil transportation expenditure greater than an amount double the local per pupil expenditure for public school transportation during the last completed school year. In the event that such per pupil expenditure for transportation to a nonprofit nonpublic school may exceed double the local per pupil expenditure, the municipality or school district may allocate its share of said transportation on a per pupil, per school basis and may pay, at its option, its share of said transportation directly to the provider of the transportation services on a monthly basis over the period such service is provided, or provide such service for a period of time which constitutes less than the entire school year. Any such municipality or school district providing transportation services under this section may suspend such services in accordance with the provisions of section 10-233c. Any such municipality or school district providing transportation as is required by this section upon the same basis and in the same manner as such municipality or school district is reimbursed for transporting children attending its public schools. The parent or guardian of any student who is denied the kind of transportation services required to be provided by this section may seek a remedy in the same manner as is provided for parents of public school children in section 10-186 and section 10-187.

Delaware

Transportation of students of Nonpublic, Nonprofit Elementary and High Schools

Title 14. Section 2905. The State Board of Education shall make rules and regulations concerning the transportation of pupils in nonpublic, nonprofit elementary and secondary (high) schools in this state. Such rules and regulations shall provide for at least the following:

(1) All rules and regulations relative to pupil transportation to nonpublic, nonprofit schools shall be the same as those applicable to public schools;

(2) Such rules and regulations shall limit transportation of pupils in nonpublic, nonprofit schools to the elementary and secondary schools, except as provisions of the title may assign such transportation responsibility to the State Board of Education in behalf of pupils enrolled at other levels in a public school system;

(3) Pupils enrolled in nonpublic, nonprofit schools shall only be entitled to transportation within the described boundaries of a public school district and not beyond those boundaries.

Driver Education Instruction in Nonpublic High Schools

Title 14. Section 127. The State Board of Education shall make rules and regulations concerning instruction in Driver Education in nonpublic high schools. Such rules and regulations shall provide for at least the following:

(1) The qualification of teachers for Driver Education in nonpublic high schools shall be the same as the qualification for teachers in the public high schools.

(2) The ratio of teachers to pupils for assignment of Driver Education teachers in nonpublic high schools shall be based upon one teacher for each 140 tenth grade pupils enrolled in the nonpublic high school; or one-fifth of a teacher assignment for each full 28 tenth grade pupils.

(3) General supervision for the program of instruction in Driver Education in nonpublic high schools shall be under the jurisdiction of the State Board of Education or as this supervision may be assigned to a local public school district.

(4) Assignment of teachers to nonpublic high schools shall be by authority of the State Board of Education and the Board shall have the authority to require from the nonpublic high schools a statement of certified enrollment on such date and in such form as the Board may require for making the decision relative to assignment.

(5) Salary for teachers in nonpublic high schools, when paid from funds of the State of Delaware, shall be in accord with the regularly adopted salary schedule set forth in Chapter 13 of this Title.

(6) Any local salary supplement paid to Driver Education teachers assigned to nonpublic high schools may be paid by the public school district to which such teacher is assigned.

(7) For purposes of administration and supervision, the teachers of Driver Education in nonpublic high schools shall be assigned to the faculty of a public high school. The State Board of Education shall be responsible for designating such assignment. The assignment of a teacher to a public high school for purposes of driving instruction in a nonpublic high school shall be made as an assignment in addition to any assignment authorized to that public high school in accord with the unit program set forth in Chapter 17 or any other portion of this Title.

(8) Funds of the payment of the State portion of any salary due to teachers of Driver Education in nonpublic high schools shall be appropriated to a contingency fund to be administered by the Budget Director for the State of Delaware and to be paid in accord with appropriate fiscal documents presented by the public school district to which the teacher has been assigned.

(9) A teacher of Driver Education may be assigned to several nonpublic or nonpublic and public high schools in accord with the ratio for assignment as set forth in this section.

Florida

Section 299.834. Services to other than public school students.

Diagnostic and resource centers are authorized to provide testing and evaluation services to nonpublic school pupils or other children who are not enrolled in a public school.

Hawaii

Driver Education

Section 299-1. Driver education. (a) The department of education may establish and administer a motor vehicle driver education and training program to be conducted at each public high school in the state after regular school hours, on Saturdays, and during the summer recess, (b) The department shall, for the purpose of this section:

(1) Set the prerequisites and priorities for enrollment in the course of driver education and training which shall be open to every resident of the state who is fifteen years of age or older and under nineteen years of age;

(2) Establish the requirements for and employ necessary instructors, who are certified to have completed satisfactorily an approved instructor's course, to conduct the course in driver education and training;

(3) Issue a certificate of completion to every student upon satisfactory completion of the course in driver education and training;

(4) Purchase, rent, or acquire by gift materials and equipment necessary for the program established by this section; and

(5) Cooperate with the chief of police in each county in promoting traffic safety.

(c) The department may promulgate rules and regulations, in conformance with chapter 91 necessary for the purposes of this section and Section 299-1.

Vision and Hearing Screening Program

Section 321-101. (a) The department of health shall conduct, as it deems advisable, a screening program to detect vision and hearing deficiencies in school children and recommend to their parents or guardians the need for further evaluation of children who are found to have hearing or vision deficiencies, or both.

(b) The departments of health and education, in cooperation with each other may conduct classes and lectures in sight and hearing conservation and prevention of blindness and hearing loss for teachers and public health nurses and others engaged in like work. The departments may also cooperate with public and private organizations and societies in an effort to educate the public in the importance of sight and hearing conservation.

Idaho

Driver Training Courses

Section 33-1703. Eligible pupils — Time courses offered. Reimbursable programs shall be open to all residents of the state, of the ages fourteen (14) through eighteen (18) years whether or not they are enrolled in a public, private or parochial school. Residents living within any school district operating, or participating in the operation of, an authorized driver training program, shall enroll, when possible, in the training program offered in the school district of residence.

No charge or enrollment fee, not required to be paid by public school pupils for driver training, shall be required to be paid by residents not then attending public schools.

Driver training programs herein authorized may, at the discretion of the board of trustees, be conducted after school hours, or on Saturdays, or during regular school vacations.

Illinois

Transportation — Pupils attending other than a public school

Chapter 122, Section 29-4. The school board of any school district that provides any school bus or conveyance for transporting pupils to and from the public schools shall afford transportation, without cost, for children who attend any school other than a public school, who reside at least 1½ miles from the school attended, and who reside on or along the highway constituting the regular route of such public school bus or conveyance, such transportation to extend from some point on the regular route nearest or most easily accessible to their homes to and from the school attended, or to or from a point on such regular route which is nearest or most easily accessible to the school attended by such children. Nothing herein shall be construed to prevent high school districts from transporting public or non-public school children on a regular route where deemed appropriate. The elementary district in which such pupils reside shall enter into a contractual agreement with the high school district providing the service, make payments accordingly, and make claims to the State in the amount of such contractual payments. The person in charge of any school other than a public school shall certify on a form to be provided by the State Superintendent of Education, the names and addresses of pupils transported and when such pupils were in attendance at the school. If any such children reside within 1½ miles from the school attended, the school board shall afford such transportation to such children on the same basis as it provides transportation for its own pupils residing within that distance from the school attended.

Nothing herein shall be construed to preclude a school district from operating separate regular bus routes, subject to the limitations of this Section, for the benefit of children who attend any school other than a public school where the operation of such routes is safer, more economical and more efficient than if such school district were precluded from operating separate regular bus routes.

If a school district is required by this Section to afford transportation without cost for any child who is not a resident of the district, the school district providing such transportation is entitled to reimbursement from the school district in which the child resides for the cost of furnishing that transportation, including a reasonable allowance for depreciation on each vehicle so used. The school district where the child resides shall reimburse the district providing the transportation for such costs, by the 10th of each month or on such less frequent schedule as may be agreed to by the two school districts.

Community School Lunch Programs—Free Breakfast and Lunch Programs

Section 712.1. Definitions. For the purpose of this Act:

"School board" means school principal, directors, board of education and board of school inspectors of public and private schools.

"Welfare center" means an institution not otherwise receiving funds from any governmental agency, serving lunches to children of school age or under, in conformance with the authorized school lunch program.

"Free breakfast program" means those programs through which school boards may supply needy children in their respective districts with free school breakfasts.

"Free lunch program" means the program whereby certain types of lunches called balanced, nutritious lunches adopted as standard types and designated by the State Board of Education, are furnished to students.

"Comptroller" means Comptroller of the state of Illinois.

Section 712.2. Reimbursement of Sponsors. The State Board of Education is authorized to reimburse school boards, welfare centers, and other designated sponsors of school lunch programs for a portion of the costs of food served in balanced, nutritious lunches, and served to students in schools operated not for profit, in nonprofit public or parochial schools and nonprofit welfare centers. The State Board of Education shall reimburse the amount of actual cost not to exceed $0.15 to School Boards for each free lunch and $0.15 for each free breakfast supplied by them. This appropriation shall be in addition to any federal contributions for Free Lunch Programs.

Shared Time. Basis for Apportionment to Districts

Chapter 122, Section 18-8.1. (d) Pupils regularly enrolled in a public school for only a part of the school day may be counted on the basis of 1/6 day for every class hour of instruction of 40 minutes or more attended pursuant to such enrollment.

Driver Education Course

Chapter 122, Section 27-27.2. Any school district which maintains grades 9 through 12 shall offer a driver education course in any school which it operates. Both the classroom instruction part and the practice driving part of such driver education course shall be open to a resident or nonresident pupil attending a non-public school in the district wherein the course is offered and to each resident of the district who acquires or holds a currently valid driver's license during the term of the course and who is at least 15 but has not reached 21 years of age without regard to whether any such person is enrolled in any other course offered in any school that the district operates. However, a student may be allowed to commence the classroom instruction part of such driver education course prior to reaching age 15 if such student will then be eligible to complete the entire course within 12 months after being allowed to commence such classroom instruction.

Such a driver education course may include classroom instruction on the safety rules and operation of motorcycles, or motor driven cycles.

Such a course may be commenced immediately after the completion of a prior course. Teachers of such courses shall meet the certification requirements of the Act and regulations of the State Board as to qualifications.

Reimbursement Amount

Section 27-24.4. Reimbursement amount. Each school district shall be entitled to reimbursement, for each pupil who finishes either the classroom instruction part of the practice driving part of a driver education course that meets the minimum requirements of this Act. Such reimbursement is payable from the Drivers Education Fund in the State treasury.

Each year all funds appropriated from the Driver Education Fund to the State Board of Education, with the exception of those funds necessary for administrative purposes of the State Board of Education, shall be distributed to the school districts by the State Board of Education for reimbursement of claims from the previous year.

The base reimbursement amount shall be calculated by the State Board by dividing the total amount appropriated for distribution by the total of:

(a) the number of students who have completed the classroom instruction part for whom valid claims have been made times 0.2; plus (b) the number of students who have completed the practice driving instruction part for whom valid claims have been made times 0.8.

The amount of reimbursement to be distributed on each claim shall be 0.2 times the base reimbursement amount for each validly claimed student who has completed the classroom instruction part, plus 0.8 times the base reimbursement amount for each validly claimed student who has completed the practice driving instruction part. The school district which is the residence of a pupil who attends a non-public school in another district that has furnished the driver education course shall reimburse the district offering the course, the difference between the actual per capita cost of giving the course the previous school year and the amount reimbursed by the State.

By April 1 the nonpublic school shall notify the district offering the course of the names and district numbers of the nonresident students desiring to take such course the next school year. The district offering such course shall notify the district of residence of those students affected by April 15. The school district furnishing the course may claim the nonresident pupil for the purpose of making a claim for State reimbursement under this Act.

Section 22-10. Payments and grants in aid of church or sectarian purpose. No country, city, town, township, school district or other public corporation shall make any appropriation, or pay from any school fund anything in aid of any church or sectarian purpose or to support or sustain any school, academy, seminary, college, university or other literary or scientific institution controlled by any church or sectarian denomination; nor shall any grant or donation of money or other personal property be made by any such corporation to any church or for any sectarian purpose. Any officer or other person having under his charge or direction school funds or property who perverts the same in the manner forbidden in this Section shall be guilty of a Class A misdemeanor.

Indiana

Transportation

Chapter 7, Section 20-9.1. When school children who are attending any parochial school in any school corporation of this state reside on or along the highway constituting the regular route of a public school bus, the governing body of such school corporation shall provide transportation for them on the bus. This transportation shall be from their homes, or from some point on the regular route nearest or most easily accessible to their homes, to such parochial school or to and from the point on such regular route which is nearest or most easily accessible to such parochial school.

Iowa

Sharing Instructors and Services

Section 257.26. 1. The state board, when necessary to realize the purposes of this chapter, shall approve the enrollment in public schools for specified courses of students who also are enrolled in private schools, when the courses in which they seek enrollment are not available to them in their private schools, provided such students have satisfactorily completed prerequisite courses, if any, or have otherwise shown equivalent competence through testing. Courses made available to students in this manner shall be considered as compliance by the private schools in which such students are enrolled with any standards or laws requiring such private schools to offer or teach such courses.

2. The provisions of this section shall not deprive the respective boards of public school districts of any of their legal powers, statutory or otherwise, and in accepting such specially enrolled students, each of said boards shall prescribe the terms of such special enrollment, including but not limited to scheduling of such courses and the length of class periods. In addition, the board of the affected public school district shall be given notice by the state board of its decision to permit such special enrollment not later than six months prior to the opening of the affected public school district's school year, except that the board of the public school district may, in its discretion, waive such notice requirement. School districts and area education agency boards, may when available, make public school services, which may include health services, special education services, diagnostic services for speech, hearing, and psychological purposes; services for remedial education programs, guidance services, and school testing services available to children attending nonpublic schools in the same manner and to the same extent that they are provided to public school students. However, services that are made available shall be provided on neutral sites or in mobile units located off the nonpublic school premises as determined by the boards of the school district and area education agencies providing the services, and not on nonpublic school property, except health services and diagnostic services for speech, hearing, and psychological purposes which may be provided on nonpublic school premises with the permission of the lawful custodian.

Section 283A.10. The authorities in charge in nonpublic schools may operate or provide for the operation of school lunch programs in schools under their jurisdiction and may use funds appropriated to them by the general assembly, gifts, funds received from the sale of school lunches under such programs, and any other funds available to the nonpublic school. However, school lunch programs shall not be required in nonpublic schools. The department of public instruction shall direct the disbursement of state funds to nonpublic schools for school lunch programs in the same manner as state funds are disbursed to public schools.

Section 285.1 14. Resident pupils attending a nonpublic school located either within or without the school district of the pupil's residence shall be entitled to transportation on the same basis as provided for resident public school pupils under this section. The public school district providing transportation to a nonpublic school pupil shall determine the days on which bus service is provided to public school pupils which shall be based upon the days for which bus services are provided to public school pupils, and the public school district shall determine bus schedules and routes. In the case of nonpublic school pupils the term "school designated for attendance" means the nonpublic school which is designated for attendance by the parents of the nonpublic school pupil.

15. If the nonpublic school designated for attendance is located within the public school district in which the pupil is a resident, the pupil shall be transported to the nonpublic school designated for attendance as provided in this section.

16. a. If the nonpublic school designated for attendance of a pupil is located outside the boundary line of the school district of the pupil's residence, the pupil may be transported by the district of residence to a public school or other location within the district of the pupil's residence. A public school district in which a nonpublic school is located may establish school bus collection locations within its district from which nonresident nonpublic school pupils may be transported to and from a nonpublic school located in the district. If a pupil receives such transportation, the district of the pupil's residence shall be relieved of any requirement to provide transportation.

b. As an alternative to paragraph "a" of this subsection, subject to section 285.9, subsection 3, where practicable, and at the option of the public school district in which a nonpublic school pupil resides, the school district may transport a nonpublic school pupil to a nonpublic school located outside the boundary lines of the public school district if the nonpublic school is located in a school district contiguous to the school district which is transporting the nonpublic school pupils, or may contract with the contiguous public school transporting the nonpublic school pupils, or may contract with the contiguous public school district in which a nonpublic school is located for the contiguous school district to transport the nonpublic school pupils to the nonpublic school of attendance within the boundary lines of the contiguous school district.

c. If the nonpublic school designated for attendance of a pupil is located outside the boundary line of the school district of the pupil's residence and the district of residence meets the requirements of subsections 14 to 16 of this section by using subsection 17, paragraph "c," of this section and the district in which the nonpublic school is located is contiguous to the district of the pupil's residence and is willing to provide transportation under subsection 17, paragraph "a" or "b," of this section, the district in which the nonpublic school is located may provide transportation services, subject to section 285.9, subsection 3, and may make the claim for reimbursement under section 285.2. The district in which the nonpublic school is located shall notify the district of the pupil's residence and shall be relieved of the requirement for providing transportation and shall not make a claim for reimbursement for these nonpublic school pupils for which a claim is filed by the district in which the nonpublic school is located.

17. The public school district may meet the requirements of subsections 14 to 16 by any of the following:

a. Transportation in a school bus operated by a public school district.

b. Contracting with private parties as provided in section 285.5. However, contracts shall not provide payment in excess of the average per pupil transportation costs of the school district for that year.

c. Utilizing the transportation reimbursement provision of subsection 3.

d. Contracting with a contiguous public school district to transport resident nonpublic school pupils the entire distance from the nonpublic pupil's residence to the nonpublic school located in the contiguous public school district or from the boundary line of the public school district to the nonpublic school.

Textbooks

Section 301.1. Adoption-Purchase and Sale. The board of directors of each and every school district is hereby authorized and empowered to adopt textbooks for the teaching of all branches that are now or may hereafter be authorized to be taught in the public schools of the state, and to contract for and buy said books and any and all other necessary school supplies at said contract prices and to sell the same to the pupils of their respective districts at cost, loan such textbooks to such pupils free, or rent them to such pupils at such reasonable fee as the board shall fix, and said money so received shall be returned to the general fund. Textbooks adopted and purchased by a school district may, and shall to the extent funds are appropriated by the general assembly, be made available to pupils attending nonpublic schools upon request of the pupil or the pupil's parent under comparable terms as made available to pupils attending public schools.

Money for Sectarian Purposes

Section 343.8. (Repealed 1981.) Public money shall not be appropriated, given, or loaned by the corporate authorities of any county or township, to or in favor of any institution, school, association, or object which is under ecclesiastical or sectarian management or control.

Funding Media and Other Services

Section 442.27. Media services and educational services provided through the area education agencies shall be funded, to the extent provided, by an addition to the district cost of each school district, determined as follows:

1. For the budget year beginning July 1, 1975, the total amount funded in each area for media services shall be the greater of an amount equal to the costs for media services in the area in the base year times the sum of one hundred percent plus the state percent of growth, or an amount equal to five dollars times the enrollment served in the area in the budget year. The costs for media services in the area in the base year beginning July 1, 1974, shall be a proportionate part of the budget expenditures by county school systems and joint county systems formerly serving pupils in the area based upon the enrollment served in that area in the base year by each county school system and joint county system compared to the total enrollment served by that county system or joint county system.

2. For the school year beginning July 1, 1978 and each succeeding budget year through the budget year beginning July 1, 1981, the total amount funded for each area for media services excluding the cost for media resource material shall be the total amount funded in the area for media service in the base year times the sum of one hundred percent plus the state percent of growth plus the costs for media resource material for the budget year.

11. "Enrollment served" means the basic enrollment plus the number of nonpublic school pupils served with media services or educational services, as applicable, except that if a nonpublic school pupil receives services

through an area other than the area of the pupil's residence, the pupil shall be deemed to be served by the area of the pupil's residence, which shall by contractual arrangement reimburse the area through which the pupil actually receives services. For the budget year beginning July 1, 1975, the total number of nonpublic pupils served by each area education agency and the number of nonpublic school pupils residing within each school district in the area to be served by the area education agency for media and educational services shall be submitted by the department of public instruction as approved by the state board to the state comptroller within one week after this Act is duly published. For school years subsequent to the school year beginning July 1, 1979, each school district shall include in the second Friday in September enrollment report the number of nonpublic school pupils within each school district for media and educational services served by the area.

12. For the school year beginning July 1, 1978, and for each subsequent school year, if an area eduation agency does not serve nonpublic school pupils in a manner comparable to services provided public school pupils for media and eduational services, as determined by the state board of public instruction, the state board shall instruct the state comptroller to reduce the funds for media services and educational services one time by an amount to compensate for such reduced services. The media services budget shall be reduced by an amount equal to the product of the cost per pupil in basic enrollment for media services in the budget year times the difference between the enrollment served and the basic enrollment recorded for the area for the budget year beginning July 1, 1975. The educational services budget shall be reduced by an amount equal to the product of the cost per pupil in basic enrollment for educational services in the budget year times the difference between the enrollment served and the basic enrollment recorded for the budget year beginning July 1, 1975.

The provisions of this subsection shall apply only to media and educational services which cannot be diverted for religious purposes.

Notwithstanding the provisions of this subsection, an area education agency shall distribute to nonpublic schools media materials purchased wholly or partially with federal funds in a manner comparable to the distribution of such media materials to public schools as determined by the state board of public instruction.

Kansas

Hearing Testing Programs

Section 72-1204. Definitions. As used in this act and the act of which this section is amendatory: (a) "Board of education" means the board of education of any school district or the governing authority of any accredited nonpublic school.

(b) "Accredited nonpublic school" means all nonpublic elementary and secondary schools accredited by the state board of education.

(c) "School district" means any school district organized under the laws of this state.

(d) "Basic hearing screening" means a hearing testing program conducted with a calibrated audiometer.

Section 72-1205. Free tests required; when and by whom tests performed; reports to parents. (a) Every pupil enrolled in a school district or an accredited nonpublic school shall be provided basic hearing screening without charge during the first year of admission and not less than once every three years thereafter.

(b) Every pupil enrolled in a school district shall be provided basic hearing screening by the board of education of the school district in which the pupil resides and is enrolled.

(c) Every pupil in an accredited nonpublic school shall be provided basic hearing screening either (1) by the board of education of the accredited nonpublic school in which the pupil is enrolled, or (2) upon request thereof by the pupil's parent or guardian, by the board of education of the school district in which the pupil resides. No board of education of a school district shall be required to provide basic hearing screening outside the school district. If the accredited nonpublic school in which the pupil is enrolled is located within the school district, basic hearing screening shall be provided in the nonpublic school. If the accredited nonpublic school in which the pupil is enrolled is located outside the school district, basic hearing screening shall be provided in a school of the school district.

Section 72-5393. *Same, Conditions for Provision; Location; Transportation.*

Any school district which provides auxiliary school services to pupils attending its schools shall provide on an equal basis the same auxiliary school services to every pupil, whose parent or guardian makes a request therefor, residing in the school district and attending a private, nonprofit elementary or secondary school whether such school is located within or outside the school district. No school district shall be required to provide such services outside the school district. Any such school district may provide auxiliary services to all pupils attending a private nonprofit elementary or secondary school located within the school district whether or not all such pupils reside in the school district. Speech and hearing diagnostic services and diagnostic psychological services, if provided in the public schools of the school district, shall be provided in any private, nonprofit elementary or secondary school which is located in the school district. Therapeutic psychological and speech and hearing services and programs and services for exceptional children, which cannot be practically provided in any private, non-profit elementary or secondary school which is located in the school district, shall be provided in the public schools of the school district, in a public center, or in mobile units located off the private, nonprofit elementary or secondary school premises as determined by the school district; and, if so provided in the public schools of the school district or in a public center, transportation to and from such public school or public center shall be provided by the school district.

Section 72-5394. Same; provision in connection with religious activity prohibited.

No auxiliary school services shall be provided in connection with religious courses, devotional exercises, religious training, or any other religious activity.

Kentucky

Transportation

Section 158.115. Conduct of schools. Supplementation of school bus transportation system by county out of general funds. . . . Each county may furnish transportation from its general funds, and not out of funds or taxes raised or levied for educational purposes or appropriated in aid of the common schools, to supplement the present school bus transportation system for the aid and benefit of all pupils of elementary grade attending school in compliance with the compulsory school attendance laws of The Commonwealth of Kentucky who do not reside within reasonable walking distance of the school they attend and where there are no sidewalks along the highway they are compelled to travel; and any county may provide transportation from its general funds to supplement the present school bus transportation system for the aid of any pupil of any grade who does not live within reasonable walking distance of the school attended by him in compliance with the compulsory school attendance laws and where there are no sidewalks along the highway he is compelled to travel.

Section 159.030. Exemptions from compulsory attendance.

(1) The board of education of the district in which the child resides

shall exempt from the requirement of attendance upon a regular public day school every child of compulsory school age:

(a) Who is a graduate from an accredited or an approved four-year high school; or

(b) Who is enrolled and in regular attendance in a private or parochial regular day school approved by the State Board of Education; or

(c) Who is less than seven (7) years old and is enrolled and in regular attendance in a private kindergarten-nursery school with a permit issued pursuant to KRS 158:310; or

(d) Whose physical or mental condition prevents or renders inadvisable attendance at school or application to study; or

(e) Who is enrolled and in regular attendance in state approved private or parochial school programs for exceptional children; or

(f) Who is enrolled and in regular attendance in a state supported program for exceptional children.

(2) Before granting an exemption under paragraph (d) of subsection (1) of this section the board of education shall require satisfactory evidence, in the form of a signed statement of a licensed physician, psychologist, or psychiatrist, or public health officer, that the condition of the child prevents or renders inadvisable attendance at school or application to study. On the basis of such evidence the board may exempt any such child from compulsory attendance. Any child who is excused from school attendance more than six (6) months must have two (2) signed statements from a combination of the following professional persons: a licensed physician, psychologist, psychiatrist, and health officer. Exemptions of all children under the provisions of subsection (1) (d) of this section must be reviewed annually with the evidence required being updated.

(3) For any such child who is excluded under the provisions of subsection (1) (d), home, hospital, institutional or other regularly scheduled and suitable instruction meeting standards, rules and regulations of the state board for elementary and secondary education shall be provided.

Conduct of Schools

Section 158.030. Common school defined — Who may attend. A "common school" is an elementary or secondary school of the state supported in whole or in part by public taxation. No school shall be deemed a "common school" or receive support from public taxation unless the school is taught by a qualified teacher for a term of eight (8) or more months during the school year and every child residing in the district who satisfies the age requirements of this section has had the privilege of attending it. Provided, however, that any child who is six (6) years of age or who may become six (6) years of age by October 1, 1979, and any year thereafter, shall attend public school as provided by KRS 157.315 or qualify for an exemption as provided by KRS 159.030. Any child who is five (5) years of age or who may become five (5) years of age by October 1, 1979, and any year thereafter, may enter a public school kindergarten. Any child who has successfully completed kindergarten and shall be six years of age by December 31, 1980, shall be eligible for enrollment in the first grade notwithstanding any other age requirements of this section, and any child who has attended nursery school and will be five (5) years of age on or before December 31, 1980, shall be eligible for enrollment in a public kindergarten program in the 1981–82 school year and in the first grade during the 1982–83 school year.

Louisiana

Section 361. Required Reports and Records: Cost Reimbursement to Approved Nonpublic Schools.

The superintendent of education, in accordance with rules and regulations adopted by the Board of Elementary and Secondary Education, shall annually reimburse each approved nonpublic school, for each school year beginning on and after July 1979, an amount equal to the actual cost incurred by each such school during the preceding school year for providing school services, maintaining records and completing and filing reports required by law, regulation or requirement of a state department, state agency, or local school board to be rendered to the state, including but not limited to any forms, reports or records relative to school approval or evaluation, public attendance, pupil health and pupil health testing, transportation of pupils, federally funded educational programs including school lunch and breakfast programs, school textbooks and supplies, library books, pupil appraisal, pupil progress, transfer of pupils, teacher certification, teacher continuing education programs, unemployment, annual school data, and any other education-related data which are now or hereafter shall be required of such nonpublic school by law, regulation or requirement of a state department, state agency, or local school board.

Section 422.3. Adjustments in Salaries of School Lunch Employees in Nonpublic Schools.

Beginning with the school year 1972–1973, the salary increases provided for in R.S. 17:422.1 shall be granted and made applicable to all school lunch employees in nonpublic schools of the state which are receiving state and federal funds for the operation of their programs; provided, however, that this section shall not be operative unless and until state funds are appropriated for this specific purpose and provided further that no salaries of any lunchroom emeployees or any other employees of any public school system will be reduced by the adoption of this section.

Section 2990.1. Legislative Policy.

The legislature of this state, in the exercise of its policies and general welfare powers, declares the public policy of the state as follows:

WHEREAS, one out of every six children attending schools in Louisiana attends a nonpublic elementary or secondary school, with a total of more than 163,000 children being enrolled by their parents in nonpublic schools of this state and with the cost of their education being borne by their parents and other nonpublic sources; and

WHEREAS, the state and local school districts of the state are at present (1970–71) spending approximately $737.90 annually to educate each child enrolled in a public elementary or secondary school; and

WHEREAS, the general public of Louisiana saves approximately $119.1 million annually in public school operating costs alone as a result of students' attendance at nonpublic schools; and

WHEREAS, the public interest is best served through competition in educational opportunity offered by public and nonpublic schools, provided both meet the standards established for schools by the constitution and laws for the state; and

WHEREAS, parents with lower incomes are less well able to exercise their right to choose between sending their children to public or nonpublic schools solely because of their economic condition.

THEREFORE, it is declared to be in the interest of the citizens of Louisiana that nonpublic schools continue to serve the children of Louisiana, and further that lower income parents be afforded financial assistance in order that they may exercise their constitutional right to choose between public and nonpublic schools.

It is further recognized and declared that parents should not be deprived of their right to choose between public and nonpublic schools merely because of their economic condition.

It is further declared that financial assistance to lower income parents who choose to send their children to nonpublic schools will benefit the general welfare of the state of Louisiana and of public and nonpublic schools and enable those parents to exercise fundamental constitutional rights.

Section 2990.2. Definitions.

As used herein, the following terms shall have the following meanings, unless the context clearly indicates otherwise:

(1) "Child," "children," or "student" means any child or children between the ages of six and fifteen whose attendance at a public or private day school is required by Louisiana Revised Statutes 17:221 who attends a nonpublic school and all such children beyond the age of fifteen up to the age of eighteen actually enrolled in a nonpublic school as defined herein.

(2) "Parent" or "low income parent" means the parent, tutor or other person residing within the state of Louisiana having control or charge of any child herein defined whose total annual income for the previous year did not exceed $7,500.00 or, who meets the requirements of R.S. 17:2990.3 (2).

(3) "Nonpublic school" means any nonprofit elementary or secondary school within the state of Louisiana or which may hereafter be established within the state of Louisiana, offering education to the children of this state in any grades from grades one through twelve, wherein a pupil may fulfill the requirements of the Compulsory School Attendance Law and is in compliance with the Civil Rights Act of 1964.

(4) "Total annual income" means the total amount actually earned in the tax year as reflected in the federal or state income tax return. If both parents earn income, both shall be considered in determining the total.

Section 2990.3. Assistance: Tuition and Income.

Financial assistance shall be given to any lower income parent who:

(1) Has a child or children in a nonpublic school and has paid a tuition to that school for the current school year in an amount in excess of $75.00 per child in grades 1 through 8, or in excess of $100.00 per child in grades 9 through 12, and

(2) Has a total income for the previous year which does not exceed $7,500.00. Provided, that any parent whose total annual income exceeds $7,500.00 shall receive the amount specified in R.S. 17:2990.5, less any amount of tax credit given by the state of Louisiana as a consequence of his children's enrollment in a nonpublic school. Provided further, that in no event shall the financial assistance exceed the amounts stated in R.S. 17:2990.5.

Section 2990.4. Administration: Receipts and Income Tax Returns.

The superintendent of education, or a person duly appointed by him, shall administer the provisions of this chapter. Said administration shall be as simplified as is possible. Assistance shall be given upon:

(1) The parent submitting a paid receipt showing payment of tuition for the current school year to a nonpublic school in excess of $75.00 per child in grades 1 through 8, or in excess of $100.00 per child in grades 9 through 12, and

(2) a copy of the parents' previous year's state and/or federal income tax return, as the superintendent of education may determine in administering this act, showing that the requirements of R.S. 17:2990.3 (2) are met.

Maine

Transportation

Title 30. Section 5104. Schools and Libraries.

A municipality may raise or appropriate money:

1. Providing for public schools and libraries, including construction, extensions, enlargements, repairs, improvements or maintenance to buildings for which a municipality has a contract, lease or agreement with the Maine School Building Authority pursuant to Title 20, Sections 3501 to 3517.

2. Bands. Providing for school bands and other organized activities conducted under the supervision of the school committee.

3. Physical education. Providing for physical fitness programs in the schools.

4. Maintenance. Providing for the construction, repairs and maintenance of buildings and equipment for educational institutions with which a municipality has a contract as provided in Title 20, Section 1289.

5. Transportation. Providing for the transportation of school children to and from schools other than public schools, except such schools as are operated for profit in whole or in part. Historical note for 5.

A. Such sums shall not be considered in computing the net foundation program allowance on which state subsidy is computed under Title 20, Section 3722. This paragraph shall not apply to an administrative unit which transports children to a school pursuant to Title 20, Sections 1289 and 1291.

B. The superintendent of schools in each municipality that conveys such school children shall annually on or before April 1st make a return to the Commissioner of Education, showing the number of school children conveyed to and from schools other than public schools in such manner as the commissioner may require. Any municipality which fails to make the return shall be subject to Title 20, Section 854. The commissioner shall compute the school children transportation costs in the net foundation program by deducting from the total school children transportation cost that percentage that the number of school children being transported to schools other than public schools bears to the total number of school children being transported by the municipality.

C. This subsection shall not be effective in any city until a majority of the legal voters, present and voting, at any regular election so vote, and shall not be effective in any town until an article in a town warrant so providing shall have been adopted at an annual town meeting. The question in appropriate terms may be submitted to the voters at any regular city election by the municipal officers thereof and shall be so submitted upon petition of at least 20% of the number of voters voting for the gubernatorial candidates at the last state-wide election in that municipality. Such petition shall be filed with the municipal officers at least 30 days before such regular election. When a municipality has voted in favor of adopting this subsection, said subsection shall remain in effect until repealed in the same manner as provided for its adoption.

6. Textbooks. Providing for the purchase of those secular textbooks which have been approved by the school committee or board of directors for use in public schools in the municipality or district and to loan those textbooks to pupils or to the parents of pupils attending nonpublic elementary and secondary schools. The loans shall be based upon individual requests submitted by the nonpublic school pupils or parents. The requests shall be submitted to the school committee or board of directors of the administrative

district in which the student resides. The request for the loan of textbooks shall, for administrative convenience, be submitted by the nonpublic school student or parent to the nonpublic school which shall prepare and submit collective summaries of the individual requests to the school committee or board of directors. As used in this section, "textbook" means any book or book substitute which a pupil uses as a text or text substitute in a particular class or program in the school he regularly attends.

7. Physician, nursing, dental and optometric services. Providing physician, nursing, dental and optometric services to pupils attending nonpublic elementary and secondary schools within a district or municipality. These services may be provided in the school attended by the nonpublic school pupil receiving the services.

8. Tests and scoring services. Providing for the use by pupils attending nonpublic elementary and secondary schools within the municipality or a district the standardized tests and scoring services which are in use in the public schools serving that municipality or district; and

9. Advisory organizations. For obtaining the services of educational advisory organizations. The Legislature recognizes the Maine School Management Association and the Maine School Boards Association as such nonprofit advisory organizations, and declares these associations to be instrumentalities of their member school administrative units, municipal and quasi-municipal corporations, with their assets upon their dissolution to be delivered to the Secretary of State to be held in custody for the municipalities of the State. Such educational advisory organizations may receive federal grants or contributions for their activities with respect to the solution of local problems.

No municipality shall provide health or remedial services to nonpublic school pupils as authorized by this section, unless those services are available to pupils attending the public school serving the municipality.

Health and remedial services and instructional materials and equipment provided for the benefit of nonpublic school pupils pursuant to this section, and the admission of pupils to the nonpublic schools shall be provided without distinction as to race, creed, color, the national origin of the pupils or of their teachers. No instructional materials or instructional equipment shall be loaned to pupils in nonpublic schools or their parents unless similar instructional materials or instructional equipment is available for pupils in a public school served by a municipality.

No municipality shall provide services, materials or equipment for use in religious courses, devotional exercises, religious training or any other religious activity.

Maryland

Transportation

[Thirteen of the 24 school systems in Maryland have enabling legislation which allows local governments to make some public money available for the transportation of parochial school children.]

Anne Arundel County, Laws of Maryland 1963, Chapter 854.

All children who attend any parochial schools in the county, which schools do not receive state aid, and who reside on or along or near to the public highways of the county, on which there is now or hereafter operated a public school bus or conveyance provided by the board of education of the county for transporting children to and from the public schools of the county, shall be entitled to transportation on such buses or conveyances as now are or may be hereafter established, operated or provided by the board of education of the county for transporting children to and from the public schools of the county; and the same shall be provided for them by the board of education of the county, subject to the conditions hereinafter set forth, from a point on the public highways nearest to or most accessible to their respective homes to a point on the public highways nearest or most accessible to their respective schools, without changing the routes of the buses or conveyances now or hereinafter established by the board of education of the county for transporting children to and from the public schools and such transportation shall be provided by the board of education, as aforesaid, for all the children attending schools described herein, upon the same terms and conditions as now are or as may be hereafter established by the board of education of the county for children now attending public schools. Whenever there are children attending schools, which schools do not receive state aid, except such schools as are operated for profit in whole or in part, the board of education of the county shall make rules and contracts for the transportation of such children to and from such schools; provided, however, that the transportation benefits accorded children under this section shall be governed by the same rules and standards applicable to and shall be neither more nor less than the transportation benefits accorded public school students by the board of education of the county.

[Enabling legislation for the other 12 counties uses essentially the same language as the law for Anne Arundel County. The other counties and their codes follow:

Allegany County—Laws of Maryland 1933, Chapter 399

Baltimore County—Laws of Maryland 1961, Chapter 525

Calvert County—Laws of Maryland, extra session 1948, Chapter 11

Cecil County—Laws of Maryland 1957, Chapter 70

Charles County—Laws of Maryland 1947, Chapter 918, Section 241A

Hartford County—Laws of Maryland 1955, Chapter 112

Howard County—Laws of Maryland 1943, Chapter 648, Section 291A

Montgomery County—Laws of Maryland 1945, Chapter 977

Prince George's County—Laws of Maryland 1947, Chapter 910

St. Mary's County—Laws of Maryland 1941, Chapter 609, Section 202

Talbot County—Laws of Maryland 1955, Chapter 403

Washington County—Laws of Maryland 1970, Article 77, Section 146A]

Materials of Instruction

Section 7-107. Connection with closed-circuit educational television system by private and parochial schools. On application and at no expense to the county or state, each county board may allow any private or parochial school to connect its facilities to a closed-circuit educational television system that is maintained for the use of the public school system for any program presented by way of the system.

Section 7-403. Hearing and vision screening tests.

(a) County boards or health departments to provide tests. — (1) Each county board or county health department shall provide hearing and vision screening tests for all students in the public schools; (2) Each county health department shall provide and fund hearing and vision screening tests for all students; (i) In any private school that has received a certificate of approval under Section 2-206 of this article; and (ii) In any nonpublic educational facility in this state approved as a special education facility by the Department.

(b) When administered. — (1) Unless evidence is presented that a student has been tested within the past year, the tests required under subsection (1) of this section shall be given in the year a student enters a school system and when he enters the ninth grade; (2) Further testing shall be done in accordance with the bylaws adopted by the State Board.

(c) Records. — The results of the hearing and vision tests required by this section shall be: (1) Made a part of the permanent record file of each student; and (2) given to the parents of any student who fails the tests.

(d) Adoption of standards, rules, and regulations. — In cooperation with the Department of Health and Mental Hygiene, the Department of Education shall adopt standards, rules, and regulations to carry out the provisions of this section.

(e) Students excepted. — A student whose parent or guardian objects in writing to hearing and vision testing on the ground that it conflicts with the tenets and practice of a recognized church or religious denomination of which he is an adherent or member may not be required to take these tests.

Massachusetts

Chapter 71, Section 45 *Textbooks and Other Supplies to be Provided: Lending Textbooks to Private School Pupils.*

The committee, at the individual request of a pupil in a private school which has been approved under section one of chapter seventy-six, and which does not discriminate in its entrance requirements on the basis of race or color, shall lend free of charge to him textbooks which shall be the same as those purchased by the committee for use in the public schools. Such textbooks shall be loaned free to such pupils subject to such regulations as the committee may prescribe.

Chapter 71, Section 57. *Examining for Defective Sight, etc.*

The committee, or the board of health in those municipalities where school health services are the responsibility of the Board of Health, shall cause every child in the public schools, and at the individual request of a parent or guardian of a pupil in a private school which has been approved under section one, and which does not discriminate in its entrance requirements on the basis of race or color cause such pupil to be separately and carefully examined in such manner and at such intervals, including original entry, as may be determined by the department of public health after consultation with the department of education and the medical profession, to ascertain defects in sight or hearing. Postural and other physical defects tending to prevent his receiving the full benefit of this school work, or requiring a modification of the same in order to prevent injury to the child which might unfavorably influence the child's health or physical efficiency, or both, during childhood, adolescence and adult years, and shall require a physical record of each child to be kept in such forms as prescribed by the provisions of section one hundred and eighty-five A of chapter one hundred and eleven. Tests ascertaining postural defects shall be administered at least once annually in grades five through nine. Tests of sight and hearing and postural defects shall be performed by teachers, physicians, optometrists, nurses or other personnel who are approved by the department of public health for the purpose, and the examination of feet shall be made by the school physicians or podiatrists, in accordance to regulations set up by the department. Any child shall be exempt on religious grounds from these examinations upon written request of parent or guardian on condition that the laws and regulations relating to communicable diseases shall not be violated. (Amended by 1980, 111, approved April 23, 1980, effective 90 days thereafter.)

Chapter 76, Section 1. *Transportation.* Except as herein provided, pupils who attend approved private schools of elementary and high school grades shall be entitled to the same rights and privileges as to transportation to and from school as are provided by law for pupils of public schools and shall not be denied such transportation because their attendance is in a school which is conducted under religious auspices or includes religious instruction in its curriculum. Each school committee shall provide transportation for any pupil attending such an approved private school within the boundaries of the school district, provided however, that the distance between said pupil's residence and the private school said pupil attends exceeds two miles or such other minimum distance as may be established by the school committee for transportation of public school students. Any school committee which is required by law to transport any pupil attending an approved private school beyond the boundaries of the school district shall not be required to do so further than the distance from the residence of such pupil to the public school he is entitled to attend.

Section 2. Any school committee which under the provisions of this act is obligated to provide transportation services to nonpublic school pupils who were not receiving such services during the period of the nineteen hundred and eighty-three and nineteen hundred and eighty-four school year prior to the effective date of this act shall submit to the commissioner of education, as soon as possible after January first, nineteen hundred and eighty-four a proposed expenditure plan for additional transportation costs incurred during the nineteen hundred and eighty-three to nineteen hundred and eighty-four school year as a result of this act, including any supporting documentation as requested by said commissioner.

The commissioner of education shall approve the payment of state funds for the costs of such additional transportation services after said commissioner has approved such expenditure plan, and such payment shall be made forthwith and shall be deposited by the city, town or regional school district treasurer in a separate account. The school committee shall expend the funds solely for the purpose of such transportation services without further appropriations. Such funds shall also be deducted from the state aid received by the city, town, or regional school district under the provisions of sections seven A and sixteen C of chapter seventy-one of the General Laws during fiscal year nineteen hundred and eighty-five.

Section 3. The provisions of this act which affect any city, town, or regional school district which, on the effective date of this act, are not providing transportation services to non-public school pupils shall take effect on January first, nineteen hundred and eighty-four.

Section 4. Notwithstanding the provisions of said section seven A of said chapter seventy-one of the General Laws, the commonwealth shall, for fiscal year nineteen hundred and eighty-four and subject to appropriation, reimburse the costs incurred in the transportation of nonpublic school pupils whose transportation to approved private schools would not have been required but for the passage of this act; provided, however, that the amount of such reimbursement shall not exceed the average per pupil cost incurred by the city, town, or regional school district in the transportation of pupils to public schools; and, provided further, that the commissioner of education may exceed such reimbursement limit for any city or town or regional school district that demonstrates a unique and disproportionate municipal financial burden as a result of this act. The commissioner of education may, upon finding that such a unique and disproportionate financial burden exists, approve the payment of up to one hundred percent of the cost of such additional transportation services. The commissioner of education shall calculate the amount of reimbursement to which a city, town or regional school district may be entitled under the provisions of this section and shall include such amount in his calculation of transportation expenses under the provisions of section seven A and sixteen C of said chapter seventy-one of the General Laws.

Michigan

Supportive Personal Health Services

Section 14.15 (9101). Elementary and Secondary school health services plan development; contents; school nurse employment; exempt pupils.

(1) The department shall establish a plan for health services for pupils in the elementary and secondary schools of this state. The plan shall include a definition of school health services and standards for the implementation of the plan. The department shall cooperate with the department of education and the state health planning and development agency in developing the plan to ensure coordination among those agencies.

(2) The plan may include the provision of health services by and through intermediate and local school districts.

(3) The plan shall be consistent with the program of school nursing services adopted pursuant to Section 1252 of Act No. 451 of the Public Acts of 1976, being Section 380.1252 of the Michigan Compiled Laws, and shall encourage employment of individuals certified by the department of education as school nurses pursuant to that section.

(4) The plan shall not require health instructions for a pupil whose parent or guardian objects in writing and specifically requests that the pupil be excused. The plan shall not require a pupil to attend a class for which the pupil is excused pursuant to Act No. 451 of the Public Acts of 1976, as amended, being sections 380.1 to 380.1853 of the Michigan Compiled Laws.

Section 14.15 (9105). Pupil examination. Section 9105. Examinations or health services provided to school children in attendance in the elementary and secondary grades shall be provided on an equal basis to school children in attendance in both public and nonpublic schools.

Section 15.41217. Sectarian schools, restriction on application of moneys; transportation of nonpublic school pupils. Section 1217. A board of a school district shall not apply moneys received by it from any source for the support and maintenance of a school sectarian in character. This section does not prohibit the transportation to school and from school of pupils attending nonpublic schools under Sections 1321 and 1322. Transportation shall be provided on an equal basis to school children in attendance in both public and nonpublic schools.

Section 15.41217. Sectarian schools, restriction on application of moneys received by it from any source for the support and maintenance of a school sectarian in character. This section does not prohibit the transportation to school and from school of pupils attending nonpublic schools under Sections 1321 and 1322.

Section 15.41321. Transportation for pupils; provision; nonpublic schools, pupils at; provision without charge. Section 1321. (1) A board of a school district providing transportation for its resident pupils, except handicapped pupils transported under article 3, or other pupils who cannot safely walk to school, shall provide transportation for each resident pupil in the elementary and secondary grades for whom the school district is eligible to receive state school aid for transportation. These pupils shall be attending either the public or the nearest state approved nonpublic school in the school district to which the pupil is eligible to be admitted. Transportation shall be without charge to the resident pupil, the parent, guardian, or person standing in loco parentis to the pupil.

Distances and routes; nonpublic school pupils. (2) A school district shall not be required to transport or pay for transportation of a resident pupil living within 1½ miles, by the nearest traveled route, to the public or state approved nonpublic school in which the pupil is enrolled. A school district shall not be required to transport or pay for the transportation of a resident pupil attending a nonpublic school who lives in an area less that 1½ miles from a public school in which public school pupils are not transported, except that the school district shall be required to transport or pay for the transportation of the resident pupil from the public school within the area to the nonpublic school the pupil attends.

Nonpublic schools outside district. (3) A school district shall not be required to transport or pay for the transportation of resident pupils to state approved nonpublic schools located outside the district unless the school district transports some of its resident pupils, other than handicapped pupils under article 3, to public schools outside the district, in which case the school district shall transport or pay for the transportation of resident pupils attending a state approved nonpublic school at least to the distance of the public schools located outside the district to which the district transports resident pupils and in the same general direction.

Section 15.41322. Routes; rules; nonpublic school pupils, limitations on transportation. Section 1322. (1) A pupil attending public school or the nearest state approved nonpublic school available, to which nonpublic school the pupil may be admitted, shall be transported along the regular routes as determined by the board to public and state approved nonpublic schools. Transportation to public and the nearest state approved nonpublic school located within or outside the district to which nonpublic school the pupil is eligible to be admitted shall be provided under the rules promulgated by the state board. Rules shall not require the transportation or payment for transportation for nonpublic school pupils on days when public school pupils are not transported.

Construction of Section. (2) This section shall not be construed to require or permit transportation of pupils to a state approved nonpublic school attending in the elementary grades when transportation is furnished by the school district for secondary pupils only, nor to require or permit the transportation of pupils to a state approved nonpublic school attending the secondary grades when transportation is furnished by the district for elementary pupils only.

Vehicles; adequacy; capacity. (3) Vehicles used for the transportation of pupils shall be adequate and of ample capacity.

Section 15.41324. Contracting for transportation. Section 1324. The board of a school district may enter into a contract with the board of another district or with private persons to furnish transportation for nonresident pupils attending public and state approved nonpublic schools located within the district or in other districts. The price paid for the transportation shall not be less than the actual cost thereof to the district furnishing transportation.

Section 15.41296. Auxiliary services for nonpublic school pupils; state funds, use; rules of state board. Section 1296. The board of a school district that provides auxiliary services specified in this section to its resident pupils in the elementary and secondary grades shall provide the same auxiliary services on an equal basis to pupils in the elementary and secondary grades at nonpublic schools. The board may use state school aid to pay for the auxiliary services. The auxiliary services shall include health and nursing services and examinations; street crossing guards services; national defense education act testing services; teacher of speech and language services; school social work services; school psychological services; teacher consultant services for handicapped; remedial reading; and other services determined by the legislature. Auxiliary services shall be provided under rules promulgated by the state board.

Driver's Education

Section 9.2511.(3) From the money credited to the driver education fund, the legislature shall annually appropriate the sum of $100,000.00 to the department of education for state administration of the program. In addition there shall be distributed to local public school districts from the driver education fund the amount of $45.00 per student, but not to exceed the actual costs for each student completing an approved driver education course. Driver education courses by the local public school district, and enrollment in driver education courses shall be open to children enrolled in the high school grades of public, parochial, and private schools as well as resident out-of-school youth. Reimbursement to local school districts shall be made on the basis of an application made by the local school district superintendent to the department of education. (e) The department of education (may promulgate) rules, including instructional standards, teacher qualifications, reimbursement procedures, and other requirements which will further implement this legislation.

Section 15. 1927. Act construed as to distribution of primary school fund. Nothing in this act shall be construed so as to permit any parochial denominational, or private school to participate in the distribution of the primary school fund.

7.302. Refunds; assignment; sales tax deductions; payment of department of revenue; snowmobile, exclusion. Section 12. The purchaser of gasoline used for a purpose other than the operation of a motor vehicle on the public roads, streets, and highways of this state, and the state government and the federal government using gasoline in a state or federally owned motor vehicle, and a person operating a passenger vehicle of a capacity of 5 or more under a municipal franchise, license, permit, agreement, or grant, respectively, and a person operating a passenger vehicle for the transportation of school students under a certificate of public convenience and necessity issued by the Michigan public service commission pursuant to section 5 of article 2 of Act No. 254 of the Public Acts of 1933, being section 476.5 of the Michigan Compiled Laws, and a political subdivision of the state using gasoline in a vehicle owned by or leased and operated by the political subdivision for the state and community action agencies as described in title 2 of the economic opportunity act of 1964 42 usc 2781 to 2837, which are not a part or division of a political subdivision of this state, shall be entitled to a refund of the tax on the gasoline. And such community action agencies shall make the refund a state-contributed non-federal share to grants received by such community action agencies from the community services administration under title 221 of the economic opportunity act of 1964, as amended, by filing a verified claim with the revenue division of the department of treasury upon forms prescribed and to be furnished by it, within one year after the date of purchase, as shown by the invoice. A claim mailed within the one year period, as evidenced by the postmark, when received by the revenue division of the department of treasury, shall be considered as filed within the required time. An amount equal to the tax levied pursuant to section 2 shall be refunded to each person operating a passenger vehicle of a capacity of 5 or more under a municipal franchise, license, permit, agreement, or grant, respectively, and operated over regularly traveled routes expressly provided for in the municipal licenses, permits, agreement, or grants and to each person operating a passenger vehicle for the transportation of school students under a certificate of public convenience and necessity issued by the Michigan public service commission. The retail dealer shall furnish the purchaser with an invoice, showing the amount of gasoline purchased, the date of purchase, and the amount of tax on the purchase, and the dealer shall at the request of the revenue division of the department of treasury immediately supply the department with a copy of the invoice issued by the dealer during a one year period preceding the request. A claim for a refund shall have attached to the claim the original invoice received by the purchaser and when approved by the revenue division of the department of treasury shall be paid out of the Michigan transportation fund upon the warrant of the state treasurer. A claim for a refund shall not be assignable without the prior written consent of the revenue division of the department of treasury. If the verified claim of the purchaser, in form and content as prescribed by the department shall show or it shall otherwise appear that the amount of gasoline used by the purchaser for purposes on which the taxes under Act No. 167 of the Public Acts of 1933, as amended, being sections 205.51 to 205.78 of the Michigan Compiled Laws, are deductible pursuant to section 4a of Act No. 167 of the Public Acts of 1933, as amended, being section 205.54a of the Michigan Compiled Laws is not the total amount included in the statement of the transferee. ... The purchaser of gasoline used for the operation of a snowmobile as defined and regulated by Act No. 74 shall not be entitled to a refund under this section.

Minnesota

Transportation of School Children

Section 123.76. Policy

In districts where the state provides aids for transportation it is in the public interest to provide equality of treatment in transporting school children of the state who are required to attend elementary and secondary schools pursuant to Minnesota Statutes, Chapter 120, so that the health, welfare and safety of such children, while using the public highways of the state, shall be protected. School children attending any schools, complying with Minnesota Statutes, Section 120.10, Subdivision 2, are therefore entitled to the same rights and privileges relating to transportation.

Section 123.77. Definitions

Subdivision 1. The following words and terms in Sections 123.76 to 123.79 shall have the following meanings ascribed to them.

Subdivision 2. "District" means any school as defined in Minnesota Statutes, or unorganized territory as defined in Minnesota Statutes, Section 120.02.

Subdivision 3. "School" means any school as defined in Minnesota Statutes, Section 120.10, Subdivision 2.

Subdivision 4. "School Board" means the governing body of any school district or unorganized territory.

Subdivision 5. "School children" means any student or child attending or required to attend any school as provided in the Education Code, Minnesota Statutes, Chapters 120–129.

Section 123.78. Equal Treatment

Subdivision 1. General provisions. A district eligible to receive state aid for transportation under chapter 124, shall provide equal transportation within the district for all school children to any school when transportation is deemed necessary by the school board because of distance or traffic condition in like manner and form as provided in sections 123.39 and 124.223, when applicable.

Subdivision 1a. (a) The school board of any local district shall provide school bus transportation to the district boundary for school children residing in the district at least the same distance from a nonpublic school within the transportation district, if the transportation is to schools maintaining grades or departments not maintained in the district or if the attendance of such children at school can more safely, economically, or conveniently be provided for by such means.

(b) The school board of any local district may provide school bus transportation to a nonpublic school in another district for school children residing in the district or if the children attend that school, whether or not there is another nonpublic school within the transporting distance, if the transportation is to schools maintaining grades or departments not maintained in the district or if the attendance of such children at school can more safely, economically, or conveniently be provided for by such means. If the board transports children to a nonpublic school located in another district, the nonpublic school shall pay the cost of such transportation provided outside the district boundaries.

Subdivision 2. When transportation is provided, the scheduling of routes, manner and method of transportation, control and discipline of school children and any other matter relating thereto shall be within the sole discretion, control and management of the school board.

Section 123.79. Funds and aids

Subdivision 1. Such state aids as may become available or appropriated shall be governed by Minnesota Statutes, Section 124.225, be paid to the school district entitled thereto for the equal benefit of all school children, and disbursed in such manner as determined by the board.

Subdivision 2. The board of any district may expend any monies in its treasury, whether received from state or any other source for the purpose of providing equal transportation treatment of all school children attending school.

Section 124.17. Definition of pupil units

Subdivision 1. Pupil units for each resident pupil in average daily membership shall be counted as follows;

(1) In an elementary school: (a) For each handicapped prekindergarten pupil and each handicapped kindergarten pupil, as defined in section 120.03, enrolled in a program approved by the commissioner, a number of pupil units equal to the ratio of the number of hours of education services required in the school year by the pupil's individual education program plan, developed pursuant to the rules of the state board to 875, but not more than one pupil unit; (b) For kindergarten pupils, other than those in clause (a), enrolled in one-half day sessions throughout the school year or the equivalent thereof, one-half pupil unit; and (c) For other elementary pupils one pupil unit.

Subdivision 2. Average daily membership. Membership for pupils in grades kindergarten through twelve and for handicapped prekindergarten pupils shall mean the number of pupils on the current roll of the school, counted from the date of entry until withdrawal. The date of withdrawal shall mean the day the pupil permanently leaves the school or the date it is officially known that the pupil has left or has been legally excused. However, a pupil, regardless of age, who has been absent from school for fifteen consecutive school days during the regular school year or for five consecutive school days during summer school or intersession classes of flexible school year programs without receiving instruction in the home or hospital shall be dropped from the roll and classified as withdrawn. Nothing in this section shall be construed as waiving the compulsory attendance provisions cited in section 120.10. Average daily membership shall equal the sum for all pupils of the number of days of the school year each pupil is enrolled in the district's schools divided by the number of days the schools are in session. Days of summer school or intersession classes of flexible school year programs shall only be included in the computation of membership for handicapped pupils appropriately served at levels 4, 5, and 6 of the continuum of placement model described in 5 MCAR 1.0120 B 11.

Subdivision 2a. Nothwithstanding subdivision 2, pupils granted transitional year status shall continue to be counted as members on the current roll of the school for the remainder of the school year. For purposes of computing average daily membership transitional year pupils shall be considered to be enrolled every day school is in session for the remainder of the school year.

Subdivision 2b. Notwithstanding subdivision 2, pupils enrolled in the Minnesota National Guard program shall be construed to be in attendance for purposes of computing average daily membership during any period of the regular school year, but not to include summer school, during which the pupil is attending military active duty training pursuant to that program. During that period of military active duty training, the pupil shall earn all aid for the district of residence or attendance which would be otherwise earned by his presence.

Subdivision 2c. Notwithstanding the provisions of subdivision 2, in any case where school is in session but pupils are prevented from attending for more than 15 consecutive days because of epidemic, calamity, weather, fuel shortage, or other justifiable cause, the state board, upon application, may allow the district to continue to count these pupils in average daily membership. A lawful employees' strike is not a justifiable cause for purposes of this subdivision.

Subdivision 2d. In summer school or intersession classes of flexible school year programs, membership for pupils shall mean the number of fulltime equivalent pupils in the program. This number shall equal the sum for all pupils of the number of classroom hours in the programs for which each pupil is enrolled divided by 1050. Membership in summer school or intersession classes of flexible school year programs shall not include a handicapped pupil whose district of residence has been determined by section 120.17 subdivision 8a, and who is temporarily placed in a state institution or a licensed residential facility for care and treatment.

Subdivision 3. In computing pupil units for a prior year, the number of pupil units shall be adjusted to reflect any change for the current year in relative weightings by grade level or category of special assistance, any change in measurement from average daily attendance to average daily membership and any change in school district boundaries, but not for the addition for the first time in the current year of a specified category of special assistance as provided in subdivision 1, clause (4).

Driver Education

Section 171.04. Persons not eligible for driver's licenses. The Department shall not issue a driver's license hereunder:

(1) To any person who is under the age of 16 years; to any person under 18 years unless such person shall have successfully completed a course in driver education, including both classroom and behind-the-wheel instruction, approved by the department of public safety or, in the case of a course offered by a private, commercial driver education school or institute employing driver education instructor, by the department of public safety, except when such person has completed a course of driver education in another state or has a previously issued valid license from another state or country; nor to any person under 18 years unless the application of license is approved by either parent when both reside in the same household as the minor applicant, otherwise the parent having custody or with whom the minor is living in the event there is no court order for custody, or guardian having the custody of such minor, or in the event a person under the age of 18 has no living father, mother or guardian, the license shall not be issued to such person unless his application therefor is approved by his employer. Driver education courses offered in any public school shall be open for enrollment to persons between the ages of 15 and 18 years residing in the school district or attending school therein. Any public school offering driver education courses may charge an enrollment fee for the driver education course which shall not exceed the actual cost thereof to the public school and the school district. The approval required herein shall contain a verification of the age of the applicant;

(2) To any person whose license has been suspended during the period of suspension except that a suspended license may be reinstated during the

period of suspension upon the licensee furnishing proof of financial responsibility in the same manner as provided in the Minnesota No Fault Automobile Insurance Act;

(3) To any person whose license has been revoked except upon furnishing proof of financial responsibility in the same manner as provided in the safety responsibility act and if otherwise qualified;

(4) To any person who is a drug dependent person as defined in section 254-A.02, Subdivision 5.

(5) To any person who has been adjudged legally incompetent by reason of mental illness, mental deficiency, or inebriation, and has not been restored to capacity, unless the department is satisfied that such person is competent to operate a motor vehicle with safety to persons or property;

(6) To any person who is required by this chapter to take an examination, unless such person shall have successfully passed such examination;

(7) To any person who is required under the provisions of the Minnesota No Fault Automobile Insurance Act of this state to deposit proof of financial responsibility and who has not deposited such proof;

(8) To any person when the commissioner has good cause to believe that the operation of a motor vehicle on the highways by such person would be inimical to public safety or welfare;

(9) To any person when, in the opinion of the commissioner, such person is afflicted with or suffering from such physical or mental disability or disease as will affect such person in a manner to prevent him from exercising reasonable and ordinary control over a motor vehicle while operating the same upon the highways; nor to a person who is unable to read and understand official signs regulating, warning and directing traffic.

Educational aids for nonpublic school children

123.931 Declaration of policy. It is the intent of the legislature to provide for distribution of educational aids such as textbooks, standardized tests and pupil support services so that every school pupil in the state will share equitably in education benefits and therefore further assure all Minnesota pupils and their parents freedom of choice in education.

123.932 Definitions

Subdivision 1. Repealed by laws 1978, c. 733,26, effective April 6, 1978.

Subdivision 1a. As used in sections 123.931 to 123.937, the terms defined in this section shall have the meanings ascribed to them.

Subdivision 1b. "Textbook" means any book or book substitute which a pupil uses as a text or text substitute in a particular class or program in the school he regularly attends and a copy of which is expected to be available for the individual use of each pupil in this class or program, which book or book substitute or text or text substitute shall be limited to books, workbooks, or annuals, whether bound or in looseleaf form, intended for use as a principal source of study material for a given class or a group of students. The term includes only such secular, neutral and nonideological textbooks as are available and are of benefit to Minnesota public school pupils.

Subdivision 1c. "Standardized tests" means standardized tests and scoring services which are provided by commercial publishing organizations and which are in use in the public schools of Minnesota to measure the progress of pupils in secular subjects.

Subdivision 1d. "Pupil support services" means guidance and a counseling service and health services.

Subdivision 1e. "Individualized instructional materials" means educational materials which: (a) are designed primarily for individual pupil use in a particular class or program in the school the pupil regularly attends;

(b) Are secular, neutral, nonideological and not capable of diversion for religious use; and

(c) Are available and are of benefit to Minnesota public school pupils.

Subject to the requirements in clauses (a), (b), and (c), "Individualized instructional materials" include the following if they do not fall within the definition of "textbook" in subdivision 1b: published materials; periodicals; documents; pamphlets; photographs; reproduction; pictorial or graphic work; filmstrips; prepared slides; prerecorded video programs; prerecorded tapes, cassettes and other sound recordings; manipulative materials; desk charts; games, study prints and pictures; and desk maps; models; learning kits; blocks or cubes; flash cards; individualized multimedia systems; prepared instructional computer software programs; and prerecorded film cartridges.

"Individualized instructional materials" do not include the following: chemicals; wall maps; wall charts; pencils, pens, or crayons; notebooks; blackboards; chalk and erasers; duplicating fluids; paper; 16mm films; unexposed films; blank tapes, cassettes or videotape; and instructional equipment.

Subdivision 2. (Repealed by Laws 1978, c. 733 26 effective July 1, 1978.)

Subdivision 2a. "Pupils" means elementary and secondary students.

Subdivision 2b. "Elementary Pupils" means pupils in grades kindergarten through six; provided, each kindergarten pupil shall be counted as one-half pupil for all computations pursuant to sections 123.931 to 123.937.

Subdivision 2c. "Secondary pupils" means pupils in grades seven through twelve.

Subdivision 3. "Nonpublic school" means any school within the state other than a public school, wherein a resident to Minnesota may legally fulfill the compulsory school attendance requirements of Section 120.10, and which meets the requirements of Title VI of the Civil Rights Act of 1964 (Public Law 88-352).

Subdivision 3a. "Nonsectarian nonpublic school" means any nonpublic school as defined in subdivision 3 which is not church related, is not controlled by a church, and does not promote a religious belief.

Subdivision 4. "School" means any public or nonpublic school within the state wherein children receive educational services and materials provided for or recognized by the state, or children of residents of Minnesota.

Subdivision 5. "Pupil" or "student" means a child enrolled in a school and is limited to children who are residents, or children of residents of Minnesota.

Subdivision 6. (Repealed by Laws 1978, c. 733 26.)

Subdivision 7. "Intermediary service area" means a school administrative unit approved by the state board of education, other than a single school district, including but not limited to the following: (a) an educational cooperative service unit; (b) a cooperative of two or more school districts; (c) learning centers; or (d) an association of schools or school districts.

Subdivision 8. (Repealed by Laws 1978, c. 733 26.)

Subdivision 9. "Neutral site" means a public center, a nonsectarian nonpublic school, a mobile unit located off the nonpublic school premises, or any other location off the nonpublic school premises which is neither physically nor educationally identified with the functions of the nonpublic school.

Subdivision 10. "Guidance and counseling services" means all activities of a licensed counselor in counseling pupils and parents, providing counseling on learning problems, evaluating the abilities of pupils, assisting pupils in personal and social development and providing referral assistance.

Subdivision 11. "Health services" means physician, dental, nursing or optometric services provided to pupils in the field of physical or mental health; provided the term does not include direct educational instruction, services which are required pursuant to section 120.17, or services which are eligible to receive special education aid pursuant to section 124.32.

123.933. Purchase or loan of textbooks, individualized instructional materials, standardized tests.

Subdivision 1. The state board of education shall promulgate rules under the provisions of chapter 14 requiring that in each school year, based upon formal requests by or on behalf of nonpublic school pupils in a non-public school, the local districts or intermediary service areas shall purchase or otherwise acquire textbooks, individualized instructional materials and standardized tests and loan or provide them for use by children enrolled in the nonpublic school. These textbooks, individualized instructional materials and standardized tests shall be loaned or provided free to the children for the school year for which requested. The loan or provision of the textbooks, individualized instructional materials and standardized tests shall be subject to rules prescribed by the state board of education.

Subdivision 2. The title to textbooks, individualized instructional materials and standardized testing materials shall remain in the servicing school district or intermediary service area and possession or custody must be granted or charged to administration of the nonpublic school attended by the nonpublic school pupil or pupils to whom the textbooks, individualized instructional materials or standardized tests are loaned or provided.

Subdivision 3. (a) The cost per pupil of the textbooks, individualized instructional materials and standardized tests provided for in this section for each school year shall not exceed the state-wide average expenditure per pupil, adjusted pursuant to clause (b), by the Minnesota public elementary and secondary schools for textbooks, individualized instructional materials and standardized tests as computed and established by the department of education by March 1 of the preceding school year from the most recent public school year data then available.

(b) The cost computed in clause (a) shall be increased by an inflation adjustment equal to the percent of increase in the foundation aid formula allowance, pursuant to section 124.2122, subdivision 1, from the second preceding school year to the current school year.

(c) The commissioner shall allot to the school districts or intermediary service areas the total cost for each school year of providing or loaning the textbooks, individualized instructional materials and standardized tests for the pupils in each nonpublic school. The allotment shall not exceed the product of the statewide average expenditures per pupil. Adjusted pursuant to clause (b) multiplied by the number of nonpublic school pupils who make requests pursuant to this section and who are enrolled as of September 15 of the current school year.

(d) For the 1982–83 school year, 85 per cent of a district's nonpublic pupil aid shall be distributed prior to December 31 of that school year. The final aid distribution to each district shall be made prior to December 31 of the following school year.

123.935. Provisions of pupil support services

Subdivision 1. The state board of education shall promulgate rules under the provisions of chapter 14 requiring each school district or other intermediary service area; (a) to provide each year upon formal request by a specific date by or on behalf of a nonpublic school pupil enrolled in a nonpublic school located in that district or area, the same specific health services as are provided for public school pupils by the district where the nonpublic school is located; and (b) to provide each year upon formal request by a specific date by or on behalf of a nonpublic school secondary pupil enrolled in a nonpublic school located in that district or area, the same specific guidance and counseling services as are provided for public school secondary pupils by the district where the nonpublic school is located. The district where the nonpublic school is located shall provide the necessary transportation within the district boundaries between the nonpublic school and a public school or neutral site for nonpublic school pupils who are provided pupil support services pursuant to this section. Each request for pupil support services shall set forth the guidance and counseling or health services requested by or on behalf of all eligible nonpublic school pupils enrolled in a given nonpublic school. No district or intermediary service area shall expend an amount for these pupil support services which exceeds the amount allotted to it under this section.

Subdivision 2. Health services may be provided to nonpublic school pupils pursuant to this section at a public school. A neutral site, the nonpublic school or any other suitable location. Guidance and counseling services may be provided to nonpublic school pupils pursuant to this section only at a public school or a neutral site. District or intermediary service area personnel and representatives of the nonpublic school pupils receiving pupil support services shall hold an annual consultation regarding the location of the provision of these services. The district board or intermediary service area governing board shall make the final decision on the location of the provision of these services.

Subdivision 3. Guidance and counseling services provided to nonpublic school pupils pursuant to this section shall not include the planning or selection of particular courses or classroom activities of the nonpublic school.

Subdivision 4. Each school year the commissioner shall allot to the school districts of other intermediary service areas for the provision of health services pursuant to this section the actual cost of the services provided for the pupils in each respective nonpublic school for actual cost of the services provided for the pupils in each respective nonpublic school for that school year, but not to exceed the average expenditure per public school pupil for these services by those Minnesota public elementary and secondary schools which provide health services to public school pupils, multiplied by the number of pupils in that particular nonpublic school who request these health services and who are enrolled as of September 15 of the current school year.

Subdivision 5. Each school year the commissioner shall allot to the school districts or intermediary service areas for the provision of guidance and counseling services pursuant to this section the actual cost of the services provided for the pupils in each respective nonpublic school for that school year. The allotment for guidance and counseling services for the secondary pupils in each nonpublic school shall not exceed the average expenditure per public school secondary pupil for these services by those Minnesota public schools which provide these services to their secondary pupils, multiplied by the number of secondary pupils in that particular nonpublic school who request these services and who are enrolled as of September 15 of the current school year.

Subdivision 6. For purposes of computing maximum allotments for each school year pursuant to this section, the average public school expenditure per pupil for health services and the average public school expenditure per secondary pupil for guidance and counseling services shall be computed and established by the department of education by March 1 of the preceding school year from the most recent public school year data then available.

123.936. Payments for contractual obligations

In every event the commissioner shall make such payments to school districts or intermediary service areas pursuant to sections 123.931 to 123.937 as are needed to meet contractual obligations incurred for the provision of benefits to nonpublic school students pursuant to sections 123.933 or 123.935.

Mississippi

Student Loans

Section 37-51-1. Legislative Declaration. It is hereby determined and declared that the state reaffirms its commitment and dedication to public school education; that nothing contained in this chapter shall be administered in any manner whatever to be an abandonment or impairment of public school education in this state; that the state calls upon all public school trustees, administrators, teachers, parents, and the public at large to continue full support of the public school system of this state; and that, especially during these difficult times, all school officials, administrators, teachers, and others with primary responsibility for the public school system merit and need continued support and encouragement in their efforts.

Section 37-51-3. State educational finance commission shall administer chapter. The terms and provisions of this chapter shall be administered and executed by the state educational finance commission. For the purpose of this chapter, the term "commission" shall mean "state educational finance commission" except where the context clearly indicates otherwise.

Section 37-51-5. State educational loan fund created. There shall be, and there is hereby created in the state treasury, a special fund to be known as the "state educational loan fund." The said fund shall consist of such amounts as may be paid into said fund by appropriation and also such amounts as may be returned to said fund as repayments, both principal and interest from loans provided in this chapter.

Section 37-51-7. Duties and authority of the commission. It shall be the duty of the commission to receive and pass upon, allow or disallow, all applications for loans made by students who desire to receive a secular education in any of the grades one through twelve in any school in this state constituting a bona fide school as defined in a general regulation of commission, other than in the free public school system of this state, and who are acceptable for enrollment in any approved nonfree school system. The commission may make such investigation into the financial status of the parents of such students who apply for loans as it deems advisable, to determine the extent of the need for said loan. The commission may prescribe such rules and regulations as it may deem necessary and proper to carry out the purposes of this chapter.

The commission shall have the authority to grant loans from the "state educational loan fund" to such applicants as are qualified to receive them and on such terms as may be prescribed by regulation of the commission and by this chapter.

Section 37-51-9. "Secular education of children" defined. The "secular education of children" as used in this chapter shall mean the education of children in those subjects, and only those subjects, which are required to be taught by state law to the same extent as those subjects are taught in the public schools of the state or which are provided in public schools throughout the state; it shall not include the education of children in any course in religion or any course expressing religious teaching or the morals or forms of worship of any sect.

Section 37-51-11. Eligibility of applicants. In addition to the requirements set out in section 37-51-7, to be eligible for a loan an applicant must:

(a) Be a bona fide actual resident of the State of Mississippi; and

(b) Attend any bona fide approved nonfree elementary or secondary school.

Section 37-51-13. Applications for loans; transfers. An applicant shall not have to submit but one initial application for a loan; thereafter, he or she shall file a request for each additional year's loan amount up to the maximum amount allowed. Accompanying each said request shall be a certification from the school which applicant is attending certifying that the applicant is in attendance and in good standing.

Each application by or on behalf of said student shall be signed by and made also in the name of the parent or legal guardian of said student if he or she be a minor. However, the parent or legal guardian shall not be considered the applicant for the purposes of the limitations in section 37-51-15.

In the event that the applicant transfers to another approved school within the state, he shall cause the certification to immediately go forth to the commission, setting out the school from which and to which he has transferred.

Section 37-51-15. Limitations on amounts of loans. Applicants who are granted loans may receive a loan in any amount, not exceeding two thousand four hundred dollars ($2,400.00) to any one applicant. Said amount is to be paid in annual, semiannual or quarterly installments not exceeding two hundred dollars ($200.00) per school year, and shall be used to defray part of the applicant's tuition and other costs of attending said schools. The loans herein provided shall not exceed the limitations set out above, but they may be for any such lesser amounts as may be required.

Section 37-51-17. Contract agreeing to terms and conditions of loans; suits thereon. Each applicant, if an adult, or his parent or legal guardian in his behalf, if a minor, before being granted a loan shall enter into a contract with the State of Mississippi agreeing to the terms and conditions upon which the loan shall be made. Said contract shall include such terms and conditions as are necessary to carry out the full purpose and intent of this chapter. The form of said contract shall be prepared and approved by the attorney general of this state, and said contract shall be signed by the executive secretary of the commission.

The commission is hereby vested with full and complete authority to sue in its own name any applicant for any balance due the state on any such contract. Such suit shall be filed and conducted by the attorney general of the State of Mississippi, or by private counsel, which the commission is hereby authorized to employ for such purpose.

Section 37-51-19. Repayment of Loans. Any loans made or granted to any applicant shall be made and based upon the following conditions of repayment:

(a) Repayment in full of the principal of the loan may be made at any time prior to three years after graduation from or termination of attendance in an approved school, plus simple interest at the rate of three percent per annum from the date of each payment made to applicant.

(b) Repayment of the principal of the loan after three years from the date of graduation from or termination of attendance in an approved school shall be with interest at the rate of four percent per annum from the date of each payment made to applicant. From and after the fourth year following graduation or termination of attendance in an approved school, the rate of interest to be paid on the remaining unpaid balance, after such fourth year, shall increase at the rate of one-half percent per annum to a maximum of eight percent.

(c) No applicant shall be entitled to more than twelve years after said graduation or termination of attendance in an approved school within which to repay said loan.

Section 37-51-21. Credit on loans. The amount of any loan made or granted to any applicant shall be reduced by a credit at the rate of one hundred dollars ($100.00) per annum for each year that applicant continues his education at any junior college, college or university within the State of Mississippi after his graduation or termination from secondary school.

In addition, the amount of said loan shall be reduced by a credit at the rate of two hundred dollars ($200.00) per annum for each year that applicant resides within the state and teaches in any school system therein, beginning from the date of his certification or licensing by the state department of education to teach in any such system.

Driver Education and Training

Section 37-25-3. Establishing and maintaining driver education and training program. The school board of any school district maintaining a secondary school which includes any of the grades nine through twelve inclusive, may, in its discretion, establish and maintain driver education and training programs for pupils enrolled in the day secondary schools in that district.

Section 37-25-7. Pupil eligibility; temporary permits. Each school district providing driver training and education shall prescribe regulations determining who can best profit by and who shall receive instruction under this program. It is provided, however, that any student receiving instruction under this chapter shall be:

(a) Fourteen years of age or above;
(b) A regularly enrolled student in the ninth, tenth, eleventh or twelfth grades; and
(c) A full-time student in the respective secondary school.

A temporary permit issued by the Mississippi Highway Safety Patrol shall be issued and valid only while such a student is actually enrolled in an approved course of driver education which consists of thirty hours of classroom and six hours of dual driving instruction. Said temporary permit shall expire at the end of the driver training course.

Financial Assistance

Section 37-23-63. Eligibility to receive state financial assistance. Every child who is a resident citizen of the State of Mississippi under twenty-one (21) years of age, who cannot pursue all regular class work due to reasons of defective hearing, vision, speech, mental retardation, or other mental or physical conditions as determined by competent medical authorities and psychologists, who has not finished or graduated from high school, and who is in attendance in a private school or parochial school, or speech, hearing and/or language clinic shall be eligible and entitled to receive state financial assistance in the amount set forth in section 37-23-69.

Section 37-23-69. Determination and payment of financial assistance. The state department of education shall have the power to determine and pay the amount of the financial assistance to be made available to each applicant, and to see that all applicants and the programs for them meet the requirements of the program for exceptional children. No financial assistance shall exceed the obligation actually incurred by the applicant for tuition and fees. Within the amount of available state funds appropriated for such purpose, each such applicant may receive assistance according to the following allowances: 37-23-69

(a) If the applicant chooses to attend an accredited school, an accredited parochial school, or a speech, hearing and/or language clinic meeting criteria established by the state department of education, having an appropriate program for the applicant, and if the school or clinic meets federal and state regulations, then the tuition reimbursement will be one hundred percent (100%) of the first six hundred dollars ($600.00) in tuition charged by the school or clinic; or if the applicant is under six (6) years of age, and no program appropriate for the child exists in the public schools of his domicile, then the reimbursement shall be one hundred percent (100%) of the first six hundred dollars ($600.00) in tuition charged by the school or clinic; and

(b) If the applicant in the age range six (6) through twenty (20) requests the public school district where he resides to provide an education for him and the nature of the applicant's educational problem is such that, according to best educational practices, it cannot be met in the public school district where the child resides; if the public school district decides to provide the applicant a free appropriate education by placing him in an accredited private, an accredited parochial school or a speech, hearing and/or language clinic meeting criteria established by the state board of education having an appropriate program for the applicant and if the program meets federal and state regulations, then the public school district shall be reimbursed for the educational costs of the applicant up to a maximum of three thousand dollars ($3000.00). Nothing in these statements shall prevent two (2) or more public school districts from forming a cooperative to meet the needs of low incidence exceptional children, nor shall the public school be relieved of its responsibility to provide an education for all children. The state department of education may also provide for the payment of such financial assistance in installments and for proration of such financial assistance in the case of children attending school or clinic for less than a full school session and, in the event that available funds are insufficient, may allocate the available funds among the qualified applicants and local school districts by reducing the maximum assistance provided for herein.

Any moneys provided an applicant under sections 37-23-61 through 37-23-75 shall be applied by the receiving educational institution as a reduction in the amount of the tuition paid by said applicant, and the total tuition paid by said applicant shall not exceed the total tuition paid by any other child in similar circumstances in the same program in said institution. Provided, however, this limitation shall not be construed to prohibit the waiving of all or part of the tuition for a limited number of children based upon demonstrated financial need, and the state department of education shall have the power and authority to adopt and enforce reasonable rules and regulations to carry out the intent of these provisions.

Missouri

School lunch program—funds—duties of state board

Section 167-201. 1. The provisions of the National School Lunch Act as amended (60 US Stat. at large 230; 42 U.S.C.A. 1751 to 1760) are accepted, and the funds provided thereby shall be accepted for disbursement.

2. All funds under the provisions of the act shall be deposited in the state treasury to the credit of the fund to be known as the "School Lunch Fund" which is hereby established.

3. The state board of education is designated as the state educational agency, as provided in the act, and is charged with the duty and responsibility of cooperating with the Secretary of Agriculture in the administration of the act and is delegated all power necessary to such cooperation.

Montana

Transportation

20-10-123. Provision of transportation for nonpublic school children.

Any child attending a nonpublic school may ride a school bus when a permit to ride such school bus is secured from the operating district by the parent or guardian of such nonpublic school child and when there is seating capacity available on such school bus. When a nonpublic school child rides a school bus, the operating district shall charge such child his proportionate share as determined by the trustees, of the cost of operating said school bus. Money realized from such payments shall be deposited to the credit of the transportation fund.

Nebraska

79-487. Pupils; public or private schools; transportation, buses; conditions; purchase; use; State Department of Education; Duties.

The school board or board of education of any public school district may, when authorized by a majority vote of the members of such board, purchase out of the general fund of the district a school bus or buses for the purpose of providing transportation facilities for school children to and from school and to and from all school related activities. The school board or board of education of any public school district providing such transportation facilities for children attending public schools shall also provide transportation without cost for children who attend nonprofit private schools which are approved for continued legal operation under rules and regulations established by the State Board of Education pursuant to subdivision (5) (c) of section 79-328. Such transportation shall be provided for only such children attending nonprofit private school students, and such transportation shall extend only from some point of the regular public school route nearest or most easily accessible to their homes to and from a point on the regular public school route nearest or most easily accessible to the school or schools attended by such children. The governing body of such nonprofit private school, on a form to be provided by the State Department of Education, shall certify to the public school district the names, addresses, and days of school attendance of children transported and such other information useful in operating the transportation facility as may be required by rules established by the State Board of Education. Transportation shall be provided for nonprofit private school children only at times when transportation is being provided for public school children.

The school board or board of education of any public school district may enter into a contract with a municipality or county pursuant to section 19.3908

Nevada

333.490 Procurement and distribution of federal surplus property to eligible institutions and organizations; creation of surplus property administration fund.

1. The chief shall do all things necessary to secure, warehouse and distribute throughout the state federal donable surplus property to tax supported or nonprofit schools and other health and educational institutions, to organizations for emergency management, to volunteer fire departments,

and to such other institutions or activities as may be eligible under federal law to acquire such property. The chief may make such certifications, take such actions and enter into such contracts and undertakings for and in the name of the state as may be authorized or required by federal law or regulations in connection with the receipt, warehousing and distribution of federal donable surplus property received by him. He may adopt regulations, prescribe requirements, and take action as he deems necessary to assure maximum utilization by and benefit to eligible institutions and organizations from the federal donable surplus property. He shall make a charge to the schools and institutions receiving donable surplus property secured through the purchasing division, the charge to be a percentage of the cost of acquisition or of the fair value of the item requested sufficient to repay in portion or in entirety the cost of transportation and other costs incurred in acquisition of the property.

2. All money received by the chief pursuant to this section must be deposited in the state treasury for credit to the surplus property administration fund, which is hereby created as a special revenue fund. All expenses for the distribution of federal surplus property must be paid from the fund as other claims against the state are paid.

3. The chief may discontinue temporarily or terminate entirely the operation of purchasing and distribution donable surplus property at any time when there is not a sufficient flow of property to make continued employment of personnel for this purpose beneficial to the state.

Programs of Nutrition for Children

387.075 Federal money: Acceptance; disbursement.

1. The state board of education may accept and adopt regulations or establish policies for the disbursement of money appropriated by any Act of Congress and apportioned to the State of Nevada for use in connection with programs of nutrition for children.

2. The superintendent of public instruction shall deposit with the state treasurer all money received from the federal government or from other sources for programs of nutrition for children.

New Hampshire

Program of Special Education

1860A:7 Establishment of Programs.

A school district shall establish programs for handicapped children as approved by the State Board of Education, or shall pay tuition to such an approved program maintained by another school district or by a private organization. Eligibility for this type of education shall be determined by the school board under regulations promulgated by the State Board of Education.

198:20-a. Payment of governmental moneys prohibited in nonpublic school without program approval by the Board of Education for handicapped children.

No state moneys or moneys raised and appropriated by the state or any political subdivision thereof shall be paid or granted to a nonpublic school for the education and training of handicapped children as defined by RSA 186-A:2, IV which has not been approved by the state board of education pursuant to those policies adopted under the provisions thereof.

Health and Other Services Child Benefit Services

Section 189:49. Optional Services. The school board of any school district may provide the following child benefit services for pupils in each public and nonpublic school in the district, or in another school district in this state:

   I. School physician services under the provisions of RSA 200:26-41.
   II. School nurse services.
   III. School health services.
   IV. School guidance and psychologist services.
   V. Educational testing services.
   VI. Transportation under the provisions of RSA 189:9.
   VII. Textbooks and instructional materials.
   VIII. Health and welfare services equivalent to those provided by public school including speech correction and remedial and diagnostic services.
   IX. Driver Education.
   X. Educational television services.
   XI. Programs for the deaf, blind, emotionally disturbed, crippled, and physically handicapped children; audio-visual aids; and programs for the improvement of the educational studies of pupils with handicaps.
   XII. Physical education.
   XIII. Hot lunch program.

In the event that a court rules in invalid one or more of the above services the other services shall not be deemed void but shall continue in effect.

Transportation

Section 189:9. Pupils in private schools, pupils attending approved private schools, up to and including the twelfth grade shall be entitled to the same transportation privileges within any town or district as are provided for pupils in public schools.

Shared-time

Section 193.1-a. Dual enrollment.

Notwithstanding any other provision of the law, the full-time attendance requirement may be met by attendance at more than one school provided the total time spent in the school is equivalent to full-time attendance and further that the attendance at more than one school may include attendance at a nonpublic school provided that the school district and the state board of education have given prior approval to the detailed dual enrollment agreement, which is to be effectuated for this purpose.

Child Benefit Service Grants

198:22 Grants

I. Any school district which is providing any child benefit service pursuant to the authority of RSA 189:49 and 50 shall be granted the following proportion of the costs, exclusive of any part of the cost and carrying charges of any capital improvements of providing such service to any student who regularly attends a nonpublic school within the district for more than ½ each school day:

(a) Not more than 70 percent of such cost of any such service.

II. Application for any such grant shall be submitted by a district to the state board of education no later than the July first preceding the start of the school year for which it shall be applicable, provided that the board may, for good cause shown, accept any such application up to but no later than the start of the applicable school year. Payment of said grant shall be made upon submission of certified expenses prior to the end of the applicable fiscal year.

III. The board shall determine what costs shall be allowed in computing and the amount of any grant, and shall make payments of such grants from the funds appropriated therefor.

IV. In the event that for any year insufficient sums are available to pay grants in full as provided by this section to all qualified applying school districts the state board of education shall prorate such grants so that all such districts receive the same proportion thereof.

V. No pupil counted by any school for the purpose of calculating the amount of a grant to be paid pursuant to this section shall for the same school year by the same district be included in average daily membership for the purposes of funding aid or counted for the purposes of grants pursuant to RSA 198:21.

198:21 Grants

I. Any school district which has in operation an approved dual enrollment agreement under the provisions of RSA 193:1-a shall be granted for the first school year that such agreement is in operation the full operation costs of implementing such agreement, exclusive of any part of the cost and carrying charges of any capital improvements; and for the next succeeding school year, if such operation is then continued, ½ of such costs.

II. Application for any such grant shall be submitted by a district to the state board of education no later than the July first preceding the start of the school year for which it shall be applicable, provided that the board may, for good cause shown, accept any such application up to but no later than the start of the applicable school year.

III. The board shall determine what costs shall be allowed in computing the amount of any grant, and shall make payments of such grants from the funds appropriated therefor.

IV. In the event that for any year insufficient sums are available to pay grants in full as provided by this section to all qualified applying school districts the state board of education shall prorate such grants so that all such districts receive the same proportion.

V. No pupil counted by any school district for the purpose of calculating the amount of a grant to be paid pursuant to this section shall for the same school year by the same district be included in average daily membership for the purposes of foundation aid or counted for the purposes of grants pursuant to RSA 198:22.

New Jersey

Transportation to and from Schools

Section 18A:39-1. Transportation of pupils remote from schools.

Whenever in any district there are pupils residing remote from any schoolhouse, the board of education of the district may make rules and contracts for the transportation of school pupils to and from school other than a public school, except such school as is operated for profit in whole or in part.

When any school district provides any transportation for public school pupils to and from school pursuant to this section, transportation shall be supplied to school pupils residing in such school district in going to and from any remote school other than a public school, not operated for profit in whole or in part, located within the state not more than 20 miles from the residence of the pupil provided the per pupil cost of the lowest bid received does not exceed $325.00, and if such bid shall exceed said cost then the parent, guardian or other person having legal custody of the pupil shall be eligible to receive said amount toward the cost of his transportation to a qualified school other than a public school, regardless of whether such transportation is along established public school routes. It shall be the obligation of the parent, guardian or other person having legal custody of the pupil attending a remote school, other than a public school, not operating for profit in whole or in part, to register said pupil with the office of the secretary of the board of education at the time and in the manner specified by rules and regulations of the state board in order to be eligible for the transportation provided by this section. If the registration of any such pupil is not completed by September 1 of the school year and if it is necessary for the board of education to enter into a contract establishing a new route in order to provide such transportation then the board shall not be required to provide it, but in lieu thereof the parent, guardian or other person having legal custody of the pupil shall be eligible to receive $325.00 or an amount computed by multiplying 1/80 times the number of school days remaining in the school year at the time of registration times $325.00 whichever is the smaller amount. Whenever any regional school district provides any transportation for pupils attending school other than public schools pursuant to this section, said regional district shall assume responsibility for the transportation of all such pupils, and the cost of such transportation for pupils below the grade level for which the regional district was organized shall be prorated by the regional district among the constituent districts on a per pupil basis after approval of such costs by the county superintendent. This section shall not require school districts to provide any transportation to pupils attending a school other than a public school where the only transportation presently provided by said district is for school children transported pursuant to chapter 46 of this Title or for pupils transported to vocational, technical or other public school offering a specialized program. Any transportation to a school, other than a public school, shall be pursuant to the same rules and regulations promulgated by the state board as governs transportation to any public school.

Nothing in this section shall be so construed as to prohibit a board of education from making contracts for the transportation of pupils to a school in an adjoining district when such pupils are transferred to the district by order of the county superintendent, or when any pupils shall attend school in a district other than that in which they shall reside by virtue of an agreement made by the respective boards of education.

Nothing herein contained shall limit or diminish in any way any of the provisions for transportation for children pursuant to chapter 46 of this Title.

Legislative Findings and Determination

18A:46A-1. The legislature hereby finds and determines that the welfare of the State requires that present and future generations of school age children be assured opportunity to develop to the fullest their intellectual capacities. It is the intent of the legislature to insure that the State shall furnish on an equal basis auxiliary services to all pupils in the state in both public and nonpublic schools.

18A:46A-2. Definitions as used in this act:

(a) "Commissioner" means the State Commissioner of Education.

(b) "Nonpublic school" means an elementary or secondary school within the state, other than a public school, offering education for grades kindergarten through 12, or any combination of them, wherein any child may legally fulfill compulsory school attendance requirements and which complies with the requirements of Title VI of the Civil Rights Act of 1964. (P.L. 88-352.)

(c) "Auxiliary services" means compensatory education services; supportive services for acquiring communication proficiency in the English language for children of limited English-speaking ability; supplementary instruction services; and home instruction services.

(d) "Support limit" means the maximum amount which may be appropriated each year for the purposes of this act for each pupil enrolled in nonpublic schools of the state.

18A:46A-3. Nonpublic schools; receipt of auxiliary services by resident pupils. In the 1977–78 school year, and each school year thereafter, each board of education shall provide for the receipt of auxiliary services by children between the ages of 5 and 20 residing in the district and enrolled in the nonpublic schools of the state. For the purposes of this act, a child who boards at a school in a district in which his parents do not maintain a residence shall not be considered a resident of the district.

18A:46A-4. Eligibility Standard. Auxiliary services shall be provided only to those children who would be eligible for such services and for the appropriate categorical program support if they were enrolled in the public schools of the state.

18A:46A-5. Consent of parent or guardian; location. Auxiliary services shall be provided only upon the consent of the parent or guardian and shall be provided in a location determined by the local board of education, except that no such services shall be provided in a church or a sectarian school.

18A:46A-6. Transportation to location to obtain services; payment of cost. If the provision of services pursuant to this act requires transportation, the board of education shall provide for such transportation, and the cost shall be paid from state aid received by the district pursuant to this act.

18A:46A-7. Contracts for provision of auxiliary services. Any board of education may contract with an educational improvement center, an educational service commission or other public or private agency, other than a church or sectarian school, approved by the commissioner for the provision of auxiliary services.

18A:46A-8. Limitation on expenditures for administration of act and rental of facilities. No more than 6% of such aid shall be used to rent facilities needed to implement the provision of this act.

18A:46A-9. State aid: apportionment. The apportionment of State aid among local school districts shall be calculated by the commissioner as follows: a. The statewide average cost of providing the equivalent service to children enrolled in the public schools, shall be determined.

b. The appropriate average cost shall then be multiplied by the number of pupils enrolled in the nonpublic schools who are expected to receive each auxiliary service, to obtain each district's State aid for the next school year.

18A:46A-10. Annual reports by boards of education. Annually, by October 5, each board of education shall file with the commissioner a report stating the number of pupils residing in the district and enrolled in the nonpublic schools of the state on the last day of September. By October 5, 1978, and each October 5 thereafter, each board shall also file a report on the number of such pupils expected to receive each auxiliary service during the next school year.

The commissioner shall then determine the maximum appropriation for the next school year for the purposes of this act by multiplying the support limit for the next school year times the pupil enrollment in the nonpublic schools of the state on the last school day in September of the current school year.

18A:46A-11. Support Limit; determination. Annually, by November 1, the commissioner shall determine the support limit for the next school year by multiplying the support limit for the current school year times the percentage increase in the State average net current school year times the percentage increase in the State average net current expense budget per pupil in the most recent year available, and adding the product to the support limit for the current school year. The commissioner shall then determine the maximum appropriation for the next school year times the pupil enrollment in the nonpublic schools of the State on the last school day in September of the current school year.

18A:46A-12. Notification of amount of aid apportioned to each district; inclusion in budget. By November 1, 1978 and by each November 1 thereafter, the commissioner shall notify each district of the amount of aid apportioned to it pursuant to this act for the next school year and each district shall include such amount in its budget for the next school year.

18A:46A-13. Payment of state aid. In the 1978–79 school year and each year thereafter, aid pursuant to this act shall be payable in equal amounts beginning on the first day of September and on the first day of each month during the remainder of the school year.

18A:46A-14. Expenditure less than state aid; reduction of state aid. In the event the expenditure incurred by any district is less than the amount of state aid received, the district's state aid shall be reduced accordingly during the second year following the receipt of such aid.

18A:46A-15. Expenditures in excess of state aid. In any year, no district shall be required to make expenditures for the purposes of this act in excess of the amount of state aid received pursuant to this act for that year.

18A:46A-16. Insufficient appropriations; apportionment of appropriations. If in any year the amount of state aid appropriated is insufficient to carry out in full the provisions of this act, the commissioner shall apportion such appropriation among the districts in proportion to the state aid in each district that would have been apportioned had the full amount of state aid been appropriated.

18A:46A-17. Severability. If any provision of this act or the application of such provision to any person or circumstance is declared invalid, such invalidity shall not affect other provisions of this act which may be given effect to this end; the provisions of this act are declared to be severable.

18A:58-7.1. School lunch program. Each school district or nonprofit nonpublic school participating in the National School Lunch Program shall be reimbursed for each type A lunch as defined within an approved contract with the Department of Education at a rate not to exceed the maximum amount permissible under federal regulations for the general cash-for-food assistance phase of the program. Whenever the federal funds available to the Department of Education are less than the maximum amount permissible under federal regulations, the state may provide, within the limitations of available state funds, an amount which, when added to the federal funds, will equal the maximum amount permissible under federal regulations for the general cash-for-food assistance phase of the program.

18A:58-7.1A. Nonprofit nonpublic school defined. As used in this act "nonprofit nonpublic school" means an elementary or secondary school in this state, other than a public school, organized and operated not for profit, offering education for grades kindergarten through 12, or any combination thereof, wherein a child may legally fulfill compulsory school attendance requirements and which complies with the requirements of Title VI of the Federal Civil Rights Act. (P.L. 88-352.)

18A:58-7.2. School lunch program; additional state aid. Each school district or nonprofit nonpublic school participating in the special assistance phase of the National School Lunch Program as defined within an approved contract with the Department of Education shall be paid an additional state reimbursement for each Type A lunch served free or at a reduced price. Such rate of additional state reimbursement per lunch shall not exceed 50% of the total rate of reimbursement per each such Type A lunch served free or at a reduced price payable from federal funds.

18A:58-37.4. Textbooks loaned to students in nonpublic schools; free rental; length of use of designated textbook.

a. Textbooks which are loaned to students enrolled in grades kindergarten through 12 of any nonpublic school shall be textbooks which are used in any public elementary or secondary school of the state or are approved by any board of education. Such textbooks are to be loaned without charge to such children subject to such rules and regulations as are, or may be adopted by the commissioner and such board of education.

b. When a textbook has been designated for use in a school district such textbook shall not be superseded by any other book, prior to the expiration of 5 years following such designation, except upon the authorization of the board of education.

18A:58-37.5. Appropriations to districts for payment for textbooks; limitations. The commissioner shall, upon request of the local board and pursuant to the rules and regulations of the State Board of Education distribute to each school district an amount equal to the cost of textbooks purchased and loaned by the school district pursuant to this act, but in no event shall the aid appropriated to the district exceed the following amount:

A. The expenditures for the purchase of textbooks pursuant to this act made during the school year 1979–80 shall not exceed an average $10.00 for each student residing in the district, who on September 30 of the preceding school year was enrolled in grades kindergarten through 12 of a public or nonpublic school; and,

B. The expenditures for the purchase of textbooks made during the school year 1980–81, and in any subsequent year shall not exceed the state average budgeted textbook expense per public school pupil for the prebudget year for each student residing in the district, who on September 30 of the preceding school year was enrolled in grades kindergarten through 12 of a public or nonpublic school.

18A:58-37.6. Public school education act of 1975, expenditures for textbooks. State aid provided pursuant to the public School Education Act of 1975 may be expended for the purchase and loan of textbooks for public school pupils in an amount which shall not exceed the state average budgeted textbook expense for the prebudget year per pupil in resident enrollment. Nothing contained herein shall prohibit a board of education in any district from purchasing textbooks in excess of the amounts provided pursuant to this act.

Classes and Facilities for Handicapped Children. Types of facilities and programs.

Section 18A:46-13. Facilities to be furnished. It shall be the duty of each board of education to provide suitable facilities and programs of education for all the children who are classified as handicapped under this chapter except those so mentally retarded as to be eligible for day training pursuant to NJS 18A:46-9. The absence or unavailability of a special class facility in any district shall not be construed as relieving a board of education of the responsibility for providing education for any child who qualifies under this chapter.

A board of education is not required to provide any further educational program for children who have been admitted to the Marie H. Katzenbach School for the Deaf but shall be required to furnish necessary daily transportation Monday through Friday to and from the school for nonboarding pupils when such transportation is approved by the county superintendent of schools in accordance with such rules and regulations as the state board shall promulgate for such transportation. Any special education facility or program authorized and provided for a child attaining age 20 during a school year shall be continued for the remainder of that school year.

18A:46-14. Enumeration of facilities and programs. The facilities and programs of education required under this chapter shall be provided by one or more of the following:

a. A special class or classes in the district, including a class or classes in hospitals, convalescent homes, or other institutions;

b. A special class in the public schools of another district in this state or any other state in the United States;

c. Joint facilities including a class or classes in hospitals, convalescent homes or other institutions to be provided by agreement between one or more school districts;

d. A jointure commission program;

e. A State of New Jersey operated program;

f. Instruction at school supplementary to the other programs in the school, whenever, in the judgment of the board of education with the consent of the commissioner, the handicapped pupil will be best served thereby.

New Mexico

22-15-7. Students eligible; distribution

A. Any qualified student or person eligible to become a qualified student attending a public school, a state institution or a private school approved by the state board in any grade from first through the twelfth grade of instruction is entitled to the free use of instructional material. Any student enrolled in an early childhood education program as defined by Section 22-13-3 NMSA 1978 or person eligible to become an early childhood education student as defined by Section 22-13-3 NMSA 1978 attending a private early childhood education program approved by the state board is entitled to the free use of instructional material. Any student in an adult basic education program approved by the state board is entitled to the free use of instructional material.

B. Instructional material shall be distributed to school districts, state institutions, private schools and adult basic education centers as agents for the benefit of students entitled to the free use of the instructional material.

C. Any school district, state institution, private school or adult basic education center as agent receiving instructional material pursuant to the Instructional Material Law 22-15-1 to 22-15-14 NMSA is responsible for distribution of the instructional material for use of eligible students and for the safekeeping of the instructional material.

22-15-15. Instructional Material Fund.

A. The state treasurer shall establish a fund to be known as the "Instructional Material Fund."

B. The Instructional Material Fund shall be used for the purpose of paying for the cost of purchasing instructional material pursuant to the Instructional Material Law 22-15-1 to 22-15-14 NMSA 1978. Transportation charges for the delivery of instructional material to a school district, state institution, a private school or an Adult Basic Education center as agent and emerging expenses incurred in providing instructional material to students may be included as a cost of purchasing instructional material.

22-13-8. Special education; private.

A. The responsibility of school districts, institutions and the state, to provide a free public education for exceptional children is not diminished by availability of private schools and services. Whenever such schools or services are utilized, it continues to be a state responsibility to assure that all exceptional children receive the education to which the laws of the state entitle them.

B. A local school board may make an agreement with nonsectarian, nonprofit educational training centers for educating exceptional children and for providing for payment for such education. All financial agreements between local boards and nonsectarian, nonprofit educational training centers must be negotiated in accordance with regulations promulgated by the chief director of public school finance. Payment for education and services under such agreements shall be made by the local board of education from funds available.

C. All agreements between local school boards and nonsectarian, non-profit educational training centers must be approved by the state super-intendent. All agreements must provide for diagnosis and an educational program for each child which meets state standards for such programs. The agreements must also acknowledge the authority and responsibility of the local board and the department of education to conduct on-site evaluations of programs and pupil progress to ensure meeting state standards.

D. Exceptional children attending a nonsectarian, nonprofit training center shall be counted in the special education membership of the school district as enrolled in the Class D special education program.

New York

Health and welfare services to all children

Section 912. The voters and/or trustees or board of education of every school district shall, upon request of the authorities of a school other than public, provide resident children who attend such school with any or all of the health and welfare services and facilities which are made available by such voters and/or trustees or board of education to or for children attending the public schools of the district. Such services may include, but are not limited to all services performed by a physician, dentist, dental hygienist, nurse, school psychologist, school social worker, or school speech correc-tionist, and may also include dental prophylaxis, vision and hearing tests, the taking of medical histories and the administration of health screening tests, the maintenance of cumulative health records and the administration of emergency care programs for ill or injured pupils. Any such services or facilities shall be so provided notwithstanding any provision of any charter or other provision of law inconsistent herewith. Where children residing in one district attend a school other than public located in another school district, the school authorities of the district of residence shall contract with the school authorities of the district where such nonpublic school is located, for the provision of such health and welfare services and facilities to such children by the school district where such nonpublic school is located, for a consideration to be agreed upon between the school authorities of such districts, subject to the approval of the qualified voters of the district of residence when required under the provisions of this chapter. Every such contract shall be in writing and in the form prescribed by the commissioner of education, and before such contract is executed the same shall be submitted for approval to the superintendent of schools having jurisdiction over such district of residence and such contract shall not become effective until approved by such superintendent.

Transportation

Section 3635. Transportation. 1. Sufficient transportation facilities (including the operation and maintenance of motor vehicles) shall be provided by the school district for all the children residing within the school district to and from the school they legally attend, who are in need of such transportation because of the remoteness of the school to the child or for the promotion of the best interest of such children. Such transportation shall be provided for all children attending grades kindergarten through eight who live more than two miles from the school which they legally attend and for all children attending grades nine through twelve who live more than three miles from the school which they legally attend and shall be provided for each such child up to a distance of fifteen miles, the distance in each case being measured by the nearest available route from home to school. The cost of providing such transportation between two or three miles, and as the case may be, and fifteen miles shall be considered for the purposes of this chapter to be a charge upon the district and an ordinary contingent expense of the district. Transportation for a lesser distance than two miles in the case of children attending grades kindergarten through eight or three miles in the case of children attending grades nine through twelve and for a greater distance than fifteen miles may be provided by the district, and, if provided, shall be offered equally to all children in like circumstances residing in the district. School districts providing transportation to a nonpublic school for pupils living within a specified distance from such school shall designate one or more schools as centralized pick-up points and shall provide transportation between such points and such nonpublic schools for students residing in the district who live too far from such nonpublic schools to qualify for transportation between home and school. The district shall not be responsible for the provision of transportation for pupils between their home and such pick-up points. The cost of providing transportation between such pick-up points and such nonpublic schools shall be an ordinary contingent expense. The foregoing provisions of this subdivision shall not require transportation to be provided for children residing within a city school district, but if provided by such district pursuant to other provisions of this chapter, such transportation shall be offered equally to all such children in like circumstances. City school districts with a population of more than two hundred twenty-five thousand and less than three hundred thousand which elect to provide transportation shall do so in accord with the grade and distance provisions of this subdivision including transportation outside the city limits. Nothing contained in this subdivision, however, shall be deemed to require a school district to furnish transportation to a child directly to or from his home.

2. A parent or guardian of a child residing in any school district, or any representative authorized by such parent or guardian, who desires for a child during the next school year any transportation authorized or directed by this chapter shall submit a written request therefore to the school trustees or board of education of such district not later than the first day of April preceding the next shool year, provided, however, that a parent or guardian of a child not residing in the district on such date shall submit a written request within thirty days after establishing residence in the district. No late request of a parent or guardian for transportation shall be denied where a reasonable explanation is provided for the delay. If the voters, school trustees, or board of education fail to provide the transportation authorized or directed by this chapter after receiving such a request, such parent, guardian or representative, or any taxpayer residing in the district, may appeal to the commissioner of education, as provided in section three hundred ten of this chapter. Except as hereinbefore provided, the commissioner of education shall not require that such parent, guardian, or representative present a request for such transportation to any meeting of the voters, school trustees or board of education in order to appeal. Upon such appeal, the commissioner of education shall make such order as is required to effect compliance with the provisions of this chapter and this section.

3. Every contract for transportation of school children shall be in writing, and before such contract is executed the same shall be submitted for approval to the superintendent of schools having jurisdiction over said district and such contract shall not become effective until approved by such superintendent who shall first investigate the same with particular reference to the type of conveyance, the character and ability of the driver, the routes over which the conveyance shall travel, the time schedule, and such other matters as in the judgment of the superintendent are necessary for the comfort and protection of the children while being transported to and from school. Every such contract for transportation of children shall contain an agreement upon the part of the contractor that the vehicle shall come to a full stop before crossing the track or tracks of any railroad and before crossing any state highway. A copy of such contract duly certified by the trustee or trustees or clerk of the board of education of the district and approved by the superintendent shall be filed with the education department within thirty days after its execution.

4. No transportation quota or other public moneys shall be apportioned and paid as provided in this chapter to any district furnishing transportation

for pupils until the contract for transportation shall also have been approved by the commissioner of education. In defraying any expense incurred in providing transportation of any pupils or children under any provision of this chapter, public moneys apportioned to the district in which such pupils or children reside may be used therefore.

5. For the purpose of affording the greatest possible protection to school children, drive-off places on public highways may be designated by the appropriate board of education or district superintendent to permit school buses to be driven off the highway to receive or discharge school children, and the state or municipality having jurisdiction of such highway, is authorized to provide construction and maintenance of such designated drive-offs.

Article 15 — Textbooks

Section 701. Power to designate textbooks; purchase and loan of textbooks; purchase of supplies.

(4) No school district shall be required to purchase or otherwise acquire textbooks, the cost of which shall exceed an amount equal to fifteen dollars plus a minimum lottery grant determined pursuant to subdivision four of section ninety-two-c of the state finance law multiplied by the number of children residing in such district and so enrolled on the first day of October of any school year; and no school district shall be required to loan textbooks in excess of the textbooks owned or acquired by such district; provided, however that all textbooks owned or acquired by such district and so enrolled in grades kindergarten through twelve in public and private schools on an equitable basis.

Section 3601. Secular Educational Services — 1974.

Section 1. Legislative findings. The legislature hereby finds and declares that:

The state has the responsibility to provide educational opportunity of a quality which will prepare its citizens for the challenges of American life in the last decades of the twentieth century.

To fulfill this responsibility, the state has the duty and authority to evaluate, through a system of uniform state testing and reporting procedures, the quality and effectiveness of instruction to assure that those who are attending instruction, as required by law, are being adequately educated within their individual capabilities.

In public schools these fundamental objectives are accomplished in part through state financial assistance to local school districts.

More than seven hundred thousand pupils in the state comply with the compulsory education law by attending nonpublic schools. It is a matter of state duty and concern that such nonpublic schools be reimbursed for the actual costs which they incur in providing services to the state which they are required by law to render in connection with the state's responsibility for reporting, testing and evaluating.

Section 2. Definitions.

1. "Commissioner" shall mean the state commissioner of education.

2. "Qualifying school" shall mean a nonprofit school in the state, other than a public school, which provides instruction in accordance with section thirty-two hundred four of the education law.

Section 3. Apportionment. The commissioner shall annually apportion to each qualifying school, for school years beginning on and after July first, nineteen hundred seventy-four, an amount equal to the actual cost incurred by each such school during the preceding school year for providing services required by law to be rendered to the state in compliance with the requirements of the state's pupil evaluation program, the basic educational data system, regents examinations, the statewide evaluation plan, the uniform procedure for pupil attendance reporting, and other similar state prepared examinations and reporting procedures.

Section 4. Application. Each school which seeks an apportionment pursuant to this act shall submit to the commissioner an application therefor, together with such additional reports and documents as the commissioner may require, at such times, in such form and containing such information as the commissioner may prescribe by regulation in order to carry out the purposes of this act.

Section 5. Maintenance of records. Each school which seeks an apportionment pursuant to this act shall maintain a separate account or system of accounts for the expenses incurred in rendering the services required by the state to be performed in connection with the reporting, testing and evaluation programs enumerated in section three of this act. Such records and accounts shall contain such information and be maintained in accordance with regulations issued by the commissioner, but for expenditures made in the school year nineteen hundred seventy-three–seventy-four, the application for reimbursement made in nineteen hundred seventy-four pursuant to section four of this act shall be supported by such reports and documents as the commissioner shall require. In promulgating such record and account regulations and in requiring supportive documents with respect to expenditures incurred in the school year nineteen hundred seventy-three–seventy-four, the commissioner shall facilitate the audit procedures described in section seven of this act. The records and accounts for each school year shall be preserved at the school until the completion of such audit procedures.

Section 6. Payment. No payment to a qualifying school shall be made until the commissioner has approved the application submitted pursuant to section four of this act.

Section 7. Audit. No application for financial assistance under this act shall be approved except upon audit of vouchers or other documents by the commissioner as are necessary to insure that such payment is lawful and proper.

The state department of audit and control shall from time to time examine any and all necessary accounts and records of a qualifying school to which an apportionment has been made pursuant to this act for the purpose of determining the cost to such school of rendering the services referred to in section three of this act. If after such audit it is determined that any qualifying school has received funds in excess of the actual cost of providing the services enumerated in section three of this act, such school shall immediately reimburse the state in such excess amount.

Section 8. Noncorporate entities. Apportionments made for the benefit of any school which is not a corporate entity shall be paid, on behalf of such school, to such corporate entity as may be designated for such purpose of receiving apportionments made for the benefit of such school pursuant to this act.

Section 9. In enacting this chapter (adding this note) it is the intention of the legislature that if section seven or any other provision of this act or any rules or regulations promulgated thereunder shall be held by any court to be invalid in whole or in part or inapplicable to any person or situation, all remaining provisions or parts thereof or remaining rules and regulations or parts thereof not so invalidated shall nevertheless remain fully effective as if the invalidated portion had not been enacted or promulgated, and the application of any such invalidated portion to other persons not similarly situated or other situations shall not be affected thereby.

Section 10. This act shall take effect July first, nineteen hundred seventy-four.

North Carolina

Section 115C-140.1. Cost of Education of Children in Group Homes, Foster Homes, etc.

(a) Notwithstanding the provisions of any other statute and without regard for the place of domicile of a parent or guardian, the cost of a free appropriate public education for a child with special needs who is placed in or assigned to a group home, foster home or other similar facility, pursuant to State and federal law, shall be borne by the local board of education in which the group home, foster home or other similar facility is located. Nothing in this section obligates any local board of education to bear any cost for the care and maintenance of a child with special needs in a group home, foster home or other similar facility.

(b) The State Board of Education shall use State and federal funds appropriated for children with special needs to establish a reserve fund to reimburse local boards of education for the education costs of children assigned to group homes or other facilities as provided in subsection (a) of this section.

Section 115C-250. Authority to Expend Funds for Transportation of Children with Special Needs.

(a) The State Board of Education and local boards of education may expend public funds for transportation of children with special needs who have been placed in programs by a local school board as a part of its duty to provide such children with a free appropriate education, including its duty under G.S. 115C-115.

The Department of Human Resources and the Department of Correction may also expend public funds for transportation of children with special needs who have been placed in programs by one of these agencies as a part of that agency's duty to provide such children with a free appropriate public education.

If a local area mental health center places a child with special needs in an educational program, the local area mental health center shall pay for the transportation of the child to the program.

(b) Funds appropriated for the transportation of children with special needs may be used to pay transportation safety assistants employed in accordance with the provisions of G.S. 115C-245 (e) for buses to which children with special needs are assigned.

Section 115C-551. Voluntary Participation in the State Programs.

Any such school (nonpublic schools) may, on a voluntary basis, participate in any State operated or sponsored program which would otherwise be available to such school, including but not limited to the high school competency testing and statewide testing programs.

Section 115C-559. Voluntary Participation in the State Programs.

Any such school (qualified nonpublic schools) may, on a voluntary basis, participate in any State operated or sponsored program which would otherwise be available to such school, including but not limited to the high school competency testing and statewide testing programs.

North Dakota

Transportation of nonpublic elementary and high school students— Conditions.

Section 15-34. 2-16. When authorized by the school board of a public school district providing transportation for public elementary and high school students, elementary and high school students attending nonpublic schools may be transported on public school buses to and from the point or points on established public school bus routes on such days and during the times that the public school buses normally operates. The school board of a public school district may authorize and agree to the transportation of such students only when there is passenger room available on such buses, according to the legal passenger capacity for such buses, when such buses are scheduled according to this section; provided however, no payments shall be made from state funds for any mileage costs for any deviation from the established public routes which may be caused by any agreement entered into pursuant to this section.

Ohio

Transportation of Pupils

Section 3327.01. In all city, exempted village, and local school districts where resident elementary school pupils live more than two miles from the school for which the state board of education prescribes minimum standards pursuant to division (d) of section 3301.07 of the Revised Code and to which they are assigned by the board of education of the district of residence or to and from the nonpublic school which they attend the board of education shall provide transportation for such pupils to and from such school except when, in the judgment of such board, confirmed by the state board of education, such transportation is unnecessary or unreasonable.

In all city, exempted village, and local school districts the board may provide transportation for resident high school pupils to and from the high school to which they are assigned by the board of education of the district of residence or to and from the nonpublic high school which they attend for which the state board of education prescribes minimum standards pursuant to division (d) of section 3301.07 of the Revised Code.

In determining the necessity for transportation, availability of facilities and distance to the school shall be considered.

A board of education shall not be required to transport elementary or high school pupils to and from a nonpublic school where such transportation would require more than thirty minutes of direct travel time as measured by school bus from the collection point as designated by the coordinator of school transportation, appointed under section 3327.011 (33 27.01.1) of the Revised Code, for the attendance area of the district of residence.

Where it is impractical to transport a pupil by school conveyance, a board of eduction may, in lieu of providing such transportation, pay a parent, guardian, or other person in charge of such child, an amount per pupil which shall in no event exceed the average transportation cost per pupil, such average cost to be based on the cost of transportation of children by all boards of education in this state during the next preceding year.

In all city, exempted village, and local school districts the board shall provide transportation for all children who are so crippled that they are unable to walk to and from the school for which the state board of education prescribes minimum standards pursuant to division (d) of section 3301.07 of the Revised Code and which they attend. In case of dispute whether the child is able to walk to and from the school, the health commissioner shall be the judge of such ability.

In all city, exempted village, and local school districts the board shall provide transportation to and from school or special education classes for educable mentally retarded children in accordance with standards adopted by the state board of education.

When transportation of pupils is provided the conveyance shall be run on a time schedule that shall be adopted and put in force by the school board not later than ten days after the beginning of the school term.

A district receiving a payment pursuant to division (b) of section 3317.02 of the Revised Code is not eligible for reimbursement of transportation operating costs or eligible for school bus purchase subsidy payment pursuant to section 3317.06 of the Revised Code, except for transporting children who are crippled and for transporting pupils attending nonpublic schools.

The cost of any transportation service authorized by this section shall be paid first out of federal funds, if any, available for the purpose of pupil transportation, and secondly out of state appropriations, in accordance with regulations adopted by the state board of education.

No transportation of any pupils shall be provided by any board of education to or from any school which in the selection of pupils, faculty members, or employees, practices discrimination against any person on the grounds of race, color, religion or national origin.

Purchase of vocational education from private source

Page B1f, Section 3313.91. Any public board of education may contract with any public agency, board, or bureau, or with any private individual or firm for the purchase of any vocational education or vocational rehabilitation service for any resident of the district under the age of twenty-one years and may pay for such services with public funds. Any such vocational education or vocational rehabilitation (sic) service shall meet the same requirements, including those for teachers, facilities, and equipment, as those required of the public schools and be approved by the state department of education.

The state board of education may assign school districts to joint vocational districts and shall require districts to enter into contractual agreements pursuant to section 3313.90 of the Revised Code so that special education students as well as others may receive suitable vocational services.

Purchase of services

Section 3317.06. Distribution of payments for special programs. Moneys paid to school districts under division (P) of sections 3317.024 (3317.02.4) of the Revised Code shall be used for the following independent and fully severable purposes:

(A) To purchase such secular textbooks as have been approved by the superintendent of public instruction for use in public schools in the state and to loan such textbooks to pupils attending nonpublic schools within the district or to their parents and to hire clerical personnel to administer such lending program. Such loans shall be based upon individual requests submitted by such nonpublic school pupils or parents. Such requests shall be submitted to the local public school district in which the nonpublic school is located. Such individual requests for the loan of textbooks shall, for administrative convenience, be submitted by the nonpublic school pupil or his parent to the nonpublic school which shall prepare and submit collective summaries of the individual requests to the local public school district. As used in this section, "textbook" means any book or book substitute which a pupil uses as a text or text substitute in a particular class or program in the school he regularly attends.

(B) To provide speech and hearing diagnostic services to pupils attending nonpublic schools within the district. Such service shall be provided in the nonpublic school attended by the pupil receiving the service.

(C) To provide physician, nursing, dental, and optometric services to pupils attending nonpublic schools within the district. Such services shall be provided in the school attended by the nonpublic school pupil receiving the service.

(D) To provide diagnostic psychological services to pupils attending nonpublic schools within the district. Such services shall be provided in the school attended by the pupil receiving the service.

(E) To provide therapeutic psychological and speech and hearing services to pupils attending nonpublic schools within the district. Such services shall be provided in the public school, in nonpublic schools that have no religious or sectarian affiliation, in public centers, or in mobile units located off the nonpublic premises as determined by the department of education. If such services are provided in the public school or in public centers, transportation to and from such facilities shall be provided by the school district in which the nonpublic school is located.

(F) To provide guidance and counseling services to pupils attending nonpublic schools within the district. Such services shall be provided in the public school, in nonpublic schools that have no religious or sectarian affiliation, in public centers, or in mobile units located off the nonpublic premises as determined by the state department of education. If such services are provided in the public school or in public centers, transportation to and from such facilities shall be provided by the school district in which the nonpublic school is located.

(G) To provide remedial services to pupils attending nonpublic schools within the district. Such services shall be provided in the public school, in nonpublic schools that have no religious sectarian affiliation, in public centers, or in mobile units located off of the nonpublic premises as determined by the department of education. If such services are provided in the public school or in public centers, transportation to and from such facilities shall be provided by the school district in which the nonpublic school is located.

(H) To supply for use by pupils attending nonpublic schools within the district such standardized tests and scoring services as are in use in the public schools of the state.

(I) To provide programs for the deaf, blind, emotionally disturbed, crippled, and physically handicapped children attending nonpublic schools within the district. Such services shall be provided in the public school, in the nonpublic schools that have no religious or sectarian affiliation, in public centers, or in mobile units located off the nonpublic premises as determined by the state department of education. If such services are provided in the public school or in public centers, transportation to and from such facilities shall be provided by the school district in which the nonpublic school is located.

(J) To hire clerical personnel to assist in the administration of programs pursuant to divisions (B), (C), (D), (E), (F), (G), and (I) of this section and to hire supervisory personnel to supervise the providing of services and textbooks pursuant to this section. Clerical and supervisory personnel hired pursuant to division (J) of this section shall perform their services in the public schools, in nonpublic schools that have no religious or sectarian affiliation, in public centers, or mobile units where the services are provided to the nonpublic school pupil except that such personnel may accompany pupils to and from neutral service sites when necessary to ensure the safety of the children receiving the services.

Health services provided pursuant to divisions (B), (C), (D), and (E) of this section may be provided under contract with the department of health, city or general health districts, or private agencies whose personnel are properly licensed by an appropriate state board or agency.

Transportation of pupils provided pursuant to divisions (E), (F), (G), and (I) of this section shall be provided by the school district from its general funds and not from moneys paid to it under division (P) of section 3317.024 (3317.02.4) of the Revised Code unless a special transportation request is submitted by parent of the child receiving service pursuant to such divisions. If such an application is presented to the school district, it may pay for the transportation from moneys paid to it under division (P) of section 3317.0242 (3317.02.4) of the Revised Code.

No school district shall provide health or remedial services to nonpublic school pupils as authorized by this section unless such services are available to pupils attending the public schools within the district.

Materials, equipment, textbooks, and health and remedial services provided for the benefit of nonpublic school pupils pursuant to this section and the admission of pupils to such nonpublic schools shall be provided without distinction as to race, creed, color, or national origin of such pupils or of their teachers.

No school district shall provide services for use in religious courses, devotional exercises, religious training or any other religious activity.

As used in this section, "parent" includes a person standing in loco parentis to a child.

Notwithstanding section 3317.01 of the Revised Code, payments shall be made under this section to any city, local, or exempted village school district within which is located one or more nonpublic elementary or high schools.

The allocation of payments for materials, equipment, textbooks, health services, and remedial services to city, local and exempted village school districts shall be on the basis of the state board of education's estimated annual average daily membership in nonpublic elementary and high schools located in the district.

Payments made to city, local, and exempted village school districts under this section shall be equal to specific appropriations made for the purpose. All interest earned by a school district on such payments shall be used by the district for the same purposes and in the same manner as the payments may be used.

The department of education shall adopt guidelines and procedures under which such programs and services shall be provided, under which districts shall be reimbursed for administrative costs incurred in providing such programs and services, and under which any expended balance of the amounts appropriated by the general assembly to implement this section may be transferred to the auxiliary services personnel unemployment compensation fund established pursuant to section 4141.47 of the Revised Code. The department shall also adopt guidelines and procedures limiting the purchase and loan of equipment and materials under division (K) of this section to items that are in general use in the public schools of the state, that are incapable of diversion to religious use, and that are susceptible to individual use rather than classroom use. Within thirty days after the end of each biennium, each board of education shall remit to the department all moneys paid to it under division (P) of section 3317.024 (3317.02.4) of the Revised Code and any interest earned on those moneys that are not required to pay expenses incurred under this section during the biennium for which the remitted money was appropriated, the board may apply to the department of education for a refund of money, not to exceed the amount of the insufficiency. If the department determines the expenses were lawfully incurred and would have been lawful expenditures of the refunded money, it shall certify its determination and the amount of the refund to be made to the administrator of the bureau of employment services who shall make a refund as provided in section 4141.47 of the Revised Code.

Funds distributed pursuant to this section shall not exceed specific appropriations made therefor by the general assembly, unless expressly approved by the emergency board of the controlling board.

3313.063 Reimbursement of nonpublic school for mandated service costs. The superintendent of public instruction, in accordance with rules adopted by the department of education, shall annually reimburse each chartered nonpublic school for the actual mandated service adminstrative and clerical costs incurred by such school during the preceding school year in preparing, maintaining, and filing reports, forms, and records, and in providing such other administrative and clerical services that are not an integral part of the teaching process as may be required by state law or rule or by requirements duly promulgated by city, exempted village, or local school districts. The mandated service costs reimbursed pursuant to this section shall include, but are not limited to, the preparation, filing and maintenance of forms, reports, or records and other clerical and administrative services relating to state chartering or approval of the nonpublic school, pupil attendance, pupil health and health testing, transportation of pupils, federally funded education programs, pupil appraisal, pupil progress, teacher certification, unemployment and workers' compensation, transfer of pupils, and such other education related data which are now or hereafter shall be required of such nonpublic school by state law or rule, or by requirements of the state department of education, other state agencies, or city, exempted village, or local school districts.

The reimbursement required by this section shall be for school years beginning on or after July 1, 1981.

Each nonpublic school which seeks reimbursement pursuant to this section shall submit to the superintendent of public instruction an application together with such additional reports and documents as the department of education may require. Such applications, reports, and documents shall contain such information as the department of education may prescribe in order to carry out the purposes of this section. No payment shall be made until the superintendent of public instruction has approved such application.

Each nonpublic school which applies for reimbursement pursuant to this section shall maintain a separate account or system of accounts for the expenses incurred in rendering the required services for which reimbursement is sought. Such accounts shall contain such information as is required by the department of education and shall be maintained in accordance with rules adopted by the department of education. Reimbursement payments to a nonpublic school pursuant to this section shall not exceed an amount for each school year equal to one hundred dollars per pupil enrolled in that nonpublic school.

The superintendent of public instruction may from time to time, examine any and all accounts and records of a nonpublic school which have been maintained pursuant to this section in support of an application for reimbursement, for the purpose of determining the costs to such school of rendering the services for which reimbursement is sought. If after such audit it is determined that any school has received funds in excess of the actual cost of providing such services, said school shall immediately reimburse the state in such excess amount.

3317.07 School bus purchase subsidy; distribution. The state board of education shall establish rules for the purpose of distributing subsidies for the purchase of school buses under division (E) of section 3317.024 (3317.02.4) of the Revised Code. Such rules are subject to the approval of the controlling board and shall establish the following:

(A) The manner for determining the eligibility of each school district for full payment;

(B) The method for determining the need of each school district for such moneys;

(C) The method for determining the priorities among the eligible districts for payments.

No school bus subsidy payments shall be paid to any district unless such district can demonstrate that pupils residing more than one mile from the school could not be transported without such additional aid.

The amount paid for buses purchased for transportation of handicapped and nonpublic school pupils shall be one hundred percent of the school district's net cost. The amount paid for buses purchased for transportation of other pupils shall be not less than forty percent and not more than fifty percent of the district's net cost.

Oregon

Transportation

Section 332.415. Transportation of Children Attending Private or Parochial Schools.

Whenever any district school board lawfully provides transportation for pupils attending public schools, all children attending any private or parochial school under the compulsory school attendance laws shall, where the private or parochial school is along or near the route designated by said board, be entitled equally to the same rights, benefits and privileges as to transportation so provided for.

School Lunch Funds

Section 327.520. Acceptance and Distribution of Donated Commodities.

The Superintendent of Public Instruction may accept and distribute donated commodities available for either public or private nonprofit educational institutions, subject to state or federal law or regulation relating to such acceptance and distribution. He shall make a charge sufficient to cover but not exceed all costs of distribution to the individual schools. The charge may include administrative expenses, freight, warehousing, storing, processing and transshipment to the end that all participating schools shall receive such donated commodities at the same unit cost irrespective of location of the school with respect to the original point of delivery within the state.

Driver Education

Section 343.730. State Reimbursement.

(1) Each public school or facility offering a course in automobile driver or motorcycle instruction shall keep accurate records of the cost thereof in the manner required by the Superintendent of Public Instruction. Each public school or facility shall be reimbursed on the basis of the number of pupils completing the course in the public school, to the extent of the lesser of the following schedules:

(a) 90 percent of the cost of conducting the course, or if tuition is charged, 90 percent of the cost after deducting tuition; or

(b) $100.00 per pupil completing the course, including any private school pupil completing the course in a public school.

(2) If funds available to the Motor Vehicles Division for the Student Driver Training Fund are not adequate to pay all approved claims in full, public schools and facilities shall receive a pro rata reimbursement based upon the ratio that the total amount of funds available bears to the total amount of funds required for maximum allowable reimbursement.

Section 343.960. Education of Children at Certain Private Schools and Homes.

(1) The State Board of Education shall be responsible for approving the educational program for children living in or under the care of:

(a)   The Children's Farm Home;
(b)   Albertina Kerr Center;
(c)   The Salvation Army White Shield Home;
(d)   Christie School;
(e)   Edgefield Lodge;
(f)   Parry Center;
(g)   St. Mary's School;
(h)   Villa Gerard;
(i)   Villa St. Rose;
(j)   Waverly Children's Home;
(k)   The Boys and Girls Aid Society of Oregon;
(l)   The Pacific Child Treatment Center;
(m) The JANIS Project;
(n)   Poyama Land;
(o)   The Child Center;
(p)   Grande Ronde Child Center;
(q)   Southern Oregon Child Study and Treatment Center;
(r)   Mid-Columbia Children's Center;
(s)   Cascade Child Study and Treatment Center;
(t)   Lincoln County Child Day Treatment Center;
(u)   Southern Oregon Adolescent Study and Treatment Center;
(v)   Polk Adolescent Day Treatment Center;
(w) Klamath Child Treatment Center, Inc.;
(x)   Clakamas Adolescent Day Treatment Center; and
(y)   Plowshare, Inc.

(2) Subject to the availability of funds therefor and subject to the terms of the agreement between the Children's Services Division of the Department of Human Resources and the school district, the division shall be responsible for payment of the cost of such education. The payments may be made to the school district or at the discretion of the local district to the district providing the education as set forth in subsection (3) of this section, from the funds appropriated for the purpose.

(3) Such education may be provided by the school district in which the agency is located or the school district must cause the education to be provided by an adjacent school district or by the education services district in which the program is located or one contiguous thereto. The instruction may be given in facilities of such districts or in facilities provided by such agency.

(4) The children covered by this section shall be enumerated in the average daily membership of the district providing the instruction but credit for days' attendance of such children shall not accrue to such school district for the purpose of distributing state school funds.

(5) The acceptable items for educational program costs shall be the same as those items approved for special education reimbursement to school districts in this chapter.

(6) The school district may request the Children's Services Division to combine several private agency school programs into one contract with a school district, adjacent school district, or an education service district.

Section 343.965. Reimbursement to School Districts for Costs Incurred Under ORS 343.960.

Subject to the availability of funds therefor and subject to the terms of the agreement between the school district and the Children's Services Division:

(1) The district providing the education described in ORS 343.960 shall receive from the Children's Services Division as reimbursement from moneys appropriated therefor an amount equal to the agreed cost of such education.

(2) The Children's Services Division may make advances to such school district from funds appropriated therefor based on the estimated agreed cost of educating the pupils per school year. Advances equal to 25 percent of such estimated cost may be made on September 1, December 1 and March 1 of the current year. The balance may be paid whenever the full determination of cost is made.

(3) School districts which provide the education described in ORS 343.960 on a year-round plan may apply for 25 percent of the funds appropriated therefor on July 1, October 1, January 1, and 15 percent on April 1. The balance may be paid whenever the full determination of cost is made.

Pennsylvania

Parent Reimbursement for Nonpublic Education

Section 5701. Short Title.

This act shall be known and may be cited as the "Parent Reimbursement Act for Nonpublic Education."

Section 5702. Legislative Finding: Declaration of Policy.

It is hereby determined and declared as a matter of legislative finding:

(1) That parents who send their children to nonpublic schools assist the State in reducing the rising costs of public education.

(2) The welfare of the Commonwealth requires that this and future generations of school age children be assured ample opportunity to develop to the fullest their intellectual capacities. To further this objective the Commonwealth has had in force for many years a compulsory school attendance law.

(3) In the exercise of their constitutional right to choose nonpublic education for their children, parents who support such education make a major contribution to the public welfare. However, the immense impact of inflation, plus sharply rising costs of education, now combine to place in jeopardy the ability of such parents fully to carry this burden.

(4) Should parents of children now enrolled in nonpublic schools be forced by economic circumstances to transfer any substantial number of their children to public schools, an enormous added financial, educational and administrative burden would be placed upon the public schools and upon the taxpayers of the State. Without allowance for inflationary increase, the annual operating cost of educating in public schools, the five hundred thousand students now enrolled in Pennsylvania's nonpublic schools would be an additional four hundred million dollars ($400,000,000). Necessarily added capital costs to construct new facilities or acquire existing facilities would be in excess of one billion dollars ($1,000,000,000). Any substantial portion of these operating and capital costs would be an intolerable public burden and present standards of public education would be seriously jeopardized. Therefore, parents who maintain students in nonpublic schools provide a vital service to the Commonwealth.

Wherefore, it is declared to be the public policy of the Commonwealth:

That, in order to reimburse parents partially for this service so vitally needed by the Commonwealth, and in order to foster educational opportunity for all children, a program of Parent Reimbursement for Nonpublic Education is hereby established.

Section 5703. Definitions.

The following terms, whenever used or referred to in this act, shall have the following meanings, except in those instances where the context clearly indicates otherwise:

(1) "Parent" means a resident of the Commonwealth of Pennsylvania who is a parent of a child enrolled in a nonpublic school or a person standing in loco parentis to such child.

(2) "Nonpublic school" means any school, other than a public school, within the Commonwealth of Pennsylvania, wherein a resident of the Commonwealth may legally fulfill the compulsory school attendance requirements of law and which meets the requirements of Title VI of the Civil Rights Act of 1964 (Public Law Section – 352).

(3) "Student" means a resident of the Commonwealth of Pennsylvania who is enrolled in a nonpublic school.

(4) "Parent Reimbursement Fund" means the fund created by this act.

Section 5704. Pennsylvania Assistance Authority.

There is hereby created a body corporate and politic to be known as the Pennsylvania Parent Assistance Authority, which shall consist of five members appointed by the Governor and which shall have responsibility for the administration of the program created by this act. All members shall be of full age, citizens of the United States, and residents of the Commonwealth and shall be appointed for terms of five years each. The members of the authority shall select from among themselves a chairman and a vice-chairman. The authority may employ a secretary and such other employees as it may require. Three members of the authority shall constitute a quorum for its meetings. Members shall receive no compensation for their services but shall be reimbursed for their expenses actually and necessarily incurred by them in the performance of their duties under this act. The authority shall have power to make and promulgate rules and regulations for the administration of this act; provided, the policy determinations, personnel, curriculum, program of instruction or any other aspect of the administration or operation of any nonpublic school or schools.

The authority shall have no power, at any time or in any manner to pledge the credit or taxing power of the Commonwealth, nor shall any of its obligations or debts be deemed to the obligations of the Commonwealth, and all contracts between the authority and parents or other persons in loco parentis shall be satisfied solely from funds provided under this act.

Section 5705. Parent Reimbursement Fund.

There is hereby created for the special purpose of this act, a Parent Reimbursement Fund. Beginning July 1, 1971, twenty-three percent, and beginning July 1, 1972, ten percent of the tax revenue collected by the Department of Revenue, pursuant to the act of July 22, 1970 (P.L. 513), known as the "Pennsylvania Cigarette Tax Act," shall be paid into the State Treasury to the credit of the Parent Reimbursement Fund.

Moneys in the Parent Reimbursement Fund are hereby appropriated to the Pennsylvania Parent Assistance Authority, to be used solely for the purposes of this act.

All expenses incurred in connection with the administration of this act shall be paid solely out of the Parent Reimbursement Fund.

Section 5706. Eligibility.

In order to be eligible for tuition reimbursement hereunder, the parent of a student shall, at the completion of the school year but not later than July fifteenth, file with the Parent Assistance Authority a verified statement that the student has completed the school year in a nonpublic school or schools and, in addition, the following information: (i) the name and address of the parent; (ii) the name, address and birth date of the student; (iii) the name and address of the nonpublic school or schools in which the student completed the school year; and (iv) a receipted tuition bill or copy of the executed contract under which the student attended the nonpublic school or schools.

Section 5707. Tuition Reimbursement Payments to Parents.

Upon the filing by a parent of the verified statement required by Section 6, the Parent Assistance Authority shall make a tuition reimbursement payment to such parent in the amount of (i) seventy-five dollars ($75) for each elementary school student to whom the parent bears a parental relationship and one hundred fifty dollars ($150) for each secondary student to whom the parent bears a parental relationship, or (ii) the actual amount of tuition paid or contracted to be paid by a parent, whichever is lesser.

Reimbursement payments to parents hereunder shall be made not later than September fifteenth in the school year following the school year for which tuition reimbursement payments are being made.

Section 5708. Penalties.

The Parent Assistance Authority shall have power to employ means reasonably necessary to determine the accuracy of all statements submitted by parents in connection with reimbursement payments hereunder. Any person who, by means of a willfully false statement, secures or attempts to secure or aids or abets any person in securing reimbursement payment hereunder, shall be guilty of a misdemeanor, and, upon conviction thereof, shall be sentenced to pay a fine of not exceeding one thousand dollars ($1,000), or to undergo imprisonment not exceeding one year, or both, and shall also be sentenced to make restitution of any moneys he has recieved by reason of any false statement.

Section 5709. Insufficient Moneys in Fund.

In the event that, in any fiscal year, the total amount of moneys which were actually paid into the Parent Reimbursement Fund shall be insufficient to pay the total number of claims submitted by parents to the Parent Assistance Authority, the reimbursement payments provided for in Section 7 shall be proportionate in amount to the percent which the total amount of moneys in the Parent Reimbursement Fund bears to the total amount of claims.

Section 5710. Severability.

If a part of this act is invalid, all valid parts that are severable from the invalid part remain in effect. If a part of this act is invalid, in one or more of its applications, the part remains in effect in all valid applications that are severable from the valid applications.

Shared-time

Section 5-502. Additional Schools and Departments.

In addition to the elementary public schools, the board of school directors in any school district may establish, equip, furnish, and maintain the following additional schools or departments for the education and recreation of persons residing in said district, and for the proper operation of its schools, namely:

High schools,   Technical schools,
Trade schools,   Cafeterias,
Vocational schools,   Agricultural schools,

Evening schools,
Kindergartens,
Libraries,
Museums,
Reading-rooms,
Gymnasiums,
Playgrounds,

Schools for physically and
  mentally handicapped,
Truant schools,
Parental schools,
Schools for adults,
Public lectures.

Such other schools or departments, when established, shall be an integral part of the public school system in such school district and shall be so administered.

No pupil shall be refused admission to the courses in these additional schools or departments, by reason of the fact that his elementary or academic education is being or has been received in a school other than a public school.

Standardized Driver-Education Program

Section 15-1519.1. Standardized Driver Education Program.

(a) The Department of Public Instruction shall establish, for operation in the public school system of the Commonwealth, a standardized driver-education program in the safe operation of motor vehicles available to all public high school pupils and all high school pupils attending nonpublic high schools.

(b) The Department of Public Instruction shall assist school districts throughout the Commonwealth in the functioning of such program by

(1) Preparation, publication and free distribution of driver-education instructional material to insure a more complete understanding of the duties of motor vehicle operators;

(2) Making such rules and regulations as may be necessary to carry out such program.

(c) Annual expenditures of the Department of Public Instruction from the Motor License Fund for (1) salaries and expenses of employees of the Department of Public Instruction essential to the program; (2) purchase of visual training aids and psychophysical testing equipment; and (3) costs of preparation, publication and distribution of driver-education instructional material, for assistance to their driver-education programs, shall not exceed three (3) percentum of the annual total amount paid by the

Commonwealth to all school districts, or joint school organizations, on account of standardized driver-education programs.

Nonprofit School Lunch Programs

Section 13-1337.

(a) Definitions — For the purpose of this section — "school food program" means a program under which food is served by any school on a nonprofit basis to children in attendance, including any such program under which a school receives assistance out of funds appropriated by the Congress of the United States.

(b) Expenditure of Federal Funds — The Department of Education is hereby authorized to accept and direct the disbursement of funds appropriated by any act of Congress, and apportioned to the State, for use in connection with school food programs. The Department of Education shall deposit all such funds received from the Federal government in a special account with the Treasurer of the State who shall make disbursements therefrom upon the direction of the Department of Education.

(c) Administration of Program — The Department of Education may enter into such agreements with any agency of the Federal government with any board of school directors, or with any other agency or person, prescribe such regulations, employ such personnel, and take such other action as it may deem necessary to provide for the establishment, maintenance, operation and expansion of any school-food program, and to direct the disbursement of Federal and State funds in accordance with any applicable provisions of Federal or State law. The Department of Public Instruction may give technical advice and assistance to any board of school directors in connection with the establishment and operation of any school food program, and may assist in training personnel engaged in the operation of such program. The Department of Public Instruction, and any board of school directors, may accept any gift for use in connection with any school food program.

Transportation

Section 13-1361.

When provided,

(1) The board of school directors in any school district may, out of the funds of the district, provide for the free transportation of any resident

pupil to and from the kindergarten, elementary school, or secondary school in which he is lawfully enrolled, provided that such school is not operated for profit and is located within the district boundaries or outside the district boundaries at a distance not exceeding ten miles by the nearest public highway, except that such ten-mile limit shall not apply to area vocational technical schools which regularly serve eligible district pupils or to special schools and classes approved by the Department of Education, and to and from any points within or without the Commonwealth in order to provide field trips for any purpose connected with the educational pursuits of the pupils. When provision is made by a board of school directors for the transportation of public school pupils to and from such schools or to and from any points within or without the Commonwealth in order to provide field trips as herein provided, the board of school directors shall also make identical provision for the free transportation of pupils who regularly attend nonpublic kindergarten, elementary and high schools not operated for profit to and from such schools or to and from any points within or without the Commonwealth in order to provide field trips as herein provided. Such transportation of pupils attending nonpublic schools shall be provided during regular school hours on such dates and periods that the nonpublic school not operated for profit is in regular session, according to the school calendar officially adopted by the directors of the same in accordance with provisions of law. The board of school directors shall provide such transportation whenever so required by any of the provisions of this act or of any other act of Assembly.

(2) The board of school directors in any school district may, if the board deems it to the best interest of the school district, for the purposes of transporting pupils as required or authorized by any of the provisions of this act or of any other act of the Assembly, appropriate funds for urban common carrier mass transportation purposes from current revenues to urban common carrier mass transportation authorities to assist the authorities to meet costs of operation, maintenance, capital improvements, and debt service. Said contributions shall not be subject to reimbursement by the Commonwealth of Pennsylvania.

(3) The State Board of Education shall adopt regulations, including qualifications of school bus drivers, to govern the transportation of school pupils.

Section 9-971A. Nonpublic School Children, Speech and Hearing Defects, Diagnosis and Correction.

(1) Legislative Finding; Declaration of Policy. Defects in speech and hearing are health related. They are also the frequent cause of emotional

instability in children and are vitally connected to behavior and to learning ability. Services to remedy these defects can best be conducted upon the premises of the school which the child regularly attends, and forcing children to go to other premises in order to have such needed services is found by the General Assembly of the Commonwealth of Pennsylvania to be both inadequate and harmful. The General Assembly expressly finds and declares speech and hearing correctional services to be health services, and it is the intention of the General Assembly now to make these available on a general and evenhanded basis to all school children in the Commonwealth.

(2) Definitions. As used in this act: "Nonpublic school" means any nonprofit school, other than a public school within the Commonwealth of Pennsylvania, wherein a resident of the Commonwealth may legally fulfill the compulsory school attendance requirements and which meets the requirements of Title VI of the Civil Rights Act of 1964.

(3) Provision of Services. The Secretary of Education directly, or through the intermediate units out of their allocation under Section 922.1-A of the act of March 10, 1949, known as the "Public School Code of 1949," shall have the power and duty to furnish free to nonpublic school students, upon the premises of the nonpublic schools which they regularly attend, services adequate for the diagnosis and correction of speech and hearing defects provided that such services are also afforded to public school students by the public school district in which such nonpublic school is located.

Auxiliary Services

Section 9-972.1. Legislative Finding: Declaration of Policy.

(a) The welfare of the Commonwealth requires that the present and future generation of school age children be assured ample opportunity to develop to the fullest their intellectual capacities. It is the intent of the General Assembly by this enactment to ensure that the intermediate units in the Commonwealth shall furnish on an equal basis auxiliary services to all pupils in the Commonwealth in both public and nonprofit nonpublic schools.

(b) Definitions. The following terms, whenever used or referred to in this section, shall have the following meanings, except in those circumstances where the context clearly indicates otherwise:

"Auxiliary services" means guidance; counseling and testing services; psychological services; visual services as defined in Section 923.2-a; services for exceptional children; remedial services; speech and hearing services; services for the improvement of the educationally disadvantaged (such as, but not limited to, the teaching of English as a second language), and such other secular, neutral, nonideological services as are of benefit to all school children and are presently or hereafter provided for public school children of the Commonwealth.

"Nonpublic school" means nonprofit school, other than a public school within the Commonwealth of Pennsylvania, wherein a resident of the Commonwealth may legally fulfill the compulsory school attendance requirements of this act and which meets the requirements of Title VI of the Civil Rights Act of 1964.

(c) Program of Auxiliary Services. Students attending nonpublic schools shall be furnished a program of auxiliary services which are provided to public school students in the school district in which their nonpublic school is located. The program of auxiliary services shall be provided by the intermediate unit in which the nonpublic school is located, in accordance with standards of the Secretary of Education. Such services shall be provided directly to the nonpublic school students by the intermediate unit except that such services shall not be provided in a church or in any facility under the control of a sectarian school.

Such auxiliary services shall be provided directly by the intermediate units and no auxiliary services presently provided to public school students by the intermediate units and/or school districts by means of state or local revenues, during the school year 1974–75, shall be eliminated. No school districts shall be required, pursuant to any section of this act, to offer auxiliary services provided by any other school districts within such intermediate units.

(d) Allocations. In July of 1977 and annually thereafter, in July, the Secretary of Education shall allocate to each intermediate unit an amount equal to the number of nonpublic school students as of October 1 of the preceding school year who are enrolled in nonpublic schools within the intermediate unit times seventy-two dollars ($72.00). The Secretary of Education shall increase this figure on a proportionate basis whenever there is an increase in the median actual instructional expense per WADM as defined in clause 12.1 of Section 2501 of this act. The Commonwealth shall pay to each intermediate unit fifteen percentum (15%) of its allocation on August 1, seventy-five percentum (75%) on October 1 and the remaining ten percentum (10%) on the first day of February.

(e) Limitations. The intermediate unit shall not use more than six percentum (6%) of the funds it receives for administration or eighteen percentum (18%) for rental of facilities. The Department of Education shall not use more than one percentum (1%) of the funds it allocates under this section for administrative expenses. If all funds allocated by the intermediate units to administration, or rental facilities are not expended for those purposes, such funds may be used for the program costs.

(f) Interest. There shall be no adjustment in the allocation as provided in subsection (d) because of interest earned on the allocations by the intermediate units. Interest so earned shall be used for the purpose of this section but shall not be subject to the limitations of subsection (e).

(g) Preliminary Budget. Annually, each intermediate unit shall submit to the secretary a preliminary budget on or before January 31 and a final budget on or before June 15, for the succeeding year; and shall file a final financial report on or before October 31 for the preceding year.

Section 9-973. Loan of Textbooks, Instructional Materials and Equipment, Nonpublic School Children.

(a) Legislative Findings: Declaration of Policy. The welfare of the Commonwealth requires that the present and future generations of school age children be assured ample opportunity to develop to the fullest their intellectual capacities. To further this objective, the Commonwealth provides, through tax funds of the Commonwealth, textbooks and instructional materials free of charge to children attending public schools within the Commonwealth. Approximately one quarter of all children in the Commonwealth, in compliance with the compulsory attendance provision of this act, attend nonpublic schools. Although their parents are taxpayers of the Commonwealth, these children do not receive textbooks or instructional materials from the Commonwealth. It is the intent of the General Assembly by this enactment to assure such a distribution of such educational aids that every school child in the Commonwealth will equitably share in the benefits thereof.

(b) Definitions. The following terms, whenever used or referred to in this section, shall have the following meanings, except in those circumstances where the context clearly indicates otherwise:

"Instructional equipment" means instructional equipment, other than fixtures annexed to and forming part of the real estate, which is suitable for and to be used by children and/or teachers. The term includes but is not limited to projection equipment, recording equipment, laboratory equipment, and any other educational secular, neutral, nonideological equipment as may be of benefit to the instruction of nonpublic school children and are presently or hereafter provided for public school children of the Commonwealth.

"Instructional Materials" means prepared learning materials which are secular, neutral and nonideological in character and are of benefit to the instruction of school children on an individual basis and are presently or hereafter provided for public school children of the Commonwealth.

"Nonpublic school" means any school, other than a public school within the Commonwealth of Pennsylvania, wherein a resident of the Commonwealth may legally fulfill the compulsory school attendance requirements of this act and which meets the requirements of Title VI of the Civil Rights Act of 1964.

"Textbooks" means books, workbooks, including reusable and nonreusable workbooks, and manuals, whether bound or in looseleaf form intended for use as a principal source of study material for a given class or group of students, a copy of which is expected to be available for the individual use of each pupil in such class or group. Such textbooks shall be textbooks which are acceptable for use in any public, elementary, or secondary school of the Commonwealth.

(c) Loan of textbooks and instructional materials. The Secretary of Education directly, or through the intermediate units shall have the power and duty to purchase textbooks and instructional materials and, upon individual request, to loan them to all children residing in the Commonwealth who are enrolled in grades kindergarten through twelve of a nonpublic school. Such textbooks and instructional materials shall be loaned free to such children subject to such rules and regulations as may be prescribed by the Secretary of Education, due regard being had to the feasibility of making loans of particular instructional materials on an individual basis.

(d) Purchase of Textbooks and Instructional Materials. The secretary shall not be required to purchase or otherwise acquire textbooks, pursuant to this section, the total cost of which, in any school year, shall exceed an amount equal to twelve dollars ($12) for the school year 1973–1974, fifteen dollars ($15) for the school year beginning July 1, 1974, and twenty dollars ($20) for each school year thereafter for instructional materials, the total cost of which, in any school year, shall exceed an amount equal to ten dollars ($10), multiplied by the number of children residing in the Commonwealth who on the first day of October of the school year immediately preceding are enrolled in grades kindergarten through twelve of a nonpublic school.

24:　Section 9-973.1. Psychological Services.

(a) Legislative Finding: Declaration of Policy. It is today recognized that diagnostic and evaluative psychological services to children are closely related to their physical, mental and emotional health. Such services can best be rendered upon the premises of the school which the child regularly attends, and forcing children to go to other premises in order to have such needed services is found by the General Assesmbly to be both inadequate and harmful. The General Assembly expressly finds and declares diagnostic and evaluative psychological services for children to be health services, and it is the intention of the General Assembly now to make these available, on a general and even-handed basis, to all school children in the Commonwealth.

(b) Definitions. The following terms, whenever used or referred to in this section, shall have the following meanings, except in those circumstances where the context clearly indicates otherwise:

"Nonpublic school" means any nonprofit school, other than a public school within the Commonwealth of Pennsylvania, wherein a resident of the Commonwealth may legally fulfill the compulsory school attendance requirements and which meets the requirements of Title VI of the Civil Rights Act of 1964.

"Psychological services" means diagnostic and evaluative psychological services for children.

(c) Provision of Services. The Secretary of Education directly, or through the intermediate units out of their allocation under section 922.1-A of this act shall have the power and duty to furnish free to nonpublic school students, upon the premises of the nonpublic schools which they regularly attend, psychological services provided that such services are also afforded to public school students by the public school district in which such nonpublic school is located.

Section 9-973.2. Visual Services.

(a) Legislative finding; declaration of policy. Defects in vision are health related. It is today recognized that the diagnosis and evaluation of those defects and the rendering of instruction in skills appropriate for the education, safety and independence of children afflicted by visual impairments are closely related to their physical, mental and emotional health. Such services can best be rendered upon the premises of the school which the child regularly attends and forcing children to go to other premises in order to have such needed services is found by the General Assembly to be both inadequate and harmful. The General Assembly expressly finds and declares diagnostic, evaluative and instructional services for such children to be health services and it is the intention of the General Assembly now to make these available on a general and evenhanded basis to all school children in the Commonwealth.

(b) Definitions. As used in this section: "Nonpublic school" means any nonprofit school, other than a public school within the Commonwealth of Pennsylvania, wherein a resident of the Commonwealth may legally fulfill the compulsory school attendance requirements and which meets the requirements of Title VI of the Civil Rights Act of 1964 (Public Law 88-352).

"Visual Services" means diagnostic, evaluative and instructional visual services for children.

(c) Provision of Services. The Secretary of Education, directly or through the intermediate units out of their allocation under section 922.1-a shall have the power and duty to furnish free to nonpublic school students, upon the premises of the nonpublic schools which they regularly attend, services adequate for the diagnosis and evaluation of visual defects and instruction and training in skills advisable for the education, independence and safety of such children, including but not limited to mobility training, provided that such services are also afforded to public school students by the public school district in which such nonpublic school is located.

Rhode Island

Transportation

Section 16-21.1. Transportation of Public and Private School Pupils.

The school committee of any town shall provide suitable transportation to and from school for pupils attending public and private schools of elementary and high school grades, except such private schools as are operated for profit, who reside so far from the public or private school which the pupil attends as to make the pupil's regular attendance at school impractical and for any pupil whose regular attendance would otherwise be impracticable on account of physical disability or infirmity.

Loan of Textbooks

Section 16-23-2.

The school committee of every community as the same is defined in section 16-7-16 shall furnish upon request at the expense of such community, textbooks in the fields of mathematics, science, and modern foreign languages appearing on the published list of textbooks recommended by the commissioner of education as provided in section 16-23-3 of the general laws, as herein amended, to all pupils of elementary and secondary school grades resident in such community, said textbooks to be loaned to such pupils free of charge, subject to such rules and regulations as to care and custody as the school committee may prescribe.

Every such school committee shall also furnish as the expense of such community all other textbooks and school supplies used in the public schools of said community, said other textbooks and supplies to be loaned to the pupils of said public schools free of charge, subject to such rules and regulations as to care and custody as the school committee may prescribe. School books removed from school use may be distributed to pupils, and any textbook may become the property of a pupil who has completed the use of it in school, subject to rules and regulations prescribed by the school committee.

Lunches

Section 16-8-7. School Lunch Programs — Definition of Terms.

For the purposes of sections 16-8-7 to 16-8-13, inclusive:

The term "school board" shall include city or town school committees or any person or group responsible for the operation of a private or parochial school.

The term "school" shall be construed to mean any educational institution operated on a nonprofit basis, having a graded course of instruction with prescribed standards for the completion of each grade, with compulsory class attendance, and records of class work regularly maintained.

Section 16-8-8. Acceptance and Use of Federal School Lunch Funds.

The state department of education is hereby authorized to accept and direct the disbursement of funds appropriated by any act of congress and apportioned to the state in connection with the establishment and maintenance of school lunch programs. The state department of education shall deposit all such funds received from the federal government with the general treasurer, to be placed in a special account, and drawn upon only on receipt of properly authenticated vouchers signed by the department of education.

Section 16-8-9. Administration of School Lunch Program.

The state department of education may enter into such agreements, with any agency of the federal government, with any school board, or with any other agency or person, may prescribe such regulations, employ such personnel, and take such action, as it may deem necessary to provide for the establishment, maintenance, operation and expansion of any school lunch program, and to direct the disbursement of federal and state funds in accordance with existing provisions of the federal and state laws. The state department of education may give technical advice and assistance to any school board in connection with the establishment and operation of any school lunch program and may assist in training personnel engaged in the operation of such programs. The state department of education may accept any gift for use in connection with any school lunch program.

Section 16-8-10. Mandatory School Lunch Programs.

Commencing September 1, 1972, or commencing September 1, 1973, for any city or town whose fiscal year began prior to March 1, 1972, those schools identified by school boards to the department of education as needy schools for Title I ESEA purposes, and commencing September 1, 1973, all public elementary and secondary schools, shall be required to make type A lunches available to students attending those schools in accordance with such rules and regulations as are adopted from time to time by the department of education. To the extent that federal, state and other funds are available, free and reduced price type A lunches shall be provided to all students from families which meet the current specific criteria established by federal and state regulations. The requirement that type A lunches be provided shall apply to locally managed school lunch programs, and school lunch programs administered directly by the department of education or by any other public agency whether using school facilities or a commercial catering service. The department of education is further authorized to expand the school lunch program to the extent that federal, state and/or local funds are available by the utilization of one or more food preparation centers for delivery to participating schools for the purpose of providing meals to students on a more economical basis than could be provided by a community acting individually.

Section 16-7-22. Determination of Average Daily Membership.

Each community shall be paid pursuant to the provisions of Section 16-7-17 an amount based upon the provisions of either subsection (a) or subsection (b) of this section, whichever shall be the greater.

(a) On or before September 1 of each year the average daily membership of each city and town for the reference year shall be determined by the commissioner of education, from data supplied by the school committee in each community in the following manner: The aggregate number of days of membership of all pupils enrolled in grades one (1) to twelve (12), both inclusive, increased by one-half (½) the aggregate number of days of membership of all pupils in kindergarten, in all public schools in each city and town in the reference year

(i) increased by the aggregate number of days of membership of pupils residing in the particular city or town whose tuition in schools approved by the department of education is paid by the particular city or town, and

(ii) decreased by the aggregate number of days of membership of nonresident pupils enrolled in the public schools of the particular city or town, and

(iii) decreased further, in the case of a city or town which is a member of a regional school district during the first year of operation of such regional school district, by the aggregate number of days of membership of pupils residing in the city or town who could have attended the public schools in such regional school district if such regional school district had been operating during the previous year shall be divided by the number of days during which such schools were officially in session during such reference year. The resulting figures shall be the average daily membership for such city or town for the reference year; and

(b) On or before September 1 of each year the average daily membership of each city and town for the reference year shall be determined by the commissioner of education, from data supplied by the school committee in each community, which data shall be determined by said school committees from the annual census pursuant to (chapter 18 of Title 16). The commissioner of education shall determine the average daily membership in the following manner: The aggregate number of days of membership of all pupils enrolled in grades one (1) to twelve (12), both inclusive, increased by one-half (½) the aggregate number of days of membership of all pupils in kindergarten in all schools (public, private or parochial) in each city and town in the reference year

(i) increased by the aggregate number of days of membership of pupils residing in the particular city or town in schools approved by the department of education in other cities and towns and

(ii) decreased by the aggregate number of days of membership of nonresident pupils enrolled in the schools of the particular city or town and

(iii) decreased further, in the case of a city or town which is a member of a regional school district during first year of operation of such regional school district, by the aggregate number of days of membership of pupils residing in the city or town who would have attended the schools in such regional school district if such regional school district had been operating during the previous year, shall be divided by the number of days during such reference year. The resulting figures shall be the average daily membership for such city or town for the reference year; and

(c) The average daily membership of pupils attending public, parochial and private schools as determined in subsection (b) shall apply for the purposes of determining the percentage of the state's share under the provisions of Subsection 16-7-16 (d), 16-7-16 (e), 16-7-18, 16-7-19, 16-7-20, and 16-7-21.

For the purpose of applying the percentage so determined the cost of the basic program in Subsection 16-7-17 and 16-7-20 shall be determined in accordance with the provisions of subsection (a).

(d) In the case of regional school districts, the aggregate number of days of membership by which each city or town is decreased in subsection (a) (iii) above divided by the number of days during which the schools attended by such pupils were officially in session shall determine the average daily membership for such regional school district during the first year of operation. After the first year of operation, the average daily membership of each regional school district, except the Chariho Regional High School District and the Foster-Glocester Regional School District shall be determined by the commissioner of education, from data supplied by the school committee of each regional school district for the reference year in the manner provided in paragraph (a) above.

Funds for Nonpublic School Record Keeping

Section 16-40.1-1. Legislative Findings.

The general assembly hereby finds and declares that:

The state has the responsibility to provide educational opportunity of quality which will prepare its citizens for the challenges of American life in the last decades of the twentieth century.

In public schools these fundamental objectives are accomplished in part through state financial assistance to local school districts.

Substantial numbers of pupils in the state comply with the compulsory education law by attending nonpublic schools. It is a matter of state duty and concern that such nonpublic schools be reimbursed for the actual costs which they incur in providing services to the state which they are required by law to render in connection with the state's responsibility for reporting, testing and evaluating.

Section 16-40.1-2. Definitions.

1. "Commissioner" shall mean the state commissioner of education.

2. "Qualifying school" shall mean a nonprofit school in the state, other than a public school with provides instruction in accordance with Title 16.

Section 16-40.1-3. Apportionment.

The commissioner shall annually apportion to each qualifying school, for school years beginning on and after July 1, 1982, an amount equal to the actual cost incurred by each such school during the preceding school year for providing services required by law to be rendered to the state in compliance with the requirements of administration, grading and the compiling and reporting of the results of tests and examinations, maintenance of records of pupil enrollment and reporting thereon, maintenance of pupil health records, and the preparation and submission to the state of various other reports required by law or regulation.

Section 16-40.1-4. Application.

Each school which seeks an apportionment pursuant to this chapter shall submit to the commissioner an application therefor, together with such additional reports and documents as the commissioner may require, at such times, in such form and containing such information as the commissioner may prescribe by regulation in order to carry out the purposes of this chapter.

Section 16-40.1-5. Maintenance of Records.

Each school which seeks an apportionment pursuant to this chapter shall maintain a separate account or system of accounts for the expenses incurred in rendering the services required by the state to be performed in connection with the reporting, testing and evaluation programs enumerated in Section 16-40.1-3. Such records and accounts shall contain such information and be maintained in accordance with regulations issued by the commissioner, but for expenditures made in the school year 1982, the application for reimbursement made in 1982 pursuant to Section 16-40.1-4 shall be supported by such reports and documents as the commissioner shall require. In promulgating such record and account regulations and in requiring supportive documents with respect to expenditures incurred in the school year 1981–82, the commissioner shall facilitate the audit procedures described in this chapter. The records and accounts for each school year shall be preserved at the school until the completion of such audit procedures.

Section 16-40.1-6. Payment.

No payment to a qualifying school shall be made until the commissioner has approved the application submitted pursuant to Section 16-40.1-4.

Section 16-40.1-7. Audit.

No application for financial assistance under this chapter shall be approved except upon audit of vouchers or other documents by the commissioner as are necessary to insure that such payment is lawful and proper.

The state department of audit shall from time to time examine any and all necessary accounts and records of a qualifying school to which an apportionment has been made pursuant to this chapter for the purpose of determining the cost to such school of rendering the services referred to in Section 16-40.1-3. If after such audit it is determined that any qualifying school has received funds in excess of the actual cost of providing the services enumerated in Section 16-40.1-3, such school shall immediately reimburse the state in such excess amount.

Section 16-40.1-8. Noncorporate Entities.

Apportionments made for the benefit of any school which is not a corporate entity shall be paid, on behalf of such school, to such corporate entity as may be designated for such purpose pursuant to regulations promulgated by the commissioner. A school which is a corporate entity may designate another corporate entity for the purpose of receiving apportionments made for the benefit of such school pursuant to this chapter.

Section 16-40.1-9 Severability of Provisions.

If any provisions of this chapter or the application thereof to any person or circumstances is held invalid, its invalidity does not affect other provisions or applications of the chapter which can be given without the invalid provision or application, and to this end the provisions of this chapter are severable.

South Carolina

Section 43-25-60. Itinerant teachers shall assist in schools; visually handicapped pupils shall be reported to Commission.

The Commission may employ qualified itinerant teachers to assist teachers in public or private schools who are responsible for the teaching of visually handicapped students. The itinerant teacher shall assist the public or private school teacher by providing methods and materials for teaching such student. The State Department of Education shall report to the Commission the schools having visually handicapped students. All principals or heads of privae schools shall report to the Commission the names of visually handicapped students in attendance.

Grants to Students Attending Private Schools

Section 59-41-10. Definitions.

The following words and phrases as used in this chapter shall, unless a different meaning is plainly required by the context, have the following meanings:

(a) "School child" shall mean any person between the ages of six and twenty whose domicile is with his or her parent within the State and who is otherwise qualified to attend the public schools of any school district in which he or she resides.

(b) "Parent" shall mean the natural or adoptive parent or guardian having legal custody of a child eligible and entitled to receive a scholarship grant under this chapter and who is actually paying or who will pay the tuition cost of attendance of such child at a school which qualifies such child to receive a grant under the terms of this chapter.

(c) "Private school" shall mean a private or independent elementary or high school which is not operated or controlled by any church, synagogue, sect or other religious organization or institution.

Section 59-41-20. Children Eligible for Grants: Amount.

Subject to the terms and provisions of this chapter every school child in the State who has not yet finished or graduated from high school and who desires to attend a private school located within the State shall be eligible for and entitled to receive a State scholarship grant in an amount equal to the per pupil cost to the State of public education as certified by the Governor.

Section 59-41-30. Grants Payable from Appropriations.

The State scholarship grants provided for in Section 59-41-20 shall be payable from funds appropriated by the General Assembly for the payment thereof.

Section 59-41-40. School Districts Shall Provide Supplements to Grants; Levy of Taxes.

It shall be prerequisite to the grant above permitted that the local school district in which the school child resides make available a grant of local funds to such school child and to that end the trustees of each school district within the State are hereby authorized to appropriate funds in addition to the State scholarship grants provided for in Section 59-41-20 in such amount that is equal to the per pupil cost to the school district exclusive of State funds received for such purposes. The trustees of each school district are authorized to levy taxes where the school district has the power to tax, to raise funds for the payment of such local supplements to the State scholarship grants. The State Board of Education shall render such assistance to the trustees as may be necessary to determine annual per pupil expenditures of the school district for the purpose of fixing the amount of any supplement to be paid under this section.

Section 59-41-50. Grant and Supplement Shall not Exceed School Tuition.

The total of the annual scholarship grant provided for each child by this chapter shall not exceed the actual cost of tuition at the private school attended by the child.

Section 59-41-60. State Board Authorized and Directed to Promulgate Rules and Regulations.

The State Board of Education is hereby authorized and directed to promulgate such rules and regulations, consistent with the terms of this chapter, for the receiving and processing of applications for scholarship grants, the payment of grants and the administration of this chapter generally as it may find necessary or desirable. Such rules may, among other things, provide for the payment of scholarship grants by the school districts of the State to the parent of any child entitled to receive a scholarship grant in installments or otherwise, and for the proration of scholarships for children attending school less than a full school year; they shall include a minimum academic standard that shall be met by any school in order to entitle children attending such school to receive a scholarship grant; provided, however, that no rule promulgated under the authority of this chapter shall restrict, or in any way affect, the requirements of such school concerning the eligibility of pupils who may be admitted thereto or specify minimum physical plant facilities of any such school.

Section 59-41-70. Obtaining or Expending Scholarship Funds Other than for Tuition Unlawful.

It shall be unlawful for any person to obtain, attempt to obtain, expend or attempt to expend, any scholarship funds provided by this chapter for any purpose other than in payment of, or reimbursement for, the tuition cost of the child to whom such scholarship has been awarded at the institution he or she is authorized to attend under his or her scholarship grant.

Section 59-41-80. Penalties.

Any person convicted of violating the provisions of this chapter shall be punished by imprisonment for a term not to exceed three years or by a fine not to exceed two thousand dollars, or by both, in the discretion of the court.

Section 59-41-90. Effect of Invalidity.

If any portion of this chapter, or the application thereof to any person or circumstance is, for any reason declared unconstitutional, such declaration shall not affect the validity of the remaining portions of this chapter or its application to other persons and circumstances.

South Dakota

Driver Education

Section 22-5-50. Dealers Participating in Driver Education Program — Application to Commissioner of Motor Vehicles — Fee — Violation as Misdemeanor.

Any motor vehicle dealer licensed under the provisions of chapter 32-6 who participates in the driver education program in the schools of the state by furnishing any school or schools with a motor vehicle used in such program shall upon application to the department of motor vehicles and payment of a fee of one dollar, receive from said department of motor vehicles a public school corporation license plate for the operation of such vehicle upon the highways of the state. A violation of this section is a class 1 misdemeanor.

Section 13-34-16.2.

It is declared to be the policy of this state that the common good and general welfare of the state are promoted by an educated and enlightened citizenry and, to assist in achieving those goals and in accord with the child benefit doctrine, there shall be loaned without charge to any persons ages five through nineteen such nonsectarian textbooks and text related workbooks designed for individual use as are normally furnished by the school boards of the several public school districts of this state to the students enrolled in the public schools of such respective districts. It is further declared to be the policy of this state that, in the loaning of such materials to such persons, the state shall be neutral to and between all such persons.

Section 13-34-16.3.

To implement Section 13-34-16.2 each public school board shall loan without charge to all persons ages five through nineteen who are either enrolled in a public school, or in a school supervised in accord with Chapter 13-4, or who are engaged in a course of instruction pursuant to Section 13-27-3, within the school district under such board's jurisdiction, or who are residing in such district but are not enrolled in any such school or engaged in any such course of instruction, such nonsectarian textbooks and text related workbooks designed for individual use as are normally furnished by such school board to individual students enrolled in the public schools of the district under such board's jurisdiction. All such textbooks and text related workbooks shall be approved by the respective school boards.

Utah

Section 53-14-13.5. Enrollment of private school pupils in driver education classes. Local school districts maintaining automobile driver education classes shall allow pupils enrolled in grades nine to twelve, inclusive, of regularly established private schools located in said school district to enroll in the most accessible public school in said school district for the purpose of receiving driver education. The enrollment of such pupils of regularly established private schools shall be on the same terms and conditions as applies to the pupils of public schools within said school district, as such terms and conditions relate to the driver education classes only.

Vermont

Driver Education

Section 1045. Driver training course. A driver education and training course, approved by the department of education and the department of motor vehicles shall be made available to pupils whose parent or guardian is a resident of Vermont and who have reached their fifteenth birthday and who are regularly enrolled in a public or private high school approved by the state board.

Maintenance of Public Schools

Section 821. School district to maintain public elementary schools or pay tuition. Each school district shall provide, furnish, and maintain one or more approved schools within the district in which elementary education for its pupils is provided unless:

(1) The electorate authorizes the school board to provide for the elementary education of some or all of the pupils residing in the district by paying tuition in accordance with law to public elementary schools in another school district. However, a school board without previous authorization by the electorate may pay tuition for elementary pupils who reside near an elementary school in an adjacent district upon request of the pupil's parent or guardian, if in its judgment the child's education can be more conveniently furnished there, or

(2) The school district is organized to provide only high school education for its pupils.

(3) Otherwise provided for by the general assembly.

Added 1969. No. 298 (Adj. Sess.), Section 52, eff. July 1, 1970.

Section 822. School districts to maintain high schools or pay tuition.

(a) Each school district shall provide, furnish, and maintain one or more approved high schools in which high school education is provided for its pupils unless:

(1) The electorate authorizes the school board to close an existing high school and to provide for the high school education of its pupils by paying tuition in accordance with law. Tuition for its pupils shall be paid to a high school, public or private, approved by the state board, to be selected by the parents or guardians of the pupil, within or without the state. The school board may both maintain a high school and furnish high school education by paying tuition elsewhere as in the judgment of the board may best serve the interests of the pupils, or

(2) The school district is organized to provide only elementary education for its pupils.

Section 823. Elementary tuition. Tuition for elementary pupils shall be paid by the district in which the pupil is a resident. The tuition paid shall be at a rate not greater than the calculated net cost per elementary pupil in average daily membership in the receiving school district for the year of attendance.

Section 824. High school tuition. (a) Tuition for high school pupils shall be paid by the school district in which the pupil is a resident. The district shall pay the full tuition charged its pupils attending an approved public high school in Vermont or an adjoining state, or a public or private school in Vermont functioning as an approved area vocational center; or for its pupils enrolled in a private school not functioning as a Vermont area vocational center, but which has been approved by the Vermont State board or by comparable authority, an amount not to exceed the average announced tuition of Vermont union high schools for the year of attendance or any higher amount approved by the electorate at an annual or special meeting warned for that purpose. However, any increased amount approved by the electorate may not be included as a current expenditure of the district for the purposes of aid paid under chapter 123 of this title.

Section 3445. Use of funds. State aid may be used by a town school district or an incorporated school district only for legitimate items of current expense, including, but without limitation, the following: transportation, advanced instruction, supervision and teachers' salaries. It may be used for aid to schools other than public schools as defined in section 3441(2) of this title.

Student Tuition

Section 3441. (2) Public school means any school which provides elementary or secondary school education as defined in this title, and which received its principal support from public funds; and shall also include a private school to which a Vermont school district pays tuition from public funds on behalf of a pupil.

Washington

Section 28A.24.065. Authorization for Private School Students to Ride Buses — Conditions.

Every school district board of directors may authorize children attending a private school approved in accordance with RCW 282.02.201 to ride a school bus or other student transportation vehicle to and from school so long as the following conditions are met:

(1) The board of directors shall not be required to alter those bus routes or stops established for transporting public school students;

(2) Private school students shall be allowed to ride on a seat available basis only; and

(3) The board of directors shall charge an amount sufficient to reimburse the district for the actual per seat cost of providing such transportation.

Section 28A.58.107. Commencement Exercises — Lip Reading Instruction — Joint Purchasing, Including Issuing Interest Bearing Warrants — Budgets.

Every board of directors, unless otherwise specifically provided by law, shall:

(1) Provide for the expenditure of a reasonable amount for suitable commencement exercises;

(2) In addition to providing free instruction in lip reading for children handicapped by defective hearing, make arrangements for free instruction in lip reading to adults handicapped by defective hearing whenever in its judgment such instruction appears to be in the best interests of the school district and adults concerned;

(3) Join with boards of directors of other school districts or an educational service district pursuant to RCW 28A.21.086(3), as now or hereafter amended, or both such school districts and educational service district in buying supplies, equipment and services by establishing and maintaining a joint purchasing agency, or otherwise, when deemed for the best interests of the district, any joint agency formed hereunder being herewith authorized and empowered to issue interest bearing warrants in payment of any obligation owed: Provided, however, that those agencies issuing interest bearing warrants shall assign accounts receivable in an amount equal to the amount of the outstanding interest bearing warrants to the county treasurer issuing such interest bearing warrants: Provided further, that the joint purchasing agency shall consider the request of any one or more private schools requesting the agency to jointly buy supplies, equipment, and services, and, after considering such request, may cooperate with and jointly make purchases with private schools of supplies, equipment and services so long as such private schools pay in advance their proportionate share of the costs involved in such purchases;

(4) Consider the request of any one or more private schools requesting the board to jointly buy supplies, equipment and services, and, after considering such request, may provide such joint purchasing services: Provided, that such private schools pay in advance their proportionate share of the costs or provide a surety bond to cover their proportionate share of the costs involved in such purchases; and

(5) Prepare budgets as provided for in Chapter 28A.65 RCW.

West Virginia

Section 18-28-4. Voluntary Participation in State Programs.

Any private, parochial or church school or school of a religious order or other nonpublic school complying with the provisions of this article may, on a voluntary basis, participate in any state operated or state sponsored program otherwise made available to such schools by law.

Wisconsin

[Constitution Article 1-23]: Nothing in this constitution shall prohibit the legislature from providing for the safety and welfare of children by providing for the transportation for children to and from any parochial or private school or institution of learning.

Notes

Chapter I

[1] Edgar W. Knight and Clifton L. Hall, *Reading in American Educational History* (New York: Appleton-Century-Crofts, 1951), pp. 62–63.

[2] Robert A. Koenig, *The Courts and Education* (Chicago: University of Chicago Press, 1978), p. 1.

[3] Peter H. Rossi and Alice S. Rossi, "Some Effects of Parochial School Education in America," in *Society and Education: A Book of Readings,* ed. Robert J. Havinghurst, Bernice L. Neugarten, and Jacqueline M. Falk (Boston: Allyn, 1967), p. 204.

[4] M.A. McGheney, *Control of the Curriculum* (Chicago: University of Chicago Press, 1978), p. 140.

[5] Mary Perkins Ryan, *Are Parochial Schools the Answer?* (New York: Holt, Rinehart and Winston, 1964), p. 32.

[6] Ronald F. Campbell et al., *The Organization and Control of American Schools* (Columbus, Ohio: Charles E. Merrill, 1970), p. 528.

[7] James D. Richardson, ed., *Compilation of the Messages and Papers of the Presidents,* 1889–1897, vol. 7, record, 1876, 4, 175–181 (Washington, D.C.: Government Printing Office, 1898).

[8] Vincent P. Lannie, *Public Money and Parochial Education* (Cleveland: Press of Case Western Reserve University, 1968), p. 3.

[9] Samuel Eliot Morison, Henry Steel Commager, and William Luechtenberg, *The Growth of the American Republic* (New York: Oxford University Press, 1969), 1, p. 452.

[10] Ibid. See also Elwood P. Cubberley, *Changing Conception of Education* (Boston, 1909), pp. 15–16. Professor Cubberley insisted that southern and eastern Europeans, considerably different from northern Europeans, were "illiterate, docile, lacking in self-reliance and initiative, and not possessing the Anglo-Teutonic conception of law, order, and government, their coming has served to dilute tremendously our national stock, and to corrupt our civic life." Public education must, continued Professor Cubberley, "assimilate and amalgamate these people as a part of our American race, and to implant in their children, so far as can be done, the Anglo-Saxon conception of righteousness, law and order, and popular government, and to awaken in them a reverence for our democratic institutions and for those things in our national life which we as a people hold to be of abiding worth."

[11] Edwin Scott Guastad, *A Religious History of America* (New York: Harper and Row, 1966), pp. 212–213.

¹²Rossi and Rossi, p. 205.
¹³Elywn A. Smith, *Religious Liberty: The Development of Church and State Thought Since the Revolutionary Era* (Philadelphia: Fortress Press, 1972), p. 103.
¹⁴Ibid., p. 105.
¹⁵Ibid.
¹⁶Ibid., p. 101.
¹⁷Ibid.
¹⁸Ibid.
¹⁹Lemon v. Kurtzman, 91 S. Ct. 2111, 2133 (1971).

Chapter II

¹Norman A. Graebner, Gilbert C. Fite, and Philip W. White, *A History of the United States,* vol. 1 (New York: McGraw-Hill, 1970), pp. 49–50.
²Ibid.
³Ibid.
⁴*Compton's Encyclopedia,* vol. 9 (Chicago: William Benton, 1967), p. 193.
⁵Graebner, Fite, and White, *History of the United States,* vol. 1, p. 51.
⁶Ibid., pp. 50–53; see also Saint Augustine, *The City of God* (New York: Modern Library, Random House, 1950). Saint Augustine, fifth-century Bishop of Hippo (Bona), in this literary masterpiece — a theology of history — promulgates an eschatology that includes a temporal theocracy. See also John Calvin, *Institutes of the Christian Religion.* The *Institutes* is probably the most notable work in all Protestant theology and provided the Puritans with a theological framework for governing their colonies. John Calvin established a theocratic republic in Geneva, Switzerland, and under his rule (1541–1564) banished at least twenty-six heretics, executed one child for striking his parents, closed all theaters and amusement establishments; the council of elders inspected every household and examined all citizens concerning theology, dress, politics, and sex.

In America, the "City of God" theology — establishing a theocratic republic — has returned as an important political force. With the election of President Richard Nixon, America began moving unmistakably in a conservative direction. Emerging with and from the conservative influence is the New Right. Now, the New Right wishes to be called Populists, a political description from an earlier era of America's political history. Also emerging within the New Right, hand in glove and providing the spiritual direction, and in reality the energizing force behind the New Right are the fundamentalist religions. Over the last eighteen years riding on a pale white horse from West to East — from San Francisco to San Diego in California to Virginia — with a bulge in Ohio and headquarters in Dallas, Texas, a new Bible Belt, corresponding geographically to the Sun Belt, has emerged. Using the electronic media, they are preaching a gospel of gloom and doom, that the world is coming to an end at any moment but you still have time to send one more check. The New Right fundamentalist preachers are preaching a religious-political gospel that sounds remarkably similar to John Calvin's *Institutes of the Christian Religion* — a theocratic republic. The leading theoretician of the New Right is Frances A. Schaeffer, who resides in Switzerland. See Frances A. Schaeffer, *A Christian Manifesto* (Crossway Books, Illinois). See also his son Franky Schaeffer, *A Time for Anger* (Crossway Books, Illinois, 1982). In this publication Franky Schaeffer insists: "What is the use of preaching a gospel and spreading the teachings of Christ when the gospel and those teachings are seen as irrelevant to the ways in which we value life, to the issues of infanticide and euthanasia — if it is no longer to be allowed to provide a sure humane moral base for education?" Franky Schaeffer acknowledges that this book is a polemic against the "secular humanistic elite." See also John W. Whitehead, *The Second American Revolution* (Westchester, Ill.: Crossway Books, 1982); Tim La Haye, *The Battle for the Mind* (Fleming H. Revell, Old Tappan, N.J., 1980); Erling Jorstad, *The Politics of Doomsday* (Abingdon Press, Nashville, Tenn., 1970).

[7]Graebner, Fite, and White, *History of the United States,* vol. 1, p. 52.

[8]Nathaniel Hawthorne, *The Scarlet Letter* (New York: Washington Square Press), p. 49. The first edition of *The Scarlet Letter* was published in 1859 by Ticknor, Reed and Fields, Boston.

[9]Ibid., pp. 267–68.

[10]Paul Monroe, *Founding of the American Public School System* (New York: Halner, 1970, facsimile of 1940 ed.), 1, p. 11.

[11]Elwood P. Cubberley, *Public Education in the United States* (Boston: Houghton Mifflin, 1934), p. 14.

[12]_____. *Readings in the History of Education* (Boston: Houghton, Mifflin, 1920), p. 298.

[13]Richard G. Boone, *Education in the United States* (New York: D. Appleton, 1980), pp. 47–53.

[14]Edgar W. Knight, *Education in the United States* (Boston: Ginn, 1929), p. 144.

[15]Ibid., pp. 146–56; see also Cubberley, *Public Education,* p. 14.

[16]Elwood P. Cubberley, *Changing Conception of Education* (Boston: Houghton Mifflin, 1909), p. 28; see also Knight, *Education in the United States,* pp. 153–56; see also P.A. Siljestrom, *The Educational Institution of the United States,* trans. F. Rowan (London: John Chapman, 1853), p. 16.

[17]Monroe, *American Public School System,* 1, p. 295.

[18]Elwood P. Cubberley, *Public Education,* p. 89.

[19]Ibid.

[20]Ibid.

[21]Ibid.

[22]Ibid., p. 90.

[23]Ibid.

[24]Ibid.

[25]Ibid.

[26]Graebner, Fite, and White, *History of the United States,* vol. 1, pp. 230–34, 340–44.

[27]Cubberley, *Public Education,* p. 97.

[28]Knight, *Education in the United States,* p. 144; see also Boone, *Education in the United States,* pp. 47–53.

[29]Cubberley, *Public Education,* p. 164.

[30]Charles Beard and Mary Beard, *The Rise of American Civilization* (New York: Macmillan, 1927), 1, p. 443.

[31]*Twelfth Annual Report of the Board of Education, Together with the Twelfth Annual Report of the Secretary of the Board* (Boston, 1849), p. 84, quoted in Lawrence A. Cremin, *The Transformation of the School* (New York: Alfred A. Knopf, 1961), p. 9.

[32]Lawrence A. Cremin, *The Transformation of the School* (New York: Alfred A. Knopf, 1961), p. 11.

[33]Ibid., p. 9.

[34]*Sixteenth Annual Report of the Board of Directors of the St. Louis Public Schools* (St. Louis, 1871), p. 28.

[35]*Seventeenth Annual Report of the Board of Directors of the St. Louis Public Schools* (St. Louis, 1872), p. 58.

[36]John Dewey, *Democracy and Education* (New York: Macmillan, 1916), pp. 87–88.

[37]John Dewey, *The School and Society* (Chicago, 1899), p. 43.

[38]Abraham Lincoln, "Gettysburg Address," *Compton Encyclopedia* (Chicago: Compton, 1967), 1, p. 284h.

[39]Cremin, *Transformation of the School,* p. 13.

[40]Stuart v. Kalamazoo, 30 Mich. 69 (1874).

[41]P.A. Siljestrom, *Educational Institutions of the United States* (New York: Arno Press, 1969), p. vii.

[42]Roland F. Campbell et al., *The Organization and Control of American Schools* (Columbus, Ohio: Charles E. Merrill, 1970), p. 528.

[43]Stephen Goldstein, *Law and Public Education—Cases and Materials* (Indianapolis, Indiana: Bobbs-Merrill), p. 7.

[44]M.R. Smith and Joseph E. Bryson, *Church-State Relations: The Legality of Using Public Funds for Religious Schools* (Topeka, Kansas: National Organization on Legal Problems on Education, 1971), pp. 20–31.

[45]Peter H. Rossi and Alice S. Rossi, "Some Effects of Parochial School Education in America," in *Society and Education: A Book of Readings,* ed. Robert J. Havinghurst, Bernice L. Hevgarten, and Jacqueline M. Folk (Boston: Allyn, 1967), p. 204.

[46]Constitution, First Amendment.

[47]Graebner, Fite, and White, *History of the United States,* p. 367.

[48]James Madison, "Memorial and Remonstrance Against Religious Assessments," quoted in *Church and State* 36, no. 3 (March 1983): pp. 3–4.

[49]Moses C. Tyler, *Patrick Henry, American Statesman* (Boston: Houghton Mifflin, 1887), 3, p. 53.

[50]Ibid., pp. 208–9.

[51]John Foley, *Jefferson Encyclopedia* (New York: Funk and Wagnalls, 1900). Also from the same source is this interesting note from President Jefferson to Attorney General Levi Lincoln (before sending this reply to the Danbury Baptists, Jefferson enclosed a copy of it to Levi Lincoln, his attorney general) in which he said: "The Baptist address admits of a condemnation of the alliance between Church and State, under the authority of the Constitution. It furnishes an occasion, too, which I have long wished to find, of saying why I do not proclaim fastings and thanksgivings, as my predecessors did. I know it will give great offence to the New England clergy; but the advocate of religious freedom is to expect neither peace nor forgiveness from them. Will you be so good as to examine the answer, and suggest any alterations which might prevent an ill effect, or promote a good one among the people? You understand the temper of those in the North, and can weaken it, therefore, to their stomachs; it is at present seasoned to the Southern taste only."

[52]Henry Steele Commanger, *The American Mind* (New Haven: Yale University Press, 1950), pp. 26–27.

[53]Alexis de Tocqueville, quoted in Commanger, *The American Mind,* p. 163.

[54]Vincent P. Lannie, *Public Money and Parochial Education* (Cleveland: The Press of Case Western Reserve University, 1968), p. 2.

[55]Neil G. McCluskey, *Catholic Education in America: A Documentary*

History (New York: Columbia University Press, 1964), p. 6.

[56]Vincent P. Lannie, *Public Money,* p. 3.

[57]Editorials, *Literary Digest* 27, no. 9 (August 29, 1903): p. 261.

[58]"The Separation of the Church from the Tax-Supported School," *Education Review* 26 (October 1903), p. 38.

[59]William T. Harris, *Morality in the Schools,* Tract 12, quoted in Neil Gerard McCluskey, *Public Schools and Moral Education* (New York: Columbia University Press, 1958), p. 169.

[60]Ibid.

[61]Regional A. Neuwien, ed., *Catholic Schools in Action* (South Bend, Ind.: University of Notre Dame Press, 1966), p. 3.

[62]Lannie, *Public Money,* p. 6.

[63]Ibid.

[64]Diane Ravitch, *The Great School Wars* (New York: Basic Books, 1974), p. 47.

[65]Ibid.

[66]Ibid.

[67]Ibid.

[68]Lannie, *Public Money,* p. 6.

[69]Ravitch, *School Wars,* p. 48.

[70]Lannie, *Public Money,* p. 33.

[71]Ravitch, *School Wars,* pp. 49–51. Professor Ravitch's book, especially chapters 4–7, provides a beautiful and documented narrative of the Catholic struggle for public funds.

[72]Lannie, *Public Money,* pp. 47–48.

[73]Ibid., p. 256.

[74]*Congressional Record,* 44th Cong., 1st sess. (1876), vol. 4, 5245, 5246, 5562, 5568, 5580, 5595.

[75]Andrew M. Greeley and Peter H. Rossi, *The Education of Catholic America* (Chicago: Aldine, 1966), p. 2.

[76]Benton Patterson, "What's Behind the Shutdowns—and What's Ahead," *School Management* 13 (April 1969): p. 49.

[77]"Defining Religion," *University of Chicago Law Review* 32 (1965): pp. 550–51.

[78]Arval A. Morris, *The Constitution and American Education* (St. Paul, Minn.: West, 1977), p. 374.

[79]*The Random House College Dictionary,* rev. ed. (New York: Random House, 1975), pp. 1114–15.

[80]*Webster's Ninth New Collegiate Dictionary* (Springfield, Mass.: G. and C. Merriam, 1967), p. 724.

[81]Wolman v. Walter, 433 U.S. 299, 93 S. Ct. 2593 (1977).

[82]William T. Blackstone, *The Problem of Religious Knowledge* (Englewood Cliff, N.J.: Prentice-Hall, 1963); Mortimer J. Adler, *How to Think About God* (New York: Macmillan, 1980); Carl Sagan, *The Dragons of Eden* (New York: Random House, 1977); Robert Jastrow, *God and the Astronomers* (New York: W.W. Norton, 1978).

[83]Morris, *Constitution,* p. 377.

[84]Ibid.

[85]Constitution, First Amendment.

[86]Everson v. Board of Education, 330 U.S. 1, 67 S. Ct. 504.

[87]Morris, *Constitution,* p. 377.

[88]330 U.S. 1 at 15 (1947).
[89]Committee for Public Education and Religious Liberty v. Regan, 63 L. Ed. 2d 94 (1980), p. 108.
[90]Ibid.
[91]Quick Bear v. Leupp, 210 U.S. 50 at 8 (1908).
[92]Grand Rapids School District v. Ball, 105 S. Ct. 3216 (1985).
[93]Lemon v. Kurtzman, Dicenso v. Robinson, 91 S. Ct. 2111 (1971).
[94]210 U.S. 50, 78 (1908).
[95]Ibid.
[96]Ibid., p. 81.
[97]Ibid., p. 82.
[98]Meyer v. Nebraska, 262 U.S. 390 (1923).
[99]Ibid., p. 400.
[100]Frothingham v. Mellon 262 U.S. 447 (1923).
[101]Ibid., p. 490.
[102]Pierce v. Society of Sisters, 268 U.S. 510.
[103]Ibid., p. 530.
[104]Ibid., p. 535.
[105]Cochran v. Louisiana State Board of Education, 281 U.S. 370 (1930).
[106]Ibid., p. 374.
[107]Ibid., p. 375.
[108]Ibid., p. 374.
[109]Ibid., p. 375.
[110]Cantwell v. Connecticut, 310 U.S. 296 (1940).
[111]Ibid., p. 303.
[112]Ibid.
[113]Everson v. Board of Education, 330 U.S. 1 (1947).
[114]Ibid., p. 15.
[115]Ibid., p. 18.
[116]Ibid., p. 24.
[117]Ibid.
[118]Ibid., p. 51.
[119]Ibid., p. 29.
[120]63 L. Ed. 2d 94 (1980), p. 108.
[121]McCollum v. Board of Education, 333 U.S. 203 (1948).
[122]Ibid., p. 205.
[123]Ibid., p. 210.
[124]Ibid., p. 212.
[125]Zorach v. Clausen, 343 U.S. 306 (1952).
[126]Ibid., p. 324.
[127]Engel v. Vitale, 370 U.S. 421 (1962).
[128]Ibid., p. 422.
[129]Ibid., p. 431.
[130]Ibid., p. 437.
[131]Ibid., p. 443.
[132]Abington School District v. Schempp, 374 U.S. 203 (1963).
[133]Ibid., p. 222.
[134]Ibid., p. 225.
[135]Ibid., p. 228.
[136]Ibid., pp. 229–30.
[137]Lemon v. Kurtzman, 91 S. Ct. 2111 (1971).

[138]Board of Education v. Allen, 392 U.S. 236 (1968).
[139]Ibid., p. 240.
[140]Ibid., p. 243.
[141]Ibid., p. 248.
[142]Ibid., p. 253.
[143]Ibid., p. 265.
[144]Ibid., p. 266.
[145]Flast v. Cohen, 392 U.S. 83 (1968).
[146]Frothingham v. Mellon, 262 U.S. 447 (1923).
[147]Flast v. Cohen, 392 U.S. 83 (1968).
[148]Ibid., p. 113.
[149]Ibid.
[150]Walz v. Tax Commissioner of New York City, 38 U.S.L.W. 4347 (1970).

Chapter III

[1]Constitution, First Amendment.
[2]Everson v. Board of Education, 330 U.S. 1, 15 (1947).
[3]Fourteenth Amendment.
[4]Cantwell v. Connecticut, 310 U.S. 296 (1940). To the contrary, Justice William Hand in Jaffee v. Board of School Commissioners of Mobile County, 554 F. Supp. 1104, 1128 (S.D. Ala. 1983) insisted that "Alabama has the power to establish a state religion if it chooses to do so."
[5]Zorach v. Clausen, 343 U.S. 306, 314 (1952).
[6]Virginia Constitution, Article I, Section 16 (1971).
[7]Ibid.
[8]Montana Constitution, Preamble (1972).
[9]Montana Constitution, Article I, Section 5 (1972).
[10]Alabama Constitution, Article I, Section 3.
[11]Nebraska Constitution, Article I, Section 4.
[12]Colorado Constitution, Article IX, Section 8.
[13]Arizona Constitution, Article XI, Section 7.
[14]Georgia Constitution, Article I, Section 2-103.
[15]Arizona Constitution, Article XI, Section 7.
[16]Massachusetts Constitution, Article XVIII, Section 2.
[17]Montana Constitution, Article X, Section 6.
[18]Virginia Constitution, Article IV, Section 16.

Chapter IV

[1]AASA, *Private School Participation in Chapter 2 of the Education Consolidation and Improvement Act* (Arlington, Va.: AASA, 1984), p. 2. See also Felton v. Secretary, United States Department of Education, 739 F.2d 48 (2d Cir. 1984).
[2]Minnesota Statutes, §290.09(22) (1982).
[3]Mueller v. Allen, 103 S. Ct. 3062 (1983).
[4]Title V, Subtitle D of Public Law 97-35 (95 Stat. 357). See also Felton v. Secretary, United States Department of Education, 739 F.2d 48 (2d Cir. 1984). See also Aguilar v. Felton, 105 S. Ct. 3232 (1985).

[5]Chapter I of the Education Consolidation and Improvement Act of 1981 (Subchapter D of Title V in P.L. 93-35).

[6]Follow-Through Act (Subchapter C of Title VI of P.L. 97-35).

[7]Law Related Education Program, P.L. 97-35, Subchapter D, Sec. 583.

[8]Arts in Education Program, P.L. 97-35, Subchapter C, Sec. 385.

[9]Alcohol and Drug Abuse Program, P.L. 97-35, Subchapter D, Sec. 583.

[10]Inexpensive Book Distribution Program, P.L. 97-35, Sec. 583.

[11]Higher Education Act, Title V-B, Sec. 532.

[12]Women's Educational Equity Act Program, P.L. 97-35, Subchapter C.

[13]Education of the Handicapped Act, P.L. 94-142, Part C, Sec. 623.

[14]Ibid., P.L. 94-142, Part D, Sec. 633.

[15]Ibid., P.L. 94-142, Part F.

[16]Ibid., P.L. 94-142, Part C, Sec. 624.

[17]Ibid., P.L. 94-142, Part D.

[18]Special Milk Program, P.L. 84-752.

[19]National School Lunch Act of 1946, P.L. 85-478.

[20]Child Nutrition Act of 1966, P.L. 85-478.

[21]Michael Schwartz, *Tax Funds for Private Education: Louisiana's Success Story* (Milwaukee: Catholic League for Religious and Civil Rights, 1984). *Note:* On December 2, 1985, Americans United filed suit in federal district court in New Orleans challenging an array of religious-school programs supported by state and federal funds.

[22]Smith-Hurd Illinois Annotated Statutes, Chapter 122, Section 18-8,1(a).

[23]Public Laws of Pennsylvania, Section 5-5-2.

[24]Public Laws of California, Section 41902.

[25]Ibid., Section 60315.

[26]Public Laws of Minnesota, Section 123.932.

[27]Public Laws of Massachusetts, Chapter 76, Section 1.

[28]Everson v. Board of Education, 330 U.S. 1 (1947).

[29]Public Laws of Connecticut, Section 10-215A.

[30]Public Laws of Kansas, Section 72-5393.

Chapter V

[1]Kermit S. Buckner, *An Analysis of the Impact of Chief Justice Warren Burger on Supreme Court Decisions Affecting Public Education,* Ed.D. dissertation, University of North Carolina—Greensboro, 1980; see also George Robert Deakon, *The Burger Court and the Public Schools,* Ed.D. dissertation, University of North Carolina-Greeensboro, 1978.

[2]H.C. Hudgins, Jr., *The Warren Court and the Public Schools,* (Danville, Ill.: Interstate, 1970).

[3]Lemon v. Kurtzman, DiCenso v. Robinson, 91 S. Ct. 2111 (1971).

[4]Ibid.

[5]Committee for Public Education and Religious Liberty v. Regan, 63 L. Ed.2d 94 (1980).

[6]Mueller v. Allen, 103 S. Ct. 3063 (1983).

[7]Lemon v. Kurtzman, DiCenso v. Robinson, 91 S. Ct. 2111 (1971).

[8]Ibid., p. 2112.

[9]Ibid., p. 2114.

[10]Ibid., p. 2115.

[11]Ibid.

[12]Ibid., p. 2116.

[13]Ibid.

[14]Ibid.

[15]Ibid.

[16]Ibid., p. 2117.

[17]Walz v. Tax Commission 397 U.S. 690–691 (1970).

[18]Lemon v. Kurtzman, DiCenso v. Robinson, 91 S. Ct. 2133 (1971).

[19]Cook County v. Chicago Industrial School, 125 Ill. 540, 571, 18 N.E. 183, 197 (1888).

[20]Lemon v. Kurtzman, DiCenso v. Robinson, 91 S. Ct. 2134 (1971).

[21]Ibid., p. 2125.

[22]Ibid., p. 2130.

[23]Ibid., p. 2122.

[24]Ibid., p. 2132.

[25]Johnson v. Sanders, 319 F. Supp. 421 (D.C. Conn. 1970); 403 U.S. 965 (1971).

[26]Wolman v. Essex, 442 F. Supp. 399 (D.C. 1972); Essex v. Wolman, 92 S. Ct. 1961, 406 U.S. 912 (1972).

[27]Kosydar v. Wolman, 353 F. Supp. 744 (D.C. 1972); see also Grit v. Wolman, 93 S. Ct. 952 (1973).

[28]Johnson v. New York State Education Department, 409 U.S. 75 (1972); 319 F. Supp. 271 (D.C. 1971); 499 F.2d 871 (1971).

[29]Essex v. Wolman, 92 S. Ct. 1961, 406 U.S. 912 (1972).

[30]Wolman v. Essex, 442 F. Supp. 399 (D.C. 1972); see also Essex v. Wolman, 93 S. Ct. 61, 409 U.S. 808 (1973) (motion for leave to file petition for rehearing denied June 25, 1973); Essex v. Wolman, 93 S. Ct. 3044, 413 U.S. 923 (1973); on June 25, 1973, the Supreme Court denied leave to file petition for rehearing.

[31]Kosydar v. Wolman, 353 F. Supp. 744 (D.C. 1972); see also Grit v. Wolman, 93 S. Ct. 952, 410 U.S. 903 (1973); 93 S. Ct. 3062, 413 U.S. 901 (1973).

[32]Johnson v. New York State Education Department, 409 U.S. 75 (1972); see also 319 F. Supp. 271; 499 F.2d 871 (1972).

[33]Joseph E. Bryson, "Recent Activity in Church-State Relations," in *Current Trends in School Law,* ed. M.A. McGhehey (Topeka, Kan.: National Organization on Legal Problems in Education, 1973), p. 89.

[34]Lemon v. Kurtzman, 411 U.S. 192 (1973).

[35]Ibid., p. 193.

[36]In the eighth case, Norwood v. Harrison, 413 U.S. 455 (1973), the Court, with Chief Justice Burger writing the Court's opinion, insisted that Mississippi's legislative enactment loaning textbooks to students attending racially discriminatory private schools was unconstitutional.

[37]Committee for Public Education and Religious Liberty v. Nyquist, 93 S. Ct. 2955 (1973).

[38]A *qualifying* school was a nonpublic school serving low-income families.

[39]93 S. Ct. 2962.

[40]Ibid.

[41]Ibid., p. 2963.

[42]Ibid., p. 2964.

[43]Ibid.

[44]Ibid.

[45]Ibid.

[46]Ibid., p. 2969.

[47]Ibid., p. 2970.

[48]Ibid., p. 2972.

[49]Ibid., p. 2973.

[50]Levitt v. Committee for Public Education and Religious Liberty, 93 S. Ct. 2914 (1973).

[51]Ibid., p. 2916.

[52]Committee for Public Education and Religious Liberty v. Nyquist, 93 S. Ct. 2955.

[53]Levitt v. Committee for Public Education and Religious Liberty, 93 S. Ct. 2919 (1973).

[54]Ibid.

[55]Ibid.

[56]Ibid.

[57]Sloan v. Lemon, 43 S. Ct. 2982 (1973).

[58]Sloan v. Lemon, 93 S. Ct 2982 (1973).

[59]Ibid., p. 2984.

[60]Ibid., p. 2985.

[61]Ibid.

[62]Ibid., p. 2987.

[63]Marburger v. Public Funds for Public Schools of New Jersey, 413 U.S. 916 (1973); see also Marburger v. Public Funds for Public Schools of New Jersey, 417 U.S. 961 (1974) and Griggs v. Public Funds for Public Schools of New Jersey, 417 U.S. 916 (1974).

[64]Marburger v. Public Funds for Public Schools of New Jersey, 413 U.S. 916 (1973).

[65]Public Funds for Public Schools v. Marburger, 358 F. Supp. 29 (D.C. N.J. 1973).

[66]Hunt v. McNair, 413 U.S. 734, 93 S. Ct. 2865 (1973).

[67]Ibid., p. 734.

[68]Ibid., p. 735.

[69]Essex v. Wolman, 93 S. Ct. 61 (1973).

[70]Kosydar v. Wolman, 353 F. Supp. 744 (D.C. Ohio 1972); Grit v. Wolman, 93 S. Ct. 952 (1973); 93 S. Ct. 3062 (1973).

[71]Grit v. Wolman, 93 S. Ct. 952 (1973); 93 S. Ct. 3062 (1973).

[72]Kosydar v. Wolman, 353 F. Supp. 751 (D.C. Ohio 1972).

[73]Ibid.

[74]Ibid., p. 753.

[75]Ibid.

[76]Ibid., p. 754.

[77]Ibid., p. 755.

[78]Ibid., p. 765.

[79]Ibid., p. 762.

[80]Ibid.

[81]Grit v. Wolman, 93 S. Ct. 952, 410 U.S. 903 (1973); 93 S. Ct. 3062, 413 U.S. 901 (1973).

[82]Cathedral Academy v. Committee for Public Education and Religious Liberty, 93 S. Ct. 2814, 413 U.S. 37 (1973).

[83]419 U.S. 890 (1974).

[84]419 U.S. 888 (1974).

[85]417 U.S. 961 (1974); see also Griggs v. Public Funds for Public Schools of New Jersey, 417 U.S. 916 (1974).

[86]94 S. Ct. 2276 (1974).

[87]419 U.S. 890 (1974).

[88]Ibid.

[89]419 U.S. 888 (1974).

[90]Luetkemeyer v. Kaufmann, 364 F. Supp. 378 (W.D. Mo. 1973).

[91]Ibid., p. 381.

[92]Ibid., p. 382.

[93]Ibid., p. 383.

[94]Luetkemeyer v. Kaufmann, 419 U.S. 889 (1974).

[95]Ibid.

[96]Ibid.

[97]Marburger v. Public Funds for Public Schools of New Jersey, 417 U.S. 961 (1974); see also Griggs v. Public Funds for Public Schools of New Jersey, 417 U.S. 916 (1974).

[98]Wheeler v. Barrera, 94 S. Ct. 2276, 2278 (1974). Nebraska State Board of Education v. School District of Hartington, 195 N.W.2d 161 (1972) might have become the first Title I case, but the Supreme Court denied certiorari at 409 U.S. 921, 93 S. Ct. 220, 34 L. Ed. 182 (1972).

[99]Ibid., pp. 2276–2278.

[100]Ibid., p. 2278.

[101]Ibid., p. 2282.

[102]Ibid., p. 2283.

[103]Ibid.

[104]Ibid.

[105]Ibid., p. 2284.

[106]Ibid.

[107]Ibid., p. 2289.

[108]Ibid., p. 2287.

[109]Ibid.

[110]Ibid., p. 2288.

[111]Ibid.

[112]Ibid.

[113]Ibid., p. 2289; see Justice Powell's positions in Aguilar v. Felten, 105 S. Ct. 3232 (1985).

[114]Ibid.

[115]Ibid., p. 2290.

[116]Mallory v. Barrera, 544 S.W.2d 556 (Mo. 1976).

[117]Joseph E. Bryson, "Recent Church-State Litigation," in *Contemporary Legal Problems in Education,* ed. M.A. McGhehey (Topeka, Kan.: National Organization on Legal Problems in Education, 1974), p. 249.

[118]Meek v. Pittenger, 95 S. Ct. 1753 (1975); rehearing denied 95 S. Ct. 2668 (1975).

[119]Ibid., p. 1755.

[120]Ibid., p. 1758.

[121]Ibid., p. 1760.

[122]Ibid., p. 1762.

[123]Ibid.

[124]Ibid.

[125]Ibid., p. 1766.

[126]Ibid., p. 1767.

[127]Ibid., p. 1768.

[128]Ibid., p. 1769.

[129]Roemer v. Board of Education, 96 S. Ct. 2344 (1976).

[130]Wolman v. Walters, 93 S. Ct. 2593, 433 U.S. 229 (1977).

[131]Committee for Public Education and Religious Liberty v. Regan, 100 S. Ct. 840, 444 U.S. 644 (1980).

[132]Ibid., pp. 107, 108.

[133]Roemer v. Board of Public Works, 96 S. Ct. 2337 (1976).

[134]Ibid.

[135]Ibid., p. 2344.

[136]Ibid.

[137]Ibid., p. 2345.

[138]Ibid., p. 2349.

[139]Ibid.

[140]Ibid.

[141]Ibid.

[142]Ibid., p. 2350.

[143]Ibid.

[144]Ibid.

[145]Ibid., p. 2351.

[146]Ibid., p. 2352.

[147]Ibid., p. 2353.

[148]Ibid.

[149]Ibid., p. 2354.

[150]Ibid., p. 2355.

[151]Ibid., p. 2356.

[152]Ibid., p. 2357.

[153]Ibid., p. 2358.

[154]Ibid., p. 2354.

[155]Ibid.; see also Widmar v. Vincent, 102 S. Ct. 269 (1981). Among the many important religious free-speech issues discussed, the Court did insist that university students are less impressionable than younger students.

[156]Joseph E. Bryson, "Church-State Relationship—Recent Developments," in *School Law Update—1977,* ed. M.A. McGhehey (Topeka, Kan.: National Organization on Legal Problems of Education, 1978), p. 107.

[157]Wolman v. Walters, 97 S. Ct. 2593, 433 U.S 229 (1977).

[158]Ibid., p. 2595.

[159]Ibid.

[160]Ibid.

[161]Ibid.

[162]Ibid.

[163]Ibid.

[164]421 U.S. 349 (1975).

[165]Wolman v. Walters, 97 S. Ct. 2597 (1977).

[166]Ibid.

[167]Ibid.

[168]392 U.S. 236 (1968).

[169]421 U.S. 349 (1975).

[170]Wolman v. Walter, 97 S. Ct. 2593, 433 U.S. 229 (1977).

[171]Ibid., pp. 2593–2594.

[172]For substantive differences, see Meek v. Pittenger, 421 U.S. 349, 364 (1975); Public Funds for Public Schools v. Marburger, 358 F. Supp. 29 (D. N.J. 1973), aff'd, 417 U.S. 961 (1974).

[173]Wolman v. Walters, 97 S. Ct. 2603 (1977).

[174]Ibid., p. 2602.

[175]Meek v. Pittenger, 421 U.S. 349 (1975).

[176]Lemon v. Kurtzman, 403 U.S. 602 (1971).

[177]Wolman v. Walters, 97 S. Ct. 2603 (1977).

[178]Ibid., p. 2607.

[179]Ibid.

[180]Everson v. Board of Education, 330 U.S. 1 (1947).

[181]Wolman v. Walters, 97 S. Ct. 2608 (1977).

[182]Ibid., p. 2609.

[183]Ibid., p. 2610.

[184]Ibid., p. 2612.

[185]Board of Education v. Allen, 392 U.S. 236 (1968).

[186]Wolman v. Walters, 97 S. Ct. 2611, 433 U.S. 259 (1977).

[187]Ibid.

[188]See Committee for Public Education v. Nyquist, 413 U.S. 756 (1973).

[189]Wolman v. Walters, 97 S. Ct. 2613, 433 U.S. 263 (1977).

[190]Ibid.

[191]Scopes v. State, 289 S.W. 363 (1927).

[192]Wolman v. Walters, 93 S. Ct. 2614, 433 U.S. 263 (1977).

[193]Ibid.

[194]Ibid., p. 2615.

[195]Ibid.

[196]Byrne v. Public Funds for Public Schools of New Jersey, 99 S. Ct. 2818, 442 U.S. 907 (1979); see also 590 F.2d 514 (3rd Cir. 1979).

[197]Meltzer v. Board of Public Instruction of Orange County, 577 F.2d 311 (5th Cir. 1978); 99 S. Ct. 872, 439 U.S. 1089 (1979).

[198]Flory v. Sioux Falls School District, 619 F.2d 1311 (8th Cir. 1980).

[199]Ibid., p. 1316.

[200]Ibid., p. 1319.

[201]Stone v. Graham, 101 S. Ct. 192, 449 U.S. 39 (1980).

[202]Ibid., p. 193.

[203]Ibid., p. 194.

[204]Committee for Public Education and Religious Liberty v. Regan, 100 S. Ct. 840, 444 U.S. 644 (1980).

[205]Levitt v. Committee for Public Education, 93 S. Ct. 2814 (1973).

[206]Committee for Public Education and Religious Liberty v. Regan, 100 S. Ct. 840, 444 U.S. 644 (1980).

[207]Ibid.

[208]Ibid.

[209]DiCenso v. Robinson, 91 S. Ct. 2111 (1971).

[210]Ibid., p. 2119.

[211]Committee for Public Education and Relgious Liberty v. Nyquist, 37 L. Ed. 2d 939 (1973).

[212]Levitt v. Committee for Public Education and Religious Liberty, 413 U.S. 472 (1973).

[213]Sloan v. Lemon, 413 U.S. at 835 (1973).

[214]Meek v. Pittenger, 421 U.S. 349 (1975).

[215]Roemer v. Board of Education, 96 S. Ct. 2344 (1976).

[216]Wolman v. Walter, 45 U.S.F.W. 4861 (1977).

[217]Committee for Public Education and Religious Liberty v. Regan, 100 S. Ct. 849 (1980).

[218]Ibid., p. 850.

[219]Ibid.

[220]Ibid., p. 851.

[221]Ibid.

[222]Ibid.

[223]Ibid.

[224]Ibid., p. 852.

[225]Ibid., pp. 852–53.

[226]Ibid., p. 854.

[227]Ibid., p. 856.

[228]103 S. Ct. 2017 (1983).

[229]Mueller v. Allen, 103 S. Ct. 3063 (1983).

[230]Grand Rapids School District v. Ball, 105 S. Ct. 3216 (1985).

[231]Aquilar v. Felton, 105 S. Ct. 3232 (1985).

[232]Bob Jones University v. United States, Goldsboro Christian Schools, 103 S. Ct. 2017 (1983).

[233]Ibid., p. 2017.

[234]Ibid., p. 2023.

[235]Bob Jones University v. Simon, 94 S. Ct. 2038, 416 U.S. 725 (1974).

[236]Bob Jones University v. United States, Goldsboro Christian Schools, 103 S. Ct. 2017 (1983).

[237]Ibid., p. 2023.

[238]Ibid., p. 2024.

[239]Ibid.

[240]Ibid., p. 2025.

[241]Ibid., p. 2029.

[242]Ibid.

[243]Ibid.

[244]Ibid., p. 2032.

[245]Ibid., p. 2036.

[246]Ibid.

[247]Ibid.

[248]Ibid., p. 2044.

[249]Mueller v. Allen, 103 S. Ct. 3062 (1983).

[250]Ibid., p. 3065.

[251]Ibid., p. 3065; see 514 F. Supp. 998, 1003 (D. Minn. 1981).

[252]Ibid., p. 3066.

[253]Ibid.

[254]Ibid., p. 3067.

[255]Ibid.

[256]Ibid.

[257]Ibid.

[258]Ibid.

[259]Ibid.

[260]Ibid. See also Widmar v. Vincent, 102 S. Ct. 269 (1981) for the general concept of "forum neutrally ... open to a broad class" and Sloan v. Lemon for the singled-out class concept.

261Ibid.
262Ibid.
263Ibid.
264Ibid.
265Ibid.
266Ibid.
267Ibid.
268Ibid.
269Ibid.
270Ibid.
271Ibid.
272Ibid.
273Ibid., p. 3071.
274Ibid., p. 3073.
275Ibid., pp. 3071, 3077.
276Ibid., p. 3077.
277Ibid., p. 3072.
278Ibid.
279Ibid.
280Ibid., p. 3073.
281Ibid., p. 3074.
282Ibid., pp. 3074–75.
283Ibid., p. 3075.
284Ibid., p. 3076.
285Ibid.
286Ibid., p. 3077.
287Ibid.
288Ibid., p. 3078.
289Ibid., p. 3067.
290Allen v. Wright, 53 U.S.L.W. 1007 (1984).
291Wallace v. Jaffree, 104 S. Ct. 1704 (1984); see also Wallace v. Jaffree, 103 S. Ct. 842 (1984).
292Allen v. Wright, Regan v. Wright, cases 81-7575 and 81-970, 52 U.S.L.W. 5110 (1984).
293Wright v. Miller, 656 F.2d 828 (D.C. Cir. 1979); see also Wright v. Miller, 480 F. Supp. 790 (D.C. 1979).
294Allen v. Wright, Regan v. Wright, cases 81-757 and 81-970, 52 U.S.L.W. 5114 (1984).
295Ibid.
296Ibid.
297Ibid., p. 5118.
298Ibid.
299Ibid., p. 5122.
300Wallace v. Jaffree, 104 S. Ct. 1704 (1984).
301Wallace v. Jaffree, 105 S. Ct. 2479 (1985).
302Ibid., p. 2482.
303Grand Rapids School District v. Ball, 105 S. Ct. 3216 (1985).
304Aquilar v. Felton, 105 S. Ct. 3232 (1985).
305Wallace v. Jaffree, 105 S. Ct. 3479 (1985).
306Grand Rapids School District v. Ball, 105 S. Ct. 3216 (1985).
307Ibid.

[308]Americans United for Separation of Church and State v. The School District of the City of Grand Rapids, 718 F.2d 1391 (6th Cir. 1983); 546 F. Supp. 1071 (D.C.W.D.).

[309]Ibid.

[310]Ibid., pp. 1392, 1402.

[311]Ibid.

[312]Ibid., p. 1393.

[313]Ibid.

[314]Grand Rapids School District v. Ball, 105 S. Ct. 3216 (1985).

[315]Ibid.

[316]Ibid., p. 3223.

[317]Ibid.

[318]Ibid., p. 3224.

[319]Ibid., p. 3225.

[320]Ibid.

[321]Ibid.

[322]Ibid.

[323]Ibid., p. 3226.

[324]Ibid.

[325]Ibid.

[326]Ibid., p. 3229.

[327]Ibid.

[328]Ibid.

[329]Ibid.

[330]Ibid.

[331]Ibid.

[332]Ibid.

[333]Ibid.

[334]Ibid.

[335]Ibid., p. 3231.

[336]Ibid.

[337]Ibid.

[338]Ibid., p. 3232.

[339]Ibid. See also Lynch v. Donnelly, 104 S. Ct. 1355.

[340]Ibid.

[341]Aquilar v. Felton, 105 S. Ct. 3232 (1985).

[342]Wheeler v. Barrera, 94 S. Ct. 2276 (1974).

[343]Mallory v. Barrera, 544 U.S.L.W. 2d 556 (Mo., 1976).

[344]Ibid.

[345]Aquilar v. Felton, 105 S. Ct. 3232 (1985).

[346]Ibid., p. 3235.

[347]Ibid.

[348]Ibid.

[349]National Coalition for Public Education and Religious Liberty v. Harris, 489 F. Supp. 1248 (S.D. N.Y. 1980).

[350]National Coalition for Public Education and Religious Liberty v. Harris, 739 F.2d 48 (2d Cir. 1984).

[351]Aquilar v. Felton, 105 S. Ct. 3236 (1985).

[352]Ibid.

[353]Ibid., p. 3237.

[354]Ibid.; see also McCollum v. Board of Education, 333 U.S. 203, 212; 68 S. Ct. 461, 465; 92 L. Ed. 2d 649 (1948).

[355]Ibid., p. 3238.

[356]Ibid.

[357]Ibid., p. 3239.

[358]Ibid.

[359]Ibid., p. 3240.

[360]Ibid.

[361]Ibid.

[362]Ibid., p. 3241.

[363]Ibid., p. 3242.

[364]Ibid., p. 3243.

[365]Ibid.

[366]Ibid.

[367]Ibid., p. 3244.

[368]Ibid., p. 3245.

[369]Ibid.

[370]Ibid., p. 3241.

[371]Ibid.

[372]Ibid., p. 3247.

[373]Ibid.

[374]Ibid., p. 3249.

[375]Wallace v. Jaffree, 105 S. Ct. 2479 (1985).

[376]Ibid., p. 2480.

[377]Ibid., p. 2482.

[378]Ibid.; see also Jaffree v. Board of School Commissioners of Mobile County, 554 F. Supp. 1104, 1128 (S.D. Ala. 1983).

[379]Ibid., p. 2490.

[380]Ibid.

[381]Ibid.

[382]Ibid., pp. 2491, 2493.

[383]Ibid., p. 2495.

[384]Ibid.

[385]Ibid., p. 2497.

[386]Ibid., p. 2496.

[387]Ibid., p. 2505.

[388]Ibid., p. 2501.

[389]Ibid., p. 2505.

[390]Ibid.

[391]Ibid., p. 2508.

[392]Ibid.

[393]Ibid., p. 2509.

[394]Ibid.

[395]Ibid.

[396]Ibid.

[397]Ibid., p. 2512.

[398]Ibid., p. 2513.

[399]Ibid., p. 2517.

Bibliography

Primary Sources

Constitutions and Statutes

Alabama Constitution, Article I/Section 3.

Arizona Constitution, Article XI, Section 7.

California Public Laws, Section 41902.

Career Education Incentive Act, P.L. 95-207.

Child Nutrition Act of 1966, P.L. 85-478.

Colorado Constitution, Article IX, Section 8.

Connecticut Public Law, Section 19-215a.

Economic Opportunity Act of 1964, P.L. 95-207.

Education Amendments of 1976 and 1978, P.L. 94-482, 95-561, Title III-D.

Education of the Handicapped Act, P.L. 94-142, Para C, Section 623.

Elementary and Secondary Education Act, Title I, P.L. 95-561.

Georgia Constitution, Article I, Section 2-103, Paragraph XIII.

Higher Education Act, Title V-B, Section 532.

Illinois Annotated Statutes, Chapter 122, Section 18-8, 1(a).

Massachusetts Constitution, Article XVIII, Section 2.

Massachusetts Public Law, Chapter 76, Section 1.

Montana Constitution, Preamble (1972).

Montana Constitution, Article I (1972).

Montana Constitution, Article X (1972).

National School Lunch Act of 1946, P.L. 85-478.

Nebraska Constitution, Article I, Section 4.

Pennsylvania Public Laws, Act 109.

Special Milk Program, P.L. 84-752.

Tennessee Constitution, Article I, Section 3.

U.S. Constitution, Amendment I.

U.S. Constitution, Amendment XIV.

Virginia Constitution, Article I, Section 16 (1971).

Virginia Constitution, Article IV, Section 16.

Cases

Abington School District v. Schempp, 374 U.S. 203 (1963).

Allen v. Wright, 53 L.W. 1007 (1984).

Americans United for Separation of Church and State v. The School District of the City of Grand Rapids, 718 F. 2d 1389 (1984).

Aquilar v. Fulton, 105 S. Ct. 3232 (1985).

Board of Education v. Allen, 392 U.S. 236 (1968).

Bob Jones University v. Simon, 94 S. Ct. 2038, 416 U.S. 725 (1974).

Byrne v. Public Funds for Public Schools of New Jersey, 99 S. Ct. 2812, 442 U.S. 907 (1979).

Cantwell v. Connecticut, 310 U.S. 296 (1940).

Cathedral Academy v. Committee for Public Education and Religious Liberty, 93 S. Ct. 2814, 413 U.S. 37 (1973).

Cochran v. Louisiana State Board of Education, 281 U.S. 370 (1930).

Committee for Public Education v. Nyquist, 413 U.S. 756 (1973).

Committee for Public Education and Religious Liberty et al v. Regan, 100 S. Ct. 840, 444 U.S. 644, 63 L. Ed. 2d 94 (1980).

Cook County v. Chicago Industrial School, 125 Ill. 540, 571, 18 N.E. 183, 197 (1888).

DiCenso v. Robinson, 91 S. Ct. 2111 (1971).

Engel v. Vitale, 370 U.S. 421 (1962).

Everson v. Board of Education, 330 U.S. 421 (1962).

Felton v. Secretary, U.S. Department of Education, 739 F. 48 (1984).

Flast v. Cohen, 392 U.S. 83 (1968).

Flory v. Sioux Falls School District, 619 F. 21 1311 (9th Cir. 1980); 101 S. Ct. 409, 449 U.S. 987 (1980).

Franchise Tax Board v. United Americans, 419 U.S. (1974).

Frothingham v. Mellon, 262 U.S. 447 (1923).

Grand Rapids v. Ball, 105 S. Ct. 3216 (1985).

Griggs v. Public Funds for Public Schools of New Jersey, 417 U.S. 916 (1974).

Grit v. Wolman, 93 S. Ct. 952 (1973).

Hunt v. McNair, 413 U.S. (1973).

Jaffee v. Board of School Commissioners of Mobile County, 554 F. Supp. 1104 (S.D. Ala. 1983).

Johnson v. New York State Education Department, 409 U.S. 75 (1972).

Johnson v. Saunders, 319 F. Supp. (1972).

Kosydar v. Wolman, 353 F. Supp. 744 (D.C. Ohio 1972).

Lemon v. Kurtzman, 403 U.S. 602, 91 S. Ct. 2111 (1971).

Levitt v. Committee for Public Education, 413 U.S. 2914, 93 S. Ct. 2814 (1973).

Luetkemeyer v. Kaufman, 419 U.S. (1974).

Lunch v. Donnelly, 104 S. Ct. 1355 (1983).

McCullum v. Board of Education, 68 S. Ct. 461, 333 U.S. 203 (1948).

Mallory v. Barrera, 544 S.W.2d 556 (1976).

Marburger v. Public Funds for Public Schools for New Jersey, 413 U.S. 916 (1973).

Marburger v. Public Funds for Public Schools for New Jersey, 417 U.S. 961 (1974).

Meek v. Pittenger, 421 U.S. 349 (1975).

Meltzer v. Board of Public Instruction of Orange County, 577 F. 2d 311 (5th Cir. 1978); 99 S. Ct. 872, 439 U.S. 1089 (1979).

Meyer v. Nebraska, 262 U.S. 390 (1923).

Mueller v. Allen, 103 S. Ct. 3062 (1983).

Mueller v. Allen, 103 S. Ct. 3063 (1983).

National Coalition for Public Education and Religious Liberty v. Harris, 489 F. Supp. 1284 (S.D. N.Y. 1980).

National Coalition for Public Education and Religious Liberty v. Harris, 739 F. 2d 48 (2d. Cir. 1984).

Nebraska State Board of Education v. School District of Hartington, 195 N.W. 2d 161 (1972).

Norwood v. Harrison, 413 U.S. 455 (1973).

Pierce v. Society of Sisters, 268 U.S. 510 (1925).

Public Funds for Public Schools v. Marburger, 358 F. Supp. (1973).

Quick Bear v. Leupp, 210 U.S. 50 (1908).

Regan v. Wright, 52 U.S. L.W. 5110 (1984).

Roemer v. Board of Public Works of Maryland, 96 S. Ct. 2344, 426 U.S. (1976).

School District of the City of Grand Rapids v. Ball, 104 S. Ct. 1412 (1984).

Scopes v. State, 289 S.W. 363 (1927).

Sloan v. Lemon et al, 413 U.S. 835 (1973).

Stone v. Graham, 101 S. Ct. 192, 449 U.S. 39 (1980).

Stuart v. Kalamazoo, 30 Mich. 69 (1874).

Wallace v. Jaffree, 103 S. Ct. 842 (1984).

Wallace v. Jaffree, 104 S. Ct. 1704 (1984).

Wallace v. Jaffree, 105 S. Ct. 3479 (1985).

Walz v. Tax Commission, 397 U.S. 690 (1970).

Wheeler v. Barrera, 417 U.S. (1974).

Widmar v. Vincent, 102 S. Ct. 269 (1981).

Wolman v. Essex, 342 F. Supp. (1972).

Wolman v. Walter, 97 S. Ct. 2593, 433 U.S. 229 (1977).

Wright v. Miller, 656 F. 2d 828 (1979).

Zorach v. Clausen, 343 U.S. 306 (1952).

Books

Adler, Mortimer J. *How to Think About God.* New York: Macmillan, 1980.

Beard, Charles, and Mary Beard. *The Rise of American Civilization.* Vol. 1. New York: Macmillan, 1927.

Benton, William. *Compton's Encyclopedia.* Vol. 9. Chicago: 1967.

Blackstone, William T. *The Problem of Religious Knowledge.* Englewood Cliffs, N.J.: Prentice-Hall, 1963.

Boone, Richard D. *Education in the United States.* New York: D. Appleton, 1980.

Bryson, Joseph E., and M.R. Smith. *Church State Relations: The Legality of Using Public Funds for Religious Schools.* Topeka, Kans.: National Organization on Legal Problems of Education, 1971.

Buckner, Kermit S. "An Analysis of the Impact of Chief Justice Warren Burger on Supreme Court Decisions Affecting Public Education." Ed.D. dissertation, University of North Carolina at Greensboro, 1980.

Campbell, Ronald F., et al. *The Organization and Control of American Schools.* Columbus, Ohio: Charles E. Merrill, 1970.

Commanger, Henry Steele. *The American Mind.* New Haven: Yale University Press, 1950.

Cremin, Lawrence A. *The Transformation of the School.* New York: Alfred A. Knopf, 1961.

Cubberly, Elwood P. *Changing Conception of Education.* Boston: Houghton Mifflin, 1909.

————. *Public Education in the United States.* Boston: Houghton Mifflin, 1934.

————. *Readings in the History of Education.* Boston: Houghton Mifflin, 1920.

Deakon, George Robert. *The Burger Court and Public Schools.* Ed.D. dissertation, University of North Carolina at Greensboro, 1978.

"Defining Religion." *University of Chicago Law Review* 32 (1965):533–52.

Dewey, John. *Democracy and Education.* New York: Macmillan, 1916.

Goldstein, Stephen. *Law and Public Education: Cases and Materials.* Indianapolis: Bobbs-Merrill, 1974.

Graebner, Norman A., Gilbert C. Fite, and Philip W. White. *A History of the United States.* Vol. 1. New York: McGraw-Hill.

Greeley, Andrew M., and Peter H. Rossi. *The Education of Catholic America.* Chicago: Aldine, 1966.

Guastad, Edwin Scott. *A Religious History of America.* New York: Harper and Row, 1966.

Hage, Tim La. *The Battle for the Mind.* Old Tappan, N.J.: Fleming H. Revell, 1980.

Hawthorne, Nathaniel. *The Scarlet Letter.* New York: Washington Square Press, 1950.

Hudgins, H.C., Jr. *The Warren Court and the Public Schools.* Danville, Ill.: Interstate, 1970.

Hund, Gaillard, ed. *The Writings of James Madison.* Vol. 2. New York: G.P. Putnam's Sons, 1920.

Jastrow, Robert. *God and the Astronomers.* New York: W.W. Norton, 1978.

Jorstad, Erling. *The Politics of Doomsday.* Nashville, Tenn.: Abington Press, 1970.

Knight, Edgar W. *Education in the United States.* Boston: Ginn, 1929.

_____, and Clifton L. Hall. *Readings in American Educational History.* New York: Appleton-Century-Crofts, 1951.

Koenig, Robert A. *The Courts and Education.* Chicago: The University of Chicago Press, 1978.

Lannie, Vincent P. *Public Money and Parochial Education.* Cleveland: The Press of Case Western Reserve Library, 1968.

Lipscomb, Andrew A., and Albert F. Bergh, eds. *The Writings of Thomas Jefferson.* Vol. 16. Washington, D.C.: The Thomas Jefferson Memorial Association, 1904.

McCluskey, Neil G. *Catholic Education in America: A Documentary History.* New York: Columbia University Press, 1964.

_____. *Public Schools and Moral Education.* New York: Columbia University Press, 1964.

McGheney, M.A. *Control of the Curriculum.* Chicago: University of Chicago Press, 1978.

Monroe, Paul. *Founding of the American Public School System.* New York: Hofner Publishing Company, 1940 edition.

Morison, Samuel Eliot, Henry Steele Commager, and William Leuchtenburg. *The Growth of the American Republic.* Vol. 2. New York: Oxford University Press, 1969.

Morris, Arval A. *The Constitution and American Education.* St. Paul, Minn.: West, 1977.

Neuwien, Reginald A., ed. *Catholic Schools in Action.* South Bend, Ind.: University of Notre Dame Press, 1966.

Ravitch, Diane. *The Great School Wars.* New York: Basic Books, 1974.

Richardson, James D., ed. *A Compilation of the Messages and Papers of the President,* 1897. Vol. 7. Congressional Record, 1876. Washington, D.C.: Government Printing Office, 1898.

Rossi, Peter H., and Alice S. "Some Effects of Parochial School Education in America." In *Society and Education: A Book of Readings,* by Robert J. Havighurst, Bernice L. Neugarten, and Jacqueline M. Falk. Boston: Allyn, 1967.

Ryan, Mary Perkins. *Are Parochial Schools the Answer?* New York: Holt, Rinehart and Winston, 1967.

Sagan, Carl. *The Dragons of Eden.* New York: Random House, 1977.

Saint Augustine. *The City of God.* New York: Modern Library, Random House, 1950.

Schaeffer, Frances A. *A Christian Manifesto.* Crossway Books, 1981.

————. *A Time for Anger.* Crossway Books, 1982.

Schotten, Peter M. *The Establishment Clause and Excessive Governmental Religious Entanglement: The Constitutional Status of Aid to Nonpublic Elementary and Secondary Schools.* Atlanta: Darby, 1979.

Siljestrom, P.A. *The Educational Institution of the United States,* translated by F. Rowan. London: John Chapman, 1853.

Smith, Elwyn A. *Religious Liberty: The Development of Church and State Thought Since the Revolutionary Era.* Philadelphia: Fortress Press, 1972.

Tyler, Moses C. "Patrick Henry." In *American Statesman.* Boston: Houghton Mifflin, 1887.

Van Deusen, Glyndon. *William H. Seward.* New York: Oxford University Press, 1967.

Whitehead, John W. *The Second American Revolution.* Elgin, Ill.: D.C. Cook, 1982.

Legal Aids

American Jurisprudence. Constitutional law, by the publisher's editorial staff; Rochester, New York: The Lawyer's Cooperative Publishing Company.

National Reporter System. St. Paul: West Publishing Company, 1879 to date, with weekly advance sheets. The system includes:

The Atlantic Reporter. Reports every decision of the courts of last resort of Connecticut, Delaware, Maine, Maryland, New Hampshire, New Jersey, Pennsylvania, Rhode Island, and Vermont from 1885 to date.

The California Reporter. Reports every decision of the California Supreme Court and lower courts of record in California from 1959 to date.

The Federal Reporter. Reports every decision of the United States circuit courts and other federal courts from 1880 to date.

The Federal Supplement. Reports the decisions of the United States district courts since 1932, Court of Claims from 1932 to 1960, and the United States Customs Court since 1949.

The New York Supplement. Reports all cases of the New York Court of Appeals and lower courts of record in New York from 1888 to date.

The North Eastern Reporter. Reports every decision of the courts of last resort of Illinois, Indiana, Massachusetts, New York, and Ohio from 1885 to date.

The North Western Reporter. Reports every decision of the courts of last resort of Iowa, Michigan, Minnesota, Nebraska, North Dakota, South Dakota, and Wisconsin from 1879 to date.

The Pacific Reporter. Reports every decision of the courts of last resort of Alaska, Arizona, California, Colorado, Hawaii, Idaho, Kansas, Montana, Nevada, New Mexico, Oklahoma, Oregon, Utah, Washington, and Wyoming from 1883 to date.

The South Eastern Reporter. Reports every decision of the courts of last resort in Georgia, North Carolina, South Carolina, Virginia, and West Virginia from 1887 to date.

The South Western Reporter. Reports every decision of the courts of last resort in Arkansas, Kentucky, Missouri, Tennessee, and Texas from 1886 to date.

The Southern Reporter. Reports every decision of the courts of last resort in Alabama, Florida, Louisiana, and Mississippi from 1887 to date.

The Supreme Court Reporter. Reports every decision of the Supreme Court of the United States from 1882 to date.

NOLPE (National Organization on Legal Problems of Education), *School Law Update.* Topeka, Kans.: 1977.

Encyclopedias and Dictionaries

Ebel, R.E., ed. *Encyclopedia of Educational Rsearch.* 4th ed. New York: Macmillan, 1969.

Harris, Chester W., ed. *Encyclopedia of Educational Research.* 3d ed. New York: Macmillan, 1960.

Monroe, Walter S., ed. *Encyclopedia of Educational Research.* 2d ed. New York: Macmillan, 1950.

A Uniform System of Citation. Cambridge: The Harvard Law Review Association, 1974.

Index